THE HI
STEPPI

The Hackney horse yesterday and today

TOM RYDER

J. A. ALLEN
London & New York

British Library Cataloguing in Publication Data
Ryder, Tom
The high stepper.
1. Hackney horse – History
I. Title
636.1'4 SF293.H2
ISBN 0-85131-308-6

Published in Great Britain in 1979 by
J. A. Allen & Company Limited,
1, Lower Grosvenor Place, Buckingham Palace Road,
London, SW1W 0EL
and in the United States of America by
Sporting Book Center, Inc.,
Canaan, N.Y. 12029.

Book production Bill Ireson.

Typeset by Computacomp (UK) Limited, Fort William, Scotland.
Printed and bound by Redwood Burn Limited, Trowbridge & Esher.

THE HIGH STEPPER

CONTENTS

INTRODUCTION

The first edition of *The High Stepper* gave an outline of the history of the modern Hackney horse and pony after the formation of the Hackney Stud Book Society in 1883, but in this new edition I have endeavoured to trace the development of the breed from the early days of its forerunner, the Norfolk Trotter of the eighteenth century. For the early history I have drawn extensively on Henry F. Euren's *Historical Introduction to Volume I of the Stud Book*, the result of some eight years of research mostly in East Anglian records, with added information I have gathered from many other sources.

It is interesting that in the days when horses were vital to a nation's military and commercial strength, Great Britain was almost alone among the countries of Europe in having no governmental control over its horse breeding industry. During the eighteenth and nineteenth centuries many members of "the ruling class" were greatly interested in racing and hunting, and their efforts to produce better horses for these pursuits resulted in the thoroughbred horse, the outstanding importance of which has been rightly acknowledged by most writers on horse breeding. During the same period other British breeds of horses developed in response to the needs of the farmer and the demands of the market place without any assistance from the powers that were.

The improvement of English roads towards the end of the eighteenth century, followed by the establishment of fast coach services throughout the country, led to a growing need for light horses, particularly trotters. When the railways drove the coaches off the roads, there was at first some decline in that class of horse, but the growing prosperity of the towns was already creating a new market for horses. The numbers of private carriages on the streets increased rapidly after the middle of the nineteenth century, and a stylish horse with good action came to be keenly sought after by those able to afford the best.

The dealers, the stallion owners and the farmers all played their part in responding to these changes. In Yorkshire thoroughbred blood was used extensively, but in Norfolk and South Lincolnshire there were many good trotting stallions which local breeders preferred. It was not long before the Yorkshiremen, too, recognised the excellence of the Norfolk Trotters, and it was the blending of their blood with the Yorkshire roadsters that produced some of the more important strains of the modern Hackney.

For the most part, we are indebted to the English aristocracy for the improvement of the thoroughbred horse, but it is a less exalted group of practical horsemen that we must thank for the evolution of the Hackney. The first council of the Hackney Stud Book Society was made up of fifteen farmer breeders, seven landowners, three horse dealers, two auctioneers and three wealthy "fanciers". In 1930 the council was composed of thirteen tradesmen (of whom seven were butchers), seven professional horsemen, five fanciers and only two farmers, the Hackney having by then become an expensive luxury beyond the means of most farmers. In fact, so rapid had been the changeover from horse to motors, that many farmer breeders had been caught with unsaleable horses which had to go at slaughter prices, and not a few felt bitter.

The breed at its peak was a fine example of the achievements of "free enterprise"; but that state of affairs provides no cushion against the shock of sudden change. Thus the Hackney might have gone the way of the Yorkshire Coach Horse and the Devonshire Packhorse had it not been for the fascination of its magnificent action.

It may be hard to explain in commonsense terms, but once snared by the spell of the high stepper, its attraction is irresistible. "To win at one of the top shows, the harness exhibitor", James Agate wrote, "would always sell his soul, provided he has one." He goes on to say: "Harness horse exhibitors live in a curious little world of their own, they take a wholly professional and wholly expert interest in the harness classes, and in little else at a horse show." Agate was one of them, of course, but R. S. Summerhays, who was not, described them rather differently as a "funny crowd". Both were writing of the Hackney world of the thirties, and it was in that select group that I was first enraptured by the fascination of the Hackney. The excitement and thrills of the daytime show were followed by a gathering in the lounge of some hotel to discuss the events of the day, the breeding of the winners and to swap yarns about times past. To all of this I listened spellbound, oblivious to Mussolini's guns roaring in Ethiopia, or the sounds of Hitler's jackbooted troops marching into Austria; events that were soon to put an end to that dream world of my youth.

War came and horse shows ended "for the duration". The prospect for the Hackney horse and pony seemed bleak, so bleak in fact that Mr. Claud F. Goddard, then President of the Society, appealed "for special efforts to maintain the breed". Breeders responded as best as they were able, but it was the shortage of motor fuel that had the most beneficial effect. Harness horses and ponies were needed again, and out of necessity a few people were introduced to the delights of driving. The result has been that driving is now a well established part of the horse world, and the Hackney breed has shared in this revival.

Most of the familiar faces in the "funny crowd" I knew long ago are gone now, but the new generation of Hackney folk is no less enthusiastic, if perhaps a little less narrow-minded. The horses and ponies, too, have lost none of their old fascination, and, having survived so many changes and threats in the past, it seems unlikely that the breed faces extinction in the near future.

The first edition was dedicated to my old friend and mentor, Geoffrey Bennett, who has now been dead for a quarter of a century. I alluded then to his important influence on the recent history of the breed, but I failed to mention that it was due to his foresight that we have several of the early photographs. Geoffrey found them in the studio of Albert Clark, a horse painter of Camden Town, and bought what he could afford at a shilling each. In those days most people wanted paintings to hang on their walls, not photographs, little caring whether the paintings were done from life or perhaps from a mere written description!

I would also like to acknowledge the kindess of many others who have supplied pictures, including Mr. Chauncey Stillman, Mrs. Kathleen Ryan, Mrs. Kenneth Wheeler, Mr. Barrie Dickinson, and Mr. Frank Haydon.

CHAPTER ONE

THE HIGH STEPPER

To the modern horseman the name Hackney denotes a high stepping trotter, specially bred and trained for exaggerated performance in the show ring. This meaning can be applied only to Hackney spelled with a capital "H", the form adopted when a breed society was set up in 1883 to distinguish the breed name from the older usage meaning a riding horse of general utility, as distinct from the war horse. Such a hackney may not have been a trotter at all, indeed the amble was considered a more desirable gait for a utility riding horse from the earliest recorded times until the early part of the eighteenth century; the amble being a lateral gait, a slower form of what is now spoken of in harness racing circles as "the pace". This is an artificial gait, about which E. R., Gent. wrote in his book, *The Experienced Farrier*, published at the end of the seventeenth century:

> "There is not any Motion in a horse more desirable, more useful, nor indeed more hard to be obtained unto by a right way, than the Motion of Ambling."

He goes on to describe no less than eight different ways by which the horse might be induced to adopt this most comfortable way of going. However, the popularity of the amble, and "the rack" which was an allied gait, waned in Britain in the following century. John Lawrence in *A Philosophical and Practical Treatise on Horses*, published in 1796, lists the names of the various types of saddle horses then in use as follows:

> "... whether synonymous or distinctive, Road-Horses, Saddle-Horses, Nags, Chapman's Horses, Hacks, Hackneys, Ladies's Horses or Pads, Hunters, Running Horses, Racers, Race-Horses, Gallopers, Welter-Horses, Managed-Horses, Chargers, Troop-Horses, Post Hacks, or Post Horses, Trotters, Cantering Hacks or Canters, horses which carry double, Cobs, Galloways, Ponies and Mountain Merlins."

In that long list there is now no mention of amblers, although that comfortable gait continued to be popular in some other parts of the world. Hayes, quoting from Baron de Curnieu, tells us that Napoleon I was accustomed to ride amblers in his campaigns when he had to go long distances at a fast pace. The Reverend Samuel Pegge, a Norfolk antiquary, in an *Essay on Coaches* published in 1817, wrote:

> "The French word, Haquenée, implies a common horse for all purposes of riding, whether for private use or for hire; generally an ambler as distinguished from the horses of superior orders, such as the palfrey and the great horse. The former of these are often called pad-nags and were likewise amblers, while horses for draught were called trotting horses."

The slow amble remained popular among the Dutch farmers of South Africa until very recent times and was called by them the "tripple". In North America similar gaits were favoured, including the amble or pace, and the single-foot or rack, especially among the breeders of Kentucky saddle horses.

However, in Britain it was the ability to trot fast that became a much sought after quality and, although there may have been many reasons for this change, it was not likely to have been a mere whim of fashion. Hilaire Belloc in *The Road*, published in 1923, draws attention to the increase of wheeled traffic in England from the end of the seventeenth century, and with this increase came the demand for improved roads. This in turn led to faster travel for which superior horses were needed, thus the demand for trotters, ambling not being a suitable gait for coach horses. In those days the trot was also the faster, and for the horse, the less fatiguing gait. In the Low Countries fast trotting horses, the "Hard-dravers", had been in vogue for many years, and they may well have influenced the horses of East Anglia on the opposite coast of the North Sea.

In *The History and Delineation of the Horse*, published in 1809, John Lawrence wrote:

> "Speaking of the Flanders breed, brings to my recollection an excellent variety of well-shaped black nags, both for quick draught and the saddle, generally good, and sometimes capital trotters. They have doubtless originated in Flemish stock, and their numbers appear considerable at present."

However, no definite link has ever been found between the trotters of the Low Countries and those of East Anglia.

A trotting match at The Hague in 1778, showing "Hard-draver" trotters competing for the Golden Whip presented by Prince William V of Orange. (From a print by S. Folke in the Rijksmuseum, Amsterdam.)

THE NORFOLK TROTTER

Although the improved Norfolk Trotter was a product of the eighteenth century, horses noted for their ability to trot were to be found in East Anglia at least three centuries earlier. In one of the famous Paston Letters of about 1465, Margaret Paston, writing to her husband, Sir John Paston, from their home at Heylesdon, near Norwich, describes three horses bought for him at Saint Faith's Fair:

> "... and all be trotters, right fair horses, God save them, and they be well keeped."

Riding horses were, of course, at that time almost the only means of travelling other than by "Shank's mare."

To quote Pegge again, "horses for draught were called trotting horses." He was referring to Norfolk in particular where, probably because of the nature of the soil, an active breed of farm horses had been used to work the land long before horses replaced oxen elsewhere in the country.

John Marshall in *The Rural Economy of Norfolk*, published in 1787, describes the farm horses of those parts as follows:

> "The farm horses of Norfolk were formerly a small brown-muzzled breed, light boned, but stood hard work and hard keep in a remarkable manner. Of late, stallions of the heavier black breeds of Lincolnshire, Leicestershire, etc., have been fashionable; and at present (perhaps unfortunately for the country) the true Norfolk breed is almost entirely worn out. I have heard sensible old men regret this; and complain heavily against the present breed; they eat up too much of their corn, and are not so active as their favourite 'old sort'. Whether upon the road, or on the farm, the common practice is for horses to trot with empty carriages. Formerly this admirable custom was carried too far: instead of trotting for despatch races were run at full speed upon the road. The lead was the goal contended for: a fore-horse which would, at a word or signal, break out at full speed, was, by the young men who took delight in the diversion of 'roadings', considered as invaluable. Many waggons and some necks having been broken by this dangerous amusement, it is, at present, a good deal laid aside, though not yet entirely left off. I have myself seen a race of this kind: a following team broke out upon a common, and, unmindful of the ruts, hollow-ways and roughnesses, contended for the lead; while the leading team as eagerly strove to keep it; both of them going at as full a gallop as horses in harness could go, for a considerable distance, the drivers standing upright in their respective waggons. The close of the race was the most dangerous part of it; for so soon as the fore-horse of the team which broke out found that he had gained the lead, he rushed eagerly into the road; which in that place happened to be hollow, it appeared to me miraculous that no mischief was done. Savage, however, as the custom may seem, the present spirit of activity may be in some measure indebted to it; and whenever it is wholly laid aside, I hope it will not be from a want of spirit and inclination to continue it."

In a commentary on the book *The General View of Agriculture of the County of Norfolk* by Nathanial Kent, published in 1796, *The Farmer's Magazine* of 1802 has the following:

> As the Norfolk horses are allowed to be among the best working

> horses in the island, and oxen very little used, the presumption is that the intelligent and spirited farmers had made the proper choice of the animal whose labour they preferred; and when we consider the great expedition made by the Norfolk horses in ploughing, we must see that oxen could not travel nearly so fast.

John Lawrence in his 1796 treatise, quoted above, describes the Norfolk farm horses as follows:

> There was another breed of horses in Suffolk and Norfolk (how they came there is somewhat difficult to ascertain) well fitted both for the saddle and draught. I have seen a cart horse of this description, which, bating a little coarseness of the head, was perhaps as fit to get hacks and hunters from proper mares as the best bred horse alive. I have also heard of a Norfolk farmer, who, about fifty years ago (that is about the middle of the 18th century), had a peculiar sort that he styled his Brazil breed. This blade of a farmer would, it seems, unharness one of his plough horses, ride him to a neighbouring fair, and after winning with him a leather plate, ride him home again in triumph to his wife.

During the time of war with France at the turn of the eighteenth century a tax was imposed on farm horses and this was much resented in Norfolk. H. H. Dixon, who wrote under the name "the Druid", tells in *Saddle and Sirloin* of an eccentric farmer living in the flat country bordering the Wash who sold his nag horse rather than pay the tax and rode regularly to Spilsby market on a saddled cow.

Thus we have ample evidence that there existed in East Anglia a native breed of horses well suited to form the foundation for a race of trotting horses when the demand rose. We have little information about the stallions used on the common mares before the start of the eighteenth century, and, since up to that time it was the general belief that a stallion was not able to serve more than twelve mares during the season (or fifteen "if you keep him in the stable where he hath extraordinary keeping," to quote E. R., Gent again), it is reasonable to suppose that each breeder kept his own stallion or stallions; which in most cases would not be of any special breed.

No doubt it was the growing demand for horses for the road that led to superior stallions being made available to all comers, together with the realisation that, under controlled conditions, a stallion might serve many more mares than had been supposed hitherto.

Stallions started to be advertised at public service in the country newspapers from the early years of the eighteenth century, and the following were noted by Henry F. Euren in his introduction to the *Hackney Stud Book, Volume I.*

On April 12th, 1741 an advertisement in the *Norwich Mercury* read:

> "Lately come into Norfolk a famous stallion, an Arabian, by the size 15 hands 3 inches, and strength proportioned."

Then in the same journal on May 2nd, 1741 there is advertised:

> "A very large bay stallion, exceeding strong, height 15.3 hands; sire a fine strong hunter of Squire Pulteney's near Beverley, Yorkshire, and was bred by a mare called Lady Leggs, and afterwards Painted Lady."

On May 16th, 1741 there is a stallion advertisement:

> "Incitatus, five years old: colour brown bay: height 15.2 hands: recommended as having 'the strength of a troop horse with the beauty shape and speed of a running horse.' "

Reference was made in the same issue to "the old brown Stallion" kept at the Black Swan in St. Peter's, Norwich; presumably a horse of the indigenous farmers' breed. In the 1750s and 1760s Mr. Euren noted a great many well-bred horses among the stallions whose services were advertised. There was Croft's Othello, otherwise Black and All Black, by the Alcock Arabian; Yellow Jack, a son of Blaze; a roan horse by Roundhead, by Flying Childers "out of a well-bred mare"; and, in 1763, a Yorkshire chestnut son of Creature, also by Flying Childers. This last horse is advertised as challenging any horse in walking, trotting and galloping. The following year, 1764, a seven-year-old chestnut horse named Smiling Ball is advertised to travel the country with the recommendation that he "will trot 14 miles an hour with ease."

Horses advertised as trotters became more numerous in the latter half of the eighteenth century. Wallet's Golden Farmer was a noted trotting sire in Lincolnshire about this time, and a son of his was taken to Suffolk in 1767 by Andrew Blake of Ipswich to cross on the Suffolk horses. Blake in his advertisements gives the sire of this horse as "Wallet's famous Golden Farmer, son of Rigby's Fearnought." A card for the season 1845 of the East Yorkshire coach horse, Candidate, give that horse's dam as:

> "... by Carpet Weaver, by that noted Horse, old Golden Farmer ... Old Golden Farmer was got by the Duke of Devonshire's Atlas, his dam by old Black Legs, grand-dam by Old Candidate."

Of course this might have been another Golden Farmer, but it does draw attention to Atlas as a sire of trotters. This Atlas was a thoroughbred, sired by Babraham out of a mare by Lord Halifax's Justice, and his name occurs in the pedigrees of several distinguished trotters bred in Lincolnshire, Norfolk and Yorkshire. Dr. Samuel Johnson, the great lexicographer, is said to have visited Atlas at Chatsworth shortly after the horse had won his match with Mr. Warner's Careless. The good Doctor said he would rather take the horse than all the rest of the Duke's possessions. But in *The History and Delineation of the Horse* John Lawrence names a half-bred stallion as the *fons et origo* of the best Norfolk trotters:

> "The best trotters which have appeared, and which are now to be found in Lincolnshire, Norfolk, and their vicinity, have proceeded from Old Shields (Shales). That horse was succeeded in a few years by another, the property of Jenkinson (of Long Sutton in Lincolnshire on the Wash) called Useful Cub, he was got by a black cart horse, resembling as Jenkinson informed me, the Suffolk breed, out of a Chapman's mare. Much stock has been bred from this horse. They were distinguished in the first produce by the round buttock and wide bosom of their cart-horse sire, and as I observed in many of them, speed was their best; but the stock soon improved by crossing with racing blood."

No further particulars of the breeding of this Useful Cub has been found, and in some of his writings Lawrence has confused him with other horses of Jenkinson's.

SHALES, THE ORIGINAL

This horse, variously called Shales, Schales Horse, or Shields, was foaled about 1755, and it is from him that all modern Hackneys trace their descent. Lawrence tells us that the sire of Shales was the Duke of Ancaster's Blank, but he was writing almost fifty years later and admitted that his information was only based on tradition.

Many years later Henry F. Euren, the then editor of the *Norwich Mercury*, set out to compile a history of the Norfolk Trotter, and the results of his researches are incorporated in the introduction to the *Hackney Stud Book, Volume I*, referred to above. Euren established to his own satisfaction that the sire of Shales was the thoroughbred Blaze, foaled in 1733, by Flying Childers out of the Confederate filly by Grey Grantham. He based this on an advertisement in the *Norwich Mercury*, dated April 4th, 1772, which reads:

> "The noted Scot's or Shale's Horse, now the property of Mr. Jenkin, will cover this season, 1772, at Long Sutton in Lincolnshire, at one guinea a mare, and one shilling the servant, the money to be paid at the stable door. Though he had got so much good stock out of common mares, his pedigree is but little known; he was got by a son of Blaze, and Blaze by Childers; out of a well-bred Hunter."

Euren assumed that the son of Blaze mentioned here is evidently the Original Shales, Scot Shales being a son of his.

Apart from this advertisement almost the only information we have about the Original Shales is to be found in the writings of John Lawrence who himself admits to some confusion on the subject. Euren drew his stud book records from old stallion cards and advertisements which are themselves contradictory and confusing, which is not surprising considering the repeated use of certain names. In the first volume of the stud book there are some eighty stallions called Shales and almost seventy Fireways.

Lawrence's last statement on the subject appeared in an article in *The Sporting Magazine* of June, 1821, and reads:

> Since my last letter on this subject, having occasion to look further among my memoranda, I find I have not been quite accurate. Scot was not the same horse, but a son of Old Shields, out of a hunting mare, as I was informed by a considerable dealer, who chiefly made his purchases in Lincolnshire and Norfolk, and in whose stables I then saw one or two of the horses of Louis XVIII, a very hard rider; they were rare cattle for road or field, and bred in the above districts. No great dependence is to be placed on information of a distant date relative to those matters, as it must arise from mere recollection – a most uncertain source.

Euren estimates that Shales the Original was foaled in 1755 and Blaze died in 1756, so it is possible that he was the sire. He cites an advertisement in the year 1771 of a stallion, "Hopewell; owner Charles Hawkey Thetford, got by Old Blaze out of a well-bred mare, noted for trotting," in support of his belief that Blaze sired the original Shales.

A writer in the *Livestock Journal* of May 1930, tells of some hitherto unpublished records that at least add to the possibility of Blaze being the progenitor of the Shales line. These records show that a Cambridge gentleman, Thomas Panton, owned Blaze and the horse won for him several 4 mile races between 1738 and 1743, carrying the great weight of 12 stone (168 pounds). The horse afterwards stood for service in Newmarket.

Euren then goes on to write of the only two sons of Shales, of which we know anything, namely Scot Shales and Driver. The earliest known record of Scot Shales is Jenkin's advertisement, but obviously the horse had already made his name by then. Nothing is known of Scot Shales's own performance as a trotter, but his stock were among the best of the day. In 1780 Scot Shales, now about eighteen-years-old, came into the ownership of a Mr. Saffery of Downham Market and he remained there until 1789.

A stallion card of a horse not in the stud book, Young Marshland Shales, owned by William Gant in 1835, states that this horse's grand-dam was by the old original Shales, "the property of Mr. Safery of Downham," which must be the horse Euren calls Scot Shales. Perhaps Lawrence was right in the first place when he believed that Scot and Shales the original were one and the same horse. Certainly it is odd that Jenkin's advertisement of 1772 does not name the sire of "Scot's or Schale's horse" as, if the original Shales was foaled in 1755 (Euren's estimate), his name must have been well-known by then.

The male line of Scot Shales was carried to greater success by two notable sons – Marshall's Hue and Cry, and Thistleton's Shales. Lawrence in his recollections wrote of Hue and Cry:

> "I saw him several times while he was advertised as a covering stallion, upwards of 20 years since. He was then 15 or 16 years old, perhaps 15 hands one inch high, a bright bay with some white, a good figure, and master of sixteen stone ... Of his performances I know nothing very particular, but that he was one of the speedier trotters of his day, whence his name, from the hue and cry he raised whilst dashing along the road with a posse of horses galloping on each side and behind him. He was a horse of rare temper and courage, a true trotter, and got good stock. He trotted the mile in considerably under three minutes, carrying a high weight."

Thistleton's Shales was bred by Thomas Jenkinson of Long Sutton in Lincolnshire about 1785, his dam being Jenkinson's mare, but no pedigree is given. This is a pity because Jenkinson was the breeder of other good horses, as we shall see. Lawrence recalls that Thistleton Shales "had his back accidently broken, and was killed at Walpole near Wisbech, about the year 1820, at the age of 34 years."

MARSHLAND SHALES

Thistleton's Shales' claim to fame is as the sire of Marshland Shales, probably the most famous of all the Shales family. Lawrence in *The Sporting Magazine* of March, 1824 describes the horse as follows:

> Marshland Shales, now Old Shales, or Coltishall Shales, was got by Thistleton's horse, out of a mare by Hue and Cry, which mare also bred the dam of Driver. Old Shales was foaled in 1802 and then sold to a person in the name of Chamberlayne in the Fens for 12 guineas. In 1812 he was sold by auction at Lynn for £305 ... He stands barely 15 hands, has great bone, good shape, his colour an ordinary chestnut. Ten years since he trotted seventeen miles in 58 minutes, carrying 12 stone (168 pounds). His legs and hocks are clean and beautiful.

This was the feat which made Marshland Shales famous throughout the eastern counties of England, and it was reported in the *Norwich Mercury* on August 6th, 1810, as follows:

> "On Friday last was determined the long-pending trotting match of £200 between the celebrated horse Shales (the property of Mr. John Chamberlain, of Magdalen), and Driver (the property of Mr. Richard West, of Gaywood, near Lynn). They started from the South Gates, Lynn, exactly at six o'clock, to trot to the nine-mile stone on the Swaffham Road and back, till the expiration of an hour. For nearly the first two miles Driver took the lead, when Shales pushed hard and passed him in gallant style, his rider (Mr. Osbert Spinks, of Magdalen, a respectable farmer, nearly sixty years of age) politely bidding the other good morning and adding, 'I shall see you no more till I meet you on my return.' At the expiration of the hour Shales had trotted seventeen miles, distancing the other about a mile and half with the greatest ease, notwithstanding that he was the smaller horse and carried two stone more weight than the other. Shales has three several times before trotted three miles in nine minutes."

It had been asserted of West's Driver that he had trotted $17^1/_2$ miles on the Lynn Road in one hour and turned once, carrying 15 stone. Marshland Shales was to have been ridden in the match by a youth, but on its being discovered, on the morning of the race, that the lad had been "got at" by persons betting on the result, Mr. Spinks, though he weighed over 12 stone, and was not in training, determined himself to ride the horse in which he had an interest. Marshland Shales was at the time of the match eight-years-old, and Euren was assured by old men well acquainted with the facts of the race that the actual time in which the 17 miles was trotted was 56 minutes, and not 58 minutes as mentioned by Mr. Hawes in his letter to John Lawrence.

A portrait of Marshland Shales was published in *The Sporting Magazine* of April, 1824 with a description which says in part:

Marshland Shales. (From a painting by E. Cooper of Beccles, engraved for the Farmer's Magazine, *1823.)*

> "Marshland Shales, the property of Messrs. S. and R. Hawes of Coltishall, Norfolk, was foaled in 1802. ... His crest, yet very large, was, when he was young and in high condition, immense, but gradually fell over to the off side, with a remarkable indent. When excited by any passing object, he raises it so as greatly to diminish the indent ... In his numerous trials he was never beaten; and was universally acknowledged both the speediest and stoutest trotter of the time. ... He was fully master of 20 stone (280 pounds) and most truly, as they used to style in Norfolk, 'a thundering trotter', extremely apt to throw dirt and pebbles into the eyes of those who, of necessity, come behind him. He was not, however, a remarkably high goer though he bent his knees well."

Coltishall is not far from Norwich on the road to North Walsham, and it was at the former place that George Borrow saw the horse, then more than thirty-years-old, and gave us the much quoted graphic description of the scene in his autobiographical novel, *Lavengro*, published in 1851. It is worth repeating it here:

"I was standing on the Castle Hill in the midst of a fair of horses ... An old man draws nigh; he is mounted on a lean pony, and he leads by the bridle one of these animals (horses); nothing very remarkable about that creature, unless in being smaller than the rest and gentle which they are not; he is not of the sightliest look; he is almost dun, and over one eye a thick film has gathered. But stay! there is something remarkable about that horse, there is something in his action in which he differs from the rest. As he advances the clamour is hushed! All eyes are turned upon him – what looks of interest; of respect and, what is this? People are taking off their hats – surely not to that steed! Yes; verily! Men, especially old men, are taking off their hats to that one-eyed steed, and I hear more than one deep-drawn 'Ah!'

'What horse is that?' said I, to a very old fellow, the counterpart of the old man on the pony, save that the last wore a faded suit of velveteen, and this one was dressed in a white frock.

'The best in mother England,' said the very old man, taking a knobbed stick from his mouth, and looking me in the face, at first carelessly, but presently with something like interest. 'He is old, like myself, but can still trot his twenty miles an hour. You won't live long my swain; tall and over-grown ones like thee never does; yet, if you should chance to reach my years you may boast to thy grand boys thou hast seen Marshland Shales.'

Amain, I did for the horse what I would neither do for earl or baron, doffed my hat; yes! I doffed my hat to the wondrous horse, the fast trotter, the best in mother England; and I, too, drew a deep 'Ah!' and repeated the words of the old fellows around. 'Such a horse as this shall never see again, a pity that he is so old.' "

Almost the whole of the numerous Shales family trace their descent in the male line from Marshland Shales, but the line had lost its pre-eminence by the time of the Hackney Society's first London Show in 1885. The last famous male descendant of Marshland Shales was Beart's Ambition, foaled in 1863. This red roan had three crosses of the old horse in his pedigree, and he was one of the first horses to be campaigned at the leading shows in the country, defeating some of the best Yorkshire horses on their home ground. He was sold to go to France in about 1873.

The Shales family was mostly found in East Anglia, while there and elsewhere another strain was adding to the fame of the Norfolk Trotters – the Fireaways.

JENKINSON'S FIREAWAY

It is when we come to consider this horse, the first of the Fireaways, H.S.B. 201, that Euren's story of the breed's foundation seems weak. Euren gives the sire of Fireaway as Driver, the second son of the original Shales, but we are not told the basis for this assertion. All Euren can tell us about Driver is quoted from old stallion cards, such as that of Weatherill's Prickwillow 624, a Yorkshire horse foaled in 1847, which states:

> "Old Driver was kept at Newton-upon-Ouse, and there got a mare, the great grand-dam of Prickwillow, which trotted 15 miles within the hour, carrying 15 stone on Leeman Lane."

If the stud book dates are right, this represents only four generations in more than 80 years, which is possible, but hardly likely. Of course, there were many horses named Driver, and not all were trotters, making identification difficult. One active in the Fens at about the same time was Weaver's Driver, a thoroughbred.

However, the fame of Jenkinson's Fireaway was in itself sufficient for the owners of his numerous descendants whose cards make no mention of Fireaway's sire. The most they tell us is that the horse "covered in London several years at five guineas a mare, and trotted two miles on the Oxford Road in five minutes; was afterwards sold for 1,000 guineas." Most of these notices also state that the dam of Fireaway was by the thoroughbred Joseph Andrews.

Thomas Jenkinson bred several trotting stallions before Fireaway, including, as mentioned above, the sire of Marshland Shales. Another is mentioned by Lawrence in his recollections:

> "When I was in Lincolnshire in 1770, Old Schales was at the height of his reputation. He was either rivalled or succeeded in that respect by Jenkinson's Useful Cub, a horse of very different breed, and his speed (as I judged by my own hackney – a tried one) was above the rate of twenty miles an hour, though he carried 17 stone."

An advertisement in the *Norwich Mercury* in April 1777 states that "the two trotting horses called Useful Cubb and Hero, both being brothers" were to cover in Norfolk. The advertisement ends: "Signed Thomas Jenkinson of Lutton, near Long Sutton in Lincolnshire, breeder of the above two horses." It seems reasonable to suppose that these fine trotters of Jenkinson's were all bred on the same foundation stock.

Jenkinson's Fireaway has four sons recorded in Vol. 1 of the stud book, two of which made a lasting mark on the breed. The first of them, West's

Fireaway H.S.B. 203, a bright chestnut like his sire, was foaled in 1800, his dam a noted trotter by the thoroughbred Pagan, a son of Spectator. West's Fireaway's two best sons were both out of near thoroughbred mares. One was West's second Fireaway, a bright bay known as "Silver-tailed Fireaway," and he was a son of Morley's mare by All Fours by Regulus, grand dam by Johnny by King Fergus.

The other renowned son of West's Fireaway was Burgess's Fireaway, H.S.B. 208, a chestnut roan foaled in 1815 whose dam was by the Derby winner Skyscraper, by Highflyer, and he became the most successful sire of the two.

This horse was for a time owned by Mr. Theobald, the Squire of Stockwell who had made a fortune as a linen-draper in London and became an important figure in thoroughbred history. "The Druid" in *Post and Paddock*, informs us that Theobald's highest ambition was to have the best of everything, cost what it might. Besides thoroughbreds he had a taste for trotters, and his Rochester was engaged in a famous match against Squire Osbaldeston's Rattler, an American bred horse. Osbaldeston complained that "Old Leather Breeches's", (Mr. Theobald's) horse was a "pacer" or "racker" which sometimes galloped and sometimes trotted. Rochester's time for the 5 miles was 15 minutes and 38 seconds, but the match was declared a draw to settle Osbaldeston's objections.

After leaving Stockwell, Burgess's Fireaway stood for a time at Mattam's Livery Stables, Down Street, Piccadilly, London, and an advertisement in 1822 stated:

> "... his sire West's Fireaway was allowed to be the fastest trotter in the kingdom; his dam a full-sized sporting mare, bred by Mr. Burgess of Well Fen, Norfolk, and highly esteemed round the neighbourhood as an extraordinary good mare and a fast trotter."

On July 19th, 1819 Fireaway was matched against Mr. Slade's black mare over two miles on Sunbury Common, but the black mare fell lame after half a mile and Burgess's Fireaway had a walk over. Despite that, the match was claimed as a victory for Fireaway in advertisements of him and his descendants for years after.

In 1825 Fireaway was bought by Thomas Kirby of York, a prominent bloodstock dealer of the time. In 1827 the horse travelled in the county of Essex, but subsequently returned to Yorkshire where he left some valuable stock.

Kirby called the horse Wildfire, and Yorkshire breeders always knew him as "Kirby's Wildfire".

Before he left Norfolk, however, Burgess's Fireaway got his most distinguished son, the bay Norfolk Cob (Wright and Goold's) foaled in 1819, known in the stud book by the names of his one time owners to distinguish him from his many descendants of the same name. Mr. Theobald chose this horse to replace Burgess's Fireaway and the following description of him appeared in the *Sunday Times* during May, 1839.

> "This extraordinary animal was bred by Mr. Wayman, of Lillyput (Littleport) in the Isle of Ely. He was got by Fireaway, out of a Shields mare, and is reputed to be the fastest trotter that ever stepped. He is known to have performed two miles in 5 min. 4 sec., and is also said to have trotted 24 miles in an hour (?). This surpasses the celebrated Phenomenon mare, or any performances of the fastest American horses. He has a crest resembling the Godolphin Arabian; is short-legged but standing over a great length of ground. He is as strong as a buffalo; indeed his great muscular delineation and the immensity of his bone give him the resemblance of an animal of that class. He shows,

The Norfolk Cob. (From an engraving in the Farmer's Magazine, *1845.)*

however, a vast deal of blood. His colour is bay; he has lost both eyes, but is in other respects totally free from blemish, very quiet, of excellent constitution, and a remarkably safe goer, notwithstanding his almost incredible speed."

Squire Theobald changed the horse's name to the Norfolk Phenomenon and an engraving of him under this name appeared in *The Farmer's Magazine* of October 1845. An accompanying description ends by saying that the horse ...

"... stood in Bath until the last few months, when he was purchased by Sir William Codrington, and sent out to his estates in the West Indies; rather long in the tooth, perhaps, for such a voyage, but still full of health and vigour."

The horse more usually referred to as The Norfolk Phenomenon, was John Bond's horse, a red roan son of Norfolk Cob 15.2 hands, foaled in 1825. A description of this horse in *The Sporting Magazine* says:

Phenomena. The fastest trotter of her day. (From an engraving by J. Whessel after J. N. Sartorius.)

> "... his dam was a very fast trotting mare and never was beaten. She bred Mr. Bond many valuable horses, eight of which he has sold for £1080, exclusive of Phenomenon, which now stands first as a Norfolk trotter, allowed by all competent judges to be one of the best and fastest trotters ever shown in any public market."

This horse travelled extensively in West Norfolk, Cambridge and Lincoln for several seasons, until about 1838 when H. R. Phillips, who was one of the most respected London dealers of the day, bought him for Robert Ramsdale of Market Weighton. Robert's son, Philip Ramsdale owned Phenomenon from about 1843, and in *Post and Paddock* "the Druid" reports:

> "He was sold into Scotland when he had seen his twentieth summer, and astonished his 'canny' admirers by trotting two miles in six minutes."

The Norfolk Phenomenon left several good sons in East Anglia of which the best was the blue roan Norfolk Phenomenon (Taylor's). Mr. John Armstrong Storey, a former breeder of Norfolk Trotters, in a letter to Henry Euren described Bond's horse as "an astounding goer, very fast, but a decided lumberer." He went on:

> "... to Taylor's horse I must assign the palm of pre-eminence over all the trotters I have ever seen; from 12 to 15 miles an hour he lifted himself in the air, and seemed propelled by wings rather than feet, whilst his wonderfully rounded action reminded one rather of the rotation of so many wheels than the legs of an ordinary horse."

WROOT'S PRETENDER

Throughout a remarkably long career this horse had a high reputation for his achievements both as a sire and a trotter. The stud book gives his foaling date as 1788, his sire as Jenkinson's Fireaway and dam by the thoroughbred Joseph Andrews. Pretender was sold at a public auction in February, 1806, at Christopher Wroot's in Long Sutton and it is from an advertisement of this sale that Euren took the particulars of the horse's breeding, as also did the Yorkshireman who bought the horse at the sale. However, Lawrence, whose knowledge of the horse dated from some years before 1806, wrote that "he was got by Useful Cub out of a daughter of Lord Abingdon's Pretender, the race horse, a son of Marske."

Here again we come up against the confusion caused by repeated uses of the same name. Euren tells us that Pretender was at first known as Young Pretender, which suggests that there must have been an older horse of the same name. In the stud book the entry of Frost's Adonis, No. 8, foaled in 1783 gives the dam as by Wroot's Pretender, which cannot be correct, and perhaps this was the older horse of that name.

Adding to the puzzle is the card of the stallion Pride of the Isle that travelled the northwest corner of Lincolnshire in the 1860's. This card gives a very complete record of the breeding of the horse, part of which reads:

> "Gt. gt. grandsire Old Fireway, the property of Mr. R. West, Gaywood, Norfolk: Gt. gt. grandsire Pretender from whose stock the original Fireaway descended. Pretender was a Chestnut foaled in 1771, by Marske, the sire of Eclipse; his dam by Bajazet, the son of the Godolphin Arabian."

This mystery is unlikely to be unravelled now and it may not much matter.

Read's trotting mare. A celebrated daughter of Scot Shales and the dam of Read's Fireaway 202. (From a painting by Thomas Gooch.)

One possible explanation is that Jenkinson's Fireaway was known as Useful Cub in his early life but his name was changed to Fireaway when he went to London, just as the Norfolk Cob's name was changed. An alternative explanation could be that because Jenkinson's Fireaway's dam was by Joseph Andrew it is possible that someone over the years had confused the dam of the sire with that of his son. After all Pretender was eighteen-years-old at the time of the sale.

Pretender's dam was stated to have been also the dam of Allenby's Atlas, a noted trotting stallion and a son of the Duke of Devonshire's Atlas, and she was sister to two other well-known trotters of the day. In his advertisement Wroot claims:

> "When five years old he (Pretender) trotted 16 miles in one hour, carrying 16 stone (224 pounds), beating Mr. Allenby's Atlas, for which he received 200 guineas, and which is the greatest performance ever done by any horse of the same age."

Pretender's first notable son was Fireaway (Read's), a son of a famous trotting mare by Scot Shales, and Read's Fireaway was himself a storming good trotter. In 1801 this horse was sent up to Yorkshire to compete at the Howden Show for the prize for the best trotter. In the class he beat Allenby's Atlas, and afterwards trotted 1 mile in 2 minutes, 49 seconds. Then on the same day he trotted 16 miles carrying 16 stone for 500 guineas, which he did in 58 minutes, again beating Atlas. Fireaway stayed in Yorkshire for one or two seasons and then returned to Norfolk. He was the sire of the dam of Bond's Norfolk Phenomenon.

THE BELLFOUNDERS

Pretender was also the sire of Steven's Bellfounder, foaled in 1797 and the first of an important line. Jary's Bellfounder, a son of Steven's horse foaled in 1816, has been identified as the bay Norfolk stallion imported into the United States by James Booth on July 11th, 1822, and which became an important foundation sire of the American Trotter.

The Bellfounder line flourished in East Anglia almost to the end of the nineteenth century.

European breeders were also aware of the exceptional ability of the Norfolk Trotters, as reported in 1856 by "the Druid" writing in *Post and Paddock*:

> "About a quarter of a century since Norfolk had an almost European fame for its strong-made, short-legged hackneys, which could walk five miles an hour and trot at the rate of twenty. Fireaway,

> Marshland Shales, and the Norfolk Cob were locomotive giants in those days, ... Those now left are descended from these breeders but as they arrive at maturity they are sold to go to France."

Many of these exported stallions passed through the hands of H. R. Phillips of Knightsbridge, a leading dealer who reported to the House of Lords Committee on Horse Breeding in 1873:

> "Roadster stallions are much patronised by foreigners not so much by the English."

His firm sent:

> "... from thirty to forty every year of these roadster stallions to France and Italy and different countries. The number has not increased because they (the foreigners) have always taken as many as they could get."

The House of Lords Committee had been set up because of concern that the supply of horses was not keeping pace with the demand. It was revealed that foreign buyers were taking mares as well as stallions and only the inferior animals were left behind. However, a few devoted breeders in East Anglia did keep up the standard of their studs. These breeders were nearly all substantial farmers and not members of the "landed gentry" who, for the most part, if they were interested in horses at all, were only interested in racing and fox-hunting.

CHAPTER TWO

THE YORKSHIRE ROADSTERS

I have used the word "roadster" for these Yorkshire trotting horses not because it was the appellation in general use at the time, but because the word evidently came into the language about the end of the eighteenth century, and it was used at the first show of the Yorkshire Agricultural Society in 1838 for a class of trotting stallions to distinguish them from Hunter and Coach Stallions. On stallion cards and notices at that time these horses were described as trotters if they were called anything at all. In the later half of the nineteenth century the old Saxon name "nag horse" seems to have been adopted in common parlance for the same kind of horse in Yorkshire and elsewhere.

Yorkshiremen, like the horsemen of East Anglia, became interested in fast trotters towards the end of the eighteenth century at a time when blood horses were being used extensively in the North and East Ridings.

The first horse to gain fame in Yorkshire as a sire of trotters was the thoroughbred Jalap, a well-bred son of Regulus, dam Red Rose by Devonshire Blacklegs, next dam by True Blue out of Griselle by the Oxford Arabian. Jalap ran three times, winning the Gold Cup at Chester and the Kings Plate at Nottingham about 1760. He broke down at York after winning the first heat of the King's Plate.

Jalap has a prominent place in the early history of both the Cleveland Bay and the Hackney breeds. Trotting Jalap was a son of this horse, his dam by Cade, grand dam a Yorkshire hackney mare. Trotting Jalap sired Victory, a horse registered in the *Cleveland Stud Book*, that was in turn the sire of Milner's Volunteer, registered both in the *Hackney Stud Book* and *Yorkshire Coach Horse Stud Book*. The name of Jalap crops up in the female line of many of the best Yorkshire Hackney strains.

In *The Rural Economy of Yorkshire*, by William Marshall, published in 1788, we read:

> "The Vale (of Pickering), the Wolds, the Holderness, probably employ a hundred thoroughbred stallions. One hundred mares are considered the complement for one horse; some of them, perhaps, do not get fifty. On this calculation there are from five to ten thousand

horses bred between the Eastern Wolds and the Humber.

During the last twenty years some capital hunters have been bred in Yorkshire. This change was principally effected by one horse, Jalap, a full-bred horse whose pedigree and performance are well-known upon the turf. He is still living, and, what is remarkable, last season, at the age of thirty, covered several mares. His leap, five guineas each for blood mares, two guineas each for Chapman's mares.

Almost everything depends upon the mare – what are a few guineas in the first purchase of a good mare? And what are a few days ploughing, or a few rides to market, compared with the difference between a race of good and ordinary horses?"

(Marshall's mention of "Chapman's mares" is a reference to the "Chapman's Horse" which in those days meant a horse of the type used as pack horses. They were to be found in several parts of the country. Cleveland Bays were often referred to by this name and there was a class for Chapman's Horses at the Whitby Show as late as 1844.)

The local markets for this large number of half-bred horses were found in the several fairs held in the country towns. By far the largest in South Yorkshire was the Howden Fair held each September. This great fair was described in the *Sporting Magazine* in October, 1807:

"It commences annually on September 25th, being attended by all the principal dealers from London, Edinboro', and from several of the great towns in the different counties of England. During every night there are not less than 2,000 horses in the inn stables and sent out to grass. The stables of the public-houses in the adjoining villages to the extent of 10 miles round Howden are also completely full, so that it may be estimated that 4,000 horses are every-day exposed for sale, 16,000 being disposed of at the last fair, worth altogether not less than 200,000 pounds."

The following is a local ballad *Howden Fair*, sung to the tune *Nancy Dawson*, of about 1800:

"It's I have been to Howden Fair
And, oh, what sights did I see there,
To hear my tale would make you stare
And see the horses showing.
They come from east, they come from west
They bring their worst, they bring their best,

And some they lead and drive the rest
Unto the fair at Howden
  Tal al al, All at the fair at Howden.

There were blacks and bays and duns and grays
And soreled horses, aye, and mares
And pyball'd too, I do declare
And more than I do know on,
There were blind and lame and wind gall'd too
Crib-biters were there not a few
And roarers more than one or two
  Tal al al, All at the fair at Howden.

All ages too, as I'm alive
From one to two to thirty five.
And some they scarce could lead or drive
Or in the streets could show them.
There were broken winded too, I saw,
And some for panting scarce could draw,
And there were clickers, too, I know,
  Tal al al, All at the fair at Howden.

Now some upon the stones were shown
And others found upon soft ground
And up the hills their heads were turn'd
And thats the way to show them
They can gain or lose an inch or two
By managing the hoof or shoe
Oh yes, they this and more can do,
  Tal al al, All at the fair at Howden.

Then the dealers through the streets do splash
And swing around a long whip-lash
And say "My lads come stand & swash,
And lets have room to show them,"
They crack their whips and curse and swear
And cry "My lads, be of good cheer,
For this my lads, is Howden fair.
How do you like the fair at Howden?"

As the sport of fox-hunting became increasingly popular and the demand for light harness horses for coach and carriage grew, Howden Fair became the source of supply of young unbroken horses that were developed and prepared for sale by specialists. One such hunter producer, James Hall of Scarboro', was a banker and land agent in Beverley who would buy some sixty or more young horses each year to summer at grass and produce as hunters for sale. Men from Lincolnshire were active in this market, too, as "the Druid" tells us in *Post and Paddock*:

> "Yarborough, South Wold, and Burton Hunt are the great public schools where the heads, hands and heels of a legion of 'hard-riding Dicks' are ever at work five months of the year transforming the raw one-hundred-guinea Howdenite into the finished two-hundred-guinea candidate for Horncastle ... the largest fair in England for made hunters."

The buyers at these fairs, being mostly dealers, would look out for the progeny of stallions whose stock they knew suited their trade, and this probably explains the repetition of the name of a good stallion in his sons, grand-sons, and sometimes more remote relations. This practice must have given the compilers of stud books in later years many a headache. In some cases the stallion owners, in drawing up stallion's cards for the printer, would go to considerable lengths to give as full a pedigree as possible, but even they must have been misled at times. Many hundreds of different cards were published.

William Scarth Dixon in *The Influence of Racing and the Thoroughbred Horse on Light Horse Breeding*, published about 1924, made a valiant effort to trace the thoroughbred horses that have influenced British breeds of light horses, particularly those of Yorkshire. Unfortunately his catalogue of stallions gives few dates, and, for the Hackney he has apparently only consulted Volume I of the stud book, although many of the early Yorkshire horses are actually recorded in Volume II. Volume I contains the results of Euren's researches which were spread over a period of at least twelve years and mostly among Norfolk records. One has the impression that the history of roadsters and trotters in Yorkshire and Lincolnshire was dealt with more hastily, with the Editing Committee pressing for publication.

Dixon showed that many of the same thoroughbred horses influenced all three Yorkshire breeds – the Cleveland Bay, the Yorkshire Coach Horse and the Hackney. Jalap has already been mentioned and a few of the more important ones are:

Grog by Tandem, a winner of races at Yorkshire meetings; and the sire of a stallion of the same name that travelled the Flamborough and Bridlington district.

Ruler by Young Marske out of Flora by Lofty. This horse won the St. Leger of 1780 for Mr. Bethell of Rise Park, Hull and served as a country stallion in various parts of Yorkshire. In 1790 he was standing at Middleham, the property of Mark Bulmer.

Brutandorf by Blacklock out of Mandane by Pot-8-Os. This was a good race horse that was bought for £800 to serve in Yorkshire. He travelled several seasons in the district south and east of Driffield, his leader being Dick Stockdale, a Yorkshire character whose home spun humour so tickled "the Druid" that he wrote a pen portrait of him for *Saddle and Sirloin*, and used an engraving of his portly figure in *Silk and Scarlet*. A son of his, also called Brutandorf, travelled in the same district in the 1840's. This horse's dam was by Admiral, grand dam by Sovereign, next dam by Dart, next dam by Agar's Old Rainbow – a female line replete with names renowned in Cleveland Bay history.

In the early years of the nineteenth century grey horses were in fashion for a short-time; the cards of grey stallions claimed grey horses were worth from 20 to 30 per cent more than other colours. This may have been so, but Marshall deplored "the breed of grey rats with which this island has of late years been over-run," adding "they are not a greater pest than the breed of black Fen horses" – another of his abominations. Presumably the "grey rats" were the progeny of Delpini, a well-bred horse by Highflyer that was standing then in North Yorkshire which "he filled with leggy greys," to quote another writer.

Some of these country blood horses had a racing record while others had never been trained. One such was Harpham Turk, also known as "Walmsley's Turk", a son of Bedalian by Beningborough, dam by Turk, grand dam by Engineer by Sampson. The Turk in this pedigree was by Ruler out of a mare by Turk by Regulus. The village of Harpham lies some five miles east of Driffield, not far from the birthplace of Melbourne, the great sire of race horses, in a district where the farmers had a particular fondness for blood horses. Harpham Turk has many descendants in both the Cleveland Bay and Yorkshire Coach Horse stud books, but in the Hackney stud book his name only appears in a few pedigrees, notably that of Ramsdale's Performer.

THE PRESIDENTS

Of all the hundreds of blood horses that travelled in Yorkshire before the middle of the nineteenth century, the one that was most widely known was President. He became the patriarch of a family that continued to influence the light horses of that northern county for long after he was gone, and such was his fame that, although there are many references to his excellence as a sire of hunters and coach horses, rarely is his breeding given. President was described by a contemporary as "a very stylish little brown horse about 15.1 hands". This fits very well with Henry Hall Dixon's, "The Druid's", story of the horse given in *Scott and Sebright*, published in 1862:

> "Sir Mark Sykes had four or five brood mares at Sledmere in 1804, among them the sisters Miss Teazle Hornpipe and Miss Hornpipe Teazle, by Sir Peter from a Trumpator mare. Both of them were sent to Sancho, and they returned in foal with Prime Minister and President. The former beat Tramp after a most desperate finish in the Four-year-old Subscription at York, and the latter was a little brown horse who passed into Sir Tatton's hands and was given by him to an earth-stopper. To the donor (sic.) he proved a rich treasure-trove, as he soon ranked next to Screveton in the North Riding's eyes, and nearly all the young things were fathered on the pair."

There is a well known print of a picture by H. B. Chalon, *Sir Mark Masterman Sykes and His Hounds* and, in a key to this picture given in his book *The Holderness Hunt* published in 1914, Capt. Frank H. Reynard identifies one of the figures in the foreground as John Foxton the earthstopper. The owner of President and others of his tribe was J. Foxton of Waithwith, Richmond, and all in all it seems fairly certain that the great hunter sire was this President by Sancho.

Sancho was by Don Quixote and won the St. Leger of 1804 for the free-spending Colonel Mellish who, until forced to sell his estates, owned a property in South Yorkshire.

In writing about the Yorkshire Coach Horse in *The New Book of the Horse* published in 1910, William Scarth Dixon refers to President:

> "It now remains to say a few words about the most prominent of the thoroughbred horses that may be looked on as the progenitors of the modern Yorkshire Coach Horse. First among these is Bay President than whom perhaps no horse did more good in his generation. Unfortunately there is no pedigree of him forthcoming."

The "Bay President" Dixon refers to won the prize as the "best stallion for Hunters" at the Northallerton Show of the Yorkshire Agricultural Society in 1840, and his pedigree was stated to be by Old President, dam Lady Elizabeth by Akarius (G.S.B).

At the Malton meeting of the same society in 1855 Bay President, then 22 years old, won the class for the best roadster stallion.

Another son won at Richmond in 1844, this being Politician, or Politician President, by President, dam by Soothsayer. At Hull in 1859, a son of this horse won Lord Hotham's silver cup for the best hunter sire, his name also was President, owned by E. R. Harrison, son of John Harrison of Cottingham; at this same show President Junior by Bay President, dam by Lottery (G.S.B) won the roadster stallion class for L. Hodgson of Easingwold.

The horse of this line that has an important place in Hackney history is another Bay President, foaled in 1864, a son of President Junior, dam Gaiety by Albert. This Bay President is registered in the first volume of the Yorkshire Coach Horse stud book but not in the Hackney stud book, although his sire appears in the unnumbered appendix to Volume I. Bay President was shown quite extensively by his owner William Northgraves of Sutton-upon-Hull, and won prizes at the Royal, the Agricultural Hall, London and at the East of England Show. His offspring won as lady's hacks, hunters, coach horses and Hackneys and many went overseas at high prices. Bay President was still doing yeoman service at twenty-five-years-old when owned by R. P. Langdale in Holderness. He was the last blood horse of the President line, and the last stallion to have foals registered in both Hackney and YCH books.

Several stallions by Bay President are registered in the Hackney Stud Book, but by far the most important was Cook's Phenomenon, sold when five-years-old for 500 guineas to the French Government, but not before he had made his mark on the Hackney breed, as we shall see.

The story of the Shaw Mill Trotters well illustrates President's unusual ability to improve different classes of horses. These fast trotting ponies were owned by John Atkinson, a flax spinner of Shaw Mill, north of Harrogate, Yorkshire, and were descended from a mare called William Deighton's Wonderful Girl by President. This pony was said to have been the produce of a pony brought from Scotland. One of Wonderful Girl's foals was by Merry Driver, a Norfolk Trotter and, named Jenny Lind, this pony became a noted trotter. Her owner, J. W. Scriven of Otley, was once asked to be the umpire in a trotting match over a measured mile at Blubberhouses between two 16-hand roadsters. Scriven refused the offer of a big thoroughbred, preferring to ride his own pony, then twenty-years-old. For the first half mile the race was a close one, and Scriven followed a few yards behind. Then one horse broke into a gallop and refused to trot; when they were within 100 yards of the winning post, the rider of the beaten horse invited Scriven to take the shine out of his opponent, and the old pony sailed ahead to win by a length!

Trotting matches and matches against time became common in Yorkshire as they were in other parts in the early years of the nineteenth century, and it was customary for stallions appearing at shows and fairs to show their paces. Some of these full and half-bred horses were impressive performers. After winning a prize of £5 at Howden Show in 1806, Milner's Volunteer walked 5 miles on the Beverley Road in 58 minutes, carrying 217 pounds. He followed this by trotting 1 mile in 2 minutes and 58 seconds, carrying the same burden. Trotting Jalap was credited with having trotted 16 miles "within the hour" carrying 228 pounds.

The following report of a match appeared in the *York Gazette*, on February 2nd 1843:

> "TROTTING MATCH.
>
> Match for 10 sovereigns from Escrick mill to Fulford Cross on Saturday: distance 5 miles. Mr. Herbert's bay mare by Paulinus and Mr. Dunning's mare. Time 19 min. 39 secs. Road covered with loose gravel; ridden by owners. A spectator found difficulty in steering his gallant steed without coming into collision with a farmer's cart. He rivalled the exploit of Dick Turpin by a gallant leap over the cart to the slight discomfort of Farmer Davis's egg baskets, the contents of which were speedily hatched without the aid of steam or mother hen."

The blood horse Mousetrap (Young Marske-Gentle Kitty) was a noted sire of fast trotters, and a son of his trotted a match over 10 miles on the Newark Road against West's Grey Shales for 50 sovereigns, Philip Ramsdale of Market Weighton was the umpire. Shales won in a time of 33 minutes.

Long before this particular match the Norfolk Trotters had shown their superiority, and Philip Ramsdale's father, Robert, was the prime mover in bringing some of the best Norfolk horses to Yorkshire. No doubt impromptu road races were not uncommon, and the trotters of the town of Market Weighton quickly showed others their heels. It was said that their opponents, recognising what they were up against, would pull up saying, "I'll have nae mair of tha – thoo comes fra' Market Weighton!"

Many writers at various times warned against the excessive use of the wrong kinds of thoroughbred stallions for producing "hunters and roadsters, coachers and chargers." An unnamed writer in *The Farmer's Magazine* of October, 1845, in a lengthy article on the subject attributes the falling off in quality of the coach and other horses at the Yorkshire Agricultural Show of that year to two factors. Firstly, he drew attention to the "fashion which has prevailed in the last half century, of gentlemen riding and driving mares, which was not formerly the case," with the result that the farmers had been induced to part with their best and were breeding from inferior sorts. The second cause, he claimed, was that the alteration of the conditions of a half or one mile in place of the earlier style of races over two or three miles had, he said, favoured the fastest horses but not "the stoutest blood."

The same theme is developed in a well-written piece printed on the back of a notice advertising the stallion Grey Pretender, belonging to Robert Ramsdale of Market Weighton, for the season of 1838. It reads as follows:

A WORD TO BREEDERS

"The Fever for Blood Horses having once arrived in this part of the country, it may not be amiss to caution people against falling into the same misfortunes they did during the last Blood-fever some years ago, when it would really appear as if the very name of Blood was sufficient for many persons, Blood without strength is worse than nothing, and Blood without Nag symmetry, and light action, is equally as bad, let the size and powers be what they may; for unless a Blood Horse is short legged, short coupled in his back, with good loins, and a light goer, it is quite impossible for him to get Hunters; it may be here said, that he will get Carriage Horses, so he may if the colours are good, but what is to become of his undersized or slight Stock, there is the rub, they cannot hunt, they cannot ride, they are too slight for the team, why to be sure they must be sold under £10, or £15 each, which is the error the people got into last Blood fever, when they stocked their Farms with small weedy Horses, whereas had they chosen a Horse 16 hands high, with good bone and light action, and as short and compact as is requisite for a Nag, then their small Stock would have made Hunters, and the very best of Nags, and therefore paid well for breeding; nothing will pay better than breeding from Blood, if a sound judgment is exercised in their choice of a proper Horse, altho' it must be admitted, that a Horse, three parts bred, is by far the most certain (with Nag symmetry) to breed from; these sort of Horses get the most and finest Coach Horses, they are great sizes and bloody looking, their slight Stock are excellent hunters and Nags, and such of them as are not shaped for high prices, have always power for the plough, there is no weedy Stock with them, if they err, it is on the strong side; but again, he is not thoroughbred they say (just as if they were breeding for the Turf,) did you ever hear of a country Stallion, troubled with Getting Race Horses? In nine cases out of ten, there is a defect in the system of country horses for getting Race Horses; oh! but his hunters will not do unless he is thoroughbred; such silly nonsense, did you ever see a Bloody looking hunter with fine shapes want a customer in a fair? it is these sort of horses that have done more good to Blood horses than they ever had it in their power to do for themselves. Is it not notorious, that when offered for sale, in five cases out of six, they are said to be got by blood horses, which their dams never knew?"

Grey Pretender stood 16.1 hands high and was a grand-son on the sire's side of Wroot's Pretender, the son of Jenkinson's Fireaway sold at Christopher Wroot's sale in 1806. Pretender was then eighteen-years-old, but, despite this, he was bought to go to Yorkshire with the object of rectifying the results of Yorkshire breeders having "over-egged the pudding" with too much thoroughbred blood. Euren supposed the buyer was Robert Ramsdale, but on many Yorkshire cards he is referred to as "Rotsey's Pretender." Thomas Rotsey and Robert Ramsdale were both innkeepers and stallion owners at Market Weighton, an East Riding country town on the main York-Hull road where it begins its climb on to the Wolds, with Beverley beyond. Rotsey's inn was known as The Old Pretender, but whether or not this is coincidental we now have no way of knowing. Another horse Rotsey owned was Volunteer, a grandson of Milner's Volunteer, and his taste seems to have been more for coach horses than "nags". Ramsdale kept The King's Arms which must have been the principal inn in the place at that time, for it was here that the Hull Mail from York changed horses, as did some of the stage coaches.

RAMSDALE'S PERFORMER

The most important Yorkshire-bred son of Wroot's Pretender was Ramsdale's Performer, a brown horse. Performer was bred by Francis Leake of North Cliff, near Market Weighton, from his mare described as "a first rate hackney and one of the safest ever rode. When 20 years old she could trot a mile in 3 minutes and $^1/_2$". Leake's mare was of typical East Riding coach horse breeding of the time: her sire was Haldenby and company's Prince by Pickering's horse (a coaching stallion), grand sire Walmsley's horse (Harpham Turk), great grand-sire Trotting Jalap. Nowhere have I found the height of Performer stated, but his full brother, Cliff, was a bay, 16.1 hands, and Performer was probably around that height.

Francis Leake came from an old family of horsemen, and at one time he drove the Mail from York to Hull. Later he drove the "Safety Coach" from Scarborough to Selby, via Filey, Bridlington, Driffield and Market Weighton. According to a card advertising this coach in 1839, it left Scarborough at 7 a.m. in the morning, connected with the Leeds train at Selby, reaching Leeds by 5 p.m. The card also states: "No guard and only one driver throughout"; a selling point that probably had great appeal to the Tykes – only one man to tip! This was a journey of about 70 miles in about 9 hours and a good day's work for one man. Other members of Leake's family bred some important horses in later years.

Wroot's Pretender was said to have trotted 16 miles within the hour, carrying 224 pounds, in a match for 200 pounds. He was described to "the

Ramsdale's Performer. Old Bob Ramsdale's favourite and an important foundation sire of the Yorkshire Hackney. (From an engraving by Samuel Carter after T. Freeman.)

Druid" by William Lund, a Market Weighton worthy, in an interview recorded in *Saddle and Sirloin*:

> "Old Pretender; a black, he was very blood-like – I doubt there was a better; fine legs and short fetlocks. He got Performer, a dark brown."

Euren in the introduction to the *Hackney Stud Book* quotes a letter that appeared in *The Sporting Magazine* of July, 1821 written from Kirby Stephen in Cumberland, giving an account of Pretender at 33 years of age:

> "Mr Lawrence must be mistaken respecting his age, as the horse in question is now serving mares in Westmoreland and Cumberland. He was brought last year out of the East Riding of Yorkshire by a 'break-neck dealer', being 'turned adrift,' no one suspecting it possible for him to propogate his species any longer; but I have seen 10 or 12 of his produce (yearlings) as well as foals this season which are very promising. He is a dark brown, 15.2 hands, and it appears was bred by Christopher Rook (Wroot), Long Sutton, Lincolnshire. His first

performance was in that county, when he trotted two miles in 5 min. 54 sec., with a high weight, upon green sward. I well remember his first appearance in a market town in the north. The Johnny Raws smiled at his worn out emaciated form, but the moment room was given for him to get upon his pins every other stallion that was exhibited retired into the shade in an instant. As he was rattling along, apparently at full speed, a cur dog casually crossed the road; the people imagined it would be trampled upon, but the generous animal darted over it in grand style, to the astonishment of every individual. I will mention another anecdote as a proof of the efficacious remark made by Mr. Lawrence. 'It is remarkable (says this sagacious observer, 3rd. Ed., pp. 331–2) that trotters, unlike gallopers, do not lose their speed from old age many having been known to trot as fast at 20, and even near 30 years of age, as they did in their prime.' It appears to be the case with this animal. As I was anxious to witness him trot, I permitted the groom to ride a horse of mine and take him alongside. He is high bred and has great courage, and can get away at a bang-up rate, but notwithstanding the rider applied 'Birmingham' in prime style he could scarcely keep pace with Hue and Cry (Pretender)."

Although Bob Ramsdale dearly loved a trotter, we can find no record of any great achievement by Performer, other than his winning a prize of 10 guineas at the Wharfedale Agricultural Society in 1816, and other awards at West Riding shows. The following description of old Ramsdale was written by "the Druid" and published in 1870 in *Saddle and Sirloin*:

> "Old Bob Ramsden (sic.) of Market Weighton had Pretender and Reformer (sic.) – both trotting sires from Norfolk. At eighty he dressed the character to the life, in white stockings and shoes, long black coat, low broad hat, and kerseymere breeches. Even at that age he could show a trotter's paces with any man at Market Weighton each market Wednesday in May. He was never in a hurry about it, but sat in his chimney corner, and let the others trot on till his pipe was finished. Then he would reach down his spurs, and mount his galloway to show off his stallion. Performer was his delight; he would gallop his galloway by his side on the turnpike, and then shift his saddle on to the horse, and, as he was want to say, 'Trot over their backs.' No horse could trot with Performer and he trotted faster than he could gallop. Old Bob was six feet high when in his prime, and game to the back bone. He was considerably above seventy when he fetched the cap and jacket of other days out of a drawer, and it was all his friends could do

to prevent him coming up to London then and there to ride a friend's horse for a ten mile trotting match."

MERRYLEGS

Ramsdale's Performer left several sons, some of which have not been recorded in the stud book, and of those that were registered the most important were Lund's Merrylegs and Harrison's Black Rattler. Merrylegs was bred by the same character who spoke to "the Druid", old Lund, who also had something to say about Merrylegs, beginning with the story of his dam:

> "T'auld mare was tremendous fast; some days beat out in the world – some days couldn't mak' nowt of 'er. When she was 22 years old, she carried Little Bill 2 miles 200 yards in 5 min. 16 sec. with a flying start. I knew when I went into the stable i't morning whether she meant trotting or not. If she was in one of her tantrums she would rear up and squat on the ground. She had a way of whisking her tail round if she didn't want to act.
>
> "I once ploughed a yacre of ground with her, and then trotted 16 miles to Beverley races and back. T'auld bay meer come of a black meer by Harrison's Sportsman, gitten with syke a horse as come of Jerry Boughton – little bit of fash down the legs, but go for yae summer day after another. They lived like racehorses – there never was noe mair syke. We had Merrylegs, and good job if we'd never had him. We selt him for 630 pounds to Squire Dennison. Old Pretender ... he got Performer, a dark brown; and Merrylegs was gitten with Performer. He had a queer white mark on foot that all the Performers had. It was white round the coronet and down the front of the hoof. Merrylegs was about the last, and got bad ones. They tried to cross the blood and stronger animals didn't do."

The Little Bill referred to as the rider of "t'auld mear" is featured in another of old Lund's anecdotes:

> "Little Bill rode the black mare the 100 miles in 11 hours and 48 minutes. She had 13 hours 15 minutes to do it in. She was only three that Spring. If we had only roped her in that 100 miles we'd have broken all Weighton."

Little Bill was the son of William M. Lund, the breeder of the black filly. Bill was only seven-years-old when he rode the 100 miles match which started from Bielby, a village a few miles from Market Weighton where Lund lived, on to Lobster House on the York and Malton Road. From there he rode on the 10 miles to Whitewall, Malton, and continued to shuttle back and forth between these two places until the 100 miles was finished. Afterwards he rode the filly back to Bielby. This filly was a full sister to Merrylegs, which horse was foaled in 1830, so the 100 miles match may have taken place in the early 1830's. On February 5th, 1843, the *Yorkshire Gazette* reported:

> "William Lund, jockey of Bielby has been appointed head rider and trainer to the Emperor of Russia and leaves Hull in April with a lot of horses."

Probably this was a shipment of Thomas Kirby's who did a great deal of business with the Russian royal household at that time. William Lund evidently did not stay long in Russia but returned to the family farm at Bielby where his son, Thomas Lund, was still breeding a few Hackneys in the early 1920's.

The stud book gives the sire of Merrylegs as Performer or Kirby's Lottery, by Tramp, a thoroughbred, and his dam by Earle's Sportsman. Sportsman's dam was described as a nearly thoroughbred mare that had trotted the nine miles from Beningborough Hall, Captain Earle's home, to York on several occasions. Merrylegs card states that Captain Earle's mare was by Jenkinson's Fireaway, but this seems open to doubt.

Lund, in his conversation with "the Druid", refers to "Harrison's Sportsman" as the sire of Merrylegs dam. Sportsman seems to have been a popular name among Yorkshire breeders over a number of years, but the relationship, if any, in many cases is so remote that it would be mistaken to think of a Sportsman family. For instance, the closest link of Hart's Sportsman (foaled in 1852) to another horse of the same name was to the sire of his grand-dam, a horse known as Wright's Sportsman. The latter was an unregistered son of Lund's Merrylegs whose dam, according to the stud book, was by Earle's Sportsman.

Merrylegs himself trotted 1 mile in July, 1834 on the road between Market Weighton and Holme-on-Spalding Moor in 2 minutes and 47 seconds carrying 168 pounds. In three successive years, 1835–37, Merrylegs won the Premium at the East Riding Agricultural Association's Show at Beverley; at the Royal Show at York he was judged the best roadster stallion, and he won at many smaller Yorkshire shows. He travelled the same district for twelve years and sired a great many valuable horses despite old Lund's disparaging remarks reported by "the Druid".

Sons of Merrylegs travelled in the East and West Ridings of Yorkshire, in Lincolnshire and East Cheshire. Many others were exported. One of his best sons was Aughton Merrylegs, foaled 1838, whose dam was by Templeman's Creeper, a son of Wright's Creeper out of a mare by Lord Fitzwilliam's Blacklegs (G.S.B.) and his name comes into the pedigrees of many good Yorkshire Hackneys. When old Merrylegs died in March, 1846, his fame was such that the *Yorkshire Gazette* took note of his passing.

BLACK RATTLER

Harrison's Black Rattler, foaled 1833, was one of several good stallions owned by John Harrison of Cottingham, near Hull. His dam was by Ramsdale's Atlas, a great grand-son in the male line of the Duke of Devonshire's Atlas. Mares by Black Rattler figure in several successful Yorkshire Hackney strains.

John Harrison was a timber merchant at Hull, with a residence in Cottingham, and he was a keen member of the Holderness Hunt. Crowther M. Harrison, one of his two sons, became Sheriff of Hull in 1852, and was also the founder of a successful stud of thoroughbreds. The Derby winner of 1887 was of his breeding. Most of the stallions Harrison owned and travelled in Yorkshire were of a generally useful description, fitted to get road horses or hunters. He owned a son of Black Rattler, which he also called Black Rattler to confuse posterity, and whose dam was by Brown Shales, grand-dam by Sancho (TB), great grand-dam by Atlas, great great grand-dam by Bethel's Ruler (TB). Here we might say a few words about Brown Shales, a horse

Harkaway. A celebrated roadster owned by John Harrison of Cottingham, Yorkshire. (From an engraving in the Farmer's Magazine, *1843.)*

foaled in Lincolnshire about 1825, a son of Chadd's Black Shales, his dam Hewson's Roan Mare by Taylor's Primo, a grandson of Jenkinson's Fireaway.

Black Shales was advertised as "the champion of England", and travelled Cambridgeshire, West Norfolk and Lincolnshire at a fee of 3 guineas, a fairly high fee for those days, indicating a superior sort of horse. Black Shales's dam was Captain Ogden's Trotting Mare by Wroot's Pretender. Thus Brown Shales was in-bred to Jenkinson's Fireaway, and, although we don't know a great deal about him, his name is found in some distinguished Yorkshire Hackney families.

Harrison had a son of Brown Shales named Harkaway, and this horse won the Roadster Stallions class the first time the Yorkshire Show came to Hull in 1841. Harkaway's dam was by Harpham Turk, and a description of the horse appeared in *The Farmer's Magazine* of May, 1843. It probably expresses Harrison's views on what a roadster stallion should be, and the following is an extract:

> "A celebrated roadster, Harkaway is a strong, vigorous and active animal, capable from his formation of enduring great fatigue; his body is round and compact, and his limbs are remarkable for their strength ... The roadster should have good fore and hind legs, feet sound, be even-tempered and quiet in whatever situation he may be placed; not heavy in hand and not dispossed to stumble. The general notion that the hackney should lift his legs well and he will never come down is erroneous; the higher the feet are raised the greater the force in coming to the ground, and the greater the danger in case of a stone or other casualty in the road; in addition to which is the unpleasantness which the rider feels as well as the battering and wearing of the feet; more dependence is to be placed on the manner in which the horse puts his feet to the ground than on the knee action in raising them up; more on the foot being placed at once flat on the ground, or perhaps the heel coming first in contact with it, than on the highest or most splendid action."

KIRBY'S WILDFIRE

Thomas Kirby, who bought the ten-year-old Burgess's Fireaway and took him to Yorkshire in 1825, was born in 1769 and when still a young man he became one of the leading exporters of thoroughbred and other horses to Europe. He first went to Russia in 1791 with a string of horses sent out by a Market Weighton brewer. The voyage down the Baltic often took three weeks in those days, and, when his business was at its peak, Kirby would charter a vessel from Hull for the journey out and back. The horses were kept in stalls built on the ballast-sand in the ship's hold, and Kirby travelled with every one of his shipments until he was nearly sixty. His stables at York were at Walmgate Bar Without, and some good thoroughbred stallions were at stud there at different times.

Kirby bought other classes of horses for his noble European customers, and it may have been with a view to improving the Yorkshire horses for this trade that he bought Burgess's Fireaway.

ROBERT RAMSDALE'S WILDFIRE

R. Ramsdale's Wildfire, foaled 1827, was the elder of the two best Yorkshire-bred sons of Burgess's Fireaway. The stud book states that the dam of this horse was a mare by Marshland Shales, grand-dam by Chadd's Smuggler, but his card, of which I have a copy, states:

> "Wildfire's dam was the mare lately rode by Mr. Maw of Thornton, well known to be one of the best hackneys and fastest Trotters in Yorkshire; she was got by Mr. Wetherill's noted Horse of Skelton, near Guisboro'."

Now Guisborough is in North Yorkshire in the heart of the Cleveland Bay Country, and William Scarth Dixon who compiled the first volume of the Cleveland Bay stud book writes of a John Weatherill as an important breeder, and owner of the stallion Farmers' Glory, better known as "the Hob Hill Horse." Whether or not this horse was the sire of Wildfire's dam is impossible to say, but it seems probable that the mare had some Cleveland blood. Wildfire was "a good bay, with Black legs, stands 15 hands 3 inches high, with bone and strength sufficient to carry 20 stone," and Burgess's Fireaway was a chestnut roan, so the colour must have come from the mare.

The card of Wildfire has his virtues proclaimed in verse, as was common at the time:

Comes! (Make way – stand clear;)
The Horse of matchless pace;
And wondering, view his swift career,
He boasts a useful race!

He has perform'd – his Stock's been try'd,
'Tis not an empty sound;
His progeny are fam'd to ride,
Where'er he takes his round.

At least it is not any worse than some of those commercial "jingles" that assault our ears from "the box" these days!

All we know of Wildfire's performance is that he took second place in the Roadster Stallion class at the Yorkshire Show of 1839 at Leeds. According to a report in the *Yorkshire Gazette* on November 24th, 1841 he was one of fifteen stallions shipped from Hull to the Grand Duke of Hesse. That he was the only horse named in this report, must mean that he was a stallion of some renown, but we do not know very much about his achievements as a stallion.

Two sons of R. Ramsdale's Wildfire are recorded in Vol. I of the stud book and about the elder one, Philip Ramsdale's Phenomenon, we know very little. This horse appears to have been a brown foaled in 1835, his dam being Lund's mare by Sportsman, the dam of Merrylegs. Three sons of this Phenomenon are recorded in Vol. I, but of these Leake's Telegraph and Cook's Old Times are shown by old stallion cards to have been sons of P. Ramsdale's Bay Phenomenon, a horse foaled in 1848 and registered in Vol. II. Luckily, both these Phenomenons come from the same line, so perhaps it does not matter greatly now. However, the third son of P. Ramsdale's Phenomenon, was Taylor's Performer 550, a dark chestnut foaled in 1840, so he could not have been a son of the Bay Phenomenon. Taylor's Performer has a most important place in the history of the modern Hackney, and about him there is a fascinating story.

TAYLOR'S PERFORMER

Performer was bred by James Newby, a farmer of Givendale on the Yorkshire Wolds, who, being lame, was wont to travel the countryside sitting sideways on a donkey. Young James Taylor was employed as a groom by James Singleton, grandson of the celebrated jockey, John Singleton, who had purchased the Givendale estate of some 640 acres of wold land, and which James Singleton now owned in partnership with his mother.

Newby's mare was by Lund's Merrylegs and her chestnut foal of 1840 was much admired by the local horsemen, among them Taylor who saw in the colt his opportunity of rising to fame and fortune. Accordingly he begged a loan of £19 from his master, bought the colt and made a pact with the brothers Askwith, Mr. Singleton's tenants on Callis Wold, to keep the colt until he was three-years-old in return for a half share in him. Taylor carefully watched as the colt grew into a handsome young stallion, becoming increasingly convinced of his potential as a money maker. Performer was used on a few mares in his two-year-old year, and the following year Taylor left Mr. Singleton's service to lead the stallion on his rounds.

The handsome young stallion and his proud young owner made many friends that spring and had a most successful season. But when Taylor went to

Callis Wold to settle his account with the Askwiths, he was brusquely informed that he owned no part of the horse, had only been employed as a servant and, as such, he was only entitled to a small sum for wages and groom's fees. To clinch matters the Askwiths took the horse and secured him in a large brick barn, bolting and locking the door. Deeply angered, Taylor hurried off to seek the advice of his old master. Mr. Singleton sent him to George Leeman, than a rising lawyer in York, later to become Member of Parliament for that city for many years. Leeman warned Taylor that to break a lock was to break the law, but that, if he could gain possession of the horse in some other way, the Askwith's would be forced to take action against him to recover their share.

The barn in which Performer was secured happened to be built on a steep hillside and had a window at the back, almost on a level with the field behind. Taylor enlisted the aid of a friend who was a brick-layer, and they planned to remove the window at dead of night, lead the horse out, then replace the bricks and the window as before. On the appointed night the two set out for Callis Wold, taking with them Taylor's galloway and the tackle worn by the horse on his rounds. No time was lost in taking out the casement, and, once inside, the two set feverishly to work building a ramp of litter up to the window. Luckily the horse recognised his companion of recent weeks and remained calm throughout this unusual activity. At last all was ready and, wearing the familiar tackle, Performer calmly followed Taylor out through the window.

Sniffing the night air the horse caught the scent of the galloway tied to a nearby fence and whinnied loudly in greeting. The horrified conspirators expected lights to appear in the house at any moment and that they would be caught in the act. Happily, the brothers Askwith slumbered blissfully on; Taylor mounted his pony and thankfully led the horse away, leaving his friend to set all to rights in the barn.

Horse and man travelled south, not stopping through the day following till Callis Wold was 36 miles behind them. The horse was hidden away for the night not far from Doncaster, and the following night they set off again, making for Leicestershire. No doubt the Askwiths had by then started enquiries about the missing horse, but they had no news of him until the trio boldly returned to Givendale more than a week later. Taylor was promptly arrested, charged at Pocklington with the theft of the horse, and committed to York assizes. Naturally the case aroused great interest in the Yorkshire farming community, and on the appointed day the court was crowded. Mr. Leeman defended Taylor and was able to prove his ownership of a half share in the horse, so Taylor was acquitted. Performer was then put up for auction and knocked down to Taylor at 150 guineas. It is possible that Lawyer Leeman was the real buyer as at the Great Yorkshire Show at Bridlington in 1851

Performer was shown in his name, taking second prize in his class to his son, Sir Charles, then owned by James Taylor.

Later Taylor took the tenancy of Field House Farm, Barmby Moor near Pocklington and from there, during the season, he set off on Mondays to Sutton-on-Hull, via Routh and Wawne, calling at High Grange Farm, Market Weighton 9 miles from home where he took breakfast. This was a journey of at least 30 miles in the day, calling at farms on the way.

Sir Charles was bred by Richard Beal of Painsthorpe, not far from Givendale, his dam being by Lund's Merrylegs, next dam by Alfred (G.S.B.), a useful race horse that won four races out of seven starts. Mr. Mansfield Harrison, an eminent authority on Hackneys who knew the horse well, wrote in a letter to a friend:

> "Sir Charles got horses with more quality and action than any horse I have ever known. You could tell them by their style of walk a mile off. Quite ninety out of every hundred of them were high goers; he was by Taylor's Performer who, I am told, had a cross of Coaching horse in him."

I wonder if the coaching blood came through the dam of R. Ramsdale's Wildfire, but there are many gaps in his pedigree that might hide the secret of this.

Both Performer and Sir Charles remained in James Taylor's ownership, and were the most popular stallions in Yorkshire for many seasons. They did not compete at many of the horse shows that were now being held in many of the market towns, and the show of 1851 at Bridlington was their only appearance at the county show, the Great Yorkshire. Sir Charles competed at a few shows in whichever district had been chosen for that season's round, and he won his class at Bridlington three seasons running, then at Howden in 1855, and at Hackness (near Scarborough) in 1857, 58 and 59.

These two horses certainly made Taylor's fortune, and through their descendants at one time threatened to swamp the breed with their chestnut colour, but more of that later. One of Taylor's sons farmed Field House after him, and another became a clergyman, but Taylor was not a breeder of horses and no member of his family showed much interest in nag horses after the old man was gone.

PHILIP RAMSDALE'S FIREAWAY

Foaled in 1834, Ramsdale's Fireaway was the other good stallion sired in Yorkshire by Kirby's Wildfire (Burgess's Fireaway). In his case there is no doubt about the breeding of his dam, a mare owned by Francis Cook of

Huggate, the founder of the first large breeding stud of Hackneys, in Yorkshire. This mare was almost thoroughbred, sired by Ponteland (G.S.B.) by Waxy, out of a mare by Trip, a son of Granby (G.S.B.) from a mare by Richard Well's horse of Ripon (probably a half-bred horse), next dam by Jalap (G.S.B.). Burgess's Fireaway himself had a good proportion of thoroughbred blood in his pedigree, thus Ramsdale's Fireaway's ancestry was more than half thoroughbred, and further reinforcement of this Eastern blood was usual in Yorkshire Hackneys for several more generations.

Fireaway, a bay horse, 15.2 hands, was the first stallion owned by Philip, Old Bob Ramsdale's son. He bought the horse in 1837 as a three-year-old, and won with him at the East Riding Show at Beverley that same year. An engraving of him appeared in *The Farmer's Magazine* with the report of the show.

In 1838 he competed in the class for roadster stallions at the first show of the Yorkshire Agricultural Society at York. He was placed second below Lund's Merrylegs, then owned by Squire Denison, but at the same show at Leeds in 1839 Fireaway won the class with his older half-brother R. Ramsdale's Wildfire, standing second.

These are the only show appearances of which we have any record, although he doubtless appeared in impromptu contests at many of the markets and fairs in the East Riding. He became a consistently good sire, and was still in Yorkshire until about the mid-1850s. The Ramsdale's had a great many stallions during those years, and some travelled in the West Riding and parts of Lincolnshire in districts away from the main breeding centres of Hackneys, and no records of their achievements survive.

The most important son of Ramsdale's Fireaway was another Fireaway, foaled in 1838 and bred by James Scott, a well-to-do corn merchant from Market Weighton. This horse, known also as Little Wonder, was out of a mare by Ramsdale's Performer, grand-dam by Cockfighter (G.S.B.), great grand-dam by Palafox (G.S.B.). He won the roadster class at the Yorkshire Show at Thirsk in 1850, and was afterwards sold to John Ramsbottom of Doncaster.

Several sons of Scott's Fireaway are recorded in Volume I of the stud book, but the historically important one was Hairsine's Achilles, a red roan foaled in 1854. This attractive colour came from his dam, a mare by Bond's Norfolk Phenomenon, next dam by Borodino (G.S.B) by the Derby winner Smolensko. Achilles was shown a good deal in his early years; as a two-year-old he stood second to P. Ramsdale's Wildfire at Market Weighton show and in 1858 he won as far afield as Liverpool and Manchester. From the age of four he was owned by G. Sonley and G. Rodmell of Stoneferry, Hull and he appears to have spent all of a long life in the East Riding. There are records of

The Norfolk Phenomenon. An important sire in East Anglia and Yorkshire. (From a painting by T. Freeman.)

foals by him as late as 1874, and it was said that his stock paid farmers better than any others. Several of his sons went overseas.

In his conversation with "the Druid" Old Lund said Norfolk Phenomenon "did no great good" in Yorkshire, and perhaps he was not quite the marvel his connections claimed him to be, but his name is associated with many good Yorkshire-bred horses, such as Achilles. His best son in Yorkshire was Wilkinson's Shakespeare, a horse foaled about 1843 near Market Weighton. Wilkinson also bred Harrison's Black Rattler, and the two may have come from the same strain. Shakespeare's dam was by Lund's Merrylegs, granddam by Kirby's Wildfire. This horse was also a roan, a colour not common in Yorkshire Hackneys and where it appeared it was mostly through Norfolk Phenomenon.

CHAPTER THREE

THE COOKS OF HUGGATE AND THIXENDALE

The success of Philip Ramsdale's Fireaway may have drawn attention to the horses bred by the Cooks on the Yorkshire Wolds at Huggate and, later at Thixendale. Certainly from that time this stud developed into the most renowned in all Yorkshire. Through four generations members of the Cook family remained at the hub of the Hackney world and horses bred by them were shipped to the four corners of the earth.

Francis Cook had two foundation mares. One, "the Old Black Mare" by Trip, was the grand-dam of Ramsdale's Fireaway; the other was a mare, known as Miss Simpson, by Wroot's Pretender. Careful records were kept of all the progeny of these two mares.

The Ponteland mare, Fireaway's dam, is referred to on old cards as "Mr. Cook's celebrated trotting mare," and she had a filly by Templeman's Creeper that was also known as "Cook's Trotting Mare." The latter mare had three fillies that were kept for breeding, one by the Sledmere stallion Hampton (G.S.B.) the second by Black Overton (G.S.B.), and the third by Norfolk Phenomenon. Miss Simpson had two daughters, both by Ramsdale's Performer.

Francis Cook and his wife, Eleanor, had a large family, and, when Francis retired to Pocklington in the late 1840s, the breeding stock was evidently divided among three of his sons. Richard, the eldest, remained at Huggate Wold, and Francis Junior and Thomas kept their horses at Rigg's Farm, Thixendale. Francis and Thomas were both bachelors, Thomas being a draper and silk merchant at 30 Market Place, Hull. According to family tradition, for several years he travelled the thirty and more miles from Thixendale by train daily, using the station at Bilsdale on the Malton-Driffield line.

Two full brothers, both named Wildfire, and sired by P. Ramsdale's Wildfire, were bred at Thixendale in 1849 and 1853. Their dam was the Black Overton mare, and the elder of the pair, known as Cook's Wildfire, sired a horse called North Star in 1854, out of the mare, Jet, by P. Ramsdale's Fireaway, from the Miss Simpson strain. North Star was bought by Colonel Frederick Barlow of Woodbridge, Suffolk and sold by him in 1860 to the Austro-Hungarian Government. This horse went to the government farm at

Cook's North Star. The founder of an important strain of warm blood horses in Hungary. (From an engraving by Samuel Carter after E. Corbet.)

Mezohegyes where the breeding of half-breds had been started in 1842, using the English thoroughbred Furioso. North Star was mated mostly with Arabian mares to develop a dual purpose type of horses that is still known as the North Star line. Most have a good trotting gait, and Baka of the North Star line achieved a trotting record of 1 minute, 20.6 seconds for 1 kilometre.

The younger of these two Wildfire's was bought by Philip Ramsdale. This Wildfire was shown as a yearling to win at Pocklington in 1854, and in 1856 he won at Market Weighton, Hedon, Bridlington and Driffield. He grew into a 15.3 hands dark brown horse, and his place in Hackney history rests on a son, St. Giles, bred by F. Rickell of Warter-on-the-Wold and foaled in 1858. St. Giles left some good horses in Yorkshire before he was sold to be exhibited at the Paris Exhibition of 1864 where he won first prize. This is the first record of an English-bred Hackney winning at a horse show overseas. Philip Ramsdale died about 1860 and this, his second Wildfire, was one of the last stallions he owned.

Evening Star, a full sister to North Star foaled in 1855, was the best mare in the Thixendale Stud in the 1860s and 1870s. Her first foal, a filly, was by Richard Cook's horse British Champion, one of "the Old Black Mare's" family, thus in Evening Star's foal the two founding Cook strain were blended together; the filly was named British Queen and won many prizes at local and county shows. In 1862 Evening Star was put to Rickell's St. Giles and produced the good brown stallion Eclipse. When old enough, this horse was put on the road in parts of the East Riding, his conductor being Robert Drake of Everingham.

To own a popular stallion was a lucrative business in those days, and Drake, who bought Eclipse after a year or so, owned a succession of stallions in the boom years of the Hackney, covering a period of about thirty years. Unfortunately, poor Drake was what we might call today "a soft touch", and when he died he left little more than a desk stuffed with worthless IOU's. He may also have been the local "horse doctor", as were many stallion men at the time, and I have his dog-eared copy of *Brown's Manual of Modern Farriery*, published in parts by Virtue about 1840, which sold at one shilling each. Stitched into this old book are some interesting hand-written remedies, one of which is "for cough's, colds, or fever in either Man, Horse or Beast." This is made of liquorice, aniseed, saltpetre, raisins, and saffron, and is said to be "kind in operation, opening the lungs, working gently by stool and urine."

It would be tedious to catalogue all the good stallions that went out from Thixendale during the forty years that the Cooks were there to produce light harness horses for the growing needs of Victorian England and many overseas countries, but we cannot overlook the spectacular Star of the East. The dam of this horse was a mare by North Star in-bred to the Miss Simpson strain, and his sire was Charley Merrylegs by Beal's Sir Charles. His first appearance in the show ring was as a four-year-old at the Yorkshire Show at Skipton when, owned by George Holmes, a well-known veterinarian, of Beverley, he took the first prize for roadster stallions, defeating the Stand Stud Company's Norfolk bred Perseverance. Horse showing had by that time attracted the interest of the well-to-do and a class of professional showmen began to emerge. The "hand" classes, especially those for trotting stallions, were keenly fought and aroused much excitement. A ring filled with stepping trotters, each urged on by his wild-eyed whooping runner, must have been an electrifying spectacle, that caused otherwise sedate and respectable middle-aged gentlemen, very models of decorum in everyday life, to be so carried away as to fling their hats into the air and to give vent to heathen yells with complete abandon. "Trotting sires conductors", writes "the Druid", "are a set of Wild Indians and show their paces with remarkably jealous zest." Mr. Burdett-Coutts, on the other hand, tells of the "artistry" of Bob, the

Brookfield head runner. The aforementioned George Holmes had a runner "who had the knee-and-curb-chain action to perfection, and could teach his charges to step," so "the Druid" tells us.

It was said that Lord Ellesmere was among those with a financial interest in the Stand Stud Company and, with its extensive farm near Manchester and sale yard in London's Piccadilly, it must certainly have had some strong backing. Prestige demanded that its representatives in the show ring should be invincible, and so it was that Star of the East took the place of Perseverance shortly after the Skipton show. Between 1876 and 1883 he won almost £1,000 in prizes at all the leading shows in Britain, and many gold and silver trophies in addition. His greatest triumph was at the Paris Exhibition in 1878 when he won the Gold Medal as the best half-bred stallion. Long ago an eye witness described to me how, while the representatives of the great European state studs were being paraded round by their top-hatted and frock-coated attendants, Star of the East burst into the arena at a storming trot; his runner at the end of a long line, in shirt sleeves and a low-crowned pot hat, stepping with action to match that of the horse, which responded instantly to his sharp words of command. Sad to say the old horse was campaigned too long and, at the London Show of 1886, he was left ignominiously among the tail-enders of his class. Not long afterwards he met an undignified end. He was returning home to Manchester and, while he was being led down Deansgate, a she-ass, left unattended between the shafts of a two-wheeled flat cart, happening to be in season caught his scent and dashed after him, running the point of the shaft into his side.

Francis Cook of Thixendale died in 1878, but his brother Thomas carried on the stud for several more years. It was said that he did not care for Denmark, or his 5,000 guinea son Danegelt, then the most sought after sires in Yorkshire. Perhaps he had clashed at some time with George Bourdass their owner, a veterinary surgeon from Hunmanby whose black-bearded figure was often to be seen in a high gig travelling the chalk roads of the Wolds. Whatever the reason, I can find no record of any foal by Denmark having been born at Thixendale. The Cook brothers liked to reinforce the thoroughbred foundation of their roadsters by using a blood stallion from time to time. Well-bred stallions abounded in Yorkshire in those days; Sledmere was but a few miles away, while Lord Middleton's Birdsall House was just the other side of Birdsall Brow. Barefoot by Sleight-of-Hand, Hampton, Fingal and other good horses were all used, but the horse that had the greatest influence at the Thixendale stud in its later years was Northgrave's Bay President.

Thomas was the cleverest of the Cook brothers as a breeder, and he used Bay President's services a good deal. He must have given up "commuting" from Thixendale in his later years and bought a house at 7 Albert Terrace,

Anlaby Road, Hull. Thomas would have seen a good deal of Bay President, whose owner lived only a few miles away at Sutton, and the horse appeared regularly in the roadster classes at local shows. William Burdett-Coutts said of him:

> "He could generally win all before him when properly shown ... (he was) a beautiful type of 'real nag', and the most experienced Hackney breeders of England will today readily breed their grandest mares to his sons, for they know that therein lies quality, and quality with tremendous action is what catches the market."

It would seem that Thomas Cook was the first notable Hackney breeder to use Bay President, and then only when the horse was growing old. The first son of his that Cook bred was Pluto, dam Evening Star, a horse that was bought by the Askwith brothers of Callis Wold, who figured as the villains in the story of Taylor's Performer. Pluto was a good stallion, but the best of Bay President's sons in the Hackney stud book was Phenomenon 584 foaled in 1875, a dark chestnut son of the mare Eclipse by Drake's horse of that name. Phenomenon is also registered in Volume I under the name of Luck's All in the ownership of John Cook. This horse was bred by Francis Cook of Thixendale and, after Francis died, Thomas Cook became the owner. For the next few years Thomas Cook was an exhibitor at the Great Yorkshire and some local shows. At Barnsley in 1880 Phenomenon stood third to J. P. Crompton's Dorrington and Star of the East. In the class for roadster mares at this show all three entries were of Cook brothers breeding; the winner, R. Martin's Lady Mary bred by Richard, and the others were Rosalind by Eclipse and Portia by Bay President, both owned by Thomas Cook.

In 1881 at Hull, Star of the East took first place, Dorrington was second and Phenomenon again third. Not long afterwards Phenomenon was sold at a long price to go to France where he was most successful at stud. Fortunately he was one of those sons of Bay President to which, as Mr. Burdett-Coutts pointed out, "experienced breeders readily sent their grandest mares." Two important stallions were by him and several notable mares. Ford's Pioneer was one son, his dam by Denmark from a mare of the same lineage as that great horse. The other great son was Wreghitt's Wildfire, one of the key stallions in the story of the modern Hackney.

It was a tragic loss when Thomas Cook died in 1886 at no great age and the Thixendale stud was broken up. Several horses were bought by Thomas Shaw of Garstang in North Lancashire, a well-known stallion owner in the horse-breeding Fylde district who had a fondness for the Thixendale blood. Shaw had seven or eight stallions from there, but there were few well-bred mares in the

Fylde at that time and Shaw's horses had little chance to play much part in Hackney history. It was a son of Black Auster, a Shaw stallion, that sired one of the last foals Thomas Cook bred, from his favourite Portia. There may have been a reason for calling this colt Accident, but whatever the reason, it was under that name that he repeated Star of the East's triumph by winning the Gold Medal at Paris in 1889 for Mr. Burdett-Coutts.

Accident was one of several Hackney stallions taken to Vermont in the United States by Dr. William Seward Webb, and this horse was presented to the town of Middlebury to stand at a nominal fee with the object of improving local stock. Accident was described as "a charming little black-brown horse, a little over the 15 hand mark, of symmetrical form, well rounded, with good shoulders and short flat legs." Black Auster, too, crossed the Atlantic, to Illinois which was then developing its horse-breeding industry.

The dispersal at Thixendale was by no means the end of the Cook family's part in the Hackney story. Richard Cook's eldest son, Francis the third, was already established a few miles away at Nab Farm, Fimber (what a quaint Nordic ring there is about these East Riding names!), when his father died in '66. Mrs. Ann Cook, Richard's widow, carried on farming at Huggate Wold, and the horses were apportioned between mother and son. Besides farming, this Francis was an auctioneer, and his tall figure and high-pitched voice were well-known at Malton and Driffield markets for many years. He bred horses on quite a large scale, but he was not such a meticulous record keeper as his Thixendale uncles had been, and, although a number of horses of his breeding went overseas, he bred none of any particular note. Frank Cook held a great dispersal of some 100 head of Hackneys in 1911 and that ended his connection with the breed.

Far more successful was Robert Martin, and his son William who succeeded him at Gate Helmsley near Stamford Bridge. Robert Martin bought some of Richard Cook's best mares from Mrs. Ann Cook after Richard died. Lady Mary was one he bred from a mare of the Miss Simpson family, and with her he won 151 prizes in saddle, harness and brood mare classes. The Martin's were good show men and their stud enjoyed a good run of success, especially with the brothers Lord Derwent and Lord Derwent 2nd, both by Denmark, the horse the Cooks would not use, out of Lady Mary. Pilot and Pilot 2nd by Lord Derwent from Lady Webster, a mare of the Old Black Mare's line, also did well for William Martin. In more recent years, it was a descendent of Martin's Lady Mary that produced Fleetwood Viking, one of the best show horses of the 1930s and '40s. Another mare from the same line foaled the good show jumper Hoo-Doo, that was dam in her turn of the Misses Machin-Goodall's jumpers Neptune, Venus and King's Rhapsody.

Here I would like to digress with the story of what seemed at the time a

Fleetwood Viking. One of the best show harness horses of the 1930s, driven by George Lancaster. (Photograph by Rouch.)

small personal triumph. In the 1930s my imagination was fired by the story of these wonderful horses from Thixendale, and I hoped one day to find some survivors of Cook breed. By chance I heard of an old stallion that belonged to an ancient gentleman who lived a few miles from Sheffield. The horse was known as Wadsley Jack, but he was not eligible for the stud book because his dam was unregistered. His sire was a well-bred son of Polonius and his dam's sire was Blaze 2nd, both horses being grandsons of Cook's Phenomenon, and Blaze 2nd had the added interest of coming from Leak's strain, the family of Bob Ramsdale's Performer. Wadsley Jack was probably the closest blood relative of the Thixendale breed that I was likely to find, and I could hardly wait to see him in the flesh.

The horse's owner was a retired cutler named Willis Crookes, a rather frail old bachelor in his middle eighties, and, when I called one day he sent his almost equally ancient groom, James Caborn, to bring Wadsley Jack out for my inspection. He was a typical roadster of the old sort; plenty of good flat bone; deep through the heart with a strong back and muscular quarters. His neck had the somewhat pronounced crest of the Polonius breed, and, moving round his yard, he put on a storming show of action and energy. He was not for sale, I was told, but I was able to arrange to send him two mares.

Old Mr. Crookes had, as a young man, visited Thixendale, and had a great fund of stories of men and horses of the distant past which, seated in front of a roasting fire, he was happy to pour into my eager ear. In 1939 I joined the army and early in 1940 a curious letter arrived from my old friend. Would I, he wrote, call to see him as soon as possible on a matter of great urgency the nature of which he could not disclose in a letter that might be opened and read before reaching me. I was able to arrange a few days leave and hurried off to Sheffield wondering what lay behind this mysterious summons.

I found Mr. Crookes stricken with bronchitis and confined to the house facing a domestic crisis of the first magnitude, so he said. His housekeeper and James, his groom of long standing, had been at loggerheads for years, and they had now delivered an ultimatum that one of them would leave unless the other was dismissed. In his present condition it was out of the question for him to let his housekeeper go, so the only possible solution seemed to be to sell the old horse and pension off James. Would I buy Wadsley Jack?

My army pay at the time was two shillings a day, less stoppages, but despite such slender resources we were able to strike a bargain. I was asked to get the horse away as quickly as possible, and warned not to tell a soul about the transaction, especially James "who was a vindictive man and might poison the horse", so I was told. The following day was a Sunday and the best arrangements I could make was to book a horse-box on the train leaving Sheffield six miles away at 7 a.m. I slept that night at a local pub where the landlord roused me at 3 a.m. to a breakfast of ham cut from a huge home-cured specimen hanging from a beam in the kitchen. Not long afterwards I arrived in pitch darkness at Mr. Crookes stable yard to find the main gate locked and bolted and, in boots and spurs, I had to scramble over to break the lock. Despite the unavoidable noise of this and other forced entries, no one stirred and soon afterwards Wadsley Jack left his birthplace for the last time. Tram cars were running by the time we neared the city and their hissing wires alarmed the old horse more than a little, but, in spite of being misdirected several times, we got to the station with ten minutes to spare. The horse travelled well, and walked on to the platform at Hull still full of bounce, ready for the three mile walk to my uncle's farm on the eastern outskirts.

Probably because the horse was not registered my uncle would not use him, but he did kindly offer to keep him for me. I got the required license from the Ministry of Agriculture and engaged a man to travel the horse on a small circuit in part of Holderness. In the hope of being able to get approval for the

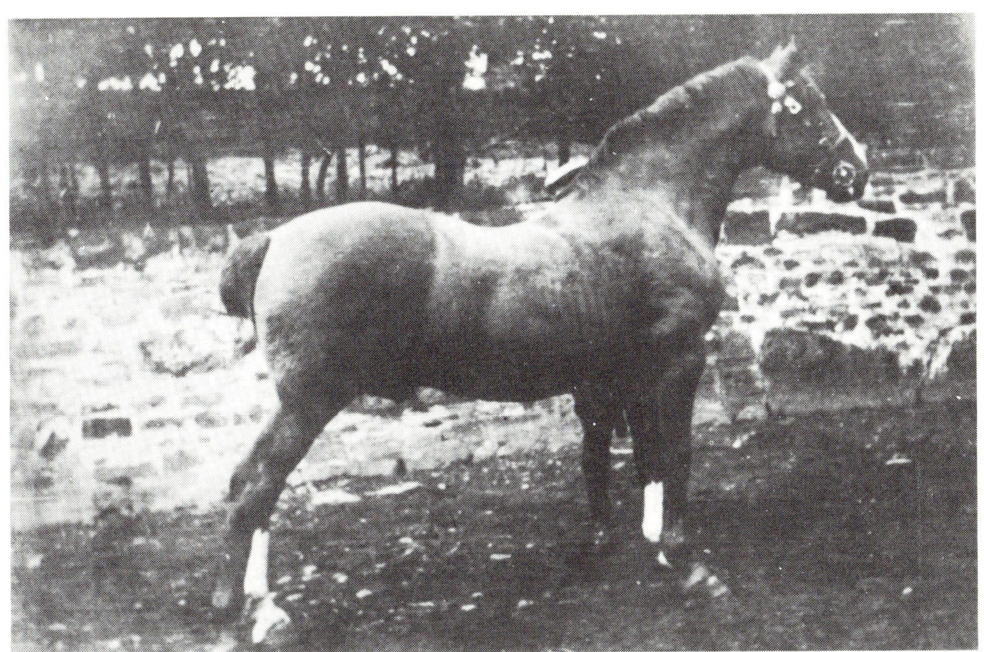

Wadsley Jack. A stallion foaled in 1919 that was in-bred to Cook's Phenomenon.

registration of Wadsley Jack's foals, I contrived to attend a meeting of the Council of the Hackney Horse Society at 12 Hanover Square, probably the last ever held at that historic London address. The phoney War was over by then and the battle for France had begun, but there was a good attendance of old stalwarts nevertheless. Claud Goddard was in the chair, Nigel Colman, M.P., had rushed over from the House of Commons, dear old Dr. Alex Bowie sat opposite me nodding his head and winking, perhaps involuntarily. Major Harry Faudel-Phillip sat next to me and did his best to put me at ease by making witty assides, *sotto voce*, or so he thought, about others in the room. His remarks began with a monotone rumbling sound deep in the lower recesses of his body, gathering volume as it neared his lips, to emerge as an articulated growl plainly audible to our neighbours. Dr. Bowie grinned a little and nodded and winked harder than ever, but I was feeling conspicuous enough in my uniform with its lone lance-corporal's stripe, and the gallant major did little to bolster my self confidence. They were rising to leave before I had managed to make my case for the horse, and as they put on their hats someone said, "Put it all in a letter, dear boy, we'll look into it."

Almost a year later a letter that had been chasing me for months found me sitting under a carob tree in a Lebanese valley, and I read how a bomb had fallen on my uncle's farm and Wadsley Jack was one of several horses killed.

CHAPTER FOUR

THE MODERN HACKNEY

The Hackney Stud Book Society was formed following a meeting in Norwich on June 30th, 1883, for the purpose of "the publication of a Stud Book for Hackneys, Roadsters, Cobs and Ponies." The registered office of the Society was at the *Norwich Mercury* office, and a branch office was set up at 11 Chandos Street, Cavendish Square, London in 1889. The name was changed to the Hackney Horse Society in 1891, and soon afterwards the office was moved to 12 Hanover Square where the Shire Society and some others were already installed.

The first show was held at the Agricultural Hall, Islington in March, 1885, with six classes for stallions, three for mares and two for thoroughbred stallions. By that time a few notable horses had begun to dominate the breed, and these same horses came to have considerable influence on the developing Hackney pony breed. The champion stallion at the first show, William Flander's Reality, was a Norfolk bred horse, but of the five stallions that came to be seen as the founding fathers of the modern Hackney four were Yorkshire bred, three of them having close blood links to the Cook strains.

Taken in chronological order the histories of these horses are given below.

FIREAWAY (TRIFFIT'S) 249

Fireaway was a black brown horse foaled in 1859 at Holme in Yorkshire, standing 15.2 hands. He lived to the age of thirty years and, although he had lost an eye in his early years, he was seldom beaten in the show ring over a period of some ten years. "The Druid" described his win at the Great Yorkshire Show at Wetherby in 1868:

> "Two blacks, father and son, the latter rejoicing in the name of Sir Edwin Landseer, headed the roadster class. There was only three years between them, but still the six-year-old was fairly beaten."

He goes on:

> "Trotting sires conductors are a set of wild Indians, and they show

their horses' paces with remarkably jealous zest. They trot them with a long rein and use words in an almost unknown tongue! ..."

... this tradition seems to die hard!

Fireaway won at the Royal Show at Manchester the following year. His line was highly esteemed by that eminent breeder Mr. Burdett-Coutts and sons and daughters of Fireaway were important members of his Brookfield Stud near London. One of Fireaway's great rivals in the show ring was Northgrave's Bay President. Old Philip Triffit told Mr. Burdett-Coutts of their decisive encounter at Sutton-in-Holderness, saying "he used to bother us a good bit wi' t'owd 'oss (Fireaway)" and at this meeting the judges had tried the two horses up and down in the grass field for a long time until at last someone suggested taking them on the road, the true place to try a Hackney. Thither they went followed by a large and keenly excited crowd. The horses' side-reins were taken off, and then – how the old man's eyes sparkled with the memory of this distant triumph! – "didn't t'owd 'oss fly oop in t'air," and it was never in doubt afterwards.

"A medal recording each fresh victory is attached to a conqueror's neck collar, and one horse which came to Wetherby and 'took nothing by his motion' wore a breeching of medals as well."

Thus "the Druid" again and nearly forty of Fireaway's medals are still prized by the Triffit family.

Fireaway was by Hairsine's Achilles, his dam Philip Triffit's good mare, Nancy, a brown that won the brood mare class at York in 1857 and at several other shows. Nancy was by Ward's Roan Performer, a horse also known as Young Phenomenon and Roan Phenomenon, which was a son of Norfolk Phenomenon out of a mare by Ramsdale's Performer. Nancy's dam was by Johnson's Harkaway, grand-dam by Templeman's Creeper. Fireaway's long list of show successes included a first at the Manchester Show of the Royal Agricultural Society in 1869. A great many of his sons went overseas. Of those that remained in Britain Foston Fireaway was perhaps the best known and this horse spent his later years at W. Burdett-Coutts's Brookfield Stud. Caxton was another; he was bred at Henry Moore's Burn Butts Stud, out of his great foundation mare Poll 3rd, but spent some time at the Terrington Stud where he sired some good mares. Winnal Fireaway was probably the best goer by him, and this horse's annual tussle with Polonius in the under 15 hand class was one of the liveliest features of the Agricultural Hall show. Winnal Fireaway scored most victories, even though just before leaving for London one year the horse nearly died of inflammation of the kidneys. He was saved

Fireaway (Triffit's). Part of the string of medallions recording the show ring victories of this great stallion and worn by the horse when shown at country fairs.

by the sovereign remedy of slaughtering a sheep and laying its skin, warm from the carcass, across his back.

None of Fireaway's sons equalled his performance as a sire and the male line died out in the early years of this century, but his daughters were wonderful breeders. Tom Jones Evans told me that some farmers on the sandy soil of the Vale of York worked the land with fine big Fireaway mares, and made a substantial addition to their incomes with the foals which found eager buyers. Mansfield Harrison rated Fireaway as the next best sire to Sir Charles. He remembered seeing ten stallions in the ring together all by Fireaway.

Phillip Triffit moved up in the farming world as his great horse added to his fortune; from Holme he went to Allerthorpe Hall, then in '79 he had Huggate Wold and moved from there to Scalla Moor, Howsham. He retired to Malton after the old horse died in 1889.

DENMARK 177

Denmark was a chestnut horse 15.2 hands, foaled in 1862. His sire was Beal's Sir Charles, the best son of Taylor's Performer whose story I have already told. His breeder, William Rickell, had an old and valuable strain of Hackneys on the Wolds near Water Priory, and he was a regular winner in the roadster classes at Yorkshire Shows in the 1850's. Denmark's dam (then 23 years old) won at the Great Yorkshire in 1862 with Denmark as a foal at foot. Her dam was by Kirby's Wildfire (Fireaway 208) and grand-dam by the thoroughbred All Fours.

Denmark himself was shown over a long period, first by Rickell, and after 1868 by George Bourdass of Bridlington. He was a regular winner at Scarborough, Bridlington and Driffield, but Beart's Ambition came up from Norfolk to beat him at the Yorkshire Show in 1869. However, as a sire he was in the very top class, getting foals with size and quality, many of them becoming great show horses.

Denmark travelled a circuit in the East Riding for more than twenty seasons and at the height of his popularity his fee was only three guineas. The best mares in Yorkshire were put to him, and a few from farther afield. At the first Islington Show his son Confidence (Moore's) was second to champion Reality, and his daughter won both classes for mares. In 1886 Candidate, full brother to Moore's Confidence, was champion stallion, and the mare championship went to Apology by Denmark after a tremendous fight between that mare and Lady Watton 2nd, also by Denmark.

Of Denmark's many famous sons, the best known was Danegelt, also a chestnut bred by Francis Rickell at Warter in 1879. George Bourdass bought Danegelt as a two-year-old, and he was sent round the East Riding farms when he was four at a fee of £2. His dam was Nelly by St. Giles, grand dam

Danegelt when he was eight years old. A photograph taken in Bourdass's yard at Hunmanby.

by Roan Napoleon by Scott's Roan Horse. At the shows Danegelt was never quite in the first flight; at the Royal at Manchester in '83 he stood third below the seasoned campaigner Star of the East, and at the first Islington show he was fourth to Lord Derby 2nd, the Norfolk bred Lord Bang and Star of the East in the under 15.2 hands class. As a sire he was reckoned at least the equal of Denmark, and when it was heard in 1892 that "the foreigners" were after buying him, Sir Walter Gilbey hastened to Yorkshire to prevent such a calamity, the great Denmark having died in 1888. George Bourdass had moved from Bridlington to Hunmanby near Filey, where he lived in a double-fronted house overlooking the green and which he named Denmark House, presumably in memory of the horse whose earnings had bought the place. Local gossip had it that Bourdass had "the foreigners" in one of the two front rooms, and Sir Walter in the other, while he himself crossed from one to the other with bid and counter-bid. In the end Sir Walter had to part with 5,000 guineas for the thirteen-year-old horse, setting a record high price for the breed that stood for many years.

Candidate was bought by Mr. Burdett-Coutts after winning the championship at Islington and was not shown again. His stock had quality and style and mares by him were good breeders.

Fred Childerhouse's M.P., champion in 1892, was by Candidate and was described as a "mass of quality." Unfortunately his dam, though registered, was of unknown breeding and there was much discontent about this lack of pedigree in a champion. Such feelings were disregarded, however, and the horse won again in '93, but he proved a complete failure at stud. Old Willis Crookes told me a curious tale of how one day a man walked into his yard, leading a stallion and asked if the horse could be stabled for the night. Mr. Crookes obliged, and, when the horse's rugs were removed there seemed something familiar about the horse.

"I know that horse," he said. "That's champion M.P."

The man looked shocked, and looking over his shoulder, he said: "Don't tell anyone what you have seen. He has been sold without pedigree to a farmer up north, and I am walking him up there so no one will know where the horse came from."

Another horse that must be mentioned was Connaught, a dark chestnut foaled in 1884, dam Fanny by Fireaway 249, the London champion in 1891. Connaught was bred by Richard Tennant of Kirkburn Grange, Driffield in whose ownership he remained and the horse became a very good sire.

Danegelt's sons included three breed champions; the double champions Royal Danegelt and Ganymede, and the treble champion Rosador. Royal Danegelt was bred by Sir Walter Gilbey from his good Yorkshire-bred mare Dorothy by Lord Derby 2nd, and he was a horse of great quality. Ganymede was bred by John Wreghitt of Londesborough, near Market Weighton, his dam Patience by Cook's Phenomenon, a full sister to Wildfire 1224 whose story follows. Ganymede was a fine upstanding horse and a great mover. As a four-year-old he had stood reserve to Connaught after a protracted battle. The illustration of this horse in Vol. XII of the stud book is taken from a painting done by Ganymede's owner, Tom Mitchell of Bradford, and the horse served him well as a sire, some of his offspring being winners in harness, which was not the case with all of the Denmark breed.

Indeed Rosador's stock had a bad reputation in harness, but many were good winners "in hand." Rosador, a bright chestnut with a white face and four white legs, was a veritable gold-mine for his breeder, Frank Buttle of Thirkleby, and his story well illustrates the part chance plays in men's lives. When Frank was five-years-old he was taken to visit his uncle, Frank Cook, the auctioneer, who lived at Nab Farm, Fimber. Young Buttle was told he might have his pick of a number of fillies running in a field and he chose the two-year-old Jessie because of her red chestnut colour and white legs. After a few years service as the "trap" horse on the Buttle farm, Jessie was mated first to Phillip Triffit's Duke of Connaught and then to Fireaway himself. Rosador was foaled in 1892 and showed great promise from the start. Jessie was by Beal's Sir Charles, thus Rosador was in-bred to that great horse, and was quite his equal in the show ring. As a three-year-old he took reserve to Ganymede for the championship, beating a lot of good older horses. His championships were won in '97 and '99 and the show rules did not allow a horse to compete for a third time. This rule was changed for the show of 1907 and at fifteen years of age, Rosador became the second horse to win the honour for the third time.

The Denmark family produced horses of size and quality, but for a time there was a danger of its chestnut colour swamping the breed. The Rosadors were a particularly colourful lot, quite the reverse of what was wanted for the high-class carriage horse trade. Denmark and his sons mated well with Fireaway and Lord Derby 2nd mares, and some good harness horses came from this cross. The male line has now almost died out in Hackney horses.

D'OYLEY'S CONFIDENCE. 158

Confidence was a handsome 15.2 hands brown horse of almost pure Norfolk trotter blood, having four crosses of Jary's Bellfounder, one of the foundation sires of the American Standardbred Trotter. He also had seven crosses of Marshland Shales, the horse immortalised by George Borrow in the oft-quoted passage in *Lavengro* in which he describes doffing his cap to the majestic old horse at Norwich Fair. Confidence was a great great grandson in the male line of Bond's Norfolk Phenomenon, while his dam's sire traced back through the Yorkshire bred Flying Buck to Wroot's Pretender. He was the sire of Leed's Monarch which Mr. R. C. Irving, a well-known London veterinarian, described as having higher front action than any horse he ever saw, and high action was found in most of his stock; but there was a flaw in the gem and that astute judge Mr. Burdett-Coutts writes:

> "There is a strain of softness and a strain of cartiness somewhere in the blood of the old horse (Confidence), both of which come out in hundreds of his stock bred from ordinary Hackney mares. The softness can best be got rid of by an infusion of thoroughbred blood or, better still, by using him or his sons on the harder basis of the Yorkshire Hackney. Foreign buyers have taken away great numbers of coarse underbred stallions by him – wonderful dealers' or 'yard' horses, that come out bursting with short-lived courage and 'dash it' up to the sky just long enough for the price to be settled. Give them twenty five minutes on the road and they are helpless passengers. The heavy shoulders and heavier neck, the pounding dishing action, the cut-away

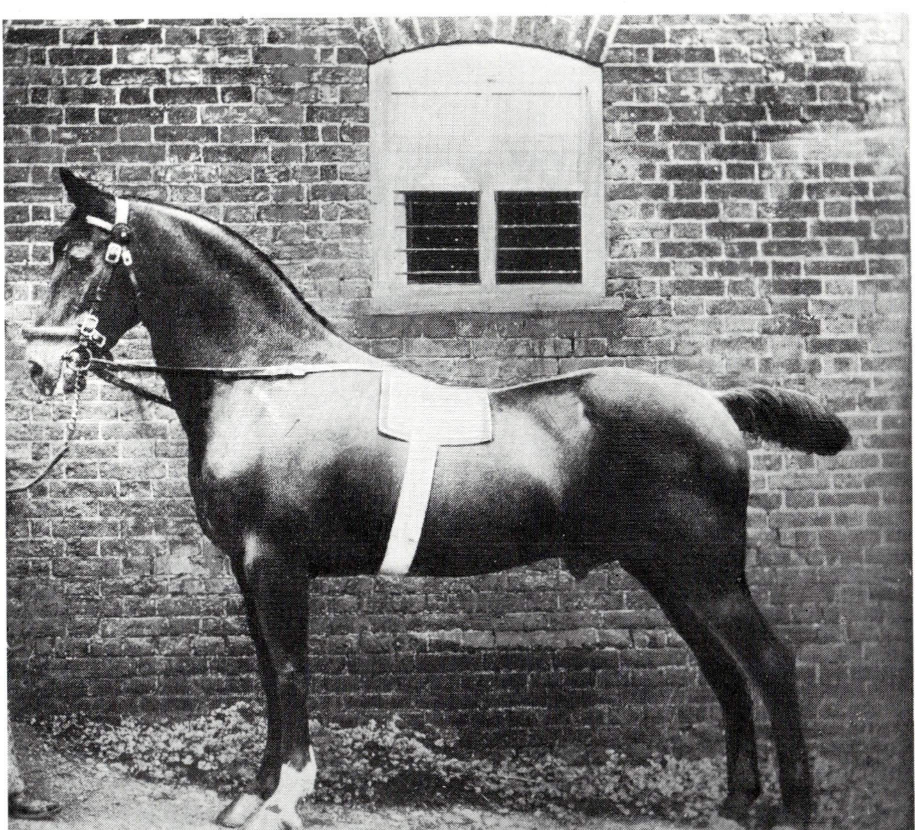

D'Oyly's Confidence. The most important Norfolk-bred stallion in modern Hackney history.

bone below the knee, the round dray-horse quarters with the dock springing from nearly half-way down their back profile, the 'punchy' character all over: these things must be acceptable to many buyers, it is a matter of taste, but what they do not know, and what is hidden from them, is the fatal strain of 'softness', the 'no heart', of these horses. With his mares correctly chosen old Confidence could get – and has got – the finest and best Hackneys that ever lifted a knee; but at the same time he has got countless brutes of the first order, who collectively have made up the worst curse that any breed of horses in our time has had to bear. In order that this criticism should not be misunderstood, I will add that I so fully appreciate what the horse could do when properly mated, I would readily give £10,000 to buy him and keep him in this country."

But Mr. Burdett-Coutts did not have to spend anything to keep the horse at home – he was not for sale at any price. It was said that half the population of Wymondham, the little town in Norfolk where Confidence was kept, owed their livelihood to him through the amount of money spent in the district to buy his stock. The first London champion, Reality, was by Confidence, his dam by the thoroughbred Tamworth, bearing out Mr. Burdett-Coutts opinion. One of the best sons of Confidence was Canvasser whose dam was by American trotter Shepherd F. Knapp, next dam by Harrison's Harkaway, a Yorkshire roadster.

The Confidence male line died out years ago in horses, but it is still of great importance in Hackney ponies.

LORD DERBY 2nd 417

Lord Derby 2nd, foaled in 1871, was another 15.2 hands brown, of Yorkshire breeding and owned throughout his life by Mr. J. R. Burnham of Frodingham Hall near Withernsea. He, too, was descended in the male line from Burgess's Fireaway through Ramsdale's Wildfire. His dam brought more of this same strain through her sire Hairsine's Achilles, sire of Triffit's Fireaway, and through several crosses of that other son of Burgess's Fireaway, Fireaway 222, the first good sire of the Cook strain. Lord Derby was a good winner in the show ring, winning his class at the first London Hackney show, and only narrowly going down to Reality for the stallion championship. As a sire he was held in the highest regard, nowhere more than in his native Holderness where ...

> "... many a poor farmer in that bleak stretch of country, swept by the winds of the German Ocean, from Withernsea to Hull, will mourn his loss, looking ruefully at his old farm mare, for whom £30 would have been a high price at any time, had not her three-year-old by Lord Derby so often sent him to his rent audit happy and independent with a fat roll of notes in his pocket."

This an extract from a tribute by Mr. Burdett-Coutts, written after the horse's death in August 1889.

Lord Derby's stock were not only good looking horses "wearing two good ends" as they say, but they were alert and active and possessed of that unquenchable spirit that brought them stepping as gaily homeward after a long journey as they had when setting out. The very qualities needed in the show harness horse, and several early winners in leather were by Lord Derby, including Duke of York, Lady Watton, Princess and Brunette. His best remembered stallion sons were David Sowerby's lovely Gentleman John;

Lord Derby 2nd. The old hero of Holderness, and probably the most influential foundation sire of the modern show Hackney and Hackney pony.

Cadet, bought at eight years of age by Mr. A. J. Cassatt, the first President of the American Hackney Horse Society; and Grand Fashion 2nd.

To digress for a moment, there is a story told of Gentleman John and David Sowerby, one of the many outrageous pranks played by that rugged and pugnacious veterinary surgeon from Hull. Gentleman John was shown in a stallion class at Doncaster in 1895 when the judges were two well-known members of the Council of the Hackney Horse Society. They considered Gentleman John insufficiently masculine and left him out of the awards. Sowerby was greatly offended and swore to have his revenge. He had two leather medals struck. On one side they bore an ass's head and on the reverse the inscription: "To ... for judging, Doncaster 1895."

After having great sport displaying these to his cronies Sowerby despatched them to the offending judges. The matter was raised at a subsequent Council meeting and our friend was summoned to appear before that august body. Sir Walter Gilbey presided at the fateful meeting and, after hearing both sides of the case, the Council considered what action must be taken. When Sowerby re-appeared to hear the verdict he was addressed by Sir Walter.

"Mr. Sowerby, the Council considers your conduct to have been unworthy of a member of this Society and, accordingly, I must ask for your resignation".

Whereupon Sowerby replied: "Yes, Sir Walter, and when do I send the 'osses?"

"You don't understand," replied Sir Walter, "I said nothing about your horses, I am merely asking for your resignation from the Society."

"But sure-lie",came the reply, "if I can't be a member of your Society I can't keep 'osses, can I?" and he mockingly left the room.

Of course, it made no difference whatever as Sowerby's elder son was made a member in his father's stead and the horses were registered in his name from then on.

Though many of his daughters were great brood mares, Lord Derby's chief influence today is through Grand Fashion 2nd, sire from the great Ophelia of the stallions Mathias and Sir Augustus. Mathias became by far the best sire of show harness horses of his day, and most of the present day show harness horses are descended from Mathias in the direct male and several colateral lines. Many horsemen thought Sir Augustus the handsomer horse of the two, and he might have proved at least as great a sire had his destiny not been to spend his days in the remoteness of Western Ireland owned by the eccentric Lord Ashtown.

Lord Derby 2nd died on December 7th, 1889 and his passing was mourned throughout Yorkshire. An anonymous poet published a commemorative pamphlet with the following:

Lines on the Death of the Celebrated Horse
Lord Derby 2nd

Lord Derby the Second of world-wide renown
Has finished his course and his honours laid down;
He has died all too soon – in his nineteenth year –
And finished Alas! a most splendid career,
A horse of such merit and symmetry, he,
That none could compete with him, all did agree,
When in his full vigour, none could him surpass,
Forty prizes he won as the best in his class,
He was gentle and docile, in colour dark brown,

As proud as a peacock when e'r he was shown,
So grand was his carriage, so bold was his walk;
He had neck like a rainbow, and eye like a hawk;
His style and his action were so highly prized
That Lords, Dukes and Earls have him patronised
The sire of more winners his record will bring
Than any before ever shown in the ring,
His loss is a great one, and long felt will be
By all who prize action with good quality.
But thanks to the giver of every good gift!
His owner has still got a son of his left
Who is of such promise that in years to come,
He will carry the fame of Lord Derby still on.

WILDFIRE (WREGHITT'S) 1224

Wreghitt's Wildfire was a bay roan horse, 15.1½ hands, foaled in 1880, a son of Cook's Phenomenon and Polly Horsley by Triffit's Fireaway, granddam by P. Ramsdale's Bay Phenomenon. Polly Horsley won many prizes as a

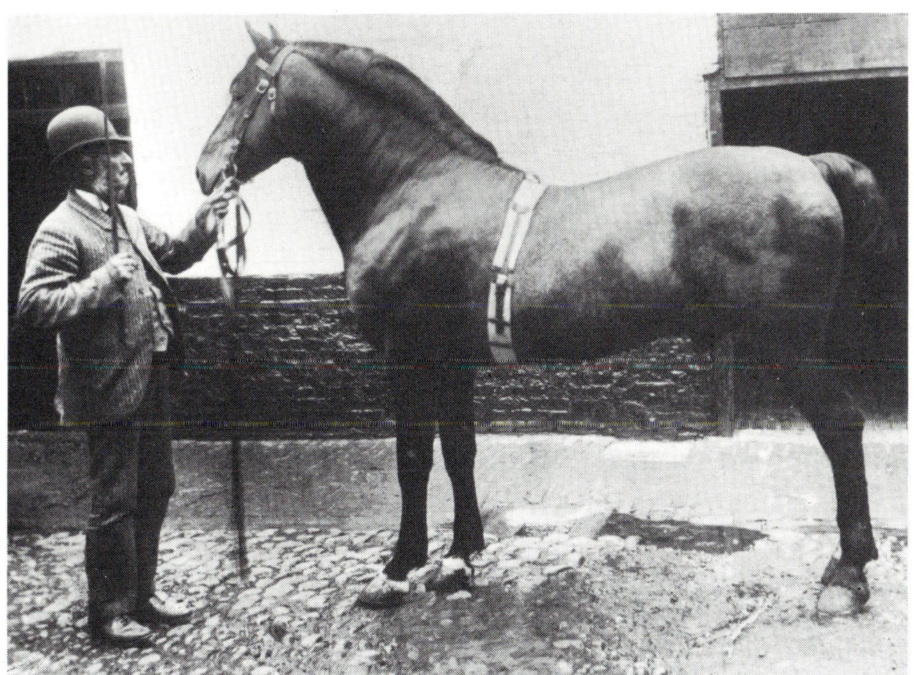

Wreghitt's Wildfire. The sire of Polonius and other good horses. Exported to Philadelphia at fifteen years old.

roadster under saddle and as a brood mare. Wildfire himself had a good show record, although the reviewer of the Islington Show of 1887 thought him lucky to have placed third in the under 15.2 hands class, calling him light of bone below the knee and inclined to fight in his action. He was a forceful style of goer, and this may have pleased North Country judges. However, he sired a number of good show horses and they made his reputation. One of his first show ring stars in harness was the roan Amazement that won at the great Manchester and Liverpool Horse Show at three-years-old for Sir Gilbert Greenall, and for different owners this horse stayed in the winning circle for at least twelve more years. His best harness horse was Heathfield Squire, the only horse ever to beat the great Forest King. Squire was a son of Ophelia, the Earl of Londesborough's great mare, making him full brother to Polonius. The latter stallion became the leading sire of show harness horses at the beginning of this century until overtaken by his half-brother Mathias about 1910.

In 1895 Wildfire was bought by Mr. Mitchell Harrison for his Chestnut Hill stock Farm near Philadelphia in the United States. He won his class at the Philadelphia Horse Show that same year, beating Alexander Cassatt's Cadet, a son of Lord Derby 2nd. Wildfire's fee in the United States was $50.00.

His best American born son was the brown stallion, Alarm, the champion at Long Branch, New Jersey, in 1900, and the winner of several harness classes at the same show. Alarm was bought by Robert Beith of Bowmanville, Ontario in 1902.

Some good Wildfire mares were also bred at Chestnut Hill, the best being Rushlight, a winner in hand and harness. Wildfire was still active in 1902, but I can find no record of what became of him after then.

CHAPTER FIVE

SOME IMPORTANT BREEDERS

Although the champion stallion at the first Hackney Stud Book Society's shows at Islington was the Norfolk-bred Reality, the champion mare, Moore's Princess, was Yorkshire-bred. Indeed it was to be almost forty years before there was a champion mare from a Norfolk strain. Rivalry between the two breeding districts was so keen that for many years the Show Committee had to ensure that one of the three judges was a Yorkshireman, one an East Anglian, and the third from elsewhere. The show results usually showed Yorkshire having the best of it, and the reason for this may have been that the modern Hackney, then emerging, was largely the result of using Norfolk Trotter sires on mares with a preponderance of thoroughbred blood, as was more commonly the case in Yorkshire. Most of the leading studs of those early days owed their success to one or two outstanding foundation mares, as we have already seen in the case of the Cooks of Thixendale, but there were others.

LOWTHORPE

John P. Crompton of Lowthorpe near Bridlington was a founder member of the Hackney Stud Book Society and the owner of a great strain of roadsters. He lived in that part of the East Riding where they loved a good "blood 'oss." Crompton, like Cook, had two foundation mares, one probably nearly thoroughbred was by Baronet (G.S.B.) a noted hunter sire. Of this line the most important was Fireaway Mare, foaled in 1870, by Triffit's Fireaway, dam by P. Ramsdale's Bay Phenomenon, grand-dam by Sir Tatton Syke's Conservative (G.S.B.) and so on down to the Baronet mare.

The second foundation mare was by Ramsdale's Performer, and her most distinguished descendant was Crompton's Bay Mare, by Rickell's St. Giles, dam by Crompton's Tom Thumb, grand dam by Lund's Merrylegs, great great dam by Borghese by Brutandorf (G.S.B.).

Tom Thumb was the earliest stallion on record of Crompton's breeding; foaled in 1849 he was by Wilkinson's Shakespeare by the Norfolk Phenomenon. Eight other stallions that were bred at Lowthorpe are recorded in Volume I of the stud book, and all played some part in the developement of the Hackney.

Goldfinder 6th. In-bred to Denmark, this stallion was noted for the quality of his offspring, both horses and ponies. (From a water colour by P. Palfrey.)

John Crompton died about 1884 and, although his son Thomas carried on breeding from the old strain at Houndales, Nafferton, a large part of the stud was sold by auction. Already its worth was widely known, and mares went to many of the breeding studs then being formed by wealthy enthusiasts including Alexander Morton of Kilmarnock, W. Burdett-Coutts and others. In later years the Crompton blood was sought out by John Makeague of Manchester and Sir Gilbert Greenall, and helped largely towards the success of both their studs.

BURN BUTTS

Probably the most prominent Yorkshire stud at the time of the founding of the Hackney Stud Book Society was Henry Moore's Burn Butts Stud at Southburn, a few miles from Driffield on the Yorkshire Wolds. The champion mare at the first London Show, Princess, was his, as also was Confidence, the reserve champion stallion. Moore's foundation mare was Poll 3rd, a mare foaled in 1866 by Shaw's Fireaway, a Norfolk-bred grandson of Burgess's Fireaway, next dam Poll 2nd by Black Rattler, grand-dam Poll 1st, foaled in

1817 by Ramsdale's Performer. Candidate, the head stallion at the Brookfield Stud, was bred at Burn Butts, as were Sweetbriar, reserve champion mare in 1887; Primrose the champion of '88; Caxton the winning three-year-old in '91; and Chocolate Junior, a winner in '93.

The champion stallion of '89 was Henry Moore's Rufus, a bright chestnut four-year-old that had been bought two years before from his breeder, Robert Peacock of Hockwold, Brandon, Norfolk. Peacock had one of the best Norfolk strains of those days, and a reporter at the show described Rufus as "one of the best Hackneys seen in recent years." The following year the same writer was even more laudatory in his description of Rufus's second victory, and there were few judges who saw the horse at that show who did not wholeheartedly agree. Unfortunately, Rufus died that same year and left few descendants.

Despite this calamity, the Burn Butts stud remained a force to be reckoned with for some years. It was dispersed after Henry Moore died in 1912.

AQUILA KIRBY OF MARKET WEIGHTON

One of the most valued mares in the Brookfield Stud was the bay Primrose by the American bred trotter Shepherd F. Knapp. Primrose had been a great winner at Yorkshire shows for her breeder, Aquila Kirby, and her dam, Nelly, had an even better show yard career during the late 1870's. The story of this family is interesting. Sall, Nelly's dam, was a thoroughbred mare by Melbourne, dam by the St. Leger winner Launcelot, grand-dam by Irish Birdcatcher. Sall, when thirteen-years-old, was sold at York for 235 guineas and given by J. B. Broudly of Scarborough to his friend and advisor, Robert Kirby. Robert passed the mare on to his son Aquila who, to the father's dismay, put her to the "nag horse" Achilles, sire of Triffitt's Fireaway, and Nelly, foaled in 1867, was the resultant foal.

Shepherd F. Knapp, American Trotting Registry No. 281, Vol. IV, was a chestnut horse, foaled in 1857, got by the Eaton Horse, dam a fast pacing mare by Whalebone (the Clark horse), a son of Sherman by Justin Morgan. He was bred by George Snell of Turner, Maine. The Shepherd had a record of 2.41 as a trotter, and was taken to Europe in 1872 to be exhibited at the Paris Exhibition. There he was admired and bought by Major Stapylton, a Yorkshire landowner, who travelled the horse in Yorkshire and East Anglia. He was the sire of Washington, whose daughter Movement was a renowned high stepping show horse.

Aquila Kirby bred many good horses from Sall's family, and probably made good money from them, but if so he used it badly. His farm failed and he earned a living for a time as the ostler at the Londesborough Arms Hotel in Market Weighton, later ending his days in the workhouse at Pocklington.

Shepherd F. Knapp trotting against the Hackney, Morning Star. (From a painting by E. P. Lambert.)

Geoffrey Bennett, who had met Aquila in his ostler days, heard of the poor old man's misfortune and tried to send him a package of his favourite biscuits. They were returned by the unfeeling Workhouse Master with a note saying he could not allow inmates to receive gifts of that kind as it might disturb the others! Before Aquila died, Bennett was able to collect him from Pocklington to see the Hackney Show at Doncaster in 1926 where Sall's most famous descendant, Buckley Courage, won the stallion championship for the first of seven times.

THE PEACOCK AND FLANDERS STRAINS

So far as I know these two families of East Anglian Hackney breeders were not related, but I have put them together because their horses were bred on similar lines, which is not surprising as both had farms a few miles apart on the border of Suffolk and Norfolk. In both cases the foundation stock had a greater infusion of thoroughbred blood than was found in most Norfolk Hackneys, much of it from the horse Tamworth by Outlaw. This horse

Authority. A son of Ganymede that was a big winner under saddle and in harness, as he appeared at the Hackney Show in 1930 driven by his owner, Mr. Nigel Colman, M.P., the horse then being 30 years old.

achieved little as a race horse, but his daughter, Foundation, was the dam of Flanders' Reality, the first champior stallion, and his name occurs five times in the pedigree of Rufus. The dam of Rufus was by Jackson's Quicksilver, a red roan son of Baxter's Performer, dam a near thoroughbred mare.

The Peacocks continued breeding Hackneys until the 1930s, and one of their stallions, Hockwold Cadet, did good service in Holland during the 1920s. The roan colour of the Norfolk Phenomenon and other noted Trotters survived in their stud, but may now have died out in the Hackney breed.

The Flanders family of Mildenhall in Suffolk, and later of Witcham Fen in Cambridge, carried on breeding for about as long as the Peacocks, but without producing any worthy successors to Reality.

THE TENNANTS OF DRIFFIELD

Two generations of Tennants were successful Hackney breeders in Yorkshire, and here again is the story of a single superior strain. In this case the foundation mare was Polly, a mare Richard Tennant bought in the Selby district to use as a shepherd's cob when he moved to Kirkburn Grange on the Yorkshire Wolds. Polly was by Ramsdale's Bay Phenomenon, dam by Wetherill's Prickwillow by Taylor's Performer. She had three foals by Triffit's Fireaway; a brown gelding that was sold to the King of Italy as one of a team of four; the stallion Sir John, sold in 1882 to the Austrian government; and the brown mare Fanny. This latter mare's second foal was Connaught by Denmark, the champion stallion in 1891 at Islington, the Royal and Great Yorkshire shows. Connaught was also a great success at the stud and did the Tennants good service.

Another of Polly's foals was Sir John 2nd by the Denmark stallion Ponteland, and, from his half sister Fanny, Sir John 2nd produced the mare Success. Success was put to Lord Derby 2nd in '88 and the resulting brown colt was named Grand Fashion 2nd, destined to win the class of 39 two-year-olds at the London Show of 1891. Grand Fashion never quite lived up to this early promise in the show ring, but from the Earl of Londesborough's champion mare Ophelia he sired the stallion Mathias, the horse from which all modern Hackney horses are descended. Unfortunately Grand Fashion died of a diseased jaw-bone when still a young horse.

Connaught's full sister, Waxwork, produced to Lord Derby 2nd a brown colt that, being badly ruptured, was made a gelding. Named Duke of York this horse became one of the best show harness horses of his day, and added 1,000 guineas to the Tennant treasury.

Two sons of Richard Tennant bred Hackneys; the elder, Sam, farmed at Wold House, Driffield, and, among many good horses he bred, were the full brothers Revival, second to champion McKinley at London in 1902, and Authority, a great winner in harness. W. J. Tennant became an architect, but kept a small stud of Hackneys of the family strain near Pontefract. The best known horse he bred was the stallion Carleton Quality, a typical Denmark type and one of the last of that line.

HALL OF LANGTON

This is really the story of another money-spinning stallion, namely Garton Duke of Connaught by Connaught, a horse bred by Joseph Young of Garton Grange, near Driffield, the first foal of a mare he had bought at Thomas Cook's sale at Thixendale, and which he registered as Lady Cook. She was by Lord Derwent 4th out of Morning Star by Bay President, a mare of the Miss Simpson line, and was mated as a two-year-old to champion Connaught.

According to a story I was told by a member of the family, Thomas Hall, then living at Stamford Bridge, was offered by his father the choice of a pedigree Leicester ram or a Hackney stallion as part of his stock-in-trade when about to set up farming on his own account. He chose the horse and bought the Lady Cook yearling for 100 guineas, registering him as Garton Duke of Connaught. A few weeks later he took him to Islington, where the horse was placed fifth of twenty, the winner being H.R.H. Prince of Wales's Field Marshal. Mr. Hall's horse was then described as one of the most promising youngsters in the show, an opinion that was upheld on his next appearance two years later when he headed a class of 57 three-year-olds. As a mature horse he was not able to stay at the top, but he had already done enough to fill his list each season. Garton Duke sired champions McKinley and Administrator, the latter one of the first stallions to be shown extensively in harness, and he was noted as a sire of those great strapping horses that were in great demand for the foreign market, such as Crayke Mikado champion at the Canadian National Show in 1907, and Langton Performer, Junior Champion at New York in 1895.

Garton Duke of Connaught lived to a ripe old age, and, when he died, Tom Hall had his four hooves mounted as memento's of the horse that had made the family fortune. Garton Duke headed the list of winning sires at the London

Copmanthorpe Performer. A typical son of Garton Duke of Connaught.

Show from 1899–1906, and in his later years he stood at Arthur Hall's farm at Copmanthorpe near York where two of his sons, Copmanthorpe Performer and St. Thomas, were also available to breeders.

These horses represented the ultimate development of the big-boned "coachy" type of Hackney that, until about 1910, was appearing in increasing numbers in the hand classes at the breed show, where a great many of them were bought to go abroad. The demand for this sort fell off rapidly as motors replaced horses both for public and private transportation. The Hall brothers then turned to training race horses with considerable success, and members of the family are well-known in racing circles to this day.

SIR WALTER GILBEY

The Hackney Stud Book Society came into being partly through the support of a few wealthy and influential individuals, some of whom later set up breeding studs of their own with the object of preventing losses of the best horses to foreign breeders. Foremost among them was Mr. (later Sir) Walter Gilbey, whose energy and enthusiasm had already had some influence on the newly formed Shire Horse Society. Mr. Gilbey bought County Member by Lord Derby 2nd for 400 guineas after he had taken third place at the first Hackney Show at Islington in 1885. Bred by Tom Reed at Beeford, this Yorkshire-bred horse was described as "perhaps one of the most perfectly-topped horses in the show, and a grand mover." Crompton's Bay Mare and her daughter, Lily of the Valley by Denmark, came to Elsenham soon afterwards, and more stallions and mares of equally illustrious breeding followed as they became available, notably the fourteen-year-old Danegelt as already noted. Danegelt's best son, Royal Danegelt, and his dam, the Lord Derby 2nd mare Dorothy, were other purchases; they, like most of the Elsenham stock, being of Yorkshire strains.

Sir Walter was made President of the Society in 1887 and again in 1902, and he was an active Council member for many years. He was also a great publicist, never losing an opportunity of pointing to the breed's good qualities in the *Livestock Journal* of which he was the proprietor, and other publications.

Although the Elsenham Hall horses seldom, if ever, competed in harness classes, most were broken to harness, and in a large circular building on the farm was an arrangement for exercising up to eight horses in harness under the control of one man. The type of horse bred at Elsenham was generally a high-class carriage horse of reasonable size and good quality. Possibly Sir Walter might have selected Flash Cadet, a bay horse 15.3 hands, foaled in 1906, as his ideal sort, but, sad to say, this fine horse went to Italy in 1912. Mares bred at Elsenham produced some great show harness horses in later years, notably Flash Clara, the dam of Modern Maid.

THE BROOKFIELD STUD

Important though Elsenham was in Hackney history, the Brookfield Stud played a more important role. This stud was founded in 1887 by William Burdett-Coutts, an American-born but English educated gentleman, whose marriage to the much older and extremely wealthy Baroness Angela Burdett-Coutts had scandalised London society in 1881. A handsome and gifted man, Burdett-Coutts became Member of Parliament for Westminster, a seat he held until his death in 1921, and he was one of the founder members of the Hackney Stud Book Society. The Baroness had a "country" house at Highgate, only four miles from the centre of London, and here it was that Mr. Coutts put up the main stud buildings, but most of the mares and the young stock were kept at Purseley Farm, Shenley, 8 miles further north. The aim at Brookfield was to demonstrate that the finest harness horses and hacks in the world could be produced from native British breeds. Although Hackney horses formed the largest part of the breeding stock, Cleveland Bays, Yorkshire Coach Horses, thoroughbreds and a small number of ponies were also kept. In the 1890s more than a hundred breeding mares were kept, and Metham Hall

"A turn in the ring with the old horse." William Burdett-Coutts driving at Brookfield. (From a painting by Samuel Carter.)

Polonius. Next to Mathias this was the most successful sire of show harness horses of the years before 1914.

near Howden in Yorkshire was acquired to provide more grazing for youngstock.

Although Mr. Coutts was keenly interested in the work of the stud and was an authority on bloodlines, he appointed a Yorkshire farmer, Mansfield Harrison, as manager. Harrison and his brother farmed at Garton-on-the-Wolds near Driffield and they bred some good horses there. Harrison was a member of the first Council of the Hackney Stud Book Society. At the Highgate establishment some stallions were kept, and the young horses were trained to saddle and harness. The stud made a speciality of producing matched pairs and fours, and well-mannered horses were always available for sale. From time to time auction sales were held at Brookfield and the harness horses usually sold at prices well in advance of the general market level.

The stallion chosen to head the stud in its early years was Candidate, Henry Moore's four-year-old winner of the championship at the second show of the Hackney Society in 1886. This was a dark chestnut horse 15.2 hands, by Denmark out of Poll 3rd by Shaw's Fireaway. Although Candidate's stock had great quality and the mares were good breeders, it was the purchase of Polonius at the Earl of Londesborough's sale in 1898 that really brought the

Brookfield stock to the forefront. Many of the leading show harness horses in the early years of the twentieth century were bred at Brookfield, and the bloodlines developed there continued to influence the breed long after the stud was closed in 1912.

Mr. Coutts, being an American, made a special effort at introducing Hackneys into the United States, resulting in several large breeding studs being set up in the Eastern States on the Brookfield model. He was also aware of the growing horse-breeding industry in the Middle West, and, with this in mind, the Brookfield Stud had a stand at the Columbian Exposition in Chicago in 1893.

In Britain many wealthy men followed the Gilbey and Burdett-Coutts example and set up breeding studs of Hackneys, paying high prices for winning stock, which, together with the large export trade, made the 1890s and the early years of the twentieth century the boom years for the Hackney, and considerable fortunes were made by some of the cleverer breeders and dealers.

CHAPTER SIX

THE HACKNEY OUTSIDE ITS NATIVE LAND

At the height of its popularity at the turn of the century the Hackney breed had been introduced into almost as many countries as the English thoroughbred and was just as highly esteemed in its different way. European horse breeders became interested in the earlier Norfolk Trotter in the early years of the nineteenth century, particularly the French breeders. Indeed it was this persistent demand from abroad that brought the Norfolk Trotters to the notice of British horse breeders outside its native counties. Eager French buyers scoured the East of England for these trotting horses, taking mares as well as stallions. Among the many proven sires they secured were Beart's Ambition, the winner at the Royal Show in 1867 and '68 as well as at several other major shows; Rickell's St. Giles, the grand-sire of Danegelt; and Cook's Phenomenon, the sire of Wreghitt's Wildfire. The horses of Normandy showed the most influence from these importations, and by the 1890s the Anglo-Norman breed, as it came to be called, was firmly established and enjoyed a wide reputation.

In those days the governments of most European countries exercised some control over horse breeding in their territories with a view to ensuring an adequate supply of horses for their massive armies in time of war. This was especially true of Germany where many of the princely states had regulations concerning the selection of stallions from the eighteenth century. The great London dealer, H. R. Phillips, advised the German breeders to use Norfolk Trotters in place of the heavier Cleveland Bay stallions, and many were used in the Oldenburg, Hanoverian and Holstein breeding districts. European horse breeders for the most part do not aim at purity of blood so much as the production of a definite type of horse, the type they consider most suitable for their needs and for the prevailing demand. As demand has changed so has the type of horse produced. Thus we find that Tora, the winner of the individual gold medal in the Prix des Nations Competition at the 1936 Berlin Olympiad when ridden by Oberleutenant Hasse, is usually described as a Holstein mare even though her sire was the Hackney, Capenor Mormal Forester, while her dam was by the thoroughbred, Blaue Vogel, with more than one Hackney cross further back in her pedigree.

ITALY

The Italian Government started buying Norfolk stallions about the middle of the nineteenth century, and some famous horses ended their days in that country. The first record of these exports, published in 1888, lists sixteen stallions to Italy in that year, among them such great sires as Canvasser 114, Moore's Confidence 163 and Sir Edwin Landseer, one of the best sons of Triffit's Fireaway. Two years later no less than seventy stallions formed the year's tribute to Italy. Very few mares were taken and the stallions seem to have been used exclusively for cross breeding to produce military horses. Shipments were resumed after the First World War with some thirty stallions in 1919, but from then on there was a steady reduction in numbers. Albin Supreme was the last stallion imported by the Italian Government in 1933 and this horse continued to be used until about 1950. Although they have no shows for harness horses, the Italians like a high stepper, and a few good harness horses still go there from time to time. Some years ago an emissary arrived in England from Mussolini looking for a pair of stepping horses that could draw the Duce through the eternal city in becoming style. He took home a pair of chestnuts by Mathias that had been winning in good company. Their new owner was delighted, it was said.

JAPAN

Beginning in 1900 the Japanese Government sent an annual delegation to Britain to buy stallions for their remount breeding establishments. R. G. Heaton, a noted dealer who later became the genius behind the magnificently staged International Horse Shows at Olympia, had a virtual "corner" in the Japanese market, to his considerable profit. In 1921 and '22 he sent a total of more than one hundred Hackney stallions to Japan, ten more following in '23, but very few went after that date. In 1965 there was a surprise purchase of five Hackney Pony mares and one stallion by one of the Japanese bloodstock agencies from the Hurstwood Stud. No further shipments have been made since then so far as is known.

NORTH AMERICA

The Hackney breed has been known in North America for at least a century and a half, but the records of early shipments are difficult to trace. Jary's Bellfounder was shipped to Boston in 1822 and became one of the foundation sires of the American Standard-bred trotter. Bellfounder stood for six seasons in the stable of Colonel Jacques, where he evidently earned a high reputation for, in 1828, he was leased to a Mr. Kissam of New York State for a fee of $500 a year. He was the maternal grand-sire of Rysdyk's Hambletonian.

When the American Hackney Horse Society was formed in 1891 an attempt was made to trace the early importations of Hackneys. Customs records and newspaper files were searched and a few typical Hackney names (Shales, Fireaway, Wildfire, Merrylegs, etc.) were found but there were no details of pedigree. It was thought that the Morgan breed which so much resembles the Norfolk Cob, owed its origin to these importations, but this could not be proven.

In 1830 the Hudson's Bay Company took to Winnipeg "a horse of the Fireaway breed", undoubtedly a Norfolk Trotter, although his pedigree is not known. This horse so much improved the horses of the Red River district as to make them esteemed throughout Canada. Indeed it was claimed that his influence could be detected long afterwards among some of the herds of wild horses then roaming the prairies of the Middle West.

The first stud of pure-bred Hackneys in North America was founded by the Hon. H. M. Cochrane of Hillhurst, Quebec in 1881 with a consignment of Yorkshire-bred horses headed by the Denmark stallion Fordham. This horse won the prize for the best roadster stallion at the Montreal Show that same year.

Later in the 1880's a number of good Hackney stallions was imported into Canada, mostly to stallion owners and dealers in Ontario, such as Graham Brothers of Toronto, M. Carlyle of Dunbar, O. Scoby of Guelph, and Geo. H. Hastings of Deer Park. Senator Robert Beith of Bowmanville started at this time what was to become one of the most successful Canadian studs with the importation of the brown stallion Firefly by Triffitt's Fireaway. One of the best horses in Senator Beith's stud was Smylett Performer by His Majesty, imported in 1902.

Hackneys quickly became popular in Canada, particularly in Ontario and Quebec provinces, and the Canadian Hackney Horse Society was formed in 1892 with its own stud book published by the Federal Livestock Records Office in Ottawa. The Hackney became the general utility horse on many Canadian farms as it was in its native Yorkshire and East Anglia. Largely because of the conditions of the roads in winter, horses continued to play an important part in the lives of Canadian countryfolk until quite recent years.

Hackney stallions were used a great deal in Canada for crossing on heavy mares to produce delivery or express horses, the cross with the Clydesdale being especially popular. There was a good market for these cross-breds not only in Canada, regular shipments also went to Britain and elsewhere overseas. Some of the lighter sorts were sought after to make police horses, the Toronto mounted police had a number of them. There are a few such cross-breds born each year and they have found a new market among the growing numbers of persons who have taken up pleasure driving in recent years. Both

Little Wonder. A 14-hands son of Champion Reality that was head stallion at A. J. Cassatt's stud near Philadelphia.

pure-bred Hackney horses and ponies are bred in Canada for show purposes and harness classes are offered at most shows and fall fairs, particularly in Ontario. The Canadian Hackney Horse Society continues to be an active and enterprising body of enthusiasts.

South of the border Hackneys did not become so generally popular with farmers who preferred to drive the speedier American trotters for the most part. However, some wealthy men in the east began to show an interest in the breed early in the 1880s. In 1883 Alexander J. Cassatt of Philadelphia started the first pure-bred stud with the importation of the stallion Little Wonder by Reality and two mares by Lord Derby 2nd. Four years earlier Mr. Cassatt had imported the mare Stella by D'Oyley's Confidence, and this may have influenced him in choosing a horse of similar breeding, but in 1888 he added a number of well-bred mares of Yorkshire strains. In 1892 the stallion Cadet by Lord Derby 2nd, 15.3 hands, was imported and he headed the Cassatt stud at Chesterbrook Farm for many years. Little Wonder was shown at the first National Horse Show at Madison Square Garden in 1883 and created a favourable impression. Mr. Cassatt was a keen coaching man, and his horses were bred with this hobby in view. A number of his mares were of American trotting blood.

In 1884 another, and perhaps more spectacular, stallion appeared in New York. This was the 15 hands Fashion by D'Oyley's Confidence, a great winner in England for John Grout of Woodbridge, Suffolk. Fashion was imported by Prescott Lawrence of Newport, Rhode Island, and he was shown at most of the important shows in the east where he always attracted great interest.

By 1890 what disparagers of the breed called the "Hackney mania" had gripped many wealthy Easterners, and several breeding studs were started with a lavish outlay in stock and buildings. In that year Hilary K. Bloodgood of New Marlboro in the Berkshire Hills of Massachusetts formed a stud around the good East Anglian stallion, Star of Mepal, and, close by at Lenox, William D. Sloane brought in a consignment of mares and the stallion Berseker from the Brookfield Stud. The sire of Berseker, Matchless of Londesboro', by Danegelt, had been imported two years before by Henry Fairfax of Virginia. In 1889 Mr. Fairfax induced Nathaniel Brough, the breeder of Matchless, to come over from Yorkshire to show the horse at Buffalo where he was to do battle with the great goer Fashion. Few of the 70,000 visitors to the show had seen horses with such action before, and the spirited contest brought the breed wonderful publicity. Fashion won on this occasion, but at New York the following year Matchless had his revenge.

That same year, 1890, also saw the most valuable consignment of Hackneys ever to leave England shipped to Dr. W. Seward Webb for his Shelburne Stud

The Shelburne Stud. The buildings at Dr. W. Seward Webb's ambitious breeding farm on the shore of Lake Champlain, Vermont.

Matchless of Londesboro'. The head stallion at Shelburne. The New York champion of 1890.

on the shore of Lake Champlain in Vermont. Dr. Webb was a New York physician who had married in 1881, Lila, the daughter of William H. Vanderbilt, the railroad magnate, and the newly-weds made their country home in the Green Mountain state. Shelburne Farm was built on an estate of about 5,000 acres with buildings on an equally huge scale. Dr. Webb was set upon improving the native horse stock which he considered had degenerated through the excessive use of light trotting stallions. At first he tried to interest farmers in a French Coach stallion with little success, and, after visiting the Brookfield Stud, he was convinced that Hackneys would be more acceptable. Dr. Webb selected many of the choicest of the Brookfield Stud including Mr. Coutts's favourite phaeton pair, White Socks and Dropping Well. A few days before the horses sailed for New York on the *s.s. Denmark* they were inspected by a distinguished party which included the Duke and Duchess of Portland, the German Ambassador Count Münster, Lord Suffield, Sir Dighton Probyn (representing the Prince of Wales), General Ravenhill and Mr. H. W. Gilbey, son and heir of Sir Walter.

Mr. Coutts travelled to New York to see the Webb horses make their first public appearance at the National Horse Show. He was disappointed to find them presented in such light condition as to conceal their true class; nevertheless the mares literally won all before them, Dagmar by Denmark being made champion. In 1891 Dr. Webb bought Matchless of Londesboro' from Henry Fairfax, and shortly afterwards he published a well-illustrated book describing his farm, its occupants and objectives on the lines of Mr. Coutts's book *The Brookfield Stud*.

Unhappily, despite this lavish expenditure of cash and effort, the Vermonters remained obdurate and gave the Shelburne stallions little support. In February 1897 Dr. Webb shipped 100 of his Hackneys to be sold at the American Horse Exchange in New York, Matchless among them. This great horse, now thirteen-years-old, sold for $12,000, and the other stock sold equally well. So ended the most ambitious attempt to get the Hackney breed established in the Eastern States, but other enthusiasts carried on with moderate success in some cases.

One of the more successful ones was a fairly late starter in the field. This was Senator F. C. Stevens's Maplewood Farm at Attica in northern New York State about 30 miles east of Buffalo, which he began in 1895 with the importation of Langton Performer, a son of Garton Duke of Connaught that had, as a two-year-old, beaten champion Rosador at the Great Yorkshire Show. Some high-class Yorkshire bred mares came to Maplewood at the same time, among them the winners of the champion and reserve prizes at the National Horse Show in 1896. During the following six years the Maplewood Stud won the mare championship on four occasions, and took the reserve prize at the other two shows. Good horse though Langton Performer was, the best stallion Senator Stevens owned was Fandango, a grand-son of Lord Derby 2nd imported by F. Joy of Detroit in 1893.

The story was quite different in the Middle West where commercial horse breeding on a large scale had become an important industry by the late 1880's. A number of dealers in stallions set up large establishments, such as Galbraith Brothers at Janesville, Wisconsin, O. O. Hefner of Nebraska City; Grant and Gandy of Dakota; and Jesse Harris of Colorado. These dealers did not specialise in any one breed, some, like A. B. Holbert of Greeley, Iowa, offered a selection of Coach horses, Hackneys, Belgians, Percherons and Shires. Many were set up by English and Scottish dealers, such as the Stericker Brothers of Springfield, Illinois, and Sexton, Cornstock and Company of Iowa. One of the first of these English dealers was J. H. Truman of March, Cambridge who started his Pioneer Stud Farm at the Chicago Stock Yards in 1878, moving later to Bushnell, Illinois, where the family remained in business until the 1930's.

Jesse Harris was a great advocate of the Cleveland Bay as the horse best suited to the needs of the ranches of Colorado, but in 1889 when he chartered the Wilson liner *Buffalo* from Hull, he filled her with Clevelands, Hackneys, Clydesdales, Shires and Exmoor, Shetland and Iceland Ponies. Buyers came from the big cities of the United States and Britain to Chicago and other centres looking for horses to pull the street cars, omnibuses and city transport, the demand generally having outstripped local supplies.

Hackney stallions continued to be imported by these Middle Western dealers until about 1914.

SOUTH AMERICA

In South America, particularly in Argentina and Uruguay, there was a good market for Hackney breeding stock before the First World War. Efforts to improve the native Argentine criollo were started about 1835 with the importation of heavy Flemish stallions. Various other breeds were tried and towards the end of the nineteenth century Hackneys were brought in, annually increasing in numbers. In 1889 export certificates were issued for 46 stallions and 47 mares to Buenos Aires. Most went to the large estancia owners who bred horses for their own carriages and for sale in the cities. Best known of them was Senor Don Miguel Martinez de Hoz who owned many good horses, including Hopwood Viceroy, the London champion stallion of 1913 and '14. Martinez de Hoz was a keen coaching man who kept a fine stable of

Senor M. A. Martinez de Hoz with a team of Argentine-bred Hackneys.

driving horses at his estancia, Chapadmalal. In 1908 he shipped 45 Hackneys of his own breeding to England, and with some of them he horsed the "Reliance" coach which he ran that season between London and Guildford. In the hands of the great professional, Ted Fownes, these horses became coach horses that, in the words of Maj.-Gen. Geoffrey White, "have seldom been equalled, and never surpassed on any road coach."

Many good Hackneys were shipped to Argentina between 1900 and 1914, among them Hawsker Rosina, the champion mare of 1908 that went to Senor Augustin de Elia, and classes for Hackneys are still held at the Palermo Show.

Hackneys were introduced to Chile by Col. North, "the Nitrate King", who presented the stallion, Copenhagen, full brother to Matchless of Londesboro', to the Chilean Government in 1889. Interest in the breed developed further in the early years of the twentieth century, and two former English champion stallions, McKinley and Administrator, found their way there. For a few years the Chilean market was cultivated by Harry Ford, a colourful and swarthily handsome Yorkshire dealer, but his speculations were not always profitable and the trade ended about 1911.

SOUTH AFRICA

The first recorded shipment of Hackneys to South Africa was of 28 stallions bought by the Government of the Cape Colony in 1888 in an attempt to improve the weedy native ponies. The experiment was not a great success, possibly through faulty management, but this did not deter private horse breeders from bringing in more stallions in later years. No doubt these breeders aimed at supplying the demand for harness horses that was developing with the rapidly growing wealth of the country.

In the 1890s a few Hackneys were also shipped to breeders in the independent Boer Republics beyond the Orange River where, particularly in Johannesburg, the more successful prospectors had taken to flaunting their wealth in expensive turnouts to cut a dash through the main streets of the towns.

During the Boer War (1899–1903) among the British forces engaged was a squadron of the Imperial Yeomanry recruited in East Anglia and mounted almost exclusively on Hackneys bred in those parts. A writer in the *Livestock Journal* later claimed that these horses withstood the rigours of the campaign better than most other English horses.

After peace had returned official recognition of the merits of the Hackney for upgrading native stock came with the breed's inclusion among those eligible for importation within the free freight scheme. Before this scheme was abandoned in the 1950s it had certainly helped to set up a few pure-bred studs in various parts of the country. Some of these studs survived through the 1920s

Rillington Pilot. A four year old sent to South Africa in 1911.

and the lean years of the '30's although in those years there were few importations.

AUSTRALIA

A number of Hackneys were shipped to Australia at various times since the 1880s but few pure-bred studs were established there for many years. Australians generally, from the earliest days, have been very keen on racing and even in quite remote parts of the "outback" a race meeting would draw crowds from miles around. Not surprisingly, thoroughbred stallions, sometimes of the poorest sort, were sought after with this in mind. For many years Australia was a source of remounts for the British Army in India and these horses were known as "walers" presumably because most came from New South Wales. However, so far as is known, no official efforts were ever made to organise the breeding of these horses.

A few private individuals attempted to prove the value of Hackney stallions. Capt. Phillip Charley, of the Australian contingent in the South African war, visited England in 1903 and took home to Australia Vanity Fair, one of the head stallions from the Brookfield Stud, also another stallion Moncrieffe Statesman. The latter's name still crops up in the pedigree of some Australian ponies although he himself was a big horse. C. H. Angas of South Australia imported Gallant Crompton in 1904, a well-bred horse of Sir Walter Gilbey's breeding. Nevertheless, up to 1914 the number of Hackney horses shipped to Australia totalled less than 30 head, not enough to make any great impression in that spacious sub-continent.

CHAPTER SEVEN

THE SHOW HARNESS HORSE

Had the Hackney remained only a utility horse the breed would probably have disappeared entirely by now, but the public came to know and love him in a more glamorous role – as the prince of harness horses, the aristocrat of the show ring. Whence came the ability to step with that lofty rhythmic action is a matter for speculation. Lady Wentworth has put forward a theory that the stepping action is derived from some Spanish ancestry and, further, that these Spanish horses got it from some remote link with those Chinese horses whose effigies are seen in ancient ceramics. Whatever its origin, the trot is the natural gait of the Hackney strengthened through many generations of selective breeding. The modern Hackney has the ability to step in a more extravagant manner than any other breed, and this has been his salvation.

HARNESS CLASSES AT HORSE SHOWS

Classes for harness horses started to appear in the prize lists of some English horse shows in the latter part of the 1860s. A summer horse show at the Agricultural Hall in London was first held in 1867, and even then it was largely given over to harness classes. At the 1872 show there were classes for both ponies and horses in harness, all well supported, as for instance the class for "Park cobs, high steppers" which had twenty one entries. The stepping park phaeton horse had by that time become a part of the London scene during the social "season". It was not long before the big agricultural shows up and down the country added harness classes as a popular addition to the programme for the main ring, and the showing of harness horses as a rich man's hobby began.

The first show horses were mostly small, many little more than cobs, and one of the first to gain national fame was the skewbald Magpie that has a place in the history of the Hackney Pony. Magpie was owned by William Pope of Downham Market in Norfolk who owned many other good cobs and ponies, including the 14 hands Maritana that won more than £2,000 in prize money for him. Magpie won more than 400 first prizes during a long career, including ten successive victories at the Royal Show.

Henry Frisby, a wealthy London stockbroker, was another of the early owners of show horses. One of the best he owned was Magpie's bigger but less brilliant half-sister, Movement, sired by Washington, a son of the American trotter Shepherd F. Knapp. The same owner had a fine pair of cobs called Hard to Find and Hard to Beat, and hard to beat they certainly were.

The first professional showman we hear of was "Gipsy Jack" Robinson of Hull who was one of the finest nagsmen of his day. His black mare Lady Shrewsbury beat Movement at their first meeting at Ripon in 1884, while her mate, the Lord Derby 2nd mare Lady Julia, beat Magpie at Barnsley that same year. Encouraged by these successes Gipsy Jack challenged the pride of London at the Agricultural Horse Show for a number of seasons and invariably went back north with a goodly share of the prizes. His winnings did much to make the reputation of Lord Derby 2nd's stock in this specialised field. Lady Plaisantrie, Country Gentleman and the dark chestnut sisters Princess and Brunette were some of the many Lord Derby's that Gipsy Jack started on their winning careers in the show ring.

About the middle of the 1880s the English Horse Show Society was formed with the object of staging horse shows at various centres in the country. This society held a series of well-supported shows at Olympia, London, but its other ventures were not so successful and the society was disbanded.

The Richmond Horse Show was started about 1890 and, enjoying the advantages of a delightful setting close to the fashionable part of London, it was an immediate success. Its garden party atmosphere soon made it an important feature in the social calendar, and to win at Richmond became the ambition of all show men.

The horse show at London's Crystal Palace in 1897 was noteworthy in that it saw the first American invasion of the English show ring. No less than nineteen of the entries were for horses brought from New York by Mr. G. B. Hulme and, although seldom right at the top, they certainly gave a good account of themselves. But the horse that was to win the hearts of the American horse show public, and to clearly demonstrate the superiority of the Hackney as a "heavy harness horse", was then still an unknown stallion on his breeder's Yorkshire farm.

FOREST KING

This was the brown Forest King that was bought by R. G. Heaton, a prosperous dealer of the day, at the Hackney Show of 1901. Later that year Heaton sold Forest King to Charles Wertheimer, a wealthy art dealer, who sent the horse to F. Vivian Gooch to be produced as a show gelding. Gooch was recognised as the most accomplished and versatile horseman of the time, and his presentation of Forest King at the Richmond Show of 1902 was masterly. The horse won his class, the novice and open championships and

Forest King. Vivian Gooch driving the horse that was for many years spoken of as "the best ever".

became the talk of the horsey world. But, despite the horse being then nine-years-old, Gooch brought him out no more that season, not even on the occasion when his owner asked to have him brought round to be shown off to his luncheon guests.

"Sir", came the dignified but outraged reply from Gooch, "I will neither demean myself nor your horse by driving him on the London streets!"

The following year saw Forest King going from triumph to triumph and, at the end of the English show season, Douglas Grand, having a commission from Judge W. H. Moore to buy the best harness horse in the world, bought him for £2,500. Of his uncovering at the New York Show soon afterwards the *Breeders' Gazette* of Chicago had this to say:

> "The thanks of all interested in breeding and using the heavy harness horse are due to Judge W. H. Moore for his enterprise in

introducing to this country the most perfect and brilliant type of a gig horse that has ever been shown here, and the only genuine gig horse that has ever won the Waldorf-Astoria Cup. This is Forest King, a pedigreed Hackney which was taken from the breeding ranks not long ago and put to work in heavy leather, with a most sensational list of victories in England, now crowned with the chief honours that an American show can bestow on a horse of this type ... Moreover there was a recognition of the real heavy leather high-stepper apparent throughout the list, Mr. E. D. Jordan of Boston winning several victories with his Hackneys in harness. Forest King is a brown gelding 15.2 hands and looking higher. He is beautifully fronted, his crest rising boldly and his head and ears carried in taking fashion. His top line is faultless and his dock sets high on perfectly fashioned quarters. When set going he displays action that has not been equalled in this arena."

Forest King won the Waldorf-Astoria Cup outright by repeating his win in 1905 and 1906 after which the Judge announced that he would retire the horse.

For as long as there were some who still remembered him Forest King was spoken of as the ideal of what a show harness horse should be – a paragon of his kind against which all others were judged. There is no doubt that this horse as presented by Vivian Gooch greatly influenced British judges for many years. His Majesty, sire of Forest King, was a grand-son of Danegelt, a line not generally distinguished for producing winners in harness, but Forest King's dam was herself a good winner in harness and she was in-bred to Triffit's Fireaway. Her influence may have been dominant in this instance.

OPHELIA AND HER SONS

Among the wealthy men who had started breeding harness horses about this time was the first Earl of Londesborough at his country house, Londesborough Hall, near Market Weighton. Lord Londesborough was a member of the exclusive Four-in-Hand Driving Club in London, and, with his striking red beard and metal-rimmed blue spectacles, his was an unforgettable figure as he drove through London during the season. His lordship had first bred Yorkshire Coach Horses, but the managers of his several properties in Yorkshire were instructed to look out for promising young horses, and it fell to David Cobb, bailiff on his Selby property, to make the greatest find. This was the yearling Hackney filly, Ophelia, foaled in 1884 and registered as by Denmark or Danegelt, both horses having served her dam, Jennie Bother'em by Triffit's Fireaway, the previous season. Ophelia won the breed championship in 1890 and again in '91, and was acclaimed as the most nearly perfect specimen of her

Ophelia. The champion mare of 1890 and 1891 and the most important matron in the history of the modern Hackney.

kind, a veritable equine Venus de Milo of whom, years later, James Agate wrote: "I would give half I possess to have seen Ophelia plain!"

That may have been written at a time when Agate's fortunes were at a low ebb, as they sometimes were, but who can doubt that the following description by another awestruck devotee of Ophelia is sincere and drawn from life?

> "The first time I ever saw her was at Lord Londesboro's stud farm near Market Weighton. I was driving along the road and she was running in the fields. When she heard the rattle of the trap she raised her head, pricked up her ears and stood at attention, a living picture I shall never forget. She had a perfect head and neck, full of character

> going back with beautiful symmetry into splendidly sloping shoulders that only Denmark could hand down from his great sire Sir Charles, the grandest horse and the best that Yorkshire had then produced. We got out of our trap and walked over to the hedge where we stood looking at her, spellbound, for we recognised that we were in the presence of the finest Hackney mare we had ever seen. She looked sixteen hands high so majestic was her bearing, although as a matter of fact her height was only fifteen hands and a quarter of an inch. She was a long, low mare to the ground, with a back as level as a billiard table and her tail set right at the end of it, with no sign of a droop in her quarters. And when she walked away from us, up went her tail as if it had been set up. She stood on a set of legs made of whipcord and steel, every thew and sinew standing out clear and distinct, and her feet were made of ivory so dense and close was the texture. The thing that struck me when I saw Ophelia for the first time was the beautiful balance of her lines and proportions, and I took off my hat to her as my mistress instructor in the balance of a horse."

So wrote Alexander Gemmell, Scottish lawyer turned horse-dealer, and himself something of a spellbinder.

The dispersal of the Earl's stud, shortly before his death, took place on August 16th 1898 and was a landmark in the history of the harness horse. Not surprisingly the sale attracted a great company and high prices were realised. Ophelia brought 525 guineas from Mr. Frank Bachelor, but it was two of her sons that concern us more in this story. The elder, Polonius, was a four-year-old son of Wreghitt's Wildfire and he was bought by Mr. Burdett-Coutts for 575 guineas, highest price of the day.

Polonius became the most successful sire of show harness horses, and, in 1902, Robert Whitworth, who had leased the Londesboro' stud farm, paid £2,000 to bring Polonius back there.

The other and younger son of Ophelia sold that day, Mathias, then three-years-old, was bought on behalf of William Scott of Carluke, Scotland for 210 guineas. Although then late in the season, Mathias was given three mares on his arrival at Carluke and from one of them he produced Radiant, a horse that was to be reserve champion in harness at the Hackney Show of 1904 at the start of a brilliant career. A series of great harness horses by Mathias came out in the next few years and by 1910 he had overtaken his half-brother as the leading harness horse sire. Mathias was by Grand Fashion 2nd., a son of Lord Derby 2nd, from the same family as champion Connaught and a number of other good horses. For a description of him we can't do better than quote Alex Gemmell again:

"Mathias was a black brown horse with a coat of sheen-like satin, with a little white on his coronets and head. He stood about 15.1½ hands, had a most beautiful front with riding shoulders and short back, plenty of bone, but deceptive because of its quality and flatness and, notwithstanding his quality fitted him for the place of a harness gelding, he had an alertness and masculinity of expression that proclaimed him a sire of high degree. As to his action it was absolutely 1, 2, 3, 4, never off the chalk line; nothing tied about him, his anatomy loose, and he went from his stifles and his shoulders as high and as fast as you like."

The stock of the two half-brothers differed in many ways; in short it could be said that the stock by Mathias generally had more "class", in type, colour and action. His youngsters often showed little or no natural action when

Mathias. Ophelia's most important son and the ancestor of most modern Hackney horses. (Photograph by Brown, Carluke.)

The Earl of Londesborough driving Fortinbras, Ophelia's son by Wildfire, to an American buckboard. As Heathfield Squire this horse became one of the best show horses of his day.

running loose in a field, but they usually had plenty of scope and freedom in their shoulder action. At the Hackney Show of 1906 Menella, by Mathias out of Norah Garton by Garton Duke of Connaught, caused a great sensation not only by defeating the favourite Radiant for the championship but by reason of her extraordinary hind action. The mare appeared to snatch her hind legs up, then hold them momentarily before placing them forwards and down, all done without any apparent disturbance of the balance of her stride. Such action had not been seen before and caused much comment. It was to be seen again and sneering critics came to refer to it as "the Scotch jerk." Menella was later bought by Judge Moore and afterwards was shown in a more orthodox style.

The Polonius horses often took their sire's chestnut colour and they generally showed lofty front action of a more forceful kind. They usually took a good length of stride but some had a tendency to "go on their heels." This was especially true of Heathfield Squire, a full brother to Polonius, and the biggest winner of his time in England. However, on his only appearance at the New York Show, in 1905, he was actually "given the gate" despite appearing

Administrator. A son of Garton Duke of Connaught and Gipsy Jack's mare, Lady Salisbury, this stallion was champion in 1903 and 1904, and won the class for stallions in harness in 1908, driven by Arnold Hustler.

in the ownership of Judge Moore. American judges have generally preferred a rounder and more airy type of action. Polonius sired a few good stallions of which Antonius and Beckingham Squire were thought the best, while his grandson Leopard got a number of good harness horses and the line survives today principally through him. In Canada the Polonius horse Spartan was highly regarded as a sire of show stock.

THE INTERNATIONAL HORSE SHOW

The opening of the International Horse Show at Olympia, London on June 7th, 1907 saw the show harness horse accepted by the upper crust of society as quite respectable and no longer merely a freakish play-thing of the butcher, the baker and those lesser mortals whose money came from "trade". While the titled nobility were very few among the exhibitors they at least stayed to watch and to decorously applaud the winners. Under the presidency of the flamboyant Earl of Lonsdale, the "Yellow Earl" and "the leading sporting peer" as he was called by the popular press, the show was managed by R. G. Heaton and reached a peak of magnificence both in its ornate setting and in the presentation of exhibits that is unlikely ever to be seen again. The show's founding committee was largely made up of wealthy harness horse enthusiasts and much of the programme was devoted to harness classes for roadsters, coster-mongers' turnouts, coachman driven carriages of many different kinds as well as those for stepping show horses. Among the exhibitors at the first show were several from North America including Mrs. Beck from Canada, F. Pabst from Milwaukee, A. G. Vanderbilt's Oakland Farm from Rhode Island, and C. W. Watson from Baltimore, the latter being the most successful of them.

THE SHOW HARNESS TYPE DEVELOPS

With the London streets already heavily invaded by motor vehicles of all kinds, here was convincing evidence that the future of the Hackney now lay chiefly in the show ring, and the more discerning breeders were not slow to realise this. The first Olympia Show may be thought of as marking a shift in direction for the evolution of the Hackney. Before then the breed had been influenced for several years by a large demand for stallions from foreign countries with an emphasis on bone, weight and size as well as action and activity. The trend had been towards a decidedly coachy type, exemplified by Champion McKinley, St. Thomas and others of the get of Garton Duke of Connaught. To win in the harness classes something different was needed and the established sires of harness champions were patronised as never before.

As already noted, much of the new interest centred around two of the sons of Ophelia, Mathias and Polonius. There were other distinctly promising lines but these were allowed to disappear through neglect. One such was the sire of Forest King, named His Majesty, a son of Matchless of Londesboro' the New York Champion of 1891. Middleton King by His Majesty was the sire of Princess Sheila among others, the good harness mare shown by Paddy O'Connell for the Vauclain sisters of Philadelphia and which Paddy said was the best he ever showed.

Flash Cadet was another good son of His Majesty but he was bought by the Italians at an early age. Two of his sons kept the line alive into the 1940s, Angram Majesty in England and the roan Hockwold Cadet in Holland. The last surviving son of Hockwold Cadet was the roan Feu Sacré that somehow

Olympia, 1910. A gig class in the ring.

lived through that terrible winter of 1944/45 in the much fought over ground between Nijmigen and Arnhem, but he has left nothing of great note. Mirage, a son of the good mare Her Excellency, was the best of the Hockwold Cadets and he fathered some good show horses in Holland, including the sire of the great going cob stallion, MacArthur, that in R. K. Velstra's hands thrilled the show crowds in the Netherlands after the liberation. John Partington imported a roan son of MacArthur's sire, Chestnut Brown, in the hope of preserving the roan colour in British Hackneys as well as bringing back a much needed outcross, but breeders were not interested.

The Dutch have always loved a harness horse and there have been Hackneys in Holland for many years. The popularity of the breed there dates from 1903 when Miss Ross first showed her famous black horses at the Hague Show, and this she continued to do annually until 1912.

Before, and for a few years after the First World War, Baron Van Voorst tot Voorst had a large breeding stud near Arnhem, and there the former English double champion, Diplomatist, was the head sire. In 1920 Albert Hargreaves, who had managed the Baron's stud for some years, sold him the red roan Hockwold Cadet, and this was a great success, a few Dutch Hackneys still claiming descent from him. The fine Van Voorst stables at Elden were completely destroyed during the last war.

A few of the Gelderland horses have some Hackney blood and Hackneys are admitted to the stud book of that breed provided they meet the rigid requirements of size and type. In 1946 a Netherlands Hackney Stud Book Society was formed under the energetic direction of Dr. Peter Otjens, and this has greatly helped to maintain interest in the breed. At the present time both Hackney horses and ponies are being bred in Holland and harness classes for them continue to be popular features at horse shows, especially at the great International Show at Utrecht with its fine new covered arena.

Hopwood Viceroy, one of the later sons of Ophelia by Royal Danegelt, sired a few noteworthy harness horses including another of Paddy O'Connell's importations, the chestnut Newton Victor, but Viceroy was sold to Senor Martinez de Hoz and spent most of his days in Argentina.

Meanwhile the Polonius line was still prominent, but Antonius, undoubtedly his best son, died at eight-years-old leaving some very good daughters behind him but no son of any great note. The Polonius male line survives today only through Leopard, son of Leopold by Polonius, dam Marguerite by Candidate.

Leopard was a handsome dark chestnut horse that Arnold Hustler, one of the cleverest professional Hackney men of his time, had bought at one of the Brookfield sales. Hustler mated Leopard to Terrington Leah by Goldfinger 6th, a mare of the Crompton strain, and the resulting filly became the talk of the show world when Paddy O'Connell paid what was then a record price for her. This was The Whip and she did a lot of winning for Miss Vauclain of Philadelphia. In 1910 Leopard was bought by H. C. Callaby, a Norfolk breeder, for whom he sired a lot of good horses but few other breeders made much use of him. A recent English champion, Craigweil Maypole, represents the male line of Leopard today, and this horse has more than one line to him particularly through the good mare Garston Madge.

But as winner after winner in harness came out owning Mathias as its sire, that horse's services were fully booked each season until his death in 1919. He was a most prepotent sire and several of his sons became great stallions. Copper King was the first of them to attract notice by winning the breed championship in 1908, but he was not a typical Mathias horse, indeed there is some doubt about his real paternity.

KING'S PROCTOR

There was no such doubt about the champion of 1911. This was the three-year-old King's Proctor whose vanquishing of Antonius and Hopwood

King's Proctor. The champion stallion of 1911 and 1912, and the sire of champions Adbolton Kingmaker and Bertrano.

Viceroy caused great excitement at the time. King's Proctor was a handsome upstanding chestnut, a storming goer for so big a horse – he grew to about 16 hands – but in type and colour he was more typical of the Denmark line. It is probable that he owed his fine quality to this Denmark blood coming through Candidate, his dam's sire. Of his win in 1911 that fine judge Geoffrey Bennett had this to say:

> "I have seen all the champion stallions at the Hackney Show for the past thirty years and I have no hesitation in saying that the show put up by King's Proctor when winning as a three-year-old in 1911 was the finest of the lot, having regard to the scope and freedom of his movement."

King's Proctor died during the First World War at eight-years-old, poisoned, they said, by adulterated fodder. He left behind him a few brilliant harness horses such as Edgeware Duke and Gondolier, and two future champion stallions, Adbolton Kingmaker and Bertrano.

Kingmaker was out of a St. Thomas mare and was of the type sought by foreign governments rather than a show horse sort, but he did sire a few useful winners in harness and one stallion, Fairview King's Seal that made something of a mark in North America.

After the First World War the Hackney Show returned to the Royal Agricultural Hall, Islington, taking its old February date, the week before the Shire horse show. Two shows were held there, but the lessened support and greater expense proved too much, and in 1922 the show was moved to the Glasgow Paddocks, Doncaster, and was held there each April until 1930. In 1920 farming became severely depressed, and most of the farmer breeders finally gave up.

THE BUCKLEY STUD

However, interest in show horses was in no way lessened by this, and a few new show stables came into being. The most remarkable of these was the Buckley Stud which had its beginnings in 1917 at one of the war-time shows at Newmarket. One of the newcomers at this show was Charles F. Kenyon, a wealthy Lancashire industrialist who was bent on satisfying a lifelong ambition to own as many of the best horses and ponies as he could find. His interests were not limited to Hackneys; he also acquired the Whitewall Stud at Malton, a famous name in the history of the thoroughbred, which he used as his private training quarters. Mr. Kenyon came to an arrangement with Geoffrey D. S. Bennett to act as his advisor in Hackney matters, Bennett then being in his mid-thirties and already recognised as a good judge and an authority on blood lines. The ensuing six years were undoubtedly the high-point in Geoffrey Bennett's life; throughout he retained the confidence of his patron, and, with a seemingly bottomless purse at his command, he was able to roam the country seeking stars of the future.

The aim was to set up a breeding stud of both horses and ponies, and the stallion chosen to head the horse division was Kirkburn Leader, the breed champion of 1916, for which Kenyon paid £3,000, a very high price in those days. Although he won the championship again in 1920, Leader did not have many descendants, probably because his handlers thought him dangerous, and he was put down after only two or three years of service.

Mr. Kenyon died at the end of 1923 and the horses were sold off the following spring. It is likely that the comet-like progress of the Buckley Stud across the Hackney scene would have been quickly forgotten had it not been for Buckley Courage, the most important of the several sons of Mathias. Bennett always regarded his discovery of this horse as a foal on a farm in Leicestershire as his greatest achievement. Not being able to buy the colt himself, he patiently waited for the colt to mature sufficiently to be able to show something of his possibilities before the right customer, fearful the while lest the discerning eye of a Gemmel or a Heaton might light on his discovery.

All was well, however, and in the autumn of 1920 he sold the horse unseen to Mr. Kenyon on the platform at Crewe railway station. At the last of the London shows a few months later, Courage started his show career and was placed third of nine three-year-old stallions. He was not shown again that year and may not have been thought much of by his handlers. Indeed, according to his own account, Richard Belcher, a prominent exhibitor of the day, was the unwitting means of saving the horse for the breed. Belcher had visited Buckley to see a pony he fancied, and in the course of conversation with Mr. Kenyon afterwards he casually mentioned how he liked the young bay stallion that was to be altered next day.

"What young bay stallion?" demanded Kenyon.

"Why the three-year-old Mathias horse", was the reply.

"But he is my best horse," was the surprised comment from the horse's owner, who lost no time in seeing that Courage remained a stallion.

BUCKLEY COURAGE AND BERTRANO

Courage's dam was Westfield Surprise by Paddock Polonius, grand dam Pride of the Grange by Danegelt, next dam Aquila Kirby's Primrose 2nd. At five-years-old he was reserve to Bertrano for the stallion championship at the breed show, and these two were to be the chief contenders for the honour for the next decade. Courage was the winner for the first time in 1926.

Bertrano was out of Ophelia's Daughter Grace by Royal Danegelt and was a dark chestnut standing fully 16 hands. Shown and managed throughout his career by Robert Black, Bertrano won the stallion championship on five occasions at the breed show. He was reasonably well patronised and must be reckoned one of the best sires of his day, although some of his progeny could be difficult. Most were big but not all lacked quality, though there were some that were rather "on the leg", i.e. lacking in depth of body. Alasa Farms' Fata Morgana was by him, as was Heyl Pony Farm's Ashley Lady Campion, a mare of exceptional quality, and in England three fine big chestnuts shown by Robert Black for Claud Goddard come to mind. They were Gay Huzzar, Holywell Squire and Erlegh Paramount.

During the 1920s there were two schools of thought among Hackney judges. There were those who maintained that Hackney breeders should aim to preserve those useful qualities that had made the breed so much in demand as an improver of native stock in other lands; while the other school was more realistic in believing that the show ring now offered the only worthwhile market, and, so long as the North American demand continued, they were right.

A good instance of this occurred at the Hackney Show of 1925, and here is Geoffrey Bennett's account from *The Rider and Driver*:

Buckley Courage. Seven times champion stallion in the 1920s and 1930s, and a most influential sire.

> "Buckley Courage has grand quality, almost faultless conformation, and is bigger and at least as stallion-like as his renowned sire, grand-sire and great grand-sire – Mathias, Grand Fashion 2nd, and Lord Derby 2nd. Yet, when it came to the championship, R. G. Heaton could not dissuade his colleagues – F. W. Buttle, a once famous breeder, and R. B. Nielson, an amiable amateur – from giving the coveted honour to the 16 hand four-year-old Albin King's Heir 'because he was more of a stallion!' Time will prove which gets more winners."

It is probable that both views could have been accomodated if the breed society had maintained the kind of control over breeding policy that is exercised by many of the European authorities, but the British temperament prefers a *laissez faire* attitude in such matters.

THE GLENAVON STUD

From the Hackney Society's early years there had been breeders in Scotland, and the great stallion Mathias spent all his useful days north of the border.

One of the most ardent of the Scottish fanciers was Enoch Glen who started the Glenavon Stud in 1908. His aim was simply to produce show horses, and in 1918 Glen engaged one of the most successful trainers of the time, Arnold Hustler as manager. Hustler had made a great name as the producer of several good harness horses for W. Burnell Tubbs, a wealthy Londoner. These included the pair Gongelt and Grangelt, the stallion Administrator, The Whip and many more.

The head stallion at Glenavon through 1920s was Ophelius, a handsome son of Mathias and the mare Miss Terry by Garton Duke of Connaught out of Ophelia, the dam of Mathias. Glen got together a group of well-bred mares, many by Mathias. That great goer Knight Bachelor was by Ophelius from a Mathias mare, but in general this close in-breeding to Mathias was not a great success. Ophelius got some show horses from mares of other breeding, and with them Hustler demonstrated his exceptional skill as a producer of young stock.

In 1933 Ophelius was exchanged with the Seaton Hackney Farm of New Jersey for the brown stallion Seaton Seaton. This was a handsome little horse, under 15 hands, of impeccable breeding, being by Marlboro from Judge Moore's favourite, Lady Seaton by Edemynag, but Hustler had left by this time and the golden years of the Glenavon Stud were over.

None of the sons of Ophelius proved of much worth, and Seaton Seaton's name only survives now through the progeny of one or two of his daughters. A large part of the Glenavon Stud, including Seaton Seaton, was bought by John C. Sword about 1938 and the remaining part followed in 1940. Although it was one of the largest breeding studs in Britain for almost twenty years, and its owner was a keen student of pedigree, the Glenavon Stud made no lasting contribution to the history of the Hackney horse.

MERSEY SEARCHLIGHT

Several of the sons of Buckley Courage became good stallions, but the best of them was without question Mersey Searchlight whose dam was Saucy Queen by Marlboro. This horse won as a two-year-old at Doncaster in 1925, attracting favourable notice from the critics, and, had his owner been one of the big guns of the breed, it is probable that he would have won the championship early in his career; as it was this did not come his way until 1934 after he had been bought by Frank C. Minoprio. However, it was Searchlight's good fortune that on a nearby farm the well-bred mare Flash

Clara by Royal Danegelt had been barren for some seasons. As a last resort her owner sent the mare to his neighbour's young horse, and the result was Modern Maid.

As a yearling Modern Maid easily won her class at Doncaster, and the following year she was quite the sensation of the show when she took the Junior Championship with the greatest of ease. This naturally focused attention on her sire and several prominent breeders made use of his services. One of them was the future owner of Modern Maid, Sir Nigel (then plain Mister) Colman who sent several mares. Most of Searchlight's foals were uniformly good, but one out of Crystal of Nork by Mathias was quite exceptional.

This was Nork Spotlight, a dark brown stallion, under 15 hands, that became a star performer in harness during the 1930s. In addition he was a most successful sire, as he showed early in his career with the brilliant young Nork Monoplane, champion stallion as a three-year-old in 1938, and harness champion also in 1939. A significant feature of the pedigree of Nork Spotlight

Modern Maid. The great harness mare that "made" her sire, Mersey Searchlight; James Black driving. (Photograph by Rouch.)

Kentmere Searchlight. A good but neglected son of Mersey Searchlight. (Photograph by Rouch.)

is that both his dam and Mersey Searchlight's trace to the same tap-root, the black mare Princess Dagmar by Gibson's Prince Charlie. The latter horse was closely related to Lord Derby 2nd, who was also the sire of Princess Dagmar's dam, and it was from Lord Derby that Spotlight appeared to have inherited much of his type and character. Mr. Burdett-Coutts noted the tendency of Lord Derby 2nd to produce small foals, a tendency that has been of no small importance in the evolution of the Hackney pony, and this may explain Spotlight's small size, smaller in fact than either parent.

Mersey Searchlight had two other important sons. The first of these, Kentmere Searchlight, was bred by T. M. Stephenson of Liverpool, the

Solitude. The leading sire of the 1940s and 1950s.

breeder of Modern Maid, and his dam was another mare of Sir Walter Gilbey's breeding, namely Bouncing Girl by Antonius. There was plenty of size in this mare's breeding, but, curiously, she was descended from a mare of almost identical breeding to Princess Dagmar, being by Gibson's Prince Charlie from a mare by Lord Derby 2nd.

Kentmere Searchlight was bought in 1934 by Robert Speir of the Broompark Stud, Glasgow and he sold him that same year to the Dodge Stables in Michigan. For some unknown reason, the horse was shipped back to Scotland the following year, and a year or two later he went to the Craigweil Stud for a time and was shown in John Sword's name in harness with some success, but he was not used much as a stallion. Mr. Sword, or his advisors, preferred another son of Mersey Searchlight, named Fulwood Searchlight whose dam was Lavington Sylvie by Kirkburn Leader. This horse got some good show horses, including Craigweil Golden Haze and her full brother, the stallion Craigweil Ballantrae that was a championship winner in Canada. In Britain, however, Kentmere Searchlight has proved the more important horse of the two, and his line continues through his sons – Walton Searchlight, one of the best sires of recent years, and the 16.1 hands Winestead Marmion, sire of John Partington's Marfleet Raffles, whose line survives both in England and Holland.

Nork Spotlight died in 1940 when only eight-years-old, but when showing started again with the return of peace in 1945, his sons and daughters were well to the fore in the harness classes. It was expected that one of his several sons – including Nork Monoplane then at Craigweil – would carry on the line. In fact only one, Warwick Footlight, proved to be of any account as a stallion, and this horse went to Canada where his mares have been good breeders.

The first post-war Hackney Show was held in the sale-yard at Crewe in 1946, and it was there for the first time that the thirteen-year-old Solitude won the championship. Solitude was by Buckley Courage, dam Dark Vision by St. Adrian (a Norfolk-bred son of Mathias), grand-dam Wood Vision by Antonius, a mare descended from Nellie, Danegelt's dam. He was bred by Joseph Morton in Norfolk, but his name will always by linked with the Hurstwood Stud which for the past thirty years has been the dominant influence on the Hackney breed in Britain.

THE HURSTWOOD STUD

The changed economic conditions that followed the First World War brought about the gradual disappearance of the great private stables, and the leading exhibitors began to patronise public training stables. During the 1920s the most successful public trainer was Robert Black of Osbaldwick, York, working together with his brother James, who was one of the leading show men of his day. In 1932 the Black brothers moved to Reading where they ran separate stables.

The Hurstwood Stud was founded by Robert Black's son-in-law and daughter, Frank and Cynthia Haydon, as a breeding farm and public training stable in 1945, and ever since that first show at Crewe in 1946 it has been the leader in its field. Not only have a great many of the best show horses of the past thirty years been produced from this stable, several of them were bred there also. Furthermore, through their high standard of presentation the Haydons have earned the admiration and respect of the entire horse world. What might have been the fate of the Hackney horse without the Hurstwood Stud is impossible to say, of course, but it is quite certain that its healthy position today is very largely due to the influence of the Haydons.

Solitude had been used in Norfolk for a few seasons before coming to Hurstwood. In 1940 Britain was in a state of siege, and the government authorities compelled Joe Morton to sell off his horses which they said were occupying valuable land. Robert Black heard of the sale and was able to buy

Solitude and a few others. It is quite likely that his foresighted action saved this horse for the breed. Most of Solitude's foals possessed action, but not all were of the greatest quality. One of the first of his offspring to win in harness was Holywell Florette, a daughter of the good mare Lavington Flavia. Hurstwood Lonely Lady was his daughter out of the former champion mare Erlegh Maiden by Nork Spotlight, and at Crewe in 1947 Lonely Lady became the first yearling ever to win the Supreme Mare Championship. This mare and several other sons and daughters of Erlegh Maiden became prominent winners in harness, clearly showing that Solitude, given the right mares, was the best stallion of his time.

Two half-brothers, Walton Diplomat and Walton Searchlight, were later used at Hurstwood. Their dam, Walton Beauty, was sired by the well-bred horse, Lavington Demetrius, but her dam was a pony from the family that produced the dynamic Kitty Melbourne. Diplomat's son out of the legendary harness mare, Hurstwood Superlative, namely Hurstwood Consul became a valuable sire. However, Walton Searchlight has been the most successful of the Hurstwood stallions in recent years. Although small himself, his progeny from the right mares have not lacked size and many have done well in harness.

More recently Outwood Florescent, a great going son of Solitude and his daughter Holywell Florette, has been used with some success, but it is too early yet to really gauge his importance as a sire.

Elsewhere in Britain the line of Kentmere Searchlight through his son Winstead Marmion is to be found in the Warren Hill Stud of Arthur Grant, situated in Yorkshire a few miles from Market Weighton in a district steeped in Hackney history.

It is interesting to note that, apart from the line of His Majesty, the Denmark male line has not produced a really successful sire of show horses, in harness that is, while in hand classes the Denmarks at one time dominated the field entirely. The reason lies in the all-important quality of temperament. Some of the Denmark family lacked courage, that fire and unquenchable spirit without which good looks alone are of no avail. Haydon's King Rufus is a case in point. This horse became the property of Alex Gemmell in 1923 who used all his considerable power of persuasion to induce owners to send good mares to the horse, extolling the value of the almost extinct line of Taylor's Performer and so on. The foals by Haydon's King Rufus were certainly handsome enough and showed promise of action, but when the time came to put them in harness the fatal flaw of the Rosador strain came out and few ever saw the show ring.

Rather more successful was Hopwood Viceroy's son, Carleton Quality, foaled in 1913. This horse had several Denmark crosses and had all the quality expected from this breeding. The horse twice changed hands for very high prices, finally going to the long established Norfolk stud of Joseph Morton, where among his first foals he sired the good harness mare Potentilla. This mare did a lot of winning in the United States in Harley Heyl's hands, but Carleton Quality failed to sire many more of her kind and even his daughters did not breed well.

THE SHOW HARNESS HORSE IN AMERICA

As we have seen, Hackney Horses were first brought to the United States in order to produce high-class carriage horses rather than show ring steppers. According to a writer in the *Livestock Journal* in 1893 it had by then become fashionable in New York, Philadelphia and other big cities ...

> "... to drive horses with more style and action, suitable to draw heavier-made vehicles, and to wear the heavier English harness in place of those long-tailed, narrow, leggy light horses which are only fit to draw the lightest of traps."

But in 1902 Alfred Stoddart, writing under the name "Rittenhouse", reported in the *Farmer and Stockbreeder*:

> "American Hackney men have at last realised that showing Hackneys at the shows on leading straps only was not making friends for the breed. Every effort is now being made by the Hackney Society to encourage showing in harness."

The same writer also reported that a pair of horses "fit for the National Horse Show" may fetch between $5,000 and $10,000. He wrote that Mr. Hamilton McK. Twombly had refused an offer of $20,000 for his prize-winning Hackney four at that show.

One of the early American-bred winners in harness was E. D. Jordan's Lady Dilham, winner of the championship for small horses at Madison Square Garden in 1909. This mare was by Dilham Prime Minister out of Elegance III by Lord Denby 2nd. But the specialised breeding of Hackneys to make show harness horses may be dated from Judge W. H. Moore's importation of the Mathias horse Marlboro' in 1911. This horse had been shown at the London Show that same spring as one of sixteen four-year-olds over 15.2 hands. His magnificent appearance and extraordinary front action drew great applause but he had to stand second to Antonius. Marlboro's dam was Dairymaid by Dart, a mare from the valuable Yorkshire Crompton strain. The mares, selected for Judge Moore from the leading British studs, were described by Geoffrey D. S. Bennett as the best collection ever garnered into one stable.

Their progeny by Marlboro' was of a consistently high standard and he "nicked" particularly well with mares possessing some Polonius blood. His best son, Seaton Saxon, the New York champion of 1919, was out of District Belle by Polonius.

But it was another Polonius mare, the chestnut Phosphate of Brookfield breeding, that was to produce at twenty years of age Marlboro's greatest foal, the bay mare Seaton Pippin. Unfortunately the Judge did not live to relish the satisfaction of having bred what was universally acclaimed as the loveliest specimen of a Hackney mare ever, but Pippin's full brother Melancthon had won the championship for him at Madison Square Garden in 1922. Melancthon sold for $7,500 at the W. H. Moore dispersal the following April when his buyer was E. A. Stuart of Carnation Farm, Seattle. Pippin was brought out in harness for Paul Moore, son of W. H., and she had a long and triumphant career. She was not a really extravagant mover but her good looks made her the darling of the ringsiders. Mr. and Mrs. Paul Moore continued breeding and showing Hackney horses at Seaton Farm, Morristown, New Jersey until about 1942.

Seaton Pippin. Bred by "Judge" W. H. Moore and considered by many the best harness horse bred in America. (Photograph by Haas.)

Captivation. A great American-bred harness horse owned by Mrs. Loula Long Combs of Kansas City, driven by Dave Smith.

In 1919 A. W. Atkinson of Merchantville, New Jersey, imported the brown stallion A. I.'s Ambassador bred by Dr. Alex Bowie and by his great little stallion Mathias A. I., son of the old horse and Terrington Floweret, a mare, like Marlboro's dam, from the Crompton strain. A. I.'s Ambassador's dam was Commodity by Ganymede. He was a winner at New York in 1921 but it was his achievements at the stud rather than in the show ring that have earned him a place in history. Ambassador was possibly a better sire of harness horses than Marlboro', but his opportunities were fewer. Mrs. Loula Long Comb's great mare, the home-bred Captivation, was undoubtedly his most successful show horse, and this mare was unbeaten for five seasons before her retirement in 1941.

Preston Envoy, Killearn Magi and the stallion Medfield Messenger were other good horses by A. I.'s Ambassador, but his most important son was the stallion Killearn Magician whose dam was Seaton Mazeppa by Marlboro'. Magician was foaled at A. B. Maclay's Killearn Stud at Millbrook, New York in 1925, and of his many sons and daughters that were show ring winners the most distinguished was Killearn Beauty. Indeed this daughter of Beauty of

Carleton by Carleton Quality can almost be ranked with Seaton Pippin among American bred Hackneys. Beauty first came to fame at the Belbrook Stable in California and later became a valued member of Samuel J. Campbell's Argyll Stables in Illinois under the watchful eye of Mary K. Holt. Killearn Magician was kept at the Killearn Farm until Mr. Maclay's death in 1946, and the horse later came to see out his remaining years at Mrs. Combs' Longview Farm in Missouri. The good phaeton horse Salutation was by him, as also was Dr. Bartlett's Hawthorn Co-Pilot, one of the last of his offspring to be shown. Unfortunately no entire son of Magician has survived.

Other United States studs breeding horses in the 1920s and '30s included Mr. and Mrs. A. B. Dick's Dicksfield Farm at Gurnee, Illinois where the Mathias horse Thornholme was at stud; J. J. Mitchell's Ceylon Farm at Lake Geneva, Wisconsin; and Miss Gwen Martin's farm at Chestnut Hill, Philadelphia.

In 1936 Dodge Stables of Rochester, Michigan imported the dark chestnut stallion The Band Leader, a son of champion Bertrano and Carus Queen, a mare of Brookfield breeding with some Polonius blood. The horse was used on a few good mares at Dodge Stables but none of their progeny had appeared in harness before he was sold to Charles Gilbert of Toronto in 1943, one of a big

Danish Leader. A son of The Band Leader and an American saddle-bred mare, this handsome horse won the championship stake at the Devon Horse Show.

draft of horses and ponies. The Band Leader was passed on to James Franceschini who was then beginning to assemble what was to become one of the largest Hackney farms in North America. The Band Leader's stock resembled that of his sire, Bertrano, many being chestnuts and of fair size. Wallace Munro's great goer Seaton Leader was probably the best of them and was a popular winner at Canadian shows through the 1950s. Another son, Danish Leader out of an American Saddlebred mare, won the harness stake at Devon in 1954 and was a particularly handsome horse.

James Franceschini's Dufferin Farm continued to grow, adding in 1952 a number of well-bred horses and ponies from the Longview Farm through the agency of the enterprising Charles Gilbert. The show place Dufferin Haven at Mont Tremblant in the Laurentians 100 miles north of Montreal was the scene of a private showing of harness horses and ponies on most summer week-ends, providing a most memorable spectacle in the arena above the lake with its back-drop of flower-covered terraces rising on the hillside behind.

Never a man to be content with second best, Franceschini was determined to improve his horse breeding enterprise, so he sent his manager William Pinch to Britain in 1950 to seek out and bring back the best stallion he could find. Pinch chose Warwick Footlight, one of the few entire sons of the great Nork Spotlight. Three years later Franceschini imported Dufferin Haven, a son of Solitude that in the name of Hawthorn Pedler had been a sensational winner at the English Hackney Show since his yearling days. Dufferin Haven was to prove a really good sire and it was not long before a succession of winning harness horses by him began to appear, including Dufferin Gladiator, Parade Girl and Dufferin Starlight. Not long after the Dufferin Stud was dispersed following its owner's death in 1961, Haven went to Harold Patton's farm near Toronto where he continued to sire some good stock. Warwick Footlight made his mark chiefly as a sire of mares but his male line still continues in Canada. He ended his days at Ralph Sadler's farm in Ontario.

Back in the United States another son of Solitude, Hurstwood Supremo, was imported in 1951 by Harry J. Burkart of St. Louis who also collected some well-bred mares of American breeding. Unfortunately as the young horses came of age the showing of harness horses had fallen off considerably and there were few buyers. Perhaps because of this Supremo has had no notable success, but some of his daughters are at stud, and it seems unlikely that a full brother to those great goers Hurstwood Superlative and Lonely Lady would fail to have some good influence on the American Hackneys.

The breeding of show harness horses in North America has never become so firmly based as has the breeding of Hackney ponies. Throughout the twenties and thirties the most successful show horses continued to be imported and many a promising home-bred youngster must have been given no opportunity

Warwick Footlight. The most successful son of Nork Spotlight. Driver Albert Throup.

Dufferin Haven. A successful sire of harness horses in Canada in the 1950s and 1960s, owned by James Franceschini.

of showing its worth. Probably this was due to there being room for only a limited few at the top of the horse show world and, once there, those few stayed on for season after season. Many Hackney horses proved too enduring for the good of their own breed, for instance the afore-mentioned Melancthon was still bringing home ribbons when more than twenty-years-old, and there were many like him.

The present revival of interest in pleasure driving offers a market for well-broken stylish horses, and this is an opportunity that breeders of Hackney horses should not neglect.

SOUTH AFRICA

In 1947 Mr. Theunis Wessels came to Britain with a commission to buy Hackneys on behalf of a group of breeders in the Orange Free State. Eight mares and one stallion were shipped that year and eight more went to the same buyer in the next two years. In 1948 the late H. C. Haarhoff of Colesberg imported the stallion Marfleet Burlesque followed by seven mares in later years. Interest in showing harness horses was growing quickly by that time and later imports were selected with the aim of breeding high class show stock.

In the 1950s the brothers Joe and Sam Brown of Johannesburg began their breeding stud and, over the years, they bought a number of most carefully chosen horses from England. In 1957 the Browns bought Warwick Grandmaster, a handsome chestnut stallion bred by the late W. T. Collyer at the old-established Warwick Stud. This horse was a grand-son of Solitude on his sire's side and his dam was by Nork Spotlight, a combination of the most successful lines of the day that had produced many great harness horses. In South Africa Grandmaster proved himself a worthy scion of the line.

In 1961 David de Villiers of Beaufort West, Cape Province, bought Craigweil Field Marshal, another chestnut stallion that had done well in harness in England and was the best son of Nork Monoplane by Spotlight. In the past twenty years some seventy head of Hackneys has gone to South Africa, almost three times the total of the preceeding thirty years.

The determination of the South African to have the best available was well illustrated when Arthur Dyter of Kroonstad journeyed to Canada in 1963 to buy Warwick Sensation, full brother to Grandmaster and the championship winner at the Royal Winter Fair for R. A. Campbell of Montreal. Sensation has since taken his brother's place at the Grandmaster Stud, as the Brown establishment is now named, and for his new owners he won, amongst other prizes, the award for the best animal in the show at Bloemfontein in 1972.

The South African Hackney Horse Breeders Association holds its annual show in conjunction with the Central Agricultural Society at Bloemfontein, Orange Free State. The 20 harness classes and 21 inhand classes at this show

Warwick Sensation. A winner at the English Hackney Show, champion stallion at Toronto and the Rand Show, Johannesburg, this horse became an important sire in South Africa.

draw an entry of some 150 horses. In 1971 no less than 18 stallions competed in the class for four-year-olds and over.

The market for show Hackneys in South Africa has suffered somewhat in recent years through the growing popularity of American Saddle Horses of which no less than forty head have been imported in 1972 alone.

AUSTRALIA

Interest in Hackney horses has also been revived in Australia since 1951 when Tom Dwyer brought out to New South Wales the good harness mare Arden Masquerade. Another mare, Craigweil Crepe de Chine, followed in 1954 and the stallion Marden K. C. B. three years later to found the Ellmore Stud which has been carried on by his sons since Mr. Dwyer's death in 1961. Mrs. Pauline Faulkiner, owner of the renowned Haddon Rig Stud of Merino Sheep in New South Wales, in 1960 bought the young stallion Hurstwood Sultan, English Junior Champion of the previous year, from Miss F. Simmons. This same owner has also imported a few good mares and now has a sizeable stud.

As we have seen from the foregoing there is almost nowhere in the world

Hackney horses at the Sydney Royal 1972.

where Hackneys are now bred other than for the show ring. In fact but for the fascination of its unique action the breed would have disappeared half a century ago. In a belated attempt to bolster an already dying trade the Hackney Horse Society included classes in its shows during the 1920s for stallions suitable for breeding military horses. When these "overfed bus 'osses", as the show men called them, entered the ring most of the spectators turned their backs and wandered off to the beer tent. Cynics they may have been but realists for all that.

CHAPTER EIGHT

THE HACKNEY PONY

If the future of the Hackney horse seems somewhat uncertain, that of his close relative the Hackney pony is assured as long as there is a horse lover left in the world, for he is one of the most fascinating of creatures. Miniatures of any species seem to take on a special quality, a compound of self-assurance, vivacity and *joi-de-vivre* that in humans is not always attractive, but in other animals seems irresistible. We see it in the bantam cock lording it in the barnyard, or in the smaller terrier breeds, and love them for it. To horsemen this quality is "pony character", and the Hackney pony is the quintessence of pony character.

A Hackney pony should have a smallish head, with a bold eye, refined muzzle and small expressive ears. The head should be well-set on a neck of medium length with a slight crest even in mares and geldings, running back into a well-sloped shoulder. The ribs should be well-sprung and the quarters square and muscular though not coarse. He should have an active springing walk, and his trotting action should be free, lofty, sharp and clean. The slower more ponderous action of a horse is not wanted in a pony. Hackney ponies range in height from about 12 to 14 hands.

What were the origins of this little charmer? The story is a fascinating one, and it is largely the story of a few clever and discerning breeders who knew exactly what they were aiming to produce.

THE WILSON PONY

The specialised breeding of Hackney ponies really began with the successful experiments of Mr. Christopher Wilson of Rigmaden Park, Kirby Lonsdale, Westmorland. This hilly district in the northwest of England is noted for an indigenous breed of pony, the Fell pony. In the lovely setting overlooking the Vale of Lune, Mr. Wilson employed the proven principle of in-breeding to fix type. The sire used was a 14 hand brown stallion of Yorkshire breeding named Sir George, bred by William Walker of Shadwell near Leeds. Foaled in 1866, Sir George was by Hart's Sportsman 796, by the Yorkshire Prickwillow 624 by Taylor's Performer 550, the grand-sire of Denmark. Although the breeding of Polly, his dam, was not known she must have been an exceptional

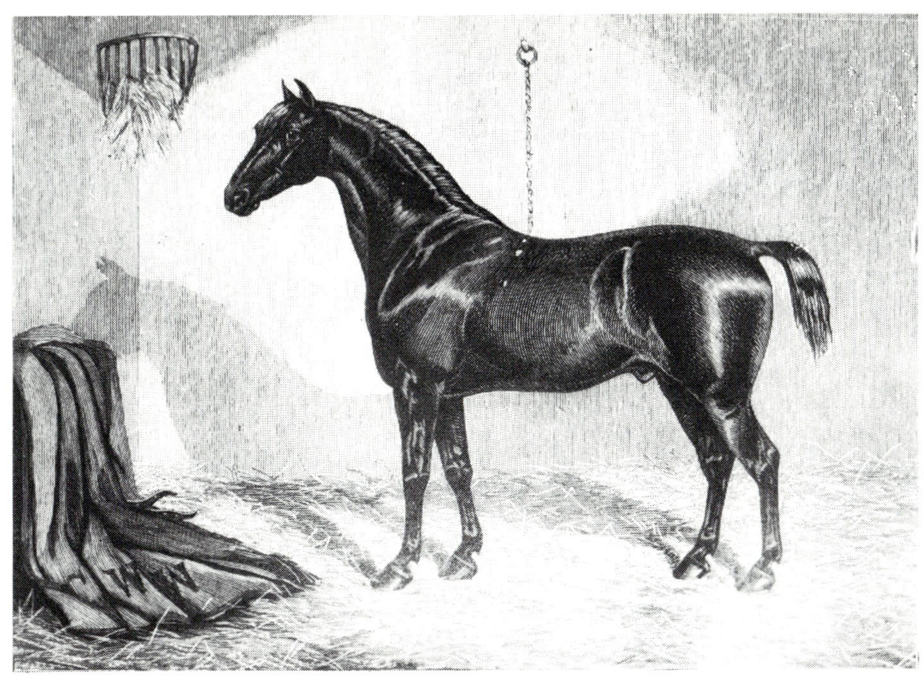

Sir George. Christopher Wilson's great foundation sire.

Snorer (standing at left) and Snorer 2nd (galloping at right). (From a water colour by P. Palfrey.)

pony for Sir George won first prize at England's Royal Show no less than eight years in succession, and he was a most prepotent sire.

Among the best of the Wilson mares was the 13.3 hands bay, The Pet, said to have been a thoroughbred, bred by Daniel Miller of Hunbridge, Worcester in 1869. The Pet was also a first prize winner at the Royal Show on at least two occasions. To Sir George this mare bred Snorer, so named, it is said, because of an odd noise she made when trotting; be that as it may, it did not prevent her from winning first prize at the Royal on five successive years, nor from taking the Queen's Gold Medal at the Great Jubilee Show at Windsor in 1887.

Snorer and two more of his daughters – Georgina and Lady Polo – were mated to Sir George and the resulting fillies bred back to him again. So successful was this policy that the Wilson ponies acheived a nation-wide renown and continued to be known by his name long after their founder's stud was dispersed.

In 1882 Mr. Wilson mated Snorer with the black-brown 13.2 hands stallion Young Confidence 1237, a Norfolk bred son of Confidence 158 out of a Welsh mare. Shown by the Stand Stud Company of Manchester under the name of Little Wonder this pony had won at the Royal Show. His mating with Snorer resulted in a brown colt registered as Little Wonder 2nd. 1610.

About 1888 Christopher Wilson bought a 13.3 Lord Derby 2nd. mare, Dorothy Derby, foaled in Cheshire the daughter of a Danegelt mare, Burton Agnes, that had been bought at the sale of John Crompton's horses in 1886, he having owned one of the most valued strains of Hackneys in Yorkshire. To Little Wonder 2nd. Dorothy Derby foaled two wonderful ponies in Sir Horace and Dorothy Derby 2nd., the dam of Julius Caesar 2nd.

Having thus established a secure foundation for the breed, Mr. Wilson sold his ponies about 1892, most of them going to Sir Humphrey de Trafford, a pioneer breeder of polo ponies who was then forming a stud in Suffolk. Polo had been introduced to England about twenty years before this (it was taken up by the Hurlingham Club in 1873), after which its popularity grew apace. There being no ready-to-hand supply of ponies to meet this new demand, the few good ones brought very high prices indeed, hence the efforts of Sir Humphrey and others to form a breed. But only four years later, on September 5th 1895, the de Trafford ponies were sold by auction at his farm at Florden. Prices unheard of before then were realised. Snorer 2nd., eight-years-old, brought 600 guineas; Georgina 5th. 300; Dorothy Derby, champion at the breed show the previous March, made 600 and her filly foal by Danegelt 105 guineas; Dorothy Derby 2nd. brought 720 and her yearling colt, Julius Caesar 2nd, made 210 guineas to John Jones of the Dinarth Hall Stud near Colwyn, Wales.

Little Wonder 2nd. The sire of Sir Horace and a winner at the Royal Show 1887.

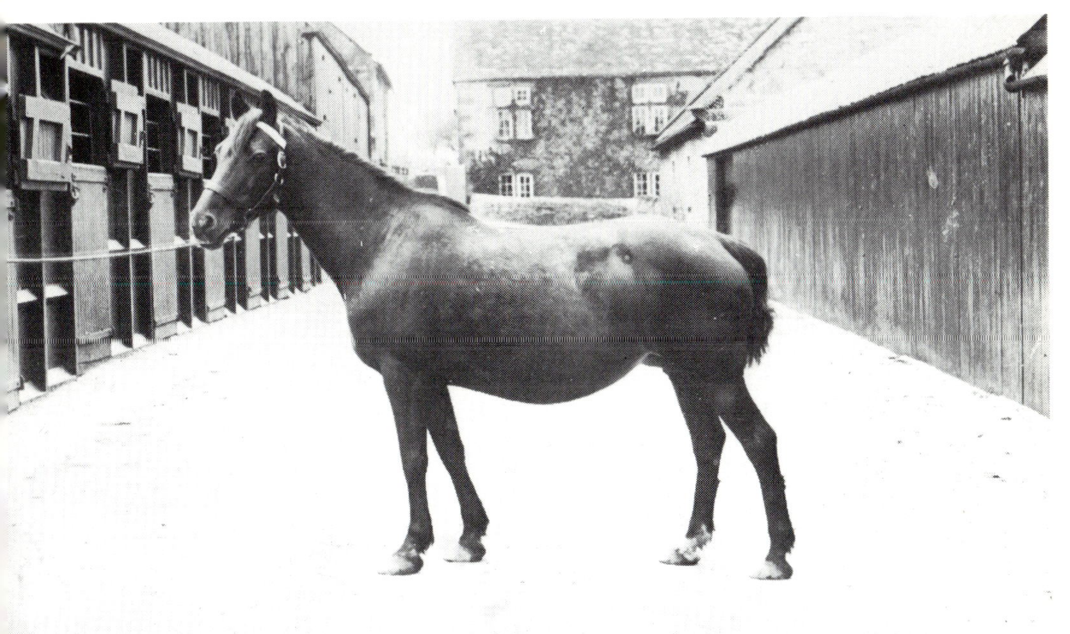

Dorothy Derby 2nd. Full sister to Sir Horace and herself champion pony mare in 1896 and 1897.

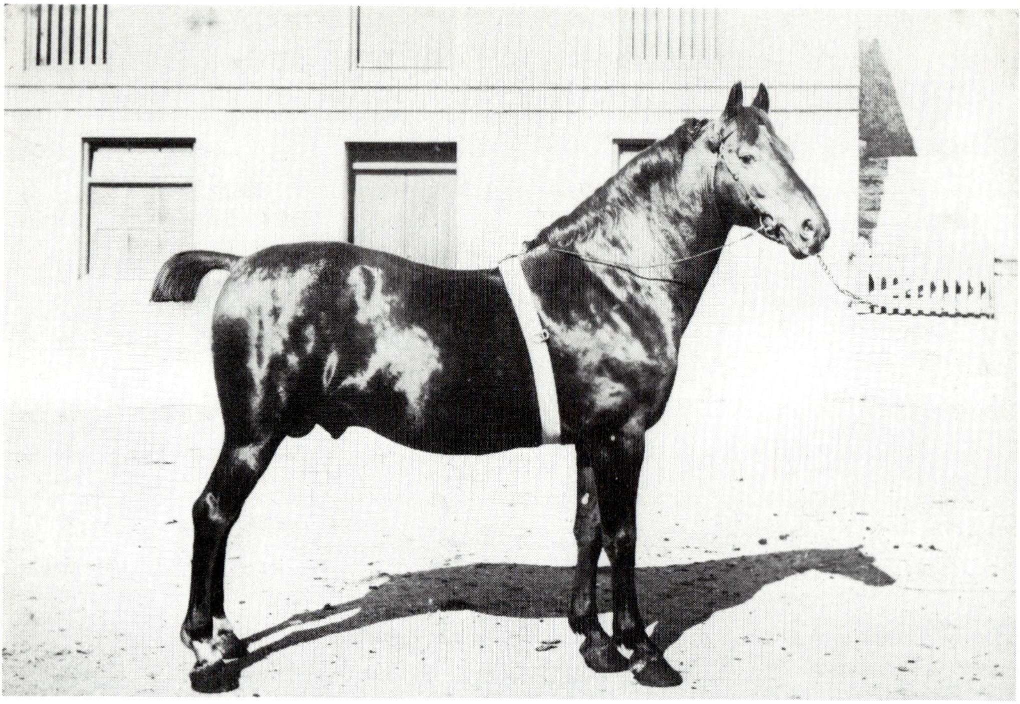

Julius Caesar 2nd. An important pony stallion, that was in-bred to Lord Derby 2nd.

Berkeley Model. The champion pony stallion of 1894 and 1895 and a great rival of Sir Horace both in the ring and at stud.

The leading buyer at this great sale was the young baronet, Sir Gilbert Greenall (later Lord Daresbury), among whose purchases were Dorothy Derby and Dorothy Derby 2nd. Sir Horace was not at the sale, he having been bought from Mr. Wilson by A. J. Scott and taken to Hampshire. Shown at the Hackney Show in 1895 as a four-year-old he had been placed second in his class and, following Mr. Scott's death a few weeks later, he was bought by Sir Gilbert for 500 guineas.

Old Sir George left very few entire sons, the most notable being Winnal George, a pony that spent some years in obscurity in wildest Wales, and Sir George 2nd, both being sons of Lady Polo by Sir George. Neither of these two sired anything of great distinction and the male line died out years ago.

THE BERKELEY STUD

The high prices at the Florden sale focused attention on the possibilities of pony breeding and a number of new studs were started, but a few years before this one or two persons had taken up the fancy, some gifted breeders among them. It is not easy to say wherein lies the secret of the breeder's art, perhaps it is something akin to the mysterious gift of "green fingers" among gardeners, but certainly some part of it lies in the ability to select the right foundation.

About 1892 a successful veterinary chemist, Mr. Alfred S. Day of Berkeley Towers near Crewe in Cheshire, decided to start breeding ponies. At the Hackney Show in March of the following year he noted a stallion that at once struck him as having the qualities he wanted to produce in his ponies, and he lost no time in buying him. This was the black-brown Heacham Model then four-years-old, sired by Leed's Monarch by Confidence 158 out of Peggy Sure by Tuck's Model by Little Model, tracing back to the best old Norfolk strains, including several crosses of Marshland Shales. Heacham Model had placed third in his class to the champion Lord Nimrod and the fifteen-year-old Winnal George.

Shown as Berkeley Model in 1894 he came out in great form to win the championship; Lord Nimrod this time standing third below him. Model repeated this success the following year when Sir Horace was in second place, as already noted the only time that wonderful pony was ever defeated in the show ring. Elated with this success, Mr. Day went off to Norfolk and bought from Alfred Lewis of Heacham the whole of Model's family – dam, brothers and sisters. One of these, Peggy Sure Two, bred to Model the great little goer Berkeley Bantam which William Carr sold to Judge W. H. Moore for £1600 in 1904.

Berkeley Model was never shown again and died in May 1900 when only eleven-years-old, but he had proved himself by then to have been a great sire of courage and action. His sire, Leed's Monarch, had most extravagant fore action and was one of the best sons of old Confidence. Many good harness horses were by him including Lord Bute, the first harness horse to be sold for more than £1000 in England, and Lady Dudley, later the dam of Edemynag. Geoffrey Bennett described Peggy Sure, Model's dam, as 'a sweet little mare, a pony in every fibre of her body.''

The pony chosen to take Model's place at Berkeley was Fireboy, a four-year-old in 1902 when he stood second to Sir Horace at the London breed show. Fireboy was by Julius Caesar 2nd, a son of Cassius by Cadet by Lord Derby 2nd and, as already described, out of Dorothy Derby 2nd whose dam was also by that great head sire. Fireboy's dam was a Norfolk mare, Lexham Fanny by Gem by Confidence 158. Fireboy also proved a great sire, but his reign at Berkeley was sadly cut short when Mr. Day died in 1905 and the stud was broken up.

THE MELBOURNE STUD

The owner of this was a wealthy Yorkshire manufacturer, Walter Cliff, who had joined the Hackney Horse Society in 1892. About 1896 he bought Melbourne Hall in the East Riding of Yorkshire and set up a breeding stud there, first of Hackney horses, but increasingly he was attracted to ponies. In the twenty years of the stud's existence he showed himself to be a breeder of great genius, producing year by year better and better ponies. He was probably the most influencial of the founders of the Hackney pony breed.

Mr. Cliff started his pony stud with two brown mares bought of John Wreghitt the owner of Wildfire 1224 and both by that horse. These were Pepper and Success, both under 14 hands, and nothing is known of the antecedents of the dam of either of them. Put to Berkeley Model, Success produced Success 2nd and this mare became dam of the Melbourne stud ponies.

A great admirer of Mr. Day's breeding enterprise, Walter Cliff also placed high value on his judgement. On a visit to Berkeley Towers in 1898 he bought two fillies, one the foal Royal Charm by Dane Royal, the other a yearling, Lovelorn by Berkeley Adonis from Alexandra by Danegelt. Adonis was a half-brother to Berkeley Model by Alfred Lewis's own stallion Tip Top Shot. The following year Lovelorn, being then merely two-years-old, was sent to Sir Horace and the progeny was a filly destined to become to the Hackney Pony what Ophelia was to the Hackney horse, her name – Wortley Bell.

To Royal Success (Royal Danegelt-Success 2nd) Wortley Bell bred the wonderful quartet of colts: Flame, Fame, Fire and Sir Eric; while to Successful she bred the fillies Melbourne Bell, Belle Melbourne, and Jennie Melbourne.

The first three colts all became the property of the greatest exhibitor of

Fireboy. A son of Julius Caesar 2nd that won the championship at London in 1903.

Wortley Bell. The great old Hackney pony matron in old age.

harness ponies of his day, William Foster and, because most harness classes in those days were restricted to mares and geldings, they were immediately rendered useless to the breed.

A slight idea of what the breed lost by this sacrifice can be got by knowing that Fame, when but two-years-old, sired from his half-sister, Melbourne Bell, the renowned stallion Fusee, sire of Bricket Fusilier, Braishfield Fuse, and a great many other great winners; while Fire at the same age got from Lovelorn's other daughter, Florence Melbourne, by Successful, the grand little sire Melbourne Shot, sire of Star Shot, Miss Freda, Buckley Fame, Vortex and many other delightful ponies.

Both Fame and Fire became great champions in harness, the former being known as Hamilton Fame in the United States, and Sir Eric, bought as a yearling at the dispersal of the Melbourne Stud by W. S. Miller, also did well in harness.

Of Wortley Bell's daughters, Melbourne Bell, as we have seen, bred Fusee; Belle Melbourne went to the United States as the match for Tissington Amity; and Jennie Melbourne became the dam of the incomparable Billet Doux and of Skirbeck Cora, in turn the dam of Highland Cora.

Melbourne Fire. One of four great sons of Wortley Bell by Royal Success; the 1913 champion.

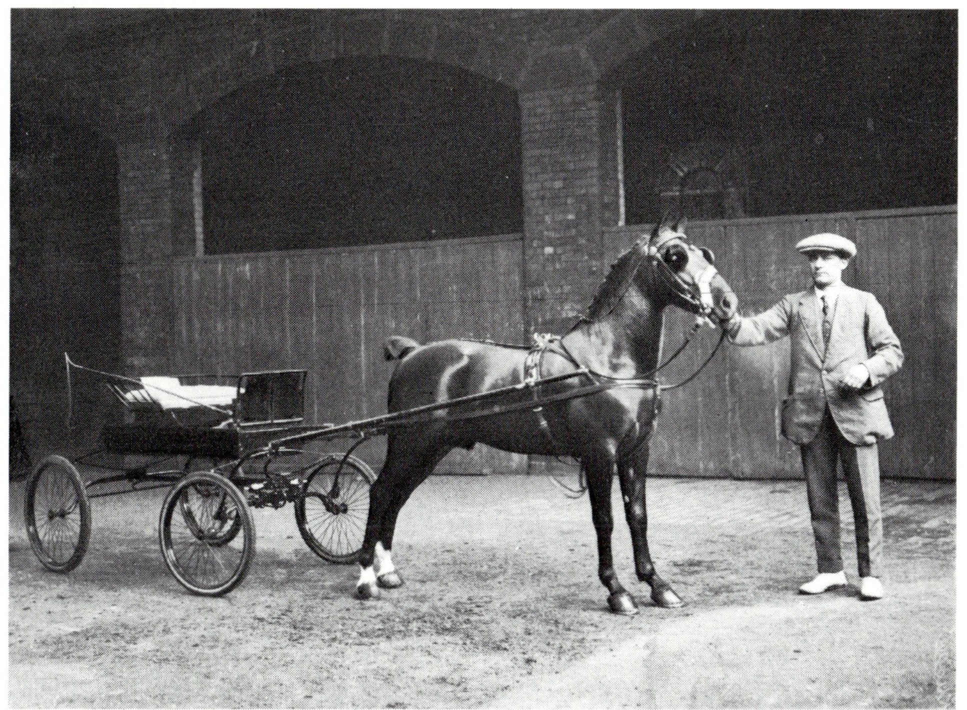

Fusee. Six times breed champion and the best sire of Melbourne breeding.

Walter Cliff was among the few breeders of his day who recognised the different characteristics of the various Hackney strains and of the great importance of blending them in the right way. He knew Lord Derby 2nd as a source of crisp action, good colour, and high courage; Wildfire brought courage again and forceful front action; while good fore action and pony character came from Berkeley Model. It was through his initiative in sending Success 2nd. to the 15.2 hands Royal Danegelt, producing Royal Success that an important line of Denmark was brought into pony breeding, although in this case he may have been seeking also the additional cross of Lord Derby 2nd that would come from Royal Danegelt's dam.

Later he reinforced the Wildfire blood of his foundation mares by using a home-bred son of Polonius, Melbourne Squire, out of the Ganymede mare Miss Walker. The union of this horse with Success 2nd resulted in Squire Melbourne, in his turn the sire of the good harness pony Olive Melbourne, as well as Minnie Melbourne the dam of the stallion Vortex that sired Carnation Rainbow and Fleetwood Storm.

Royal Success. One of the head sires at Walter Cliff's Melbourne Stud.

Walter Cliff died in 1917 and his stud was dispersed, some, in those gloomy days of the First World War, doomed to be heard of no more, but most of the best survived to leave an enduring influence on the breed.

THE TISSINGTON STUD

In 1894 Sir Gilbert Greenall, a wealthy brewer from industrial Lancashire, joined the Hackney Horse Society and set out to breed both Hackney horses and ponies, determined to have none but the best of each. He set up the Terrington stud of horses in Norfolk, and the pony stud was established at Tissington in a lovely part of Derbyshire, now a National Park. Sir Gilbert's home was at Walton Hall near Warrington and it was here that the young stock was prepared for show and, in later years, annual sales were held.

As we have seen the four-year-old Sir Horace was secured for the stud in 1895 to be joined by his full sister, Dorothy Derby 2nd, and their dam later in the same year. Some other Wilson ponies came from the de Trafford sale at the same time.

Sir Horace. A great show pony and an even greater sire.

Sir Gilbert Greenall may not have had that single-minded dedication possessed by such great pony breeders as Walter Cliff and Alfred Day, his interests were spread over a much wider field, but he knew well that the key to successful stock breeding lay in building on the solid foundation of proven female strains. His advisors in selecting suitable strains were the Walton estate manager, "Billy" Bainbridge, who was an auctioneer from Lancaster, and Christopher Wilson of Sir George fame. No doubt it was these two who had selected Sir Horace, bred by Christopher Wilson, of course, and the female line they chose to be the cornerstone of the stud was that of Sowerby's Polly.

Polly was bred at Wawne near Hull in East Yorkshire about 1878, and she was sired by Triffit's Fireaway out of a mare by Taylor's Performer, the sire of Denmark. In due course Polly was bought by a dairyman from Cottingham who used her every day to deliver his milk in Hull, that is until she chose to bolt one morning, taking herself, the dairyman and his milk into the deep drain that ran by the side of the Hull road in those days.

By a quirk of fate first on the scene of this catastrophe was David Sowerby driving his gig. He recognised the unfortunate dairyman as an old friend and bade him good morning, remarking: "Good morning, Maister, I see you have gotten your milk delivered early this morning – and all to one customer!"

Then, not being one to miss an opportunity, he proceeded to bargain for the mare and duly bought her, no doubt at a fair price considering the circumstances and the frame of mind of her late owner! Knowing the value of her breeding Sowerby at once sent Polly to stud. Her first foals were by Pride of the Isle, both colts, and history has not recorded their fate, but her foal of 1894 was a colt by Denmark which grew into the grand little brown stallion, Sir Gibbie. This pony was bought by Alexander ("Pansy") Morton of Darvel, Ayrshire, the leading breeder of Hackneys in Scotland, for whom Sir Gibbie won many prizes before he was bought by Mr. George Green of Katonah, New York, in 1892.

Sir Gibbie had made a great impression in Scotland, bringing a succession of eager customers from over the border to Sowerby's yard. James McMeeken bought Sir Gibbie's half sister, Merry Polly, and, in 1888, R. H. Walker of

Merry Polly. A daughter of Sowerby's Polly that won the London championship in 1905 at 14 years old.

Tissington Kit Cat. Sire: Sir Horace; dam: the Wilson pony, Lady Kate, the champion harness pony of 1907. Seen here at Olympia with her owner, Sir Howard Frank.

West Calder bought Polly herself, heavy in foal to Lord Derby 2nd. The foal turned out to be a filly which Mr. Walker named Lady Ethel. This mare was sold to Alex Morton in 1893 and the following year, to his stallion Goldfinder 6th, she foaled the mare Ailsa which, when four-years-old, won as a brood mare at the London Show beating three great mares – Magic, Jackdaw and Dorothy Derby 2nd.

Sir Gilbert Greenall eventually cornered practically the whole of the Polly family, including Sir Gibbie which he re-imported from America. Lady Ethel was a prolific breeder of the highest class, as also were her daughters and grand-daughters. To Goldfinder she bred two good pony sires Prospector and Golden Rule, and the mares Ailsa, already mentioned, Golden Ethel, Tissington Golden Ring and Tissington Golden Ray. To Contest, a son of Lord Derby 2nd, she threw Lady Connie and Tissington Lady Conyers, and from the latter were descended Rusper Calypso, Tissington Calypso, Braishfield Fuel and Braishfield Furore. Ailsa bred the great mares Tissington Amy and Tissington Amity, also Aillette, the dam of Ernest Kerr's champion

Sir Archie, by Sir Horace, and other good ponies. Tissington Golden Ray was the dam of Tissington Hoiden by Sir Horace, in turn the dam of Axholme Lady Edith, the dam of King of the Plain. At no less than ten of the eighteen London Hackney Shows held between 1900 and 1920 the supreme pony mare championship was won by a direct descendant of Polly; a marvellous record in those days of keen competition.

David Sowerby had another mare that has left her name in pony history. This was Bounce, bred in 1874 by Sowerby's uncle, Thomas Wakefield of Messingham in North Lincolnshire. Bounce had proved too much for the farm hands entrusted with her education so she was sent off to nephew David for a course of discipline in the "pin", or centre, position, of one of the big three-abreast wagonettes he ran from Hull carrying holiday-makers to the resort of Bridlington on the coast some thirty miles away. The round trip of more than sixty miles in one day soon changed the outlook of the most rebellious of youngsters, but Bounce was considered too good to be kept at that killing work for long. She produced her first foal in 1879 and continued to breed regularly for some years, her foals adding considerably to the Sowerby fortune to such a degree that, when her days were ended, that hard-bitten old character had a marble tablet engraved with her history set in the wall near her grave at his farm at Burstwick, where it can still be seen. It bears the following inscription:

IN MEMORY OF THE HACKNEY MARE

Bounce, H.S. B. No. 36

A mare they called Bounce in this grave lies at rest,
She's left stock behind her of the very best.
She was over fifteen hands high and her colour dark brown,
A brood mare or in harness in the show ring well known.
Her last record in the show ring to end her show career
When she was fourteen years of age she won the great Lincolnshire.
And she was plucky to the last with her action fresh and free,
The time she reigned upon this earth was thirty years & three.

Bounce was the dam of Gentleman John of the leather medals incident, and he was the sire of the great pony brood mare, Colne Marvel, one of the last two foals he left. Tip Top by Confidence was another of Bounce's sons, and the strain was carried on in the Tissington stud through her daughter Mischief by Denmark, which pony a number of high-class ponies in the United States trace their descent through Delchester Fusette.

Other distinguished families represented at Tissington included those of Snorer and Georgina of Wilson blood, and some of Alfred Day's Berkeley ponies.

Goldfinder 6th was a 14.3 hands chestnut that had been bred by Sir Walter Gilbey, being by his great Danegelt from the lovely Denmark mare, Lily of the Valley, that Sir Walter had bought at the Crompton sale in Yorkshire. She was of the important strain of Crompton's Bay Mare. Goldfinder had lost an eye through an accident and so was sold for a modest figure to Alexander Morton for whom he did noble service for many seasons, and it took three thousand of Sir Gilbert's guineas to tempt the horse away at last. Goldfinder was used in both the Tissington and Terrington studs and his mares were nearly all good breeders.

The foregoing gives some little idea of the important place the Tissington stud had in the development of the Hackney pony. It was dispersed not long before the First World War. Many of the great harness ponies of the day were bred there, including Tissington Amity, Tissington Kit Cat and Tissington Bauble, and their descendants have been responsible for innumerable show ring winners of more recent seasons.

THE HARVIESTOUN STUD

Although J. Ernest Kerr of Harviestoun Castle in Scotland started breeding Hackneys in 1898 it was not until about 1906, after he had bought the stallion Sir Archie at one of the Tissington sales, that he became seriously interested in ponies. Sir Archie won the breed championship for him the following year and, during the next few years, a selection of the annual offering at Walton Hall made its way to Harviestoun.

During a very long career Ernest Kerr bred at different times Clydesdale horses, Hackney horses and ponies, Angus cattle and Shetland ponies; always his rare flair for breeding ensured that the produce was among the best of its kind. At its peak about 1914 the Harviestoun Stud had a collection of brood mares second to none and mostly of Tissington strains. The great Sir Horace himself ended his days there, dying about 1917. Harviestoun continued for several more years the good work of Tissington and produced in its turn a goodly quota of stars. The dun stallion, Harviestoun Wattie, was reserve to Fusee for the breed championship of 1917 and he became a good sire at the Braishfield Stud. Sir Andra by Southworth Swell was another good stallion bred by Ernest Kerr, but he showed few of his ponies in harness, consequently he found Hackney men unwilling to pay high prices for the very bluest of blood without its having proved its worth in harness. Sadly, such good ponies as Harviestoun Elva, Eina, Rubra, Georgie Wood, Glenavon Cupid, Glenavon Filmstar, Broompark Mascot and many more all left their breeder at giveaway

Tissington Gideon. A son of Sir Gibbie that was the head stallion at Braishfield Manor.

Braishfield Fuse. A successful sire that was also a big winner in harness both in England and America.

prices and, not surprisingly, Kerr gave up, but his stud had made a major contribution to the progress of the breed and this cannot be ignored.

THE BRAISHFIELD STUD

Mr. and Mrs. Alfred C. King of Braishfield Manor, Romsey in the New Forest started breeding Hackney ponies in 1912, forming one of the last studs in Britain given over entirely to ponies. Acting on Geoffrey Bennett's advice, Alfred King bought a number of Tissington-bred ponies of the Polly family – the mares Tissington Golden Ring, Ripple, Calypso, Convert, Constance and Combine together with the exquisite little stallion Tissington Gideon by Sir Gibbie – at the dispersal of W. Ward-Hargrave's stud. The dun stallion Harviestoun Wattie went to Braishfield, as we have seen, where he sired some good ponies including Braishfield Lois, a pony that did well for J. R. Thompson of Chicago.

Fired by the recent successes of the great Melbourne ponies, Flame, Fame, Fire, Fusee, Kitty Melbourne and so on, about 1919 Alfred King set out to bring to Braishfield the best Melbourne blood. His purchases included Royal Success and the great matrons Wortley Bell and Success 2nd. From the latter mare, his own dam, Royal Success bred Braishfield Royal Blue, a good harness pony that was still winning in Wales when over twenty-years-old. Royal Blue sired Braishfield Monablue by Fireboy, and Monablue's foal by Braishfield History was Modern History one of the best mares at the Heyl Pony Farm, her descendants including My Desire and Master Supreme. Braishfield History was by Braishfield Furore by Fusee and out of old Success 2nd, so he was full of good Melbourne blood.

The best harness pony bred at Braishfield was undoubtedly Braishfield Fuse, by Fusee from the good show pony Monafly by Fireboy. Fuse proved himself a good sire before being gelded and his name continues to crop up in winning pedigrees. Jix, the sire of Mickey Mouse and Parkside Timothy, the sire of his mate King of the Lawn, were both by him, as also was Glenavon Mars, a pony that did well in California. Fuse also went to California after a great show career in Britain, to the stable of Ben R. Meyer of Los Angeles where he continued to distinguish himself in Jim Gilchrist's hands until he perished with his stable mate, Billet Doux, in the tragic Oakland fire.

Braishfield True Blue was the best son of Royal Blue and he was another son of Monafly. Unfortunately he was never given a great chance at stud, and ended his days in obscurity in Ireland. However, he left some good mares including the dams of Cabinteely Little Colonel and the Canadian and British champion, Simonstone Atomic. Two of the best harness ponies of the years just after the last war, namely Harlock Chiquita and Marlborough Chiconi, were both out of Braishfield Chic by True Blue. His last entire son, Harley

Boy Blue, went to Australia in 1950, where he sired a number of good ponies first at H. C. Thackeray's stud in New South Wales, and later at Mrs. M. Willsallen's stud at Harden where he was still in full vigour at twenty-four years of age.

For more than a quarter of a century ponies bearing the Braishfield prefix were a force to be reckoned with wherever they were shown, and it would be tedious to list them all. A great many found their way to North America, including Braishfield Sonnet, one of the very few ponies ever to get the better of King of the Plain. In 1938 Mrs. King, by then a widow, instructed Horace Smith, a well-known riding master and professional whip, to dispose of the remaining ponies leaving the Hackney pony in Britain about to enter a barren period while the breed was making great progress in North America.

THE HACKNEY PONY BLOODLINES

Although, as we have seen, the Hackney pony is descended in the main from the same head sires as his larger brother, I feel it is more realistic to regard the foundation stallions as those important individuals that were themselves ponies. They are:

Sir George, brown, foaled 1866.
Cassius, chestnut, foaled 1888.
Berkeley Model, bay, foaled 1889.
Sir Horace, bay, foaled 1891.
Dilham Prime Minister, brown, foaled 1891.
Royal Success, bay, foaled 1903.

The story of Sir George has already been told and his male line died out a long time ago.

Berkeley Model, Dilham Prime Minister and Sir Horace were all lineal descendants of D'Oyly's Confidence, but it is misleading to assume from this fact that Confidence was chiefly responsible for the development of the Hackney pony. I believe that the influence of Lord Derby 2nd. was more decisive and that he is the chief source of that vital energy and unquenchable spirit that we call "courage". Sir Horace was out of a mare by Lord Derby 2nd. while the name of Confidence is a generation further back. When we have this Lord Derby blood further re-inforced, as it was in many of the best of the Melbourne ponies, we get courage in superabundance. Kitty Melbourne is a good example, and of her Geoffrey Bennett wrote: "She was the only animal I have seen of whom it might truly be said that she had too much courage."

James Agate in his sparkling and evocative style tells us of another:

"Vivianette – sire Lord Hamlet by Lord Derby 2nd, dam Vivienne by Sir Horace, grand dam by Lord Derby 2nd – a trapper, was the best animal I ever owned. A bright bay, 14.3 hands, she had in overwhelming measure that supreme quality of man and horse – pluck ... She had nearly every fault of conformation and most unsoundnesses, but her temper, intelligence and courage were better than most humans. She would stand twelve hours gruelling among the Derbyshire hills and finish on her hind legs; she would do forty or fifty miles a day in tireless succession; she would strip her harness if I so much as clicked at her; and she would wait at village inns unattended for hours, finally, when she had had enough of it, tapping at the snuggery window with her nose. Vivianette wore herself so grandly in leather that, in the streets as she went by, old horsemen would snatch at their hats and children pause in their games to stare."

Add to this the influence of that remarkable Lord Derby mare, Lady Ethel, and her descendant, King of the Plain, whose lines to Lord Derby totalled one eighth of his ancestry, and we get the "hero of Holderness" in clearer perspective.

During Lord Derby's lifetime it was well known that occasionally his offspring would turn out to be mere ponies, and because of this he was shunned by some breeders. In that part of Yorkshire where I lived as a youngster there was a strain of ponies, small cobs would describe them better, known as the "Durham ponies". This strain sprang from a son of Lord Derby, Lord Durham, and they were renowned for speed and endurance; no day was too long for them nor were there many that could stay with them for more than a few miles. Not many of the Durhams became show horses and the only link I know of in modern pedigrees is through Lord Durham's son, Joe Rock, the ancestor of some good Canadian ponies.

CASSIUS

Cassius is a classic example of the tendency to produce ponies that is inherent in the Lord Derby line. It is through him that the line has survived in ponies and it is appropriate here to tell his story in greater detail. He was bred by C. E. Cooke of Litcham near Swaffam in Norfolk whose forebears had been breeders of Hackneys for at least a century. In 1886 Mr. Cooke bought Cadet, son of Lord Derby 2nd and Princess by Denmark, from his breeder, Henry Moore of Burn Butts in Yorkshire, and, though but a two-year-old, he was used that year in the stud. The Belle family was Cooke's best strain, tracing its descent from Cooke's chestnut mare foaled in 1830, by Norfolk Hero, dam by the legendary Marshland Shales, grand-dam by Stephen's

Cassius. The leading pony stallion of the male line of Lord Derby 2nd.

Bellfounder, the sire of Jary's Bellfounder. In 1886 Cooke had three mares of the Belle family, all by D'Oyly's Confidence, and the youngest of them, Belle 5th, to the service of Cadet produced Cassius. Despite his descent on both sides for several generations from fully grown horses, Cassius remained under 14 hands. In 1891 he won the pony stallion class at the London Hackney Show and the first and championship at the Royal Show the same year.

Mr. Cooke had another wonderful family, that of Spot which, though its lineage was less certain than Belle's, nevertheless left extraordinary action. Spot was a skewbald standing 14.1 hands high foaled in 1864, and sired by Gant's Premier, a horse by the thoroughbred Premier from a mare by Norfolk Hero, grand-dam by Farrer's Bellfounder by Jary's Bellfounder. Spot's dam was a skewbald by the thoroughbred Mentmore, next dam "a skewbald half-bred Arab." Two of Spot's daughters, Movement (14.3½ h.h.) and Magpie (13.3½ h.h.) were the two greatest winners in saddle and harness in Britain during the 1880s and early 1890s. Another of her daughters, Raven by Canvasser by Confidence, when put to Cadet foaled the good mare, Jackdaw, and Jackdaw when mated with Recruit 4th., by Cassius, threw the chestnut colt, Enfield Nipper, the important foundation sire of the American Hackney pony. Jackdaw also bred to Polonius the great actioned cob, King Crow, which figures in the pedigree of Southworth Noni, the sire of many good British ponies of thirty years ago.

In 1898 Cassius was bought by John Jones of the Whitegate Stud, Wrexham, North Wales, but not before his reputation as a sire had been well established. Some of his offspring had attracted favourable attention at the Florden sale, among them Julius Caesar 2nd, the yearling son of Sir Horace's full sister, Dorothy Derby 2nd. The purchaser was another John Jones, of Dinarth Hall, Colwyn Bay, North Wales. Julius Caesar 2nd turned out to be a great sire. His son, Fireboy, has already been mentioned as the successor to Berkeley Model in Alfred Day's stud, and Torchlight, another son, got Torchfire, that great source of courage and action. Torchfire was owned by Enoch Glen who used him for many seasons, and leased him for a time to Mrs. Van Nievelt for the Holland Stud. Two of his sons were widely used in North America, these being Chocolate Soldier imported in 1916 and Holland Magnate imported in 1925 by Fred Dent, then of Chicago. In 1928 Magnate was sold to James Franceschini of Toronto but returned to the United States in 1938 to Albert Buyers of Buffalo. A grand-son of Magnate, Stonehedge Brigadier by Buyer's Parader, won the championship at the English Hackney Show of 1938, but this pony left no son to keep the line alive. Milestone by Holland Manitou by Torchfire was the last British pony of this family, and his son, Glenavon Epoch, came to the Dodge Stables in 1934.

Cassius had another successful son in Whitegate Swell, sire of some great harness ponies before the First World War. His son, Whitegate Pimple, was imported to Canada in 1914 by T. A. Cox of Brantford. This pony's dam, Whitegate Queen Victoria, was also by Whitegate Swell, and his best son was Whitegate Smile whose dam was a daughter of Julia Jones, full sister to Fireboy, making Smile closely inbred to Cassius. Manor Smile, out of a mare by Nipper Junior, and Strutting Bantam, out of a mare by Royal Review by Fireboy, were sons of Whitegate Smile; while Daviburn Bantam, out of another mare by Royal Review, was a good son of the latter pony and had the distinction of winning the Junior Championship at the English Hackney Show of 1935. The ponies bred in Canada during the twenties and thirties were remarkably closely bred to Cassius lines, and they were none the worse for that. Both Manor Smile and Daviburn Bantam came to Mrs. Combs' Longview Farm about 1942 where they were used quite successfully.

SIR HORACE

The stories of his most important lineal descendants, Habrough Swell, Southworth Swell and King of the Plain follow in the story of the breed in the United States, and it is now difficult to find a pony bred in North America that is not descended from at least one of them. In British ponies, however, this is not the case, and there the only surviving line of Sir Horace comes through an imported son of Cassilis Masterpiece, named Paddock Lane Robin Rea whose

CASSILLS MASTERPIECE
Bay, foaled 1928
SOUTHWORTH SWELL
COLNE MARVEL
PINDERFIELDS HORACE
TILSTON MAID
GENTLEMAN JOHN
WARWICK WREN
SIR HORACE
LADY POMA
BERKELEY MODEL
WESTON MAID
LORD DERBY, 2nd
BOUNCE
FIRE BOY
DAINTY
LITTLE WONDER, 2nd
DOROTHY DERBY
F.S.
MONARCH
PEGGY SURE
F.S.
LORD DERBY
NANCY
PRIDE OF THE ISLE
JET
JULIUS CAESAR, 2nd
LEXHAM FANNY
F.S.

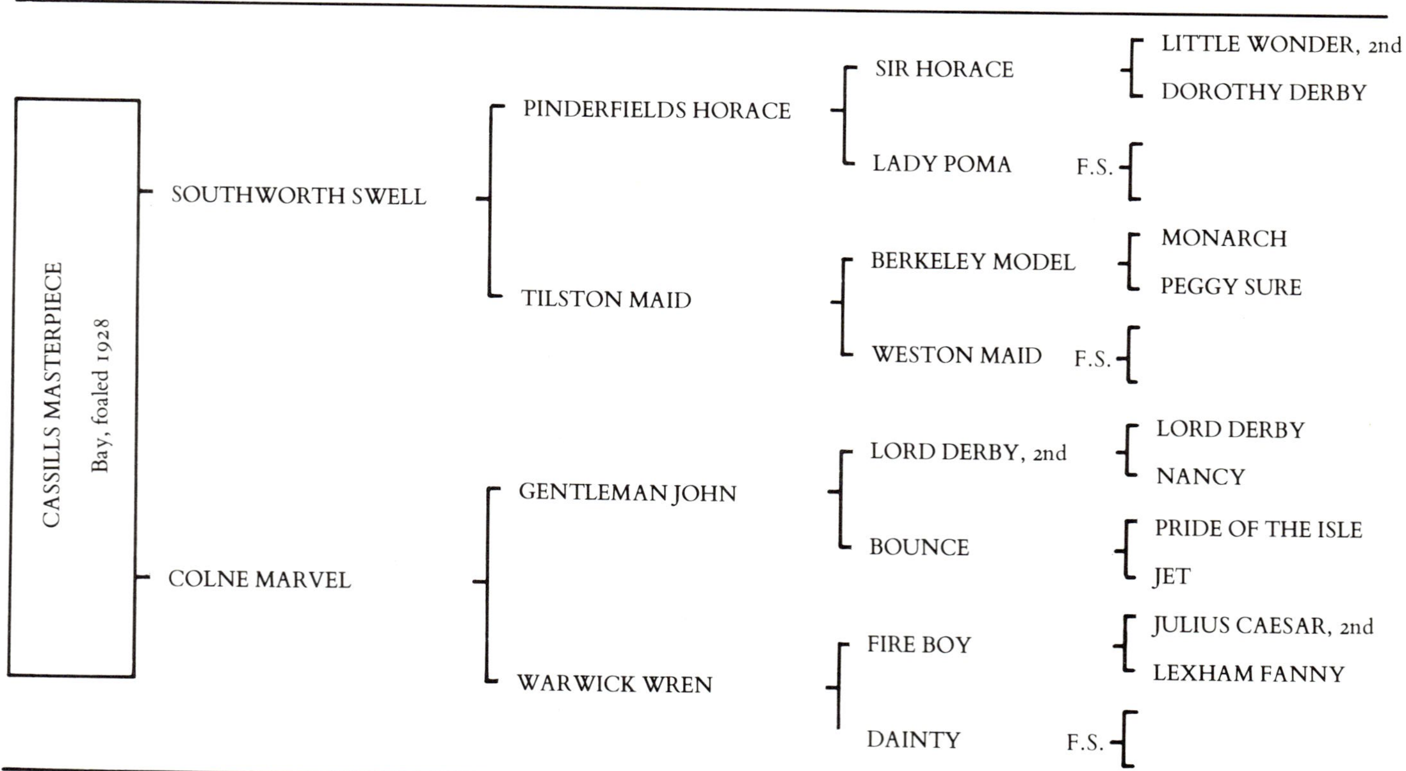

Fig. 1

dam was Masterpiece's full sister, Cassilis Marvel. Mr. Arthur Grant's Just John is a successful stallion of this strain and other branches of his family tree show further links with Sir Horace, not least among them his maternal granddam Wortley Bell.

DILHAM PRIME MINISTER

This male line comes down to us now only through Irvington Autocrat. There are still several representatives in Britain, all tracing back to Broompark Mascot, an attractive little son of Autocrat that was shipped to the United States in 1939 to perish in a tragic stable fire some years later. Mr. Frank Haydon's Oakwell Sir James is the best known stallion of this family and there are others by his sire Broompark Sir John (Mascot-Penwortham Chorus Girl by Royal Success). In recent years Cassilis Mighty Fine has been the leading representative of the Autocrat line in America. A son of Autocrat himself, Mighty Fine's dam was Cassilis Mighty Dainty by Imp. Cassilis Ladysman, next dam the famous Mighty Mite by Enfield Nipper. Ladysman was by Milestone out of Axholme Lady Edith, the dam of King of the Plain.

ROYAL SUCCESS

The direct line from Royal Success still survives in North America through Mr. Preston Graham's Cambridge Leader, but it is many generations back and the pedigree of this pony shows a greater preponderance of Cassius strains and this is apparent in his personality and type.

In Britain the line continues through Mr. Frank Haydon's Highstone Nicholas, a promising sire of his day. Nicholas's sire was Gatesheath Glitter, a delightful model of a pony stallion, but a veritable tornado to handle. He was by Onyx Zenophen, a bright star of the 1930s owned all his life by Mrs. G. Nelson Bower. Zenophen was considered the best son of the many times champion Bricket Fusilier, by Fusee. The dam of Glitter was bred by Miss Furgain Lort of North Wales, being by Castlemai Jack Snipe, next dam by Sir Horace, next dam by Cassius, next dam by Sir George, next dam probably a Welsh Mountain pony. This same family produced Tipsy Cake, Mrs. William C. Cox's winner of the thirties, and many more great-hearted ponies.

The Royal Success line is much attenuated in Highstone Nicholas, although there is some collateral support through Melbourne Shot, sire of the dam of Zenophen. The six times champion Fusee, foaled in 1912, was far and away the best entire pony descended from Royal Success and, had he not died prematurely when barely eight-years-old, he might have rivalled the great Sir Horace as a sire, but then three of his four grandparents were by that pony. Indeed it seems that most of the achievements of Royal Success and his descendants owed little to their lineage from Denmark, but came about through line breeding to other strains.

CAMBRIDGE LEADER
Bay, foaled 1949
CORONATION LADDIE
ALASA BETTY
FLEETWOOD CARNIVAL
JULIET OF MOUNT VICTORIA
ROYAL SOLDIER
HALL FARTH FREDA
FLEETWOOD STORM
FLORENCE MELBOURNE
CHRISTOPHER NORTH
JULIA JONES
CHOCOLATE SOLDIER
BERKELEY BEAUTY II
BUCKLEY ALGY
HALL GARTH KITTEN
VORTEX
BUCKLEY SUNLIGHT
SUCCESSFUL
LOVELORN
POLONIUS
PRUDENCE
JULIUS CAESAR 2nd
LEXHAM FANNY
TORCHFIRE
SYLVIA WHITNEY
TALKE FIRE ALARM
BERKELEY SWELL
SOUTHWORTH SWELL
COLNE MARVEL
MASTER SHOT
KITTEN

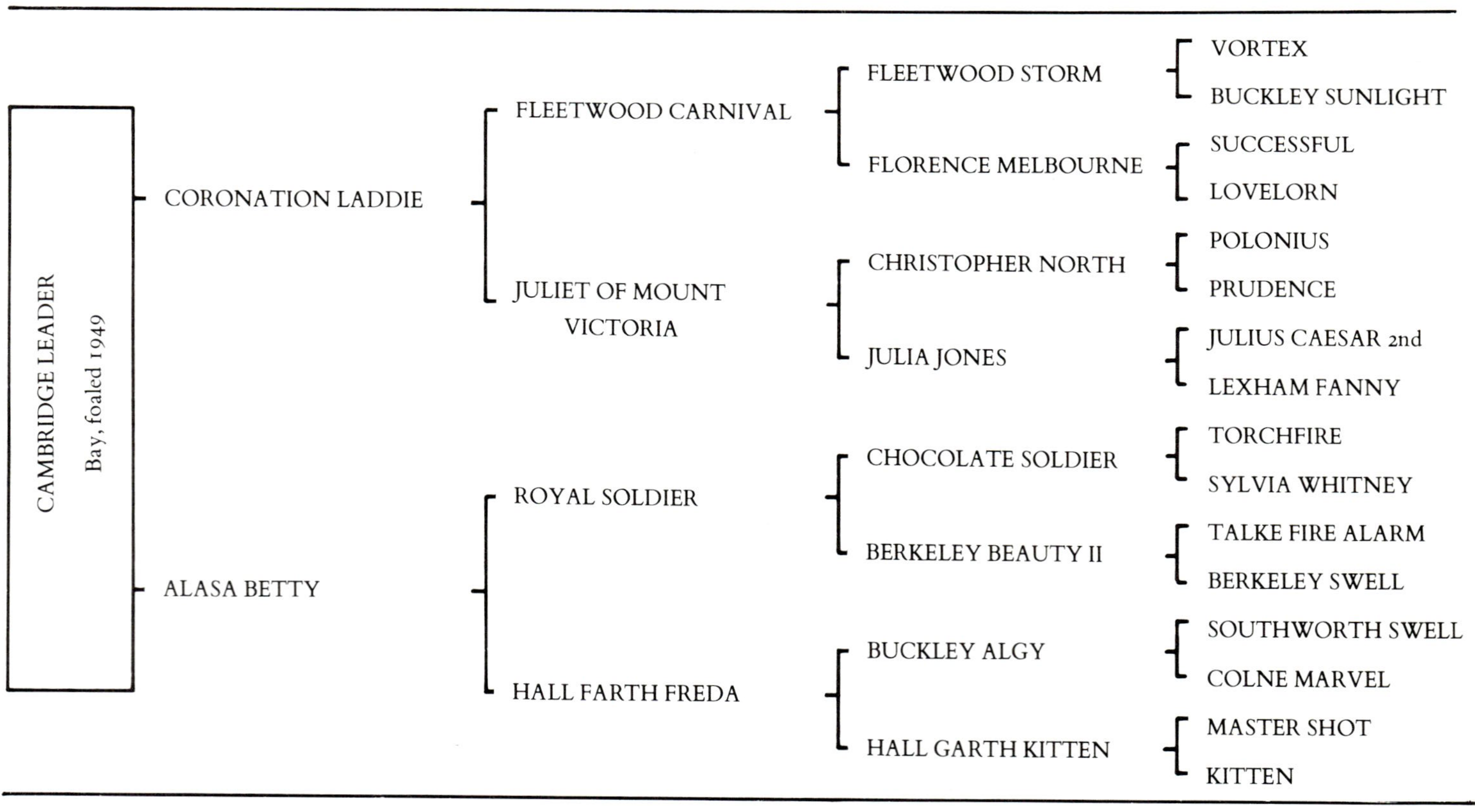

Fig. 2

Many years ago an old breeder quoted what he claimed to be his formula for success in breeding. "Return to the sire the best blood of his dam", he said, and this seems to be simply a more restricted notion of the well-tried principle of line breeding. Ever since the days of "Kit" Wilson's experiments, the best Hackney ponies have always been more or less closely bred. However, we are still a long way from absolute uniformity of type, size or colour, to say nothing of the equally important matter of temperament. The breeder has to have clearly formed in his mind the ideal he is aiming at, then he must determine what quality in his brood mare needs to be stressed to achieve this ideal. He then looks for a stallion with a bloodline that may "nick" with something in the mare's pedigree to bring this about. Of course there are a lot more considerations he must also have in mind.

Years ago when horses played an essential role in most civilised countries, the demands of the market-place guided the policies of successful breeders and ensured that producers of faulty stock were culled from their studs. Today most breeders aim only for success in the show ring. Everybody knows the deleterious effect this has had on some breeds of dogs which, through seeking to satisfy the current whim of fashion, have lost many of their distinctive and most useful qualities. An instance of this in the pony world is found in some of the modern British show riding ponies which, through aiming for exaggerated bloodlike appearance, are so hot in temperament they can only be ridden by experienced riders under expert supervision and are quite unsuitable, if not actually dangerous, for the average child. The danger for the Hackney pony breed may lie in the desire for more and more "fineness" – "lack of bone" the oldsters would have called it – and ever longer necks, leading to a strain of weeds, possible pretty in outline, but almost certainly lacking in stamina even if they remain sound.

THE HACKNEY PONY IN AMERICA

A few American horsemen had begun to be interested in the emerging Hackney pony breed from its earliest days; a class for pony stallions under thirteen hands was included in the prize list of the seventh National Horse Show in 1891 when the winner was Sir Arthur II by Alpha, a son of Sowerby's Polly. The following year the height limit was raised to fourteen hands, the winner this time being Polly's son, Sir Gibbie.

In 1898 E. D. Jordan of the Plymouth Stud imported Dilham Prime Minister, a beautiful brown grand-son of D'Oyley's Confidence out of a mare by the thoroughbred Ace of Spades. This pony was to become an important foundation sire of the American Hackney pony. In 1903 W. D. Henry of Pittsburgh imported Enfield Nipper, a stallion that came to be called "the father of the American Hackney pony". Nipper was by Recruit IV by Cassius,

OAKWELL SIR JAMES
Brown, foaled 1946
BROOMPARK SIR JOHN
CARLESTOUN SUMMER'S DREAM
BROOMPARK MASCOT
PENWORTHAM CHORUS GIRL
CARLESTOUN TORNADO
MISS APPLEBY
IRVINGTON AUTOCRAT
HARVIESTOUN ETTA
ROYAL SUCCESS
GLENAVON TORCHBELLE
CASSILIS SENSATION
CARLESTOUN CYCLONE
SOUTHWORTH SWELL
MISS APPLETON
DILHAM PRIME MINISTER
MAID OF IRVINGTON
RYBURN WONDER
LADY ETHEL
ROYAL DANEGELT
SUCCESS 2nd
TORCHFIRE
BENTON NATTY
SOUTHWORTH SWELL
JENNIE MELBOURNE
FARINGTON SWELL
GLENAVON FLAVOUR
PINDERFIELDS HORACE
TILSTON MAID
FLAME
PRINCESS VIVIA

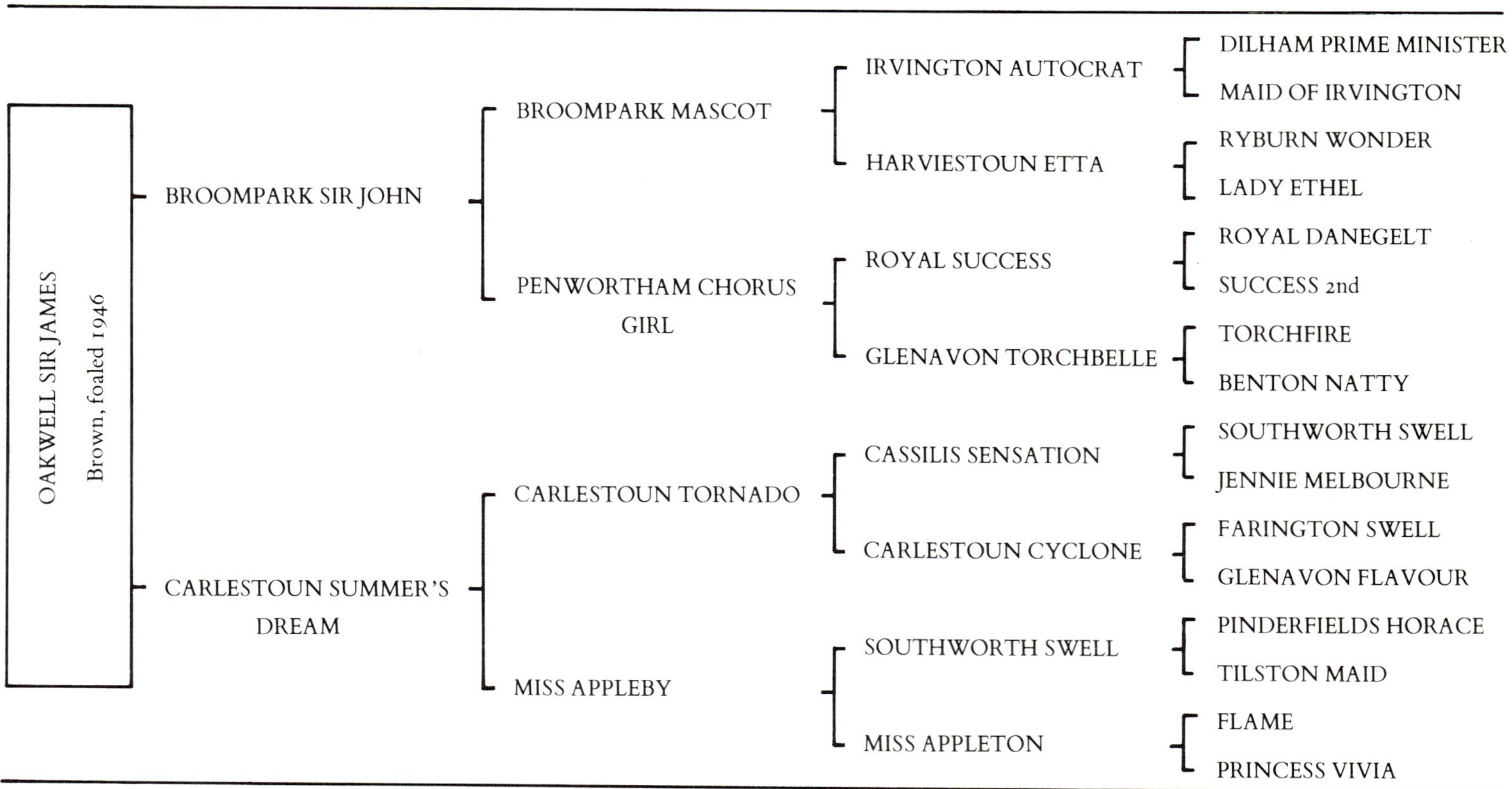

Fig. 3

dam Jackdaw by Cadet, a grand-daughter of the Skewbald Spot that had produced Magpie and Movement, two great show mares of the 1880's.

Both these stallions were used in Mr. Henry's Irvington Stud which soon became the leading pony farm in the United States. The mares at Irvington included Imp Irvington Bounce, a pony of predominantly Norfolk blood, Look-In and Welsh Queen, both by Julius Caesar II from mares of Welsh descent, and Barnston Lily by Berkeley Model and also out of a Welsh mare. When the late J. Macy Willets took up pony breeding in 1914 he made his first purchases at the Irvington Stud, and more from the same source came in succeeding years. So began the Cassilis Stud that was to have a profound influence on the breed not only in North America but in its native land as well.

THE CASSILIS STUD

Before 1914 winning harness ponies at American shows were almost all imported and, apart from Mr. Henry, no one had tried very seriously to compete with the British breeders. Now at New Marlboro, in the Berkshire Hills of Massachusetts, Mr. Macy Willets set out to change all that. In this he was ably supported by Mrs. Macy Willets whose father, H. K. Bloodgood, had been a prominent breeder of Hackney horses. The head stallion was Irvington Autocrat by Dilham Prime Minister out of Maid of Irvington by Enfield Nipper, next dam Barnston Lily. The mares included Irvington Bounce II, Irvington Bounce III, Mighty Mite, Irvington Peggy, Barnston Lily, Maid of Irvington and Look-In.

The Cassilis Stud dominated the pony breeding classes at the National Horse Show for many years after 1919. Irvington Autocrat, or one of his sons, won the stallion championship year after year, while his daughter, Irvington Bounce III, was at least four times champion mare, even defeating the redoubtable Kitty Melbourne in 1922.

In 1924 Mr. Macy Willets decided that if the stud was to make further progress new blood was needed. Characteristically, nothing but the very best would do and he determined to buy the stallion Southworth Swell, the sire of a number of harness champions including Billet Doux, the pony that had come out that very season as a three-year-old and won the coveted championship at Royal Richmond.

Southworth Swell was bred by Enoch Sankey of Croft near Warrington, and he was by Pinderfields Horace out of Tilston Maid by Berkeley Model. His grand-dam was Weston Maid, a beautiful pony that had been bred in Montgomery, probably of Welsh ancestry, though she was shown as a Hackney.

Pinderfields Horace was one of the best sons of Sir Horace, being reserve

GATESHEATH GLITTER
Bay, foaled 1939
ONYX ZENOPHEN
CRAVEN HOT BUN
BRICKET FUSILIER
CESTRIAN LADYBELL
CASTLEMAI JACK SNIPE
BETTO BROWN
FUSEE
COLNE MARVEL
MELBOURNE SHOT
SOUTHWORTH BELLE
SOUTHWORTH SWELL
MEL VALLEY BEAUTY
SIR HORACE
CASSIE BROWN
MELBOURNE FAME
MELBOURNE BELL
GENTLEMAN JOHN
WARWICK WREN
MELBOURNE FIRE
FLORENCE MELBOURNE
LORD DREWTON, 2nd
DAISY DANEGELT
PINDERFIELDS HORACE
TILSTON MAID
BURLINGTON FIRE KING
JULIET
LITTLE WONDER, 2nd
DOROTHY DERBY
CASSIUS
BIDDY BROWN

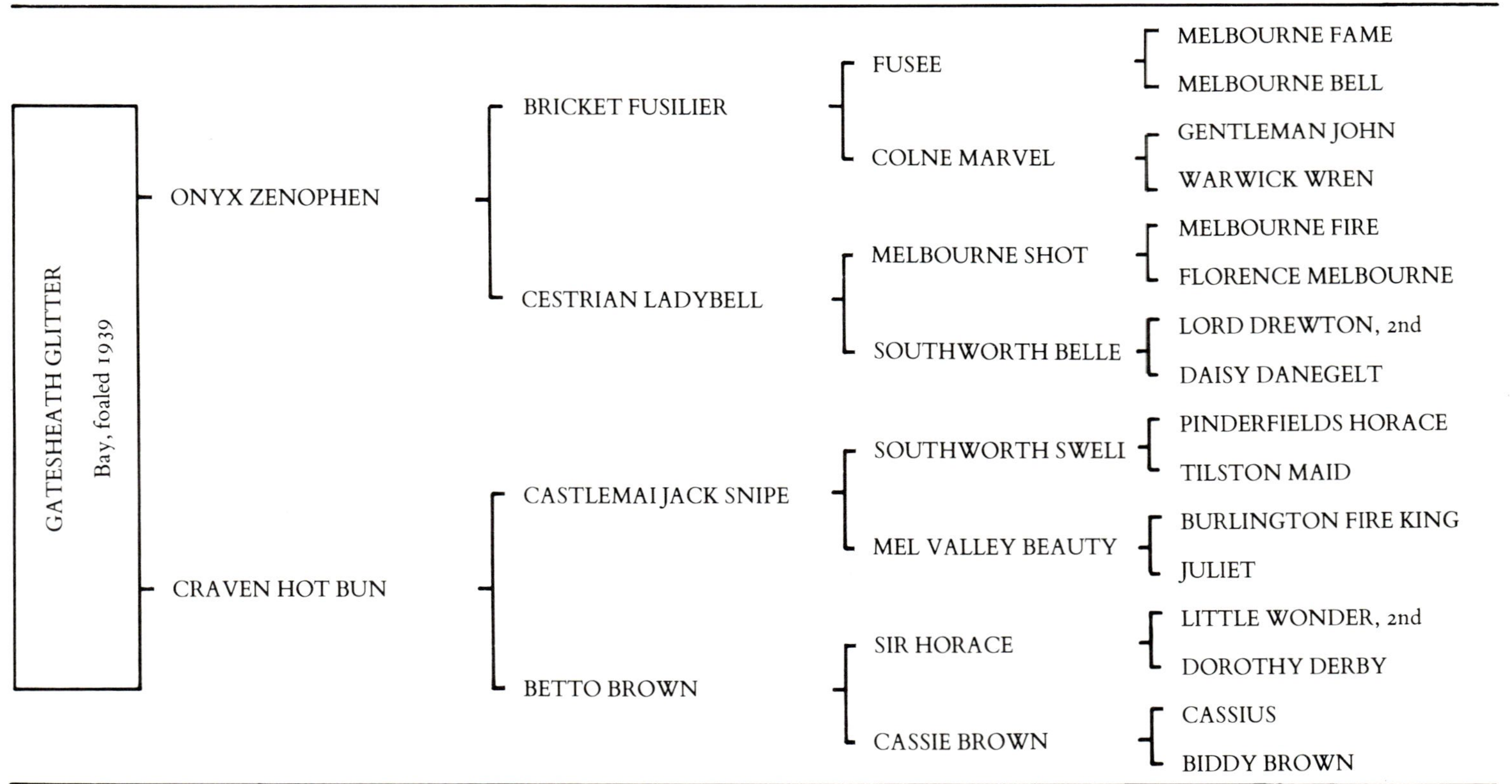

Fig. 4

Enfield Nipper. Sometimes called "the father of the American Hackney Pony." This stallion was a grandson of Cassius.

Just John. A present day descendant of Sir Horace which he closely resembles.

champion to his sire at the Hackney Shows of 1903, '04 and '05, then champion in 1906. In the following year he was bought by William Foster, the leading exhibitor of harness ponies in Britain at that time, made a gelding, under the name of Mel-Valley's Master, won numerous prizes in harness. In 1910 he was one of the Mel-Valley four-in-hand competing at the New York Show where they beat Alfred Vanderbilt's team and were afterwards sold to Mrs. Elizabeth C. Bowen. Southworth Swell was bought as a yearling by Joseph Ball of Southworth Hall, Warrington and he won first prize as a three-year-old at the Royal Show of 1910. He continued a successful career in hand and harness up to the outbreak of war in 1914, and afterwards he was brought out again at the Hackney Show, now held at Doncaster, in 1922 where he was awarded second place to Bricket Fusilier beating no less a celebrity than Braisfield Fuse.

In 1920 the first of many great ponies by Southworth Swell appeared in harness, this being Axholme Venus, the winner of the novice, open and championship classes at both the Hackney Show and the International at Olympia. Each succeeding season saw the debut of yet another stepping marvel by him; Axholme Sunbeam (later owned by Mrs. Loula Long Combs and shown as Carnation), Billet Doux already mentioned, and Easter-tide. These three with Venus are still reckoned among the best harness ponies of all time.

Lease Lend. The stallion that revived the line of Southworth Swell in Britain.

Naturally Southworth Swell was well patronised in his last few seasons in the land of his birth, but no son of anything approaching the same calibre remained to carry on the line. Talke Bonfire was perhaps the best and he sired James Agate's delightful little horse Ego as well as the stallion Fireflash.

Of his discovery of Ego James Agate wrote in the diary he published under the same title:

> "Whatever eminence I might have risen to as a dramatic critic, it would have been all the same in a hundred years ... But this can never be taken from me, that on a day in March I saw an unbroken pony shivering under a hedge, and that I had the eye to sense his quality and the wit to buy him. If ever I could conceive myself throwing aside this fleshly coil with anything approaching content, it would be because I had the ingenuity, in the high Roman sense, to bring to victory a little horse which, in his own lifetime, became a legend."

Many of Swell's daughters, however, turned out good breeders and so his blood is still quite plentiful in British ponies and it has been strengthened by some importations from the United States. In America Southworth Swell sired many more champions and several of his sons, Cassilis Masterpiece, Cassilis Magic and Cassilis Mighty Swell among them, have carried on the line. Today his name can be found at least once in the pedigrees of almost all the winning ponies of Britain and America.

In 1926 Irvington Autocrat was sold to Enoch Glen of Scotland and served at the Glenavon Stud until he returned to Cassilis in 1935 where he was used again for another four seasons. During a long career he sired a quantity of good harness ponies including Irvington Bounce III. Harviestoun Elva, Glenavon Top Hat, Glenavon Film Star and the pony stallion Broompark Mascot that was to have such an influence on British ponies. Other stallions by him include Cassilis Tip Top, Cassilis Mighty Fine and Cassilis Dictator. For the most part his stock had abundant action which in some cases tended to be "horsey".

OTHER AMERICAN STUDS

Also in 1914 the former Berkeley stud pony, Fireboy, was imported by Miss Ann Vauclain of Philadelphia whose stable was then managed by Paddy O'Connell. Fireboy was sixteen-years-old by then and he does not appear to have left many noteworthy ponies in the United States. However, the following year, his son, Talke Wildfire, was brought over by Charles E. Coxe of Willisbrook Farm, Malvern, Pennsylvania. Wildfire was out of Berkeley Lily by Berkeley Model and he had won his class at the London Hackney

Show in 1909 when two-years-old. He was again first in 1910 when Southworth Swell stood third below him. A full brother, Talke Fire King, had already achieved success as a sire, but Wildfire made no great name for himself. This may have been because Mr. Coxe did not persevere with pony breeding after about 1919 despite a promising start with mares of the highest class, including Rusper Calypso, the champion pony mare at the 1914 London Show, Kathleen Melbourne, Belle Melbourne and Tissington Amity. The last two had done great things in harness in the ownership of Dr. F. E. Judson and were sold by auction when that gentleman returned to Argentina at the outbreak of war in Europe.

About the same time breeders in the Middle West started to take an interest in ponies. In 1913 George A. Heyl of Washington, Illinois imported a number of ponies from the Dinarth Hall Stud of John Jones and Son in North Wales, the breeders of Fireboy and Torchfire. In 1916 Heyl shipped in 16 more ponies including the stallions Trillo Swell by Julius Caesar II, Dinarth Imp and Dinarth Reality; also in that year he bought the stallion Dilhamton, by Dilham Prime Minister, from Charlie Barrie of Teaneck, N.J. In the years to come the Heyl Pony Farm certainly made its mark on American pony history as will be seen later.

H. H. Truman, an English dealer living at Bushnell, Illinois, was responsible for importing several important ponies. Chocolate Soldier, a son of Torchfire that had been reserve champion to Melbourne Fire in 1913, came out in 1915 and was sold to Samuel Insull, the Chicago utilities magnate, and this pony was later passed on to J. K. Dering of Lake Villa.

Meanwhile in Canada, mostly in Ontario and a part of Quebec, people were buying pony breeding stock. T. B. Macauley, a Montreal business man with an estate at Hudson, Quebec, was among the first. He had started breeding Hackney horses about 1905, but his first batch of ponies came out in 1913. It included the Fireboy stallion, Glendermott Wildfire and mares by Julius Caesar II and Berkeley Model. Also in 1913 T. A. Cox of Brantford took up pony breeding with a consignment from the Dinarth Hall Stud amongst which were the stallions Little Briton, Trillo Fire and Talke Fire Alarm, together with the mares Isabel Melbourne, Little Marjorie and Trillo Lady, the last two by Julius Caesar II. This same breeder brought in more ponies in 1914 headed by the stallion Whitegate Pimple by Whitegate Swell by Cassius and four mares by the same sire along with two more Melbourne mares.

Senator W. C. Edwards of Rockland, Ontario had a number of ponies at this time, mostly drawn from the Tissington Stud and of impeccable breeding, but this stud does not seem to have survived long enough to have had any lasting influence.

It is interesting to note how many of the ponies imported into North

Bricket Fusilier. By Fusee-Colne Marvel this stallion was a winner in hand and harness on both sides of the Atlantic.

Highstone Nicholas. An important stallion of the past 25 years.

Irvington Autocrat. A son of Dilham Prime Minister that was used extensively both in his native America and in Britain.

Irvington Bounce 3rd. Driven by Mr. J. Macy Willets.

Southworth Swell. One of the most successful sires of harness ponies ever.

Billet Doux. The best son of Southworth Swell and one of the best ever show ponies.

Eastertide. By Southworth Swell, a winner in Britain and America.

Colne Marvel. Dam of Bricket Fusilier, Cassilis Masterpiece and several other good ponies.

America before 1920 were descendants of Cassius, while in Britain other male lines were coming to the fore.

During the ten years following the purchase of Southworth Swell by Mr. Macy Willets, he, and a few other American breeders, sought out and brought to the United States the very cream of the cream of the Hackney pony breed. The list is a long one but it includes such important matrons as Colne Marvel, herself twice breed champion mare but yet more famous as the dam of the multiple champion pony stallion Bricket Fusilier. As already noted this mare was by Gentleman John, her dam being Warwick Wren bred at the Berkeley Stud, by Fireboy from the foundation mare Dainty by the thoroughbred Zellinger, next dam by the Astbury Cob, a roadster stallion of high repute in the county of Cheshire. Bricket Fuschia, Marvel's daughter and full sister to Bricket Fusilier, came over in 1925 carrying her daughter Glen Alice.

Jennie Melbourne, daughter of Wortley Bell and dam of the peerless Billet Doux, followed in 1926, her daughter by Fusee, Skirbeck Cora, having arrived in the previous year. Buckley Poppy, from the strain of Peggy Sure that had produced Berkeley Model, came in that same year with her daughter by Southworth Swell, Flor Fina.

The list also includes Fleetwood (Carnation) Rainbow brought over in 1930 for E. A. Stuart's Carnation Farm, Glenavon Chimes that went to Mrs. Loula Long Combs in 1926, Kentmere Venus to Dodge Stables in 1934, La La Success to Heyl Pony Farm in 1933, Penwortham Creation bought for Hugh B. Wick of Cleveland by Frank Stericker in 1929, Rumney Sweet Melody to Heyl Pony Farm in 1930 and the Fusee mare, champion Harviestoun Rubra, to Dodge Stables in 1936.

KING OF THE PLAIN

Vitally important though it was, this influx of proven female strains was quite overshadowed by the importation in 1927 by J. R. Thompson of Chicago of the two-year-old stallion King of the Plain. This pony was bred by Arthur Humphrey of Morton near Gainsborough not far from Haxey where the Axholme ponies were bred. Humphrey was a close friend of Henry Gilding owner of the Axholme Stud. When the ponies were sold after Mr. Gilding's death Humphrey bought the Southworth Swell mare, Axholme Lady Edith, a descendant of Sowerby's Polly through Lady Ethel's daughter Tissington Golden Ray by Goldfinder 6th whose offspring by Sir Horace, Tissington Hoiden, was the dam of Axholme Lady Edith. Habrough Swell, sire of King of the Plain, was by Successful, a son of Sir Horace from the Melbourne mare Success 2nd, and his dam was Glenavon Ideal by Torchfire, thus King of the Plain had three near crosses of Sir Horace combined with a touch of Torchfire to strengthen the Lord Derby inheritance.

Arthur Humphrey was a blacksmith by trade with a natural eye for a good pony, and a number of good ones had passed through his hands over the years. King of the Plain had caused quite a stir when winning the class for two-year-old stallions at the Hackney Horse Society's show at Doncaster in 1927. Perfectly schooled by Harold Humphrey the pony had made his show running at the end of a long lead-rein, turning on command to make another pass before the judges.

Bertram Mills, the professional coachman who had founded Britain's leading circus, was then looking for a good pony for Mr. Thompson and King of the Plain took his eye. After some months of protracted and circuitous negotiation as is often the way in these affairs, Mills secured the pony for what was reported to be "a record figure." "Four figures" were mentioned which must have meant at least £1,000 but, whatever it was, King of the Plain must have proved a bargain.

Brought out in harness the following year by that master of his craft, Harold Jenkinson, he won the championship stakes at Toronto and Chicago, and in the ensuring decade he was to meet defeat on very few occasions. Many good judges considered his contemporary Billet Doux to have been his superior as a show pony, but their opinion was never tested in the show ring. However, towards the end of King of the Plain's show career, he was defeated at Kansas

King of the Plain. The English-bred stallion that started a mighty line in America.

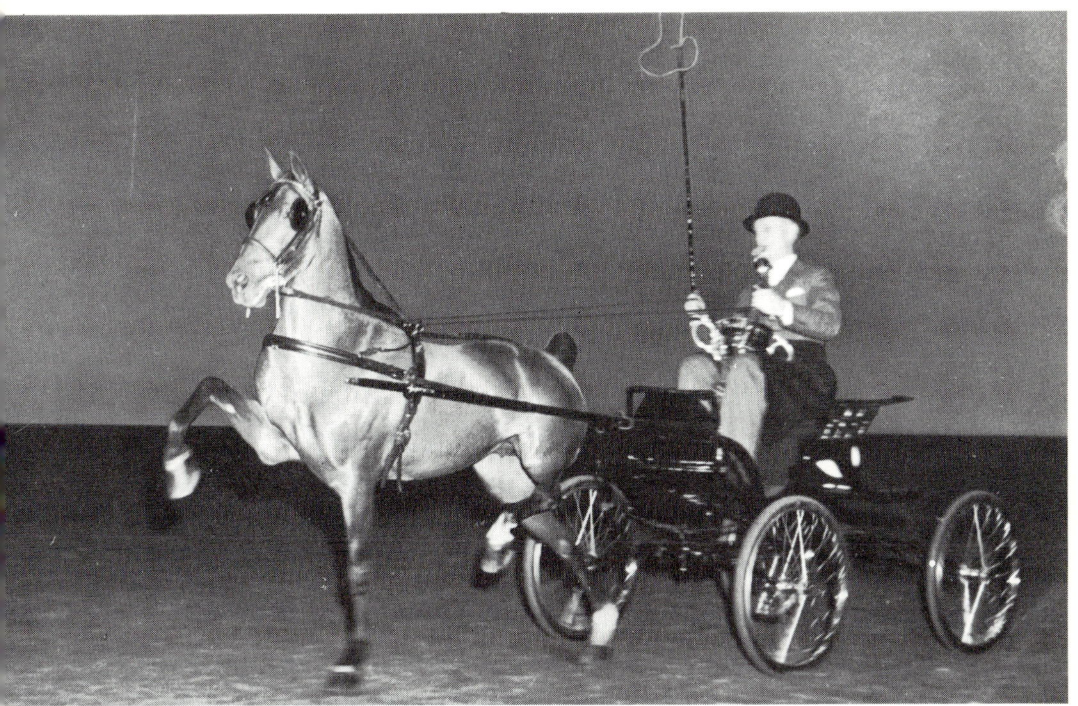

Highland Cora. After winning the stake at Madison Square Garden, driven by Reed Bridgeford for Dodge Stables.

City by Highland Cora, his own daughter out of Billet Doux's half sister Skirbeck Cora by Fusee.

In 1935 King of the Plain was bought by Frances Dodge and remained in her ownership for the rest of his days, being shown in harness very ably by manager Reed Bridgeford. At Meadowbrook Farm he sired a quantity of wonderful ponies which became widely dispersed throughout Canada and the United States when war conditions compelled the Dodge Stables to reduce their stock in 1943. Charles Gilbert of Toronto bought a large draft, among them Mrs. Elgin Armstrong's fine goer Crystal Lady and James Franceschini's Scrap Book.

Highland Cora is generally acknowledged to have been one of the best harness ponies of all time, and James Franceschini thought her not a cent too dear at $15,000 when he bought her before the war. When Italy declared war in 1940 Franceschini was interned as an enemy alien and his property, including his cherished horses, was sold. But for this nothing would have induced him to part with Cora for whom the Dodge Stables were willing to pay the full $15,000.

Not many months later Franceschini was released from custody to enter hospital after a panel of eight eminent doctors had agreed that he was suffering from an incurable disease that was expected to kill him within six months. Years later he used to delight to tell this story, adding with immense relish: "Hell! Five of dem b - - - - - - - s is dead already."

He survived for more than twenty years to enjoy his passion for horses and flowers, expecially at his "Dufferin Haven" house in the mountains North of Montreal where Cora's effigy was mounted on the gateposts.

Highland Cora was one of six exceptional ponies that Skirbeck Cora bred to King of the Plain, but the one that has had the greatest influence on the breed was Highland Magic. This pony was bought by Adrian van Sinderen and stood at his Glenholme Farm for many seasons where he sired such good winners as Killearn Victory, Glenholme Acrobat, H. J. O'Connell's Canadian champion Glenholme Radiance, and Mrs. Roth's Glenholme Troubador. When Mr. van Sinderen decided to dispose of his Hackneys in 1956, Magic and the dams of his best progeny were bought by Mrs. W. P. Roth of the Why Worry Farm, San Mateo, California, Magic dying there in 1959. E. P. Graham of Preston, Ontario bought the remaining Glenholme ponies including the brown stallion Glenholme Torchfire by Troubador, and this pony also went to Mrs. Roth in 1962.

King of the Plain was succeeded at the Dodge Stable by King's Banner, his son out of the good breeder City Star by Milestone. From his dam Banner had inherited two further crosses of Torchfire, that source of courage and extravagant action together with a tendency to coarseness. From the selected mares at Dodge Stables Banner sired some excellent harness ponies including Cupid's Beau, Top Flight, Pilot Model and Red Letter.

Another very important line of King of the Plain comes through King of the Highlands, a son of Axholme Venus. Unfortunately King of the Highlands left very few foals, but among them were the stallions Cadet Commander and Creation's King. The latter was bred by Miss Judy King of Atlanta, Georgia from her old show pony, Penwortham Creation, a daughter of Southworth Swell and the Berkeley-bred Colne Clearaway by Berkeley Claudius, next dam by Berkeley Model. Colne Clearaway was also the dam of Mrs. Combs' good harness pony Fascination (Penwortham Claudius). Harley Heyl surely never made a better bargain in his life than when he bought Creation's King early in his career, for he proved a prolific sire of high class steppers and his stock was sought after by the leading show stables. King's Ranette, shown by Mrs. Combs as Affectation, was probably the best of them all, this mare being out of Cassilis Rana by Southworth Swell, grand dam Cassilis Chiarina by Irvington Autocrat. The success of Creation's King was in large measure due to the genius of Harley Heyl who carefully chose suitable mates and brought

KING'S BANNER
Bay, foaled 1940
KING OF THE PLAIN
CITY STAR
HABROUGH SWELL
AXHOLME LADY EDITH
MILESTONE
HOLLAND MAYQUEEN
SUCCESSFUL
GLENAVON IDEAL
SOUTHWORTH SWELL
TISSINGTON HOIDEN
HOLLAND MANITOU
LADY MOON
TORCHFIRE
DIANA SOUTHWORTH
SIR HORACE
SUCCESS 2nd
TORCHFIRE
MANSFIELD QUEEN
PINDERFIELDS HORACE
TILSTON MAID
SIR HORACE
TISSINGTON GOLDEN BAY
TORCHFIRE
LADY CASS
SUCCESSFUL
MIGNONETTE
TORCHLIGHT
MISS DOT
SOUTHWORTH SWELL
SOUTHWORTH TISSINGTON

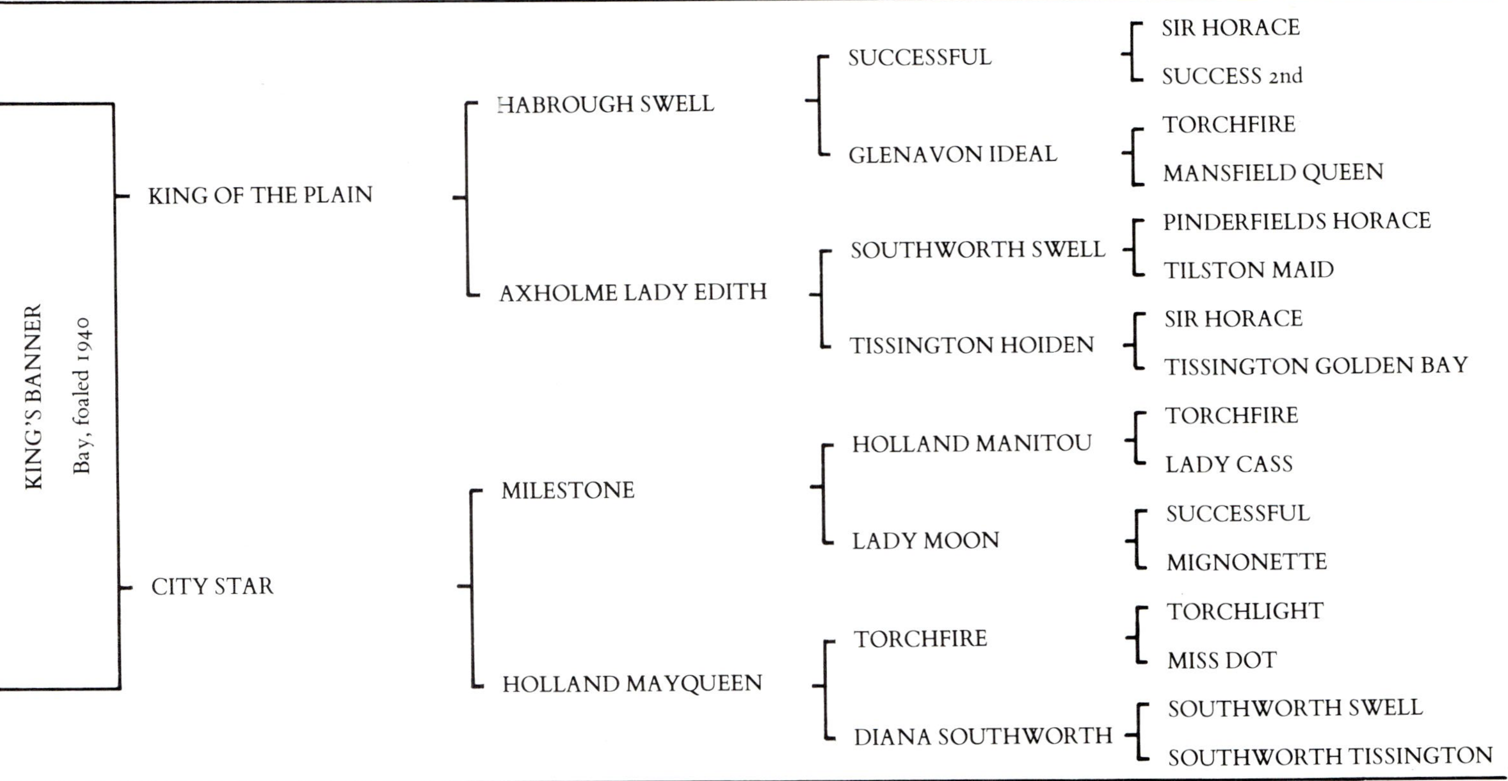

Fig. 5

CREATION'S KING
KING OF THE HIGHLANDS
PENWORTHAM CREATION
KING OF THE PLAIN
AXHOLME VENUS
SOUTHWORTH SWELL
COLNE CLEARAWAY
HABROUGH SWELL
AXHOLME LADY EDITH
SOUTHWORTH SWELL
TALKE PRINCESS
PINDERFIELDS HORACE
TILSTON MAID
BERKELEY CLAUDIUS
BERKELEY CREATION
SUCCESSFUL
GLENAVON IDEAL
SOUTHWORTH SWELL
TISSINGTON HOIDEN
PINDERFIELDS HORACE
TILSTON MAID
TALKE FIRE KING
ROYAL MAGIC
SIR HORACE
LADY POMA
BERKELEY MODEL
WESTON MAID
LORD HAMLET
PEGGY SURE FOUR
BERKELEY MODEL
LADY OF FASHION

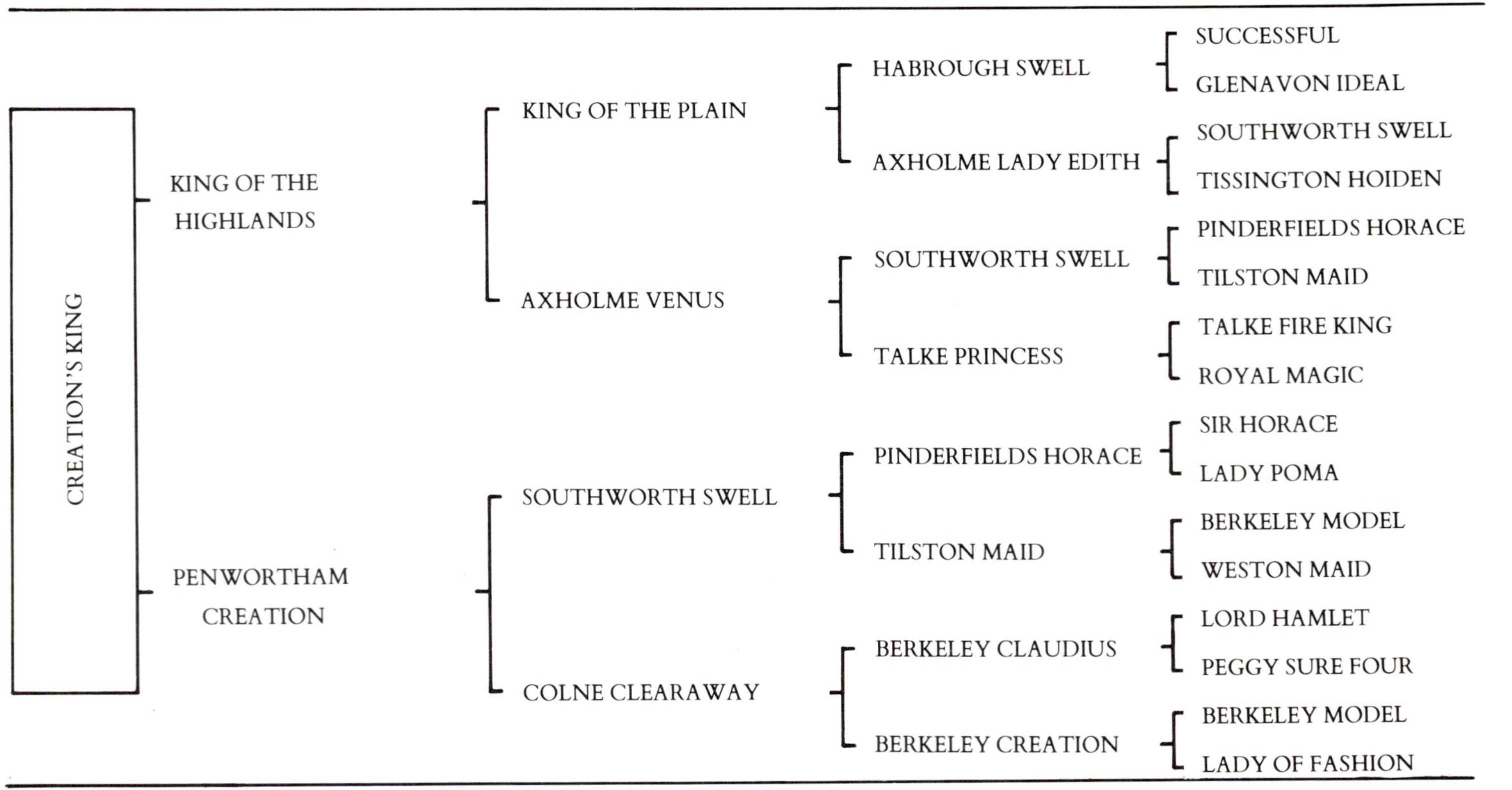

Fig. 6

the resultant progeny on with such consummate skill. Whether or not in other hands this stallion would have achieved such prominence is an unanswerable question. Some of his offspring may have been "strong", oversized and lacking in quality, but most had boundless courage and high action.

Cadet Commander, on the other hand, was far less fortunate. His dam was Penwortham Dream by Successful by Sir Horace out of Penwortham Dot by Fusee, grand dam by Cassius, great grand dam by Winnal George, great great grand dam "Kit" Wilson's favourite, The Pet. You can't find much bluer blood than this. Cadet Commander was bred by Mrs. John R. Thompson Jr., of Lake Forest, Illinois in 1937, going from there to the Nan-Su-Farm of Melville Rothschild the next year, where he was brought out in harness by James Gilchrist to start a great show career. Miss Virginia Penfield bought him in 1947 and the pony was shown for her by R. C. "Doc" Flanery to become one of the most successful ponies of his day in the show ring. At stud he did not have so much success probably through lack of opportunity, but a few of his foals did well and his line is certain to influence the breed some years yet.

King's Gaiety. One of the best of many good ponies by Creation's King, driven by Mrs. Frank Ryan of Ottawa.

Diamond's Victory. Driven by Mrs. J. Loring Brookes, a great harness show pony.

Mr. Sandman. Driven by Bill Robinson. This great little pony was registered as Equality.

Apollo Sand. Owned by Mr. and Mrs. Kenneth M. Wheeler of Virginia and trained by Gib Marcucci; winner of the A.H.S.A. High Score Award from 1974 to 1977.

Another son of King of the Plain that was slow in gaining recognition as a sire was Little Bubble, whose dam was the good harness pony Carnation Rainbow. Rainbow was one of the only seven foals by Vortex, all good ones, and her dam was Buckley Sunlight by a son of Torchfire out of Tissington Sleet by Hailstorm. Vortex was by Melbourne Shot and was also of pure Melbourne breeding on his dam's side. Little Bubble was among the draft bought from the Dodge Stables by Charles Gilbert and he had several owners before going to Miss Gayle Gray at Garastanna Farm in 1951. Little Gipsy was a good winner by him.

Coronation was a son of King of the Plain bred by Mrs. Combs from her good harness mare Carnation (Axholme Sunbeam), and he did good service at William Hunter's Croftland Stud before being sold to Dr. E. S. McClelland for his large but short lived stud in 1957. Victory Song, a pony that won many prizes for the Dodge Stables, was probably the best of Coronation's foals and Croftland's Dainty Doris was another that had a long and successful show career.

Other sons of King of the Plain that made their mark at the stud include Questionnaire out of Harviestoun Elva, Croftland Gentleman out of North View Chimes by Quo Vadis, and Delightful Delirium, a full brother to King's Banner that was used in the Canadian studs of James Franceschini and Lance Rumble.

SOME OTHER AMERICAN IMPORTATIONS

Of all the descendants of Sir Horace none has had a greater influence than King of the Plain, who has continued to pass on the vivacity, unflagging energy and bold action that has always distinguished the line. One might have expected British breeders, noting the early success of King of the Plain, to have cried enough and refused to let more ponies go, but they were too apathetic in those depressing times to really care and the steady migration went on. Habrough Swell, after standing at Albert Hargreaves' stable in Surrey for a few seasons without much patronage, was bought by Fred Dent of the Stonehedge Stud in 1931 where he was quite successful. In 1937 Heyl Pony Farm secured Lavington Lucifer, the best remaining son of Habrough Swell he being out of a Fusee mare, and used him to build up a foundation of choice mares that was to nick so spectacularly well with Creation's King a few years later.

In 1940 Albert Hargreaves brought over the last important consignment of British-bred ponies, among them Carlestoun Prince Charming, a son of Cassilis Sensation that had been taken to Scotland by W. S. Miller, Broompark Mascot and Glenavon Top Hat both by Irvington Autocrat, and Little Chief a very promising young stallion by King of the Plain's half-brother, King of the Lawn. Since then almost all the winning ponies shown in the United States have been bred in North America. The numbers of foals born there annually is now many times greater than the number bred in Britain.

AUSTRALIA

A small number of pure and part-bred Hackney ponies have been raised in Australia from the days of the first noteworthy import, the Berkeley Model stallion, Berkeley Magician, shipped to R. G. Wilson of Melbourne in 1903. H. C. Osborne of Sydney imported a few Tissington bred ponies soon afterwards, and about the same time C. H. Angas of South Australia brought in some ponies to add to his stud of Hackney horses.

This same gentleman imported the pony stallion Braishfield Lucifer, a well-bred son of Fusee, in 1920, and the Torchfire pony stallion, Glenavon Torchstar in 1923. These two are the only recorded imports into Australia in the inter-war years, but Castlemai Clansman also found his way there in that

Marfleet Cadet. The first Hackney Pony to go to Australia after the second world war, with his breeder John Partington.

period. Although registered in the Welsh Stud Book this pony was by Caslemai Jack Snipe, by Southworth Swell, and came from the same family as Tipsy Cake, a pony that distinguished herself in the States. Clansman was bred by Miss Eugain Lort in Wales who had a strain of ponies abounding in courage and vivacity that was largely of Cassius blood on a Welsh Pony foundation. Jack Snipe is not recorded in the Hackney section of the Australian Pony Stud Book, but he did sire a number of good harness ponies including H. C. Thackeray's Yonder Biddy Brown. In 1946 Mr. Thackeray imported Marfleet Cadet, a brown son of Wensleydale Recruit, by Southworth Noni and out of that good breeder Albin Nancy Melbourne by Royal Success.

At some time during the 1920's Glenavon Torchstar had been sold to New Zealand and Mr. Thackeray bought some mares there of his blood. He also bought several pony mares in England in the next few years, then in 1950 another stallion, the last entire son of Braishfield True Blue, namely Harley Boy Blue.

The Royal Sydney Easter Show continued to include classes for harness ponies and "galloways" and there Mr. Thackeray was able to present his ponies before the large crowds that that great exhibition always attracts. For

STONEHEDGE LIL' ABNER
Brown, foaled 1940
STONEHEDGE LITTLE SWELL
ALASA COQUETTE
HABROUGH SWELL
HOLLAND LORNA
CASSILIS MAGIC
WENSLEYDALE FLIRT
SUCCESSFUL
GLENAVON IDEAL
SUCCESSFUL
HOLLAND NORENA
SOUTHWORTH SWELL
COLNE MARVEL
SOUTHWORTH SWELL
GLENAVON LIGHTSOME
SIR HORACE
SUCCESS 2nd
TORCHFIRE
MANSFIELD QUEEN
SIR HORACE
SUCCESS 2nd
SIR HORACE
BENTON NINA
PINDERFIELDS HORACE
TILSTON MAID
GENTLEMAN JOHN
WARWICK WREN
PINDERFIELDS HORACE
TILSTON MAID
MATHIAS
LIGHTSOME

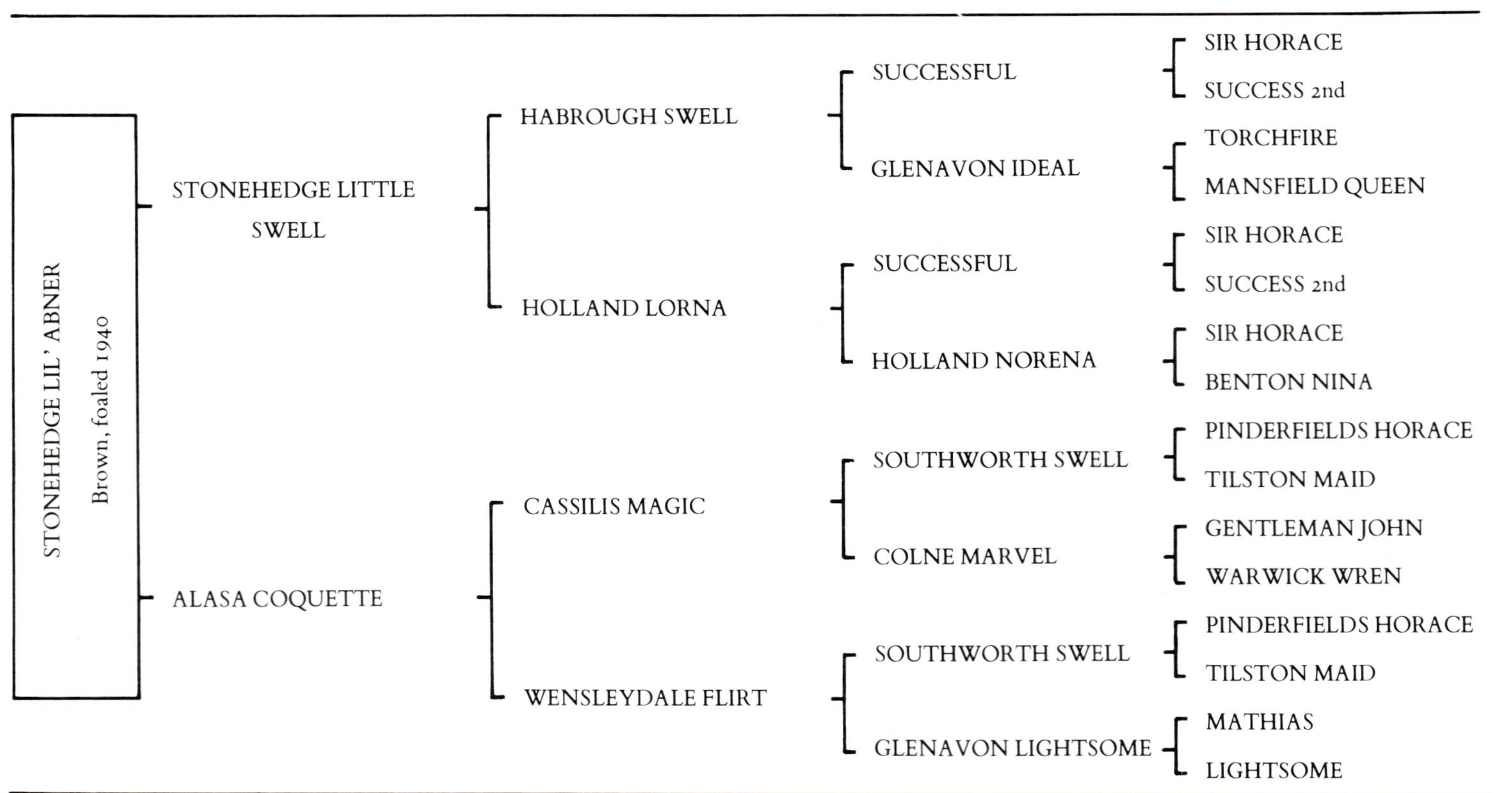

Fig. 7

several years the late John Partington gave a trophy to be awarded to the best Hackney Pony at the Sydney Show which his friend and valued customer, Cliff Thackeray, always won, but slowly the breed gathered fresh support. By the time Mr. Thackeray died in 1957 there were several new owners in both New South Wales and Victoria. In 1966 Frank Haydon shipped the stallion Marden Swell's Finality to Ken Wood of New South Wales and Marden Nureyev to Bruce Eltringham of Melbourne the next year.

When Mr. Thackeray died Mrs. Willsallen of Harden, New South Wales bought Harley Boy Blue, although the Thackeray family continued to breed ponies at Makari. In 1970 the same lady imported that year's novice harness champion, Marden Nicola, from Frank Haydon, and this mare has had a triumphant career in her hands. These and other importations have established the Hackney Pony on a firm footing in Australia and interest continues to grow there. It is unfortunate that strict animal health regulations forbid the shipping of horses to Australia direct from the United States and effectively shuts off what might become a good market for American breeders. Horses destined for Australia must travel via Britain and spend six months at least in that country before moving on.

Hackneys in Australia are registered with the Australian Pony Stud Book Society at its office in Sydney.

SOUTH AFRICA

Hackney ponies were not known in South Africa before 1961 when Mrs. Wessels imported the stallion Hurstwood Sparkle and the mare Marden Cinderella from the Hurstwood Stud. The same lady brought in three more mares in later years, and in 1966 she bought Marden Little Nick, a bay pony stallion that had won the Supreme Harness Championship at the English Hackney Show and numerous other awards.

Mrs. Viljoen of Simondium, Cape Province, imported two pony mares in 1965 and she now has the good pony stallion Hurstwood Baronet, a son of Highstone Nicholas, imported in 1972.

In 1975 Theunis Bester of the Thebes Stud, Pretoria, imported Director's Daiquirie the first American bred Hackney pony to go to South Africa, and in the same year Dr. P. G. Retief of Johannesburg bought the American stallion, Jubilee Too, and four well-bred mares.

Most major and many minor shows now offer classes for Hackney Ponies shown in both hand and harness, but usually they must compete with the horses in championship classes. Because many of the pony exhibitors also have American Saddle Horses the pony breed show is now held in conjunction with that of the South African Saddle Horse Society at Bloemfontein but on different dates from the Hackney Horse Society's show.

Weoselia's Final. Mrs. Wessels's winning South African-bred pony.

Both Hackney horses and ponies are registered with the South African Stud Book Association at its offices in Bloemfonein.

CHAPTER NINE

SELECTION AND TRAINING

To the uninformed spectator the horse world affords a range of impressions from the excitement of a tight finish on the race course, or the thrills of show jumping, or the majesty of a team of heavy horses, to the bewildering boredom of a long-drawn-out class of hunters or hacks. Each has its own devotees, but nothing can raise a crowd to its feet so readily as the sight of a great harness horse giving the show of its life – a vision of vital energy contained in balanced and rhythmic movement – an animated work of art, no less.

The training and presentation of a show horse surely falls within the definition of art, although, like a musical performance, it is a transitory form. Indeed it could be argued that the virtuoso of the ribbons has a more difficult task than the virtuoso of the keyboard, since he works with a living instrument. It is certainly true that a show horse seems to reflect something of the personality of its trainer, and certain trainers develop a style that is in some degree common to all their horses.

Training methods, details of presentation, and judges' ideals have altered somewhat through the years, and we might well begin this chapter by considering what is the perfect harness horse. In this I can only express a personal opinion.

In the early days of the century judges had in mind the ideal carriage horse; a horse of regal presence and dignity fitted to draw the elegant equipages of the day with their wealthy occupants on drives in the park or on their social occasions in town. No true gentleman was ever seen to be in a hurry, thus excessive speed was not desired. The horse must possess great quality and be well-proportioned, clean of limb, with a naturally gay and high head carriage, stepping in a free and balanced manner. Progressive action it must be, not "the knee and curb-chain business", with the hocks propelled well under the body. Naturally, good manners were of major importance also.

The days of the carriage horse are far behind us now, and the efforts of breeders and trainers have produced a horse with more extravagant action, but the basic requirements for the ideal harness horse remain the same. In action he must move with poise and balance, using the fore limbs from the shoulder, straight and true, with a light, airy and nicely rounded action, not bringing the foot to the elbow, but placing it well to the front and then returning it squarely to the ground. The hind action should follow through with the hocks well under the body and, when viewed from behind, not going wide. The whole effect should be one of extreme elegance and almost effortless movement. Dishing, or crossing of the forelegs, laboured or rolling action, going on the heels, etc. are all faults that a judge will penalise.

Different vehicles call for differing ideals. A lady's phaeton horse, for example, should be of great quality, preferably whole or almost whole-coloured, moving with poise and style at a dignified park pace, whereas a gentleman's gig requires a bolder and more sporting type of horse moving with much more dash.

SELECTION

In selecting a youngster as a potential show horse one has to consider conformation and temperament as well as breeding. Although action is an inherited characteristic developed through correct training and shoeing, there are points of conformation that have great influence on the result. The elevation of the fore-limbs of a horse is largely controlled by the muscles, which are attached to the top of the head, pass down the lower sides of the neck, over the points of the shoulders and are then attached to the middle of the upper arm bones. It follows that the greater the elevation of the head with "bridling" the greater will be the elevation of the fore-limbs – "the knee follows the nose" as the old saying has it. The head is raised and supported by muscles linking the upper part of the neck to the withers.

We also know that the range of expansion and contraction of a muscle is through about one third of its length. Knowing all this we can see that the potential stepper should have a neck of reasonable length, though certainly not over long and slender, and decidedly more muscular than that of a thoroughbred. The head should be so coupled to the neck to allow of "bridling" without hindrance to the air passages, that is clean of throat and with jaw bones that are not over large or too close together. A "swan-neck" is not necessarily undesirable provided the shoulder is well placed, but a "ewe-neck" with a badly coupled head is a serious defect.

The shoulder should be of good length and laid well back to allow of good range and freedom of fore action. A horse with a straight shoulder may have high knee action but he will certainly lack range. The withers of a show Hackney in good condition seldom show a noticeable junction with the neck, but this need not mean that they are low, nor should they be; rather does it indicate a greater development of those muscles that raise and support the head and neck. Unduly fleshy or "bullocky" withers are not wanted, however, as they usually give rise to a heavy fighting style of action.

The placing of the fore leg is particularly important in a Hackney. Legs placed too far back are seldom associated with good front action, nor should they be placed too wide apart. The width of the breast is not much indication of a horse's chest capacity. Some of the old hands used to maintain that in a good stepper "both fore legs should come out of one hole". This is taking it to extremes, but a wide breasted horse will often trot with a rolling motion.

The fore leg should be reasonably straight but, if not, one that is "over at the knee" is to be preferred to one that is "back at the knee". The latter condition imposes much more strain on the back tendons. The fore arm should be of a good length with short cannon bones, and the knee joint should be well formed and flattish to the front. The amount of bone below the knee is less regarded than in the days of the utility horse, but there should be a reasonable measurement of clean, flat bone behind which the tendons stand out clearly defined. The pasterns when viewed from the front should be straight, but feet turned slightly outwards are less objectionable than those turned inwards. Short upright pasterns are not wanted nor are those that are overlong, remembering that the longer foot grown on many show horses will add to the strain on long weak pasterns.

Above all things the back of a Hackney must be supple, as it is subjected to considerable stress when the animal is showing its paces. A horse with a long weak back will not be able to sustain its action for very long; it will begin to fade away and lose balance after a few turns of the ring. On the other hand a back that is too short and muscular may also be too rigid and, therefore, make the possessor difficult to school. A medium length of back, with well formed loins and well sprung ribs, is the ideal.

The hind quarters similarly should be neither too long nor too short. A drooping or "goose" rump is an abomination in a Hackney; not only is it unsightly but it greatly limits the range and freedom of movement of the hind limbs. The length of leg from the stifle to the hock is most important. If too great the hock will be placed too far back and, in movement, the hind legs will be left "under the wagon". The hocks must be reasonably straight, a horse with close or cow-hocks usually goes wide behind, and this is a bad defect. A fit show Hackney should show good muscular development both of the quarters and of the "second thighs". Besides providing most of the propulsion of a stepping trotter the hind limbs have much of the horse's weight to support because of the elevation of the forehand.

The feet are of the greatest importance. In the unbroken youngster they should be round and full with a good growth of strong horn, the soles concave and with a well-developed and healthy frog. Narrow upright feet, especially if they show some contraction at the heels, should be avoided, likewise those that are flat and spreading with weak and shelly walls.

TEMPERAMENT

Any horseman will tell you that it demands stamina and courage of a high order to keep up a brilliant performance for round after round of a show ring when the going is deep as it often may be. But what is this "courage"? Is it wholly a matter of innate temperament or is there something physical about it? Is it just a gritty "no surrender" determination or is it simply the release of an abundance of stored energy and vitality. Probably it is a compound of many factors and, even if we are at a loss to define or analyse it, most of us can recognise it in the finished product. But can we detect it in the raw material, in some poor half-starved gangling creature trembling and wild-eyed in the corner of a dark barn? There's the rub!

Fortunately heredity plays as great a part in determining temperament as later treatment may in forming character. It is well known, for instance, that certain strains of horse have a tendency to kick in harness, while others may be sour and resentful of any effort to hustle them. Others may be too highly strung and become fretful away from home, or in strange company, or at the sound of music. When buying a youngster it is important to find out all that is possible about the temperament of its immediate forebears. Pedigrees should be studied with this in mind, and a great deal may be learned from breeders and trainers about the characteristics of various strains.

Some of the old dealers would refuse to buy the produce of an unbroken mare. This may seem an unreasonable attitude, but there is some logic in it. I certainly do not advise buying only the progeny of successful show horses, but it is a regrettable fact that many a mare with an impressive pedigree has been sent to stud simply because she would not go in harness. This would seem to invite trouble for the future. Therefore, when buying an unbroken youngster, it is useful to find out if its dam had been broken to harness and, if not, why not.

Little can be discovered about the temperament of a wild, unbroken youngster by inspection alone. A knowledge of family traits in its antecedants is a much more reliable guide.

It sometimes happens that a certain kind of equine personality is found to be linked with some other more noticeable characteristics. For example, the black coloured females of a certain family may be notoriously untrustworthy, but it would probably be mistaken to sweepingly condemn all black mares for this reason, or indeed all those of the same breed.

Since I am really quite unable to set down any clear guide lines about temperament to help the newcomer in his search for a budding champion, I had better leave him to seek the help and advice of the most experienced person he can find.

EARLY TRAINING

Bertram W. Mills in the introduction to *Famous Harness Horses Vol. I*, wrote:

> "Success in the Show Ring by no means depends solely on good appearance, conformation and natural action of the horse, nor on the efficiency of the Coachman. Much more depends on how the horse is mouthed, mannered and broken; and this work nowadays is practically left to the head man. I would always prefer a third-rate horse with a first-class man than *vice-versa*."

To become "a first-class man" requires many years of practical experience for which the written word is no substitute. In these notes I have attempted to describe certain methods and equipment and to add some words of caution. I cannot point out any easy road to success, but if this chapter serves to help the beginner avoid some common errors and misconceptions, at the same time saving some unfortunate animal from unnecessary suffering, the writer will feel amply rewarded.

We begin then with the unbroken youngster, selected with due regard to conformation, temperament and pedigree, as only those with an inborn ability to step are worth the time, effort and expense of training. In my opinion rising three years is the best age at which to begin as at four or five years many horses have teething troubles that can make bitting a difficult business.

MOUTHING

Most particular care must be taken in mouthing a harness horse for, unlike the ridden horse, the mouth provides the driver with his only direct contact with the horse. The mouth of a young horse is extremely sensitive and pressure on the bit causes him discomfort which he will seek to alleviate. It is the trainer's job to see that relief is given as soon as the desired response is made. If there is no relief then a spirited horse will show fight, probably resulting in damage to his mouth and to the trainer's temper. The mouthing and training of a show harness horse has much in common with the training of a high school horse, both aiming at a balanced movement in which the forehand is lightened through the elevation of the head, bridling and an increased engagement of the hocks under the body.

After the horse has been taught to lead with a halter, a mouthing bit is hung in his mouth from an open bridle, or head collar, and the horse allowed to roam at liberty in his stall for a couple of hours each day for several days. A mouthing bit is usually a fairly thick straight bar mouthpiece with "keys" dangling from the centre and plain rings at each end. "Broken" mouthing bits are also used. The keys are intended to make the horse "play" with the bit so that he will more quickly get accustomed to the feel of it in his mouth.

The next stage introduces a breaking roller with crupper and side reins. This is put on with care leaving none of the straps too tight, and girthed up only sufficiently to keep the roller in place.

Two hours each day with this "tack" on for four or five days should see the horse ready to move on to working on the lunge. A special lungeing cavesson is the best tool for this work, the sort with a ring for the lungeing line fastened to the front of the nose-band. This gives far more control than would a normal halter with the line fastened behind the jaw. It is not good practice to fasten the lunge directly to the bit in the early stages. The first objective of this work is to teach the horse obedience, and the second to promote muscular development to enable the horse to support itself and to move with some degree of collection.

Work on the lunge should, if possible, be done in a special ring or an enclosed area. Even the corner of a field is better than the middle of a wide open space where the young horse will almost certainly be continually fighting to get away. The work can be done alternately at the walk and trot in both directions. When trotting, the horse must be prevented from moving faster than a fairly slow balanced gait and any attempt to rush away should be restrained. The first lessons on the lunge will be quite short, the duration being increased as the horse progresses and becomes more fit. The side reins may be gradually shortened through these lessons until the first stages of collection are achieved. A bearing rein is not brought into use until much later and the head carriage of most horses can be improved by adjustments of the position of the side reins and by the trainer urging the horse forward against the restraint of the lunge. It is important that the horse should work an equal amount of time in each direction.

When the horse accepts the bit and can be made to back away when pressure is applied to the bit it is time to start long reining. An open bridle is still used, with a straight double-ring snaffle. This is hung from the bridle by the two inner rings to which the side reins from the roller are also fastened, and the long reins are attached to the two outside rings. Work is started in a circle, preferably using the same ring or enclosed area as is used for lungeing. The horse is made to circle at a walk or slow jog guided by the inside rein while the outside rein is held quite freely and passes round the horse's quarters. To change direction the horse is first made to walk, then the trainer draws the horse towards the centre of the circle using the inside rein, at the same time he moves himself towards the outside of the circle, a little to the rear of the horse. He then uses the outside rein to turn the horse in the desired direction and, when the desired response has been made, he must smoothly and quickly adjust the length of the reins so that he again stands in the centre guiding the horses movements with what has now become the inside rein, again letting the outside rein lie easily round the horse's quarters.

When the horse has learned to respond readily to guidance through the reins, the trainer can start driving him from behind, practising stopping and reining back. The reins must never be used roughly and the trainer must be quick to relieve pressure on the reins as soon as the horse obeys their commands. Long reining is a skilled business and a vital stage in the education of the horse's mouth. Further stages of training for show harness work can be done in long reins long after the horse has been broken to harness.

When the trainer is satisfied that the young horse has learned to respond to the reins, and is no longer nervous of them making contact with his flanks and quarters, it is time to introduce him to the breaking cart. First it will be necessary to work him for a few days in a blinker bridle with a bearing rein, the latter used only at this stage to keep the head in a natural position. A long-shafted breaking cart is, of course, the safest vehicle to use for the first few times, but a jogging cart may be used with reasonable safety if precautions are taken. An active and experienced assistant is essential. For extra control should things go wrong, a lungeing line should be passed through the off-side bit ring, over the horse's head at the poll, back through the near-side bit ring, and fastened behind the chin-groove. Very great care must be taken in harnessing the horse to the cart for the first few times and especially in taking him out. Even the slightest fright in the early stages may have a lasting effect, while a more serious mishap may so alarm a young horse as to make him at best difficult to hitch for a long time to come.

It is best to stand the horse facing a wall or a stout fence and held there by his trainer, while the assistant draws the cart to him, holding the shafts high and well clear of his quarters. When in position over the horse the shafts are carefully lowered and the points passed through the tugs. Next the traces are fastened, then the belly-band tightened. It is important that the whole operation should be carried out quietly and quickly. With a fractious horse two assistants may be needed, indeed two good helpers are a great asset with any kind of horse for the first time, but both should know exactly what they have to do and when to do it.

After he has satisfied himself that the horse is properly and securely hitched the trainer takes his seat in the cart while the assistant stands to the horse's head holding the lunge line. When the trainer gives the command to walk on the assistant is ready to lead the horse off if need be, then walks at the horse's side, perhaps helping to push the horse round with the shafts when turning, and ready at any moment to restrain the horse should things go wrong. When the preparatory work has not been hurried and the horse's confidence gained

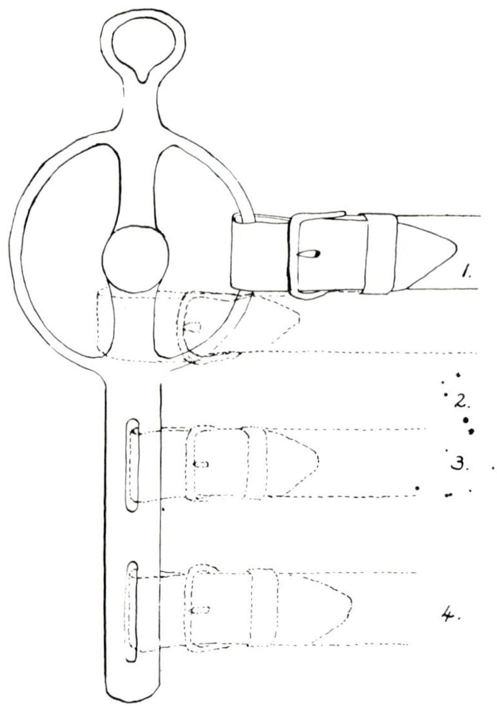

The four positions for attaching reins to Liverpool Bit.
1. Plain Cheek. *3. Middle Bar.*
2. Rough Cheek. *4. Bottom Bar.*

in the process, it is surprising how readily most take to harness. Once started, a little work in the shafts should be continued each day until the horse is fully at ease. With very nervous horses it is not a bad plan to put them in and take them out of harness two or three times a day. The bearing rein is used for these first few lessons in harness only as a safety device.

During these early stages of training it is important that the horse should not be too highly fed. He will not be called on for any great physical effort and it would be inviting trouble to allow him to become over fresh.

Once the horse is going quietly and confidently in harness a simple curb bit may be used, a Liverpool or Manchester fitted with a fairly slack curb chain and the reins in the "rough check" position. Training should continue to aim at producing a horse that moves confidently, is well-mannered and has a good mouth. His action will develop during this time, that is if nature has endowed him with any at all.

BALANCE AND HEAD CARRIAGE

Having carefully mouthed the young horse and got him going quietly in harness, we can now begin that part of the development of a high stepper that will demand all the experience and skill of the trainer. Most will have their own ideas about how this should be accomplished, but they must all follow the same basic plan. The aim is to achieve a greater elevation of the forehand, with the centre of gravity of the horse displaced towards the hind quarters. Thus, when the horse is made to increase his impulsion, the front action will be lighter and higher, and the hocks will be propelled forward under the body to maintain balance. The relationship between action and balance can be readily demonstrated. Try doing the "goose-step" with the body inclined forwards, then try again while leaning slightly backwards and the importance of the correct positioning of the centre of gravity is at once apparent. But the achievement of this new and unaccustomed position by the horse makes greater than normal demands on certain muscles so that the new position can only be sustained for lengthy periods after those muscles have been sufficiently developed. It is important to keep this in mind and to remember that for this reason training cannot be hurried but must follow a regular routine.

The centre of gravity of a horse is displaced to the hind quarters to the greatest extent when the neck is raised and bent at the poll, so that the head is held with the line of the face only a little in advance of the perpendicular, i.e., a position of extreme "collection". This collection is brought about by the horse accepting the restraining action of the bit without undue resistance. The trainer can work to this end by circling the horse on the lunge with the horse wearing breaking tackle, the side reins of which can be shortened by easy stages. The horse is made to trot round the trainer who, from time to time, makes the horse increase impulsion by using his voice or by shaking the whip behind him, at the same time restraining any attempt to increase pace unduly by means of his lunge line. The horse is thus moving between two opposing "aids" a driving aid from behind and a restraining aid in front. The effect of this will be to make him carry his head higher, and the increase of impulsion will be converted into loftier front action. If an unfit horse is made to keep this up for too long a time, sheer muscular fatigue will cause him to resist, perhaps violently, and this must be avoided.

Many trainers begin the first stages of bridling by letting the horse wear his breaking tackle while loose in a large box-stall or barn, using a bridle with a double-ring snaffle with a bearing rein and a breaking roller with side-reins. The side-reins may be attached to the roller at different positions as may be found best for that particular horse. The bearing rein must only be short enough to assist the work of the side-reins in making the horse flex his neck at the poll. The horse must never be allowed to "lean" on the bearing rein; the aim being to teach him to place his head in the desired position of his own volition. I have seen young horses braced up in tackle while cross-tied on pillar reins, but this severe restraint is too much for a sensitive animal, and his torturer will probably not observe the horse's distress until the poor creature plunges desperately and perhaps turns a somersault in his efforts to ease his aching muscles.

At this stage of training I seldom use a bearing rein because the horse's head can usually be raised sufficiently without one when working on the lunge as described, and the position can be relaxed at the very first signs of fatigue. The early and excessive use of a bearing rein is the cause of more broken harness and bad mouths – not to say bad language too – than any other single factor. When the young horse is strong enough the bearing rein may be used when he is put in harness for short periods once or twice a week. In harness he will not be wearing fixed side-reins so that his head will have more freedom of movement.

It is important to teach the horse collection before trying to raise the head too much. Draw reins, i.e., flexible reins of rawhide or similar material fastened to the roller, running through the bit rings and back to the trainer's hands, are sometimes used to make a horse "bridle". With sensitive and light hands they are useful, but harsh treatment with them can only lead to a damaged mouth. They can also be used for work in harness, for preference using a double-ring snaffle with them, but always working at a fairly slow pace, avoiding taking a strong pull and keeping the hands as steady as possible once the horse has assumed the desired head position. Resistance to bridling should not be countered by jerking the reins but by a "half-halt". The trainer should note when the horse attains a balanced and rhythmic trot and not try to maintain it for too long. Afterwards rewarding the horse by stopping and letting him relax.

The horse should now be ready to do some of his work in harness using a bit with a curb. For most horses a swivel-check Liverpool bit is best. Choose one with a mouthpiece of reasonable thickness and that is sufficiently wide to avoid pinching the cheeks. The first introduction to the curb may be made in the breaking tackle, coupling the side-reins fairly loosely to the middle bar position of the bit. The curb chain should be adjusted so that when tight the bit makes an angle of about 45° with the cheek-piece of the bridle.

When driving with a Liverpool bit the reins should be buckled in the "rough cheek" position, that is around that part of the bit cheek that is inside the ring and just below the mouthpiece. The lower bar positions are obviously more severe and should only be used by experienced drivers.

A few passes at a show pace may now be tried with the bearing rein shortened a little, but never so much as to make the horse "poke his nose". A try out in this way should not be attempted more than once or twice a week. In training a show horse the presence of an experienced man on the ground is invaluable. Only he can really judge such matters as the correct pace, elevation of the head and so on.

Most good Hackneys have a naturally high head carriage, but occasionally one meets with a horse that leans on the bearing rein and has not learned to relax his back. These cases can sometimes be improved by using a "dumb-jock". The Blackwell dumb-jock was a particularly good device which is no longer made, but similar patterns can be found. This has a gutta-percha roller with two arms of the same flexible material projecting diagonally sideways and upwards from the top to which both the side-reins and the crupper straps can be attached at various heights. The side reins have pieces of elastic let into them and run from the arms, through the bit rings to fasten back to the roller about halfway down each side. The arms being flexible, the pressure on the bit is transferred to the tail and can be relieved by flexing the neck and relaxing the back behind the withers, thus reducing the distance between tail and mouth. As with all types of tackle the roller should be put on well behind the withers and girthed fairly tightly.

Blackwell's dumb jockey and breaking cavesson.

Before leaving the subject of early training I would like to say a little more about the mouth of a horse. A good mouth is of the first importance in any trained horse, but in none more so than in the show Hackney; and in none is it more likely to suffer damage. The parts of the mouth that are in contact with the bit are the tongue and the bars, i.e., that toothless part of the gums of the lower jaw that lies between the molars and incisors of a mare or between the molars and tushes of a horse. The bars are often described as highly sensitive, though I believe they are only moderately so. Most of us probably know some odd fellow who prefers to remove his dentures to masticate even the toughest of food and, though his action may cause his more sensitive dining companions some distress, it appears to inconvenience him not at all. His gums have, in fact, becomed hardened and as insensitive as his behaviour! So it is with the horse; each injury, after it has healed, leaves the bars a little less sensitive than before until finally the horse becomes an incurable puller. Repeated sharp jabs on the reins may damage, or even fracture, the bone beneath the bars. For a time the mouth will then be painfully sore, but gradually the bone will repair itself by ossification, and have less feeling than before. There is a bony membrane running round the upper surface of the jawbone which serves to hold the teeth in place, and this continues beneath the gum of the bars between the front and back teeth. If crushed, pieces of this membrane, about the thickness of an eggshell, will work their way out, but until the healing process is completed the bars will be painfully sore. Certain nagsmen in the "good old days" used to inflict this injury on a young horse deliberately; they called it "shelling the mouth". For a time the horse would hardly touch the bit at all, and these clever fellows would boast of its light mouth, but they took care that the horse passed out of their hands before the inevitable results of their handiwork came about.

It is most important that the trainer should avoid injuring the mouth of a young horse. If he finds himself losing control of his temper he will be wise to put the colt away and hope for better results the next day. If punishment must be given *never* do it through the mouth, at least not through the horse's mouth.

It should be remembered that pain or discomfort will often cause a horse to pull, a common case being a tight noseband or narrow bit which causes the cheeks to be pressed against a sharp molar; others are where the bit is too high in the mouth and is therefore pinching the corners, or a curb chain is overtight. A young horse when he is put in harness may need some restraint for a few minutes because of excitement or *joi-de-vivre*, but the experienced driver can recognise the difference in "feel" between this sort of "pulling" and the insensitive numb feeling of a deadened mouth. In the latter case the trainer should look for the cause of the horse's distress and try to relieve it. Only by doing so will he prevent the horse becoming an incurable puller.

The variety of bits designed at different times for harness horses is only rivalled by the number now available to the jumping fraternity. In both cases there are bound to be difficulties occasionally in controlling very fit, high-couraged horses keyed up to make a considerable effort. But it must be realised that no horse can put up a free-moving, balanced and airy show when he is lifting his driver off the seat. Some horses go best when slightly "behind the bit", while others seek some support from the reins, thus bitting is often a matter of trial and error. Those horses that because of some defect in conformation find bridling difficult often become artful and they will find an answer to almost any kind of bit in time. With these horses frequent changes of bit may be necessary to keep ahead in a continuing battle of wits.

Most Hackneys are driven in some type of curb bit, and nearly all of these provide a choice of positions for attaching the reins, each giving more or less leverage on the curb. Occasionally one meets a horse that goes with no curb at all and must be driven in the plain cheek of a Liverpool bit, or perhaps in a bit with a jointed, or "broken", mouthpiece.

In choosing a bit for a particular horse the first consideration is that it must fit properly. It should be wide enough so that the corners of the mouth are not pinched and so that the upper arms of the cheek-pieces are not pressing against the horse's cheeks. Equally the bit should not be too wide so that it slides through the horse's mouth. The mouthpiece should be of a suitable thickness not only to give the necessary strength but also to suit the sensitivity of the horse's mouth, bearing in mind that a thick mouthpiece is generally less severe than a thin one.

An examination of a horse's mouth can give some idea of its likely sensitivity. In general a narrow mouth with the bars sharply angled at the inner edges and having only a thin covering of "gum" over the bone will be more sensitive than one with the jawbones wider apart and the bars well rounded and thickly covered. The first sort might be suited best with a Mullen, or half-moon, mouthpiece which will make more contact with the outer sides of the bars, and leaving more room for the tongue than will a straight bar mouthpiece. A low, or Melton, port of the proper width allows more room for the tongue while having the same contact with the bars as a straight mouthpiece. Rubber covered mouthpieces are sometimes used for sensitive or sore mouths. High port bits, and those of the Chifney type, are not always successful in single harness and then only in most careful hands.

The driving of a show Hackney follows the English school of driving, as distinct from the American or East European school. The latter is that followed in the driving of fast horses, employing snaffle bits, that is bits without a curb. The fast trotter often depends on some support from the reins for his forward poised balance, and a curb bit would be the wrong medium for this. The show Hackney, on the other hand, as I have tried to show, will be balanced in a completely different way, moving in "self carriage" as the dressage riders say. The aim, then, should be to maintain the horse's impulsion, or output of muscular energy if you like, against the restraint of the bit. Thus, to use an expression such as "set him back", implying forcing the horse to bridle by pulling on the reins, reveals a lack of understanding of the first principles. The collecting force should come from behind against the hand and not vice versa. The use of loops or handholds on the reins, possibly with some exceptions, indicates a similar lack of understanding, because using them the hands cannot be held in the most effective position. Compare the poise and hands of a master craftsman – like John Black with Stella Vane or the late Dave Smith with Affectation – with those we see sometimes today and the reader will, I hope, get the idea.

IMPROVING ACTION

Many and varied have been the devices ingenious men have contrived for developing a horse's action, ever since the price of a show horse began to be measured by the height it could raise its limbs. It had long been known that heavy shoes caused some horses to lift their feet higher at the trot and, since it seems to be normal reasoning to suppose that if a little is good more must be better, it was not long before horses were being loaded with as much as four pounds of metal on each foot. Many show organisers felt obliged to introduce regulations limiting the permitted weight of shoes, including nails, to two pounds for horses over 14 hands and one and a half pounds for ponies under that height. Of course, it was possible for anyone to control the amount put on a horse's feet in training and lead weights became widely used. Some trainers used solid weights made to be strapped round the hooves, others used bands of fine leather having several pockets that could be filled with lead shot and made to be strapped round the fetlocks.

It was also noted that the length of the foot had an influence on action and this also led some people to go to foolish extremes as remarked by Francis M. Ware in his book *Driving*, published in 1903:

> "Shoeing, the weight of the shoes and the appropriate length of the toes have much to do with developing high action. Just now, because some horse happened to go high that wore a long toe to keep him from pacing and mixing his gaits as some trotting-bred horses will, it is the fad to wear the front toes abnormally and most harmfully long, and not a few horses have been crippled by the practice."

In a book published in 1896, the German horse trainer B. H. von Hollefur

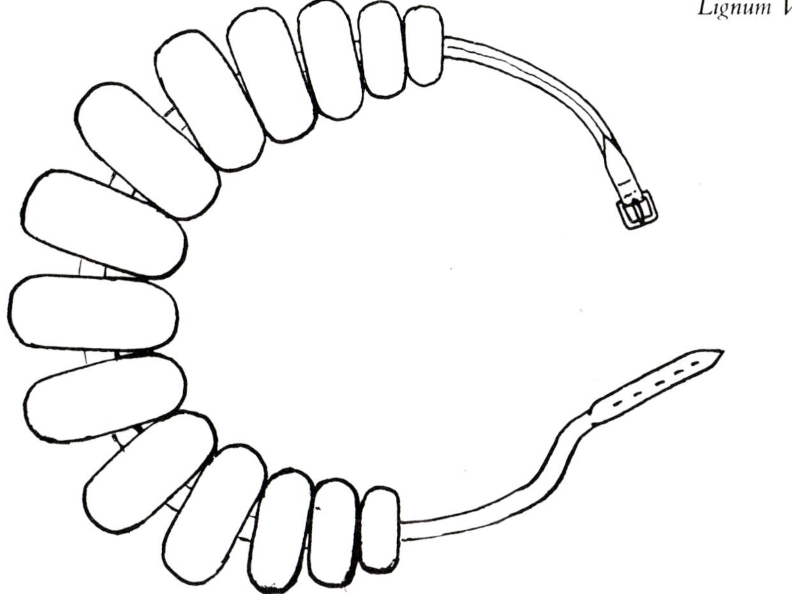

Lignum Vitae rattlers.

describes using "anklets" made of graduated wooden balls threaded on a leather thong. This is the earliest reference I have seen to the familiar "rattlers" and von Holleufor advocated their use for improving balance and cadence.

"Gipsy Jack" Robinson was the first horseman in England to specialise in the training of high steppers and, being a gifted nagsman, he was usually well ahead of his rivals. In training he made great use of what would now be called "cavaletti", using heavy railway ties for older horses while for youngsters he used straw "bottles", his name for long trusses of straw tied by a machine rather like a self-binder. The horses were regularly ridden over these objects or driven on long reins, but not before Gipsy Jack had taken great care to ensure that they had been placed at the correct intervals for the horse concerned. This training was only done for short periods after which the horses were exercised and made fit by walking under saddle for long periods. He was particularly fond of working young horses in a recently ploughed field, preferably on heavy clay soil, to develop their muscles.

The first mechanical action developer seems to have been invented by Gibson, a London saddler, in the 1890's. Gibson's developer made use of elastic cords fastened to shackles round each hoof, those on the front feet leading to rings sewn to the front of a false collar round the horse's neck, and those on the hind feet to rings on the roller girth. This device was advertised for many years and found a good market although one seldom met a trainer

Gibson's action developers.

who did not deplore its use and who swore he never used things of that sort.

The device that is talked of, but seldom seen, today is known under various names, for instance "boots", "shackles", "pulleys" and so on. This apparatus was originally used about 1885 by Prof. Norton B. Smith for controlling and taming unruly horses. The "Professor" was a Canadian "horse educator" who, after successfully touring North America for about eight seasons, put on an exhibition of horse taming at London's Crystal Palace in 1892. The show, managed by Nat Behrens, was a grandiose affair with its own ten-piece brass band, and, presumably, a resident stable of wild and vicious animals. After closing in London it toured Britain visiting most of the larger towns and local owners were invited to bring their own problem horses. Smith called his device "the double safety rope" and he describes it in his *Practical Treatise on the Breaking and Training of Wild and Vicious Horses*:

> "Buckle an ordinary hame-strap around each front limb below the fetlock joint; then take a rope twenty feet long, tie one end of this rope into the ring of the nigh front limb; then place the rope over the ring in the surcingle underneath the horse's body; now through a ring on the off front limb, back through the ring in the surcingle; this gives you a double purchase on the front limbs."

Robert Black attended one of Smith's exhibitions and he was struck by the exaggerated action produced by using a little tension on the rope. Leather hame-straps round the fetlocks were apt to chafe the skin and "boots" to fit round the hoof were devised instead. These mechanical developers work chiefly through inducing the subject to shift his balance on to his hocks and to

Nagle's high stepping hopples.

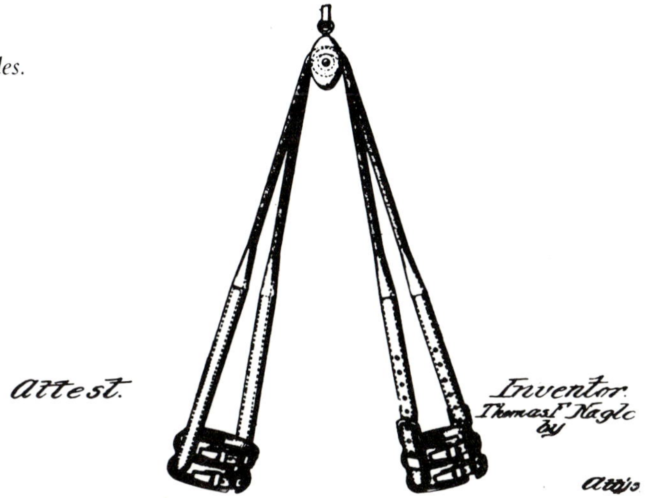

Attest.

Inventor.
Thomas F. Nagle
by

Att'ys

Professor Norton B. Smith's "double safety rope".

bring the hind action the body. If these devices are used at all it must be with great care as considerable harm may be caused through excessive use, especially of the pulley type.

This is what Ware has to say in *Driving* on the subject of developing action:

> "Lunging horses over deep straw beds, through snow or water knee-deep or less, over rails laid at certain distances apart on the ground, using "elastic action controllers" to knees and hocks when in harness, assisted by proper balancing, will temporarily help action if the horse is allowed to trot only under such circumstances and walked at all other times. The improvement, however, is rarely worth the trouble and affects chiefly animals of low breeding, naturally dull in intelligence, who are too dense to realise that, once the obstacles are removed, they need not continue to elevate the feet. Harness work will be of the most brief description – a few minutes every other day, perhaps, when every effort is directed to making him display and 'parade' himself, his exercise other wise consisting of a daily walk in hand, the idea being to keep him superlatively fresh and 'above himself', that, when shown in the ring, he may through sheer exuberance go to extremes in his action during the brief period when he is undergoing inspection by the judges, and may thus ultimately acquire as a habit the senselessly high action which show-ring requirements nowadays demand – action so absurdly exaggerated in many cases that it ceases to be graceful or useful, but degenerates into mere temporary hysterical contortion."

But Ware seems to have taken a jaundiced view of horse shows and show horses generally and later in his book he gets really worked up on the subject:

> "Much as we owe to the horse-shows which are now so universal throughout the country, we for a time have suffered hysteria to overcome us in the fancy for extravagant and useless action and pace in the selection of heavy harness horses. 'Contortionists' and 'acrobats' of all sizes (and shapes!) have been upheld as marvels provided they can hurl their knees and forefeet to extraordinary altitudes; can 'snatch' their hocks with the abruptness and awkwardness of the victim to stringhalt (from which more than one of the elect suffers); and can tear round the ring at a pace impossible and unlawful to pursue in park or on road. Like a fancy for caviar and decayed woodcock, this diseased and artificially acquired taste is, while the novelty lasts, insatiable, but cloyed palate will finally reject the

> unwholesome diet as unsatisfactory, and the level-going, nimble, true-actioned animal will again meet the reward which is his due alike from judges and from purchasers."

On both sides of the Atlantic the subject of high action in horses aroused strong feelings in those days.

SHOEING

Next to the mouth in importance to a stepper are his feet. For many years it has been the usual practice to allow the feet to grow rather longer than normal and to fit heavy shoes. Really experienced shoeing smiths are becoming more hard to find each year so that the trainer, if not actually compelled to do the shoeing himself, will almost always have to tell the smith exactly what he wants done.

While heavy shoes do increase the action of most horses that have some natural aptitude for stepping, the distribution of the weight in the shoe can be of decisive importance. As the training of the young horse proceeds his trainer must take careful note of his natural style of action. This will develop as the horse learns to move with poise and balance even though at this stage he should be wearing quite light shoes. The horse may show a tendency to straighten his fore legs before they meet the ground, perhaps even to go on his heels, and in such cases a shoe with the weight in the toe, once called the "half-moon shoe", will often correct this. If his action is short with a tendency to be under the body then a shoe with a rolled toe and the weight evenly distributed, or even weighted slightly in the heel, may help. These suggestions may run counter to the experience of blacksmiths accustomed to shoeing racing trotters but, as I have shown earlier, the balance of a race horse is totally different from that of a high stepper. As the training progresses somewhat heavier shoes can be used. It may happen that a young horse with toe-weighted shoes may begin to strike his elbows. The damage is usually done by the inner edge of the shoe, either at the toe or the inside quarter. In such cases the remedy is to go back to a lighter shoe with the weight spread evenly all round.

It is usual to fit the fully weighted shoes about ten days before a show. To alter the weight and manner of shoeing closer to the date than this could result in the horse entering the ring before he has had time to adapt his way of going to the changes. The British Hackney Horse Society has a rule limiting the weights of shoes used on horses at its shows to 32 ounces, including nails, for those over 14 hands and to 24 ounces below that height. Of course, not every horse needs heavy shoes and many very successful harness horses and ponies have been shown with quite lightweight shoes. Heavy shoes usually accentuate faults of action such as dishing or brushing, but many blacksmiths can help to correct these faults by altering the distribution of weight, lowering the walls of the hoof on the inside or outside, and so on.

The angle the foot makes with the ground is also important, indeed a difference of only a very few degrees may have a pronounced effect. This is the angle formed by the line of the hoof from the coronet to the toe and the ground surface of the wall of the hoof. A "hoof leveller" is made for measuring this angle. The angle of a normal front foot lies between 45° and 50° and of a hind foot usually greater than 55°. If the foot is allowed to grow longer more strain will be placed on the back tendons of the limb unless the angle of the foot is made steeper. A show Hackney may have front feet as steep as 50° or a little more. The most suitable angle of foot for an individual horse will also be influenced by the natural angle and length of his pasterns. A horse with short upright pasterns shod at too steep an angle will be deprived of his natural shock absorber with possible damage to the limb as a result. The angle of the foot has a definite influence on action. In general, a steeper angle tends to produce action further to the front while a lower angle may have the opposite effect. Usually the best angle must be discovered by trial and error with these rough guides in mind.

The great difficulty in trying to keep a long foot on a horse lies in preventing the heels wearing away under the shoe. In most horses the wall at the heels is less thick than at the toe and grows more slowly, thus it is important that loose shoes should be attended to at once before the heels are hammered away. It is a good practice to have the shoes removed from show horses and their feet trimmed as soon as the show season is ended, and to leave them without shoes for a time thus allowing the frog to resume its proper function. This will be especially beneficial to horses with weak heels.

Some trainers like to have a leather pad fitted under the shoe to cover the whole of the foot. The concavity of the sole beneath the pad may be packed with tow or prepared sphagnum moss. This practice prevents the normal shedding of horn from the sole and helps to support the walls. In some cases where a steep angle is desired it may be thought best to raise the heels by means of wedge shaped leather packing at the heels rather than by cutting down the toe.

It seems to be a human weakness to suppose that if a little produces a good result, twice as much will be twice as good. This is certainly no more true of horse's feet than it is of many other things we can think of. The trainer should keep a careful note of the shoeing of his horses, including details of angle, weight and type of shoe, and length from coronary band to the toe. Once he has found the best combination he should see that it is followed in later shoeings.

When preparing a horse for show nothing adds so much to a neat turnout as clean polished feet. The feet should be washed, nail holes and other cavities filled with plastic wood or other suitable material, then smoothed lightly with sandpaper and polished. Harness blacking is quite satisfactory for black hooves and clear polish for others. Hoof oil is not suitable for the dusty conditions found in many show arenas. Sandpapering must not be overdone or the supply of natural oils may be cut off. In the same way repeated painting with lacquer interferes with the natural lubrications of the hoof.

CHAPTER TEN

IN THE SHOW RING

> "We sat up the greater part of the night before the show washing her four white stockings and doing up in approved show ring fashion her charming little mane ... She was fire and air at home, and was to be fire and air in the show ring on the morrow. She was to go mountains high, with dash, pace, poise, balance, rhythm, to be pulled in after a single tour of the ring unquestionably and indisputably the winner. It was my first show. As the shiversome little beast stood outside the ring ready for the fray, the lad and I, trembling with pride, stripped the rugs off for the inspection of a well-known and friendly critic. 'She would look well' said the great authority, 'in a pie!' Before I could fathom the profundity of that dictum we were in and out of the ring seventh in a class of seven!"

So wrote the late James Agate in one of his early books describing his first essay in the ring with a "marvellous three-year-old filly", when he first experienced the feeling of dream-filled optimism and dashed hopes that are the lot of most novices at the game. How delightful if we could all emerge from the experience with such engaging good humour!

Well, we must all make a start somewhere, and it is not given to many of us to start at the top. In the horse show business, one thing we quickly learn is that an experienced judge will note, perhaps subconsciously, the top contenders from the moment they enter the ring, so first impressions are most important.

Naturally, good turnout is a first consideration and in this we include man, horse and vehicle in that order. The driver must be correctly dressed, of course, in a manner fitting the class of show, the season of the year and time of day, but what matters most in giving a good first impression is his style, made up of the manner of sitting and holding the reins and whip, together with a certain self-possession indicating that he, at least, is confident of the outcome of the competition. The novice perched on the edge of the seat with his legs tucked under, arms outstretched and whip pointing over the left shoulder, gives himself away at once and it will be entirely up to his horse to get him a place.

Many of the first professionals learned their art in the yards of the big city dealers, perhaps starting as grooms, or "strappers", and graduating to "brakesmen", able to show horses to customers. Having reached this high estate, these professional whips naturally prided themselves on their light and sensitive hands and would do no manual labour for fear of spoiling them!

The next generation of professionals developed further the art of presenting a high stepper in the show ring, and, in the writer's opinion it reached a peak in the years between the two World Wars. The best of them were real stylists.

SINGLE HARNESS

Single harness should be as light and neat as possible, black with brass furniture and faced with patent leather, breast collar, brown reins and D-shaped or round, well-cupped blinkers. Bridle fronts are usually of metal and a monogram or crest may be fitted on the blinkers, rosettes, pad and breastplate if worn. The single harness saddle used sometimes in Britain differs from the

Ardkinglass Marques. Mr. Chauncey Stillman's champion at the Royal Winter Fair, 1968, driven by Mrs. Haydon.

American pattern and is similar to a small gig saddle with slightly swelled side panels. The usual American pattern is made on a metal tree and is similar to a double-harness pad.

Tilbury or French tugs should always be used with a show wagon so that the shafts can be held quite close to the horse's sides with little free play.

The Viceroy pattern show-wagon is now the most popular style although the piano-box type is still used in Britain.

The reins should be taken in the left hand before getting into the show wagon (these, having only a single seat, may be mounted from the left); the left rein passing over the index finger and the right rein between the second and third fingers. The two reins are then firmly held in the palm of the hand with the right hand holding the whip. A firm and well balanced seat is essential, with the feet braced against the foot-rest and the body poised slightly forward so that, should the horse plunge forward, the driver will not be flung back with the risk of pulling the horse over.

When driving in the ring, the right rein is taken in the right hand, passing below the little finger and upwards through the palm. The hands should be held at about the height of the middle jacket button, elbows squared but not clamped rigidly to the sides, wrists turned inwards a little and the hands held fairly close together with the right rein still passing into the left. The whip should be tilted forward at about 45°and pointing towards the horse's left ear. Holding the hands wide apart and about level with the driver's ears is a ludicrous style that, sad to say, is occasionally seen these days.

PAIR HARNESS

When driving a pair of horses or ponies, the reins are held in the same way as for single harness, but no pair can be driven properly unless they have first been put together correctly. Great care must be taken over the proper adjustment of the harness.

A pair must trot absolutely straight, neither leaning on the pole nor pulling out with heads turned in. Pole chains or leather pole pieces must be of sufficient length to allow the horses adequate room when the traces are taut, also to allow for a little free play of the pole if it is of the fixed type. If the carriage has a drop-pole that is fastened to the shaft couplings, then a neck-yoke is needed, this being a horizontal wooden bar with a heavy leather loop at the centre through which the metal pole point passes. Two short neck-yoke straps pass through staples at the ends of the neck-yoke and are used to attach it to the kidney-link rings on the collars. The neck-yoke is commonly found on light American carriages and has the advantage of permitting the traces to be drawn up fairly tightly, thus limiting the movement backwards and forwards between horses and carriage.

Outwood Matire and Suddie Minuette, at the Devon Horse Show, owned and driven by Mrs. Frank Ryan.

Even when the coupling reins have been carefully adjusted, some pairs will develop the habit of turning their heads in and quarters out. The cause may be over-tight pole pieces or a horse with an injured mouth which he can ease by turning his head inwards. This habit can often be corrected by changing the horses over from time to time.

In America where it is the rule to drive on the right of the road, it is considered correct to have the taller horse of a pair on the off or low, side. The reverse would be correct in Britain.

A good pair should be matched not only as to colour and markings, but also as to length of stride and way of going. Both horses should carry their heads at the same height.

The harness for a show pair should be black with brass mountings; bridles with fronts and rosettes of metal; Buxton bits, pulley bridoon or French clasp bearing reins; brown reins; collars of Kay or Prince's forewale pattern; straight panel pads; hames with jointed kidney links; breastplates buckled round the inner wire of the kidney link; loin straps are optional. For a show wagon, or a "Viceroy", pole straps or neck-yokes are used, but for a spider phaeton bright pole-chains are usual with a polished pole-head.

TANDEM

The disappearance of tandem classes from many show programmes is sad as it is here Hackneys, especially Hackney ponies, show themselves to such advantage. A tandem is essentially a sporting turnout which demands the dash and action of Hackneys.

Tandem driving has been called the most difficult of all of driving; some calling it actually dangerous. Stella A. Walker in her book *Long Live the Horse*, published in 1955, quotes a saying of "Daddy" Fownes, the famous coaching personality, it goes:

> "No white man was ever born who could drive tandem. Perhaps black men can. I don't know."

It is true that a lot of practice is needed to reach perfection but any reasonably experienced driver should soon master the art if he proceeds on the right lines. Those who own harness horses or ponies and have not learned to handle a tandem are denying themselves one of the most satisfying thrills in the whole field of equitation.

Shining Star and Dufferin Pal. Winning ponies tandem, driven by Frank Ryan of Ottawa.

For show classes tandem horses need not be matched for colour, but should be well-matched for size and way of going; of course, the wheeler may be a little bigger and stronger than the leader. Bold and sharp-moving horses are most suitable, and the leader must be a gay, free-going horse.

Black brass-mounted harness is used for show classes and both horses may wear collars of Kay pattern, although it is permissible to use a breast collar on the leader. A kicking strap on the wheeler and loin strap on the leader are optional, but one should not be worn without the other.

For show classes a two-wheeled vehicle is desirable; either a gig or a tandem cart, a Whitechapel cart or similar. The driver's seat should be high enough to allow him a clear view of the leader.

The first time a tandem is put to, it is not a bad practice to dispense with the lead traces, and it goes without saying that at least one capable and active assistant on the ground is essential – two would be better. The horses should be driven a little by themselves before putting them together for the first time so that any initial high spirits may be worked off.

In a gig or other two-wheeler, the driver sits on the right so he takes up the reins from that side. They are first put into the left hand with the left lead rein over the first finger, the right lead between first and second fingers with the left wheel rein immediately under it (i.e. both reins held between the same two fingers), and the right wheel rein between the second and third fingers. After adjusting the reins to the proper length, they are passed in the same order into the right hand before mounting the carriage, and then passed back into the left hand when the driver is seated. The whip is held in the right hand.

Now have the leader stood up into his traces and adjust the reins to the proper length, noting by the splices that each rein of the two pairs is the same length so that the horses are likely to move forward in a straight line when the signal to start is given. The lead reins should be drawn back about two inches before starting so that the leader will not be "in draught". The wheeler should always start first, or both horses at the same instant. *Never* the leader first. This prevents the cart being drawn on to the wheeler's hind end which might cause trouble.

When moving freely forward on the level, the leader's traces should be slightly slack. A common fault of beginners is to allow their horses too little liberty; nervousness causes the novice driver to hold his horses back and this often upsets highly-strung horses. They should be allowed as much freedom as possible, compatible with the maintainence of control through proper contact with their mouths. Both horses must go into their bridles all the time to give a comfortable and safe drive.

If the horses are not following on the same track as they should be, a simple adjustment of the reins can put things right. If the leader is out to the left, draw back a mere inch or two the two reins held together between the first and second fingers (these being the right lead and left wheel). Similarly, if the leader is off to the right, the team can be straightened by letting out these two reins a little. When driving round a show ring it is not necessary, nor in most cases would it be possible, to "loop" the lead rein when making the turns at the end of the ring. A little pressure of the right hand on the appropriate rein or reins is usually all that is needed. Often it will be necessary to use a little "opposition" on the wheel rein to keep the horses following on the same arc of the turn. This can be done when making a turn to the left by using the right hand to draw back slightly the left lead rein to start the turn and, at the same time gripping the right wheel rein with the lower fingers of the same hand.

An alternative method is to make the opposition on the wheel reins by turning the left wrist. To do this when turning left, again the right hand starts the turn by taking up the left lead rein, the left wrist is then turned in an anti-clockwise direction and the hand drawn back slightly towards the left hip. By using a little imagination the reader can see that this action of the left wrist and hand will shorten the right wheel rein, it being between the second and third fingers. If the turn is being made to the right and the wheeler is tending to cut the corner to the right it is necessary to shorten the left wheel rein to keep him in place. This right turn can be done by taking up the right lead rein with the right fingers, then make the opposition by turning the left wrist with a clockwise motion and bringing the hand across the body to the right. This action shortens both the the left wheel and left lead, but the latter is countered by the right hand shortening the right lead rein.

With a well-trained tandem team it should be possible to make the turns in a show ring with the left hand only, turning the wrist as described, and to execute a figure of eight. Not that this is required, except by those wanting to show how smart they are.

The length of the reins can be let out, or shortened, as required by simply gripping all the reins with the fingers of the right hand, about three inches in front of the left, and then by moving the left hand forward along the reins to shorten, or by sliding it back to lengthen the reins. The lead reins alone can be shortened by taking both in the right hand, removing them out of the left hand, drawing them back and putting them back in the proper place in the left hand. All this may sound alarmingly complicated when set down on paper, but how much more complicated is it with two reins in each hand? Of course, most followers of the "two-hand school" leave the whip in its socket, or back in the barn, which simplifies matters somewhat. But no one can be called "a good whip" in truth until he can use one properly, and to use a tandem, or four-in-hand whip effectively requires much practice, which is best done under the guidance of an expert.

A tandem whip is generally a little lighter and a few inches shorter than a four-in-hand whip. It should be held where it balances best, usually somewhere close to the upper ferrule of the hand-piece. The thong is wrapped around the stick a few turns and the point is held under the right thumb.

When using the whip, try to hit the leader in front of his pad, and the thong should be caught with the fingers of the right hand as it flies back. The "double thong" is then thrown by a quick flick of the wrist and a slight turning movement, one of those knacks that looks so unbelievably simple when done by a practised hand, but is only acquired by many hours of practice.

The novice would do well to put in a few sessions of simulated practice to get the feel of the reins before tackling a live team. With a little ingenuity, it is quite easy to improvise an apparatus for this purpose, using some old reins passed over the back of a chair or tressle and weighted at the ends.

At all events, do not begin driving tandem by holding two reins in each hand hoping to take up the orthodox style later – you probably never will.

TURNOUT

The importance of turnout in the show ring cannot be too highly stressed. Nothing marks the tyro so readily as a sloppy turnout, and most judges would, rightly, be offended if badly groomed horses wearing ill-fitting and grubby harness were to be presented for their scrutiny. It is true that few owners today can afford to have their horses groomed to the perfection of yesteryear when two hours hard "strapping" daily was routine in the best stables, but there is still no excuse for a horse with a dirty skin. Good feeding can greatly assist in putting a bloom on a horse's coat, and machines are available for removing dust and scurf. The preparation of the feet has already been dealt with.

The mane should be thinned and pulled to a length of about five inches more or less, and for the show ring it is done up in narrow plaits, or braids, then tied in a neat knot with a little coloured wool or cotton cord, the knots forming a line almost along the top of the neck. There are usually about fourteen such knots. The mane is left unbraided in appointment classes. If the horse has a docked tail the hair is well damped with the water brush, parted down the centre with a comb, and then bandaged to "break" the hair over. After removing the bandage the hair is again combed out and trimmed square at the ends to that, when carried the hair hangs down each side like a flag.

In many countries, and in some of the United States, the operation of docking is now against the law and it is surely only a matter of time before it is unacceptable at all horse shows. About twenty years ago when docking was banned in England, Hackneys came to the shows with long manes and abundant tails after the fashion of the American fine harness horse, but this style was not in keeping with the character of a Hackney. Where undocked

Hackneys are shown the usual practice now is to do up the mane in the traditional Hackney fashion and to have less hair in the tail so that when carried it hangs about the level of the hocks.

A good show horse must have good manners. He should stand quietly in the ring when called to line up, standing with his head fairly erect, both pairs of legs placed together and "spread", but not too much. In open classes it is permitted to unhook the bearing rein, but in lady's and amateur classes they should remain in position.

The turnout of the driver is at least as important as that of his horse. Gloves must be worn and these should be of reasonably loose fit and made of fine leather. A driving apron is also necessary and this may be of a colour to match the colour of the vehicle. At country shows gentlemen may dress less formally than at indoor shows in the evening. At the great indoor shows gentlemen drivers were expected to appear in the evening wearing evening dress with a silk hat, but today a dinner jacket or a dark lounge suit with a black bowler (or Derby hat) is acceptable.

APPOINTMENT CLASSES

The gig class for horses is usually classified at American shows as an "appointment" class: that is, one in which the presentation of the complete turnout comes under the scrutiny of the judges. The rule book of the American Horse Shows Association (AHSA) defines it thus:

> "Gig class, single Hackney horse, stallion, mare or gelding, shown to a gig. To be shown at walk, park pace and smart trot. All horses will be required to back. To be judged on presence, manners, performance, quality; appointments to count 40%."

At some shows the class is restricted to gentlemen amateurs. The ideal gig horse should be of good conformation and commanding presence, generally being of a more muscular build than some show horses and possessed of ample bone and sound feet. He should move in great style with high brisk action, trotting straight and covering the ground with a good length of stride. He should have an active walk, not a jog. A good colour is an asset and white markings are not objectionable.

The Stanhope gig is the most usual type for these classes, painted in discreet and not garish colours. Other types of gigs such as the Park Gate, Dennett and Liverpool are also quite suitable. The harness should be black, preferably brass-mounted, and with square buckles. The bridle has square or D-shaped blinkers, bearing rein of straight or pulley bridoon pattern, Buxton or straight-cheeked gig bit and full standing martingale. The collar is of Kay or rim

Cassilis Echo's Boy. Brown pony stallion driven to a Stanhope Gig by Mrs. J. Macy Willets.

Lady Seaton. "Judge" W. H. Moore with his favourite mare to a Stanhope Gig.

pattern, shaped and leather lined with hames joined at the bottom by chain links and having anchor draft tugs. The saddle may have straight or swell panels and must be of a good width, say 4 to $4^1/_2$ inches for a horse. French or Tilbury tugs should be used with a Stanhope gig or any other type that has the Stanhope arrangement of four springs. Open tugs are used with two-wheeled vehicles having the Dennett three spring suspension. A kicking strap or breeching should be used.

A groom sits beside the driver and he should wear livery with black top hat, single breasted coat, boots and breeches. The groom should stand at a pace or two in front of the horse when the class is drawn up in the centre of the ring and he should not actually hold the horse. If the entry is called to give a further show it is usual for the groom to remain standing in the centre of the ring.

The appointments should include lamps, matches, tie-rope and halter, hoof-pick, small spool of wire, storm coats for driver and groom, waterproof apron, road blanket, spare woollen or string gloves. A leather case with spare shoe and tools may also be carried. There should be a clock in leather case on the dash and the driver carries a bow-topped whip.

Classes for lady's pair or single horse shown to a park phaeton are also invariably appointment classes. The AHSA rule book reads:

> "Lady's single Hackney horse, mare or gelding, shown to a phaeton. To be driven by a lady. Manners paramount. All around action at a park pace; speed not required. Must stand and back quietly. Must not pull. To be judged on manners, quality, performance; appointments to count 40%."

The type of phaeton used should be a George IV, Peter's phaeton or, in summer, a basket phaeton may be used. The harness should be black with brass or plated furniture to match the metal of the carriage. The bridle has D-

Mrs. Loula Long Combs and her George IV Phaeton.

Broompark Georgie Wood and Broompark Little Titch. Pony pair to a miniature Park Phaeton, driven by Mrs. Tom Ryder.

shaped blinkers, Buxton bit, pulley bridoon or straight bearing rein, bridle front of metal, or silk of a colour to match the upholstery of the carriage. The collar is of Kay pattern with anchor draft hames joined with chain links at the bottom. The saddle is of a straight pattern about 5 inches wide, with French or Tilbury tugs. A breeching is worn, also a full standing martingale. With double harness the pads are of straight pattern and used without pad cloths. A single phaeton horse should be 15.1 to 15.3 hands, of whole colour with little or no white markings, of great quality and handsome conformation. He should have a sufficiency for his work, and should move with style. A pair of phaeton horses should be perfectly matched in colour, type and action.

The appointments are: cloth lap-robe, dash clock, umbrella, tie-rope and halter, small kit of tools with a spare shoe and nails, wheel cap wrench, waterproof coat and hat cover for the groom, loin cloth or woollen cooler for the horse. A waterproof apron is folded into a case fitted on to the lower part of the dash.

A groom always accompanies a lady's phaeton seated on the dickey or rumble seat. He should wear full livery.

CHAPTER ELEVEN

THE HACKNEY IN OTHER ROLES

UNDER SADDLE

As we have seen, the early Hackney was a trotting saddle horse and most of the trotting records made at the beginning of the nineteenth century were performed under saddle. Later, when the Hackney breeders began to concentrate on producing high stepping harness horses, the Hackney came to be looked on less and less as a saddle horse. The life of the high class carriage horse of those days began on the farm of course, but at only a few specialised studs were the young horses broken to harness, schooled and presented as the finished product. Mr. Burdett-Coutts's magnificent Brookfield Stud near London was one of that few where perfectly matched pairs and magnificent single carriage horses, bred at the Hertfordshire farm and reared at Howden in East Yorkshire, were offered at regular auction sales. The tenant farmer breeders of Yorkshire and East Anglia seldom broke their young horses themselves, most being sold to country dealers who would break them to saddle and harness and, when fit and ready, take them to one of the many horse fairs (of which that at Horncastle in Lincolnshire was one of the largest), where they would be passed on to one of the city dealers or jobmasters.

These country dealers would allot two or three young horses to each of their nagsmen to break and exercise under saddle, and from their yards in the early morning a string of horses would set out for two or more hours of walking exercise interrupted most likely by occasional stops at the hostelries *en route*, for these nagsmen were notoriously thirsty characters and the country roads were dusty in summer and cold in winter.

If a young horse showed promise of becoming a show horse he might be entered in the saddle classes at the County show in the hope of attracting the notice of some wealthy exhibitor. These saddle classes filled well but, on balance, the showing of high stepping Hackneys under saddle did much damage to the breed in England and gave rise to a great deal of ridicule from the fox-hunters. At many shows these classes were described as "for the best gentleman's hack" and attracted entries often widely different in type. If the judge was a Hackney man then the daisy cutting thoroughbred types would be left at the end of the line, and if he was from the hunting fraternity out went the high-steppers.

"Gipsy Jack" Robinson of Hull "farmed" these classes for many seasons with his celebrated horse, Mornington Cannon, and it was said of him that, despite having a high trot, he could canter like a park hack. Mornington Cannon was by Saxon, a good bay son of Danegelt owned by Frederick Blanshard of Goxhill, Yorkshire. Saxon was often exhibited at the London Show and one year, Blanshard being ill, his two elderly maiden sisters were sent to report on the result. After a keenly fought battle Saxon was placed below his great Yorkshire rival, Lord Melton, to the utter disgust of the Misses Blanshard who, gathering up their skirts and clutching their bonnets, dashed off to the telegraph office to report. "Saxon second – damn the judges!" read the message. Disgruntled exhibitors were no less inhibited in those days than now it seems!

Another fine horseman, Bill Middleton, manager of the Messrs. Baxter's Hutton Stud at Brentwood in Essex, was said to have the only man able to challenge Gipsy Jack's supremacy in saddle classes. Middleton was a tall handsome man, always immaculately dressed, and equally at ease either tooling the celebrated tandem Miss Howard and Musk round the show ring or entertaining a lady friend to dinner at the Ritz. It was said that he took to the bottle for bouts sometimes lasting several days. During one such, so the story goes, he came clattering down the wrought iron stairway from his apartment

Rydedale Gertie. A winner under saddle with James Black.

in the stable yard yelling to the men: "Shut the gates, shut the gates! Can't you see the lions coming?".

Jack Major of Sledmere was another expert with a saddle horse and he had two or three good seasons with Sam Tennant's Authority before Sir Nigel Colman bought the horse.

These gentleman's hack classes were later replaced by classes described as "for Hackneys, or Hackney Ponies, under saddle", and they continued to be held at some shows in the North of England until the late 1930's. Most of the horses shown in these classes also took part in the harness classes. The riders usually wore bowler hats, highly polished brown boots with leggings and check breeches, and they sat well back on their mounts' loins with legs thrust forward. Often they used a bridle with only a long-check curb bit. A few Hackneys, like Mornington Cannon, were kept only to be shown under saddle one of the last of them being a handsome bay horse, Bay Rhum, shown in Yorkshire by that good horseman, Tom Danby of Wykeham.

Classes for Hackney horses and ponies under saddle were included in the programme of the New York National Horse Show about 1929 but they do not seem to have "caught on" in the States. Hackneys under saddle were judged at the walk and trot only and were not asked to canter as in the classes for gentlemen's hacks.

Show Hackneys, especially if they have well-developed hind action, are hardly a pleasant ride and there seems little point in trying to promote saddle classes for them. An attempt was made in the mid-1960s to revive such classes at some British shows but they failed to catch the interest of the general public. In Britain, indeed in Europe generally, there is no longer any demand for riding horses with high action, but in North America it is still much admired in certain types of saddle horses and ponies. It is not surprising, therefore, to find some Hackneys appearing under saddle there in various roles in which the natural action of the breed is wanted, but it is not developed to display quite so much snap and energy as does the harness horse. Before the American Saddle Horse became so widely popular Hackneys and part-bred Hackneys were shown in the saddle classes, particularly in the Eastern states. These classes, which would be described today as for three-gaited saddle horses, i.e. to be shown at the walk, trot and canter, attracted a variety of breeds including thoroughbreds, Hackneys, Standardbreds, even an Orloff stallion and many kinds of cross-breds, but to win some action had to be shown.

A few of the many Hackneys that did well in these classes include Mrs. Francis Hyde's Langton Director by Langton Performer from a Standard-bred mare; Mr. Penn Smith's mare Merrylegs; Mr. George Green's cobs Gipsy Queen and Badge; and the Canadian bred Copper King, brought out by Douglas Ness about 1924 and which became the champion at Boston, Toronto

Chestnut Blossom. Foaled 1913, by Irvington Model-Look In by Julius Caesar 2nd. A champion pony under saddle.

and other important shows. Three-gaited classes are now almost exclusively the province of the American Saddle Horse, but a few Hackneys and cross-bred Hackneys are still being shown in these classes in Canada.

Similar classes for saddle ponies are popular at many North American shows and a number of Hackney ponies have done well in this division. Some of them were relegated to the saddle classes because they had been considered too big for the harness pony classes, and the best have made good ponies. The late champion harness horse Killreen's Shan Og (Mr. Pepper) is an interesting case. Despite his wholly pony ancestry he grew too big for the pony harness division and was sold to make into a saddle pony. He was later found to be big enough for the harness horse division and re-appeared in harness to go right to the top.

The long-established Cassilis Stud has been the source of a great many good saddle ponies over a long period. Two well-known winners of the 1920's, Chestnut Blossom and Cassilis Look-Here, were bred at this famous stud, both being out of the imported mare Look-In by Julius Caesar II. It would be tedious to list all the Hackney ponies that have become champion saddle ponies since then and it is now generally acknowledged that this is a division in which they can more than hold their own.

Classes for parade horses are a more recent innovation. These parade horses are shown in a Western or stock saddle, heavily ornamented with trappings of chased silver and embossed leather, the rider wearing a romanticised cowboy outfit, the whole effect outdoing Hollywood at its most spectacular! Parade horses perform at an animated walk and a "parade gait" which is described as a "true high prancing trot, square, collected and balanced, not to exceed five miles per hour." Not a few Hackney horses have done well in these classes and there is a good demand for them for this work in some parts of the United States. Some shows provide classes for parade ponies which are shown in a similar manner.

In 1976 a number of Canadian Hackneys, mostly mares, were shipped to Costa Rica to improve the native saddle horses which had become undersized, but more than size the Costa Ricans wanted Hackneys to add more showy action to their saddle stock.

THE MONSON STRAIN

By the early 1920s most Hackney breeders were trying to breed winning show harness horses, but a few regretted such specialisation and tried to preserve what they called "the old riding type". Lord Ashtown of Woodlawn, County Cork was one of them, and his stud contained some fine mares of the best Yorkshire strains. The Woodlawn Stud was broken up by Government order about 1941.

The Monson family of Walpole St. Peter near Wisbech in Cambridgeshire had a very old strain that was used to breed hunters. Many of these Monson Hackneys were grey in colour, and one, Findon Grey Shales, bred in Sussex by Mrs. Hunt, was owned by H.R.H. the Prince of Wales and kept on the Duchy of Cornwall estates. This horse won the cup for stallions suitable to breed military horses at the Hackney Show of 1918 and 1920. Others of the same strain also won this award. Latterly the Monson Hackneys were registered in the Hunter Stud Book, and some good hunters were bred from thoroughbred mares. This stud also closed down during the Second World War.

The ability of Hackneys to jump well has been recognised for many years. Nelly Horsley, a half-sister to Wreghitt's Wildfire, made a name as a jumper at the end of the nineteenth century. However, it was in North America that Hackneys achieved most as jumpers. The Toronto dealers Crow and Murray produced a number of which the best known was the 16.1 full-bred Hackney, Confidence.

This horse was one of the string Crow and Murray took to the International Horse Show at Olympia in 1910, where he won and was afterwards sold to Sir Clifford Sifton, the well-known Canadian newspaper proprietor and politician. Confidence cleared 7 feet, 2 inches to win the high jump class at the

New York National in 1910. This horse's best performance was at Syracuse where he cleared 8 feet, $1^1/_2$ inches, rider Dick Donnelly.

In 1915 Crow and Murray took the 16.1 chestnut gelding, Sir Ashton, five years old, to the New York National where he won one high jump competition, was second to Confidence in another, and also won the broadwater jump, ridden by Douglas Ness. Sir Ashton was bred at Brampton, Ontario, and was sired by a Hackney from a heavy farm mare. In 1920, this horse, now named Greatheart, was owned by Mrs. Peabody when he won the high jumps at the South Shore County Club Horse Show near Chicago, establishing a world record of 8 feet, 2 inches, his rider being Fred Vesey.

Of them all the most astonishing performance was made by the 13.2 hands pony Bathgate Swell. George B. Hulme, of New York bought Swell as a show harness pony and how his unusual jumping ability was discovered is not known. Colonel P. A. Kenna, V.C., of the 21st Lancers was a member of the British Army team competing at the New York National in 1910, and it was he who rode Bathgate Swell the following year at the Olympia Show. Here Swell won second place in the competition for the Connaught Cup for serving officers of the British Army; 106 horses were entered.

Some Hackneys that have done well as show jumpers in recent years include the Canadian Black Velvet; the Misses Machin-Goodall's good mare Hoodoo; and her son King's Rhapsody, and the South African bred Oorskiet.

IN HARNESS

When the Hackney began to become popular it was subjected to much criticism, mostly on the grounds that the breed had no "bottom", i.e. that it had little stamina or power of endurance. Tom Mitchell, the owner of champion Ganymede, was one of many breeders prepared to challenge the critics. He offered to drive his registered Hackneys in a "50-mile spin" on the York-Scarborough road against horses of any other breed or cross-breed. He found no takers, but he was quoted in the *Farmer and Stockbreeder* as saying he often drove his show horse over long distances. In one day, he said, he drove the show mare Go by Triffit's Fireaway from Scarborough to Bradford, an 80 mile journey without ever touching the whip. Go was afterwards sold to Henry Fairfax of Virginia and won many prizes under saddle and in harness at Madison Square Garden and other major American shows.

In America the imported stallion, County Member Junior, a grandson of Lord Derby 2nd, was driven by his owner 100 miles on the public road in three minutes under eight hours. There were five long hills in the 50 mile route, and he was pulling two men in a gig.

In spite of these and many other convincing proofs to the contrary the belief that the Hackney had no staying power continued to be widely held among

Mr. Chauncey Stillman driving a pair of his Hackney horses at Amenia, New York. (Photograph by Freudy, New York.)

people without any intimate acquaintance with the breed. Even as recently as 1965 in an article in the *Carriage Journal*, Commodore Chauncey Stillman, the owner of the finest stable of Hackney horses in America if not the world, wrote of why he chose Hackneys:

> "My reasoning was that, since in this degenerate era and in my vicinity, the horse has no actual utility, I might as well choose an animal that gave joy by its sheer beauty, dazzle and spirit, even though – as I then ignorantly supposed – this breed was showy but lacked *bottom*, that is had no staying power. An agreeable surprise awaited me, however, for I soon discovered that besides being elegant, vivacious, and mettlesome, Hackneys were endowed with great endurance."

Cassilis Caroline. Driven by Mrs. Richard A. Kimball at Devon, Pennsylvania. (Photograph by Budd, New York.)

Park four in hand of Hackney horses. Mrs. Cynthia Haydon driving the late John McDougald's team. (Photograph by Eventer.)

Since then harness horses have attracted more notice with the developement of Combined Driving Competitions under rules drawn up by the International Equestrian Federation. Hackney horses and ponies have clearly shown their ability to hold their own in these testing competitions against other breeds. So far not many Hackneys have taken part but the achievements of some are worth mentioning.

In Britain from the start of Combined Driving one of the outstanding single harness competitors has been Miss D. Farlow's Hackney Pony, Highstone Navigator, driven by Mrs. John Dick.

The only pure-bred Hackney four to compete at international level has been the late J.A. McDougald's bay four driven by Mrs. Cynthia Haydon, and its achievements have brought the breed much favourable publicity.

The new sport arrived later in the United States, but Hackneys have done well there also. Not surprisingly ponies with the Cassilis prefix have been well to the fore: among them are Mrs. Richard A. Kimball's Cassilis Caroline;

Mrs. H. Seymour Hall's Cassilis Duncan; and Mrs. Scott Hill's Cassilis Brilliance and Alliance.

The growing popularity of driving both for competition or just for pleasure, is certain to benefit the breed that can still call itself the aristocrat of harness horses.

BIBLIOGRAPHY

The Rural Economy of Norfolk, by John Marshall, 1787.

A Philosophical and Practical Treatise on Horses, by John Lawrence, 1796.

The History and Delineation of the Horse, by John Lawrence, 1809.

The Book of the Horse, by S. Sidney, (no date).

The Hackney Stud Book, Volume I, Historical Introduction, Henry F. Euren, 1884.

The Hackney Stud Book, Volume IV, Additional Notes on the History of the Hackney Horse, Henry F. Euren, 1887.

The Brookfield Stud, W. Burdett-Coutts, M.P., 1891.

The American Hackney Stud Book, Volume I, (Reprint of Euren's Historical Introduction with notes on Importations), 1893.

The Harness Horse, Sir Walter Gilbey, Bart., 1898.

Shelburne Farm Stud of English Hackneys, Dr. Wm. Seward Webb, 1893.

Livestock Breeders' Handbook, (No. 2. Light Horse Breeds and Management), edited by James Sinclair, various editions.

The Canadian Hackney Stud Book, Volume I, Historical Introduction, R.G., 1905.

The New Book of the Horse, Charles Richardson, (no date).

Horses of the British Empire, edited by Sir Humphrey F. de Trafford, Bart., 1907.

Famous Harness Horses, Vol. I 1926, Vol. II 1932, Geoffrey D. S. Bennett.

Hackney Horses and Ponies, S. L. Righyni, 1948.

The American Hackney Stud Book, Volume XI, (Reprint of the Introduction to Volume I with a Condensed History of Importations Since the Publication of Volume I), 1949.

The Book of the Hackney, Charles Cornell and R. A. Brown, 1958.

PRIMAL ARTS

NATIVE AMERICANS, ESKIMOS,

& ABORIGINES

Cover photo: **Fish mask.** Yupik (Western Eskimo). Early 20th century. Alaska. Polychrome wood and feathers. H. 19.7".Collected by Adams Hollis Twitchell in the early 1920s. Formerly in the Museum of the American Indian, Heye Foundation, New York, the André Breton Collection, musée de l'Homme. Musée du Quai Branly, Paris.
Endpaper: **Frontal mask.** Tsimshian Indians. 19th century. British Columbia, Canada. Wood. H. 6.2". Formerly in the Claude Lévi-Strauss Collection, musée de l'Homme. Musée du Quai Branly, Paris.

Assouline Publishing
601 West 26th Street,
18th Floor
New York, NY 10001, USA
Tel: 212 989-6810 Fax: 212 647-0005
www.assouline.com

ISBN : 2-84323-824-2

Translated from French by David Wharry.

Color separation: Gravor (Switzerland)
Printed by SNP (China)

BÉRÉNICE GEOFFROY-SCHNEITER

PRIMAL ARTS

NATIVE AMERICANS, ESKIMOS, & ABORIGINES

ASSOULINE

To Cassandre and Laurent

Large ax of a parrot in the form of a stylized U. Totonac culture, classic/post-classic period. Xochicalco, Morelos, Mexico. Stone. H. 22.6". Museo Nacional de Antropologia, Mexico City. The perforations of this work fascinated the sculptor Henry Moore.

TABLE OF CONTENTS

INTRODUCTION

"THROUGH THE LOOKING GLASS"

"See how these objects justify the Surrealist vision, what a new development they can bring to it. This Eskimo mask depicts the swan who leads the white whale to the hunter in the spring—the swan, reduced here to the head and neck, is coming out of the whale's mouth. Is this or is this not poetry as we continue to understand it?"

—André Breton, *Entretiens,* 1952

Feather-haloed masks frozen in ecstasy or terror, miniature dolls parading in dream-like clothes studded with stars, the haughty silhouettes of totem poles soaring into the sky, deities out of whose gaping ribcages hang entrails that announce the horrors of sacrifice and the cosmic power of the next world: the rational or squeamish can only stare wide-eyed at these strange forms created by the inspired chisel of some Eskimoan or Mayan sculptor. Because, for the pre-Colombian and Amerindian peoples who craved for the sacred, creation was never "art for art's sake"; but it was hypnosis, dialogue, communion, a vehicle, a supplication, a prayer, a questioning within which man, so small, so fragile, so imperfect, could also dream of being a jaguar, bear, bird, bat, insect, seal, butterfly. In the headlong, sublime quest that endlessly pushed him to redefine the limits of the beautiful in order to more closely approach the spheres of the holy, the artist became demiurge,

Shaman mask. Inuit. 1860–80. Lower Kuskokwim River region, Alaska. Painted wood. H. 29.7". Private collection.
Following pages: **Yupik mask of the swan and the white whale.** Early 20th century. Alaska. Wood. H. 28.1". Formerly in the André Breton Collection. Musée du Quai Branly, Paris.
Portrait of André Breton wearing glasses. Formerly in the André Breton Collection. Private collection.

poet, and witchdoctor. With his colors he conversed with spirits, danced with the next world, ceaselessly playing out the cosmogonies celebrating man's original communion with the creatures of the animal and plant realms.

Many of these symbols have, of course, vanished, and countless languages have been silenced in the whirlwind of history and the fracas of often tragic and murderous colonial encounters. Gods have come up against one another and visions of the world have clashed, and yet this has failed to break down the barriers of preconceived ideas and arrogant dogmas.

How many populations were decimated, how many altars overturned, how many beliefs smothered, decapitated, and annihilated? It is as if the discovery of this otherness was too terrifying, too great a burden for Europeans to bear.

And how many misunderstandings between men and women whose very notion of holiness and divine equilibrium differed in so many ways? The conquistadors craving for riches and glory came face-to-face with the ancient peoples of Peru, Colombia, and Ecuador who, by worshipping gold as a god, paid homage to the fertilizing and regenerative power of the Sun. On one side, a monotheism embodied by the figure of Christ on the cross atoning for the evils of the world and on the other, a myriad of divinities and spirits that had to be reconciled through prayer and sacrifices.

Yet there were occasional moments of dialogue. In the sixteenth century, there were already traces of curiosity, wonderment even, in the writings of a young Jesuit missionary and in the work of the painter Albrecht Dürer. These savages were, in fact, not savages. They wielded the adze and brush with grace and thought. Yet their "artifacts" were for a long time considered merely charming trinkets, curios fit only for obscure, dusty cabinets of curiosities: Aztec dignitaries' feather headdresses, bison hides painted with detailed depictions of battles and initiation rites, masks and finery torn from their context.

Their resurrection in museums, many years after their initial discovery, has some-

Cover of the catalogue of the Exhibition of Surrealist Objects. Galerie Charles Ratton, Paris. 1936. Formerly in the André Breton Collection. Private Collection.
Catalogue of the Claude Lévi-Strauss auction. June 21, 1951. Archives André Breton.

thing of the miraculous about it. One could never sufficiently praise the tenacity and clairvoyance of certain curators who, ignoring the hegemony of fashion, saved these unjustly ignored works from oblivion. One example is the Eskimo masks collected by the French explorer Alphonse Pinart in 1871, then "found" over a century later in a cupboard in the museum in Boulogne-sur-Mer.

But in the long crusade to rehabilitate these arts no longer considered "primitive" (the term is now considered pejorative), many were the pioneers whose clear-sightedness and enlightened judgment toppled the preconceived ideas ranged against them: There were artists and poets such as Apollinaire, Picasso, Max Ernst, and, of course, the mentor, cacique, and high priest of Surrealism, André Breton. But also travelers and anthropologists, such as the German-born American Franz Boas who wrote *Primitive Art* in 1927 or those two mythical figures of French ethnology, Claude Lévi-Strauss and Paul-Emile Victor—the former in the Amazon rainforest, living with the Caduveo Indians, whose body paintings inspired some of the

Claude Lévi-Strauss with the Tuli-Kawahib (self-portrait). 1938.
From *Saudades do Brasil* (Paris, Plon, 1994).

finest pages of anthropological literature, and the latter in the icy, virgin wastes of the Eskimoan world.

Their inspired, uncompromising vision saw through the mirror of appearances and finally did justice to these peoples, whose masks and tattoos, chants and secret ceremonies would no longer speak had it not been for their sublime writings.

If one omnipresent figure haunts the figurines, masks, and finery of these civilizations of ecstasy and trance, it is of the shaman. The birdmen of the Amazon, spreading their wings to journey through other realms, the medicine men of the Plains Indians, healing spirits as one would a body, and the clairvoyant men of the Arctic:

Preceding pages: **Max Ernst with his collection of Kachina dolls, on Peggy Guggenheim's terrace in New York.** Early 1942.
Following pages: **Young Yanomami Indian, in Claudia Andujar's series of photographs *Yanomami—The House, the Forest, the Invisible.*** 1976. Wakatha u, Amazon, Brazil.

Paul-Emile Victor with his Inuk friend Kristian finishing Paul-Emile Victor's cabin, next to his Inuk family's communal hut at Kangerlussuatsiaq, Greenland. October 1936.

all are adepts of the supernatural and metamorphoses. They are neither magicians nor sorcerers, but rather conveyers of energy and dreams—poets, men of science, and artists all at once. It is hardly surprising, therefore, if Westerners in search of new spiritual foundations have turned to these "voyagers of the invisible" for enlightenment. In their own way, they embody the reconciliation of our origins, a harmony of species at last recovered.

In the Musée du Quai Branly, these masks and statues in wood, feathers, and stone can again whisper the voices of the wind and the murmur of the spirits in our ears. These prayers once proffered to the gods, these shreds of memory saved from oblivion are there to remind us of their origins. As Claude Roy wrote in *Arts sauvages* in 1998: "Art, with love and knowledge, is the only real escape that can tear man from the nightmare of time, from that little hell colonized after a fashion we call life."

THE TAINOS,

or the First Encounter

"To die free, one has to climb
Very high, higher, ever higher
O sacred mother, O holy mountain
Who will dare to seek us in your arms
And in your hair."
—Cacique Henri

Wandering in the labyrinth of the Musée de l'Homme forty years ago, the collector Jacques Kerchache was enchanted by a duho. Its elegance and singularity fascinated him. "Orphaned in the midst of other pre-Colombian objects" and sculpted in a beautiful dark wood, it was probably once the ceremonial seat of a Taino chief, one of the caciques (a hereditary title apparently passed down on the mother's side) Christopher Columbus met during his first voyage, in 1492. Shortly afterward, André Breton would tell the fascinated young man more about the Arawak Indians ("Arawak" is a magic word in itself) and their culture scattered in museums all over the world like the pieces of a lost jigsaw puzzle. The fruit of this initiatory meeting was the remarkable exhibition Jacques Kerchache organized in Paris in 1994, "The Art of the Taino Sculptors." Beneath the majestic cupola of the Petit Palais, it brought forth the quintessence of this Caribbean tribal art haunted by the specter of death.

Duho (ceremonial seat). 13th–14th century. Haiti or Dominican Republic. Wood. H. 16.4" L. 30.4" L. 11.9". M. and Mme David Weill Donation. Formerly in musée de l'Homme. Musée du Quai Branly, Paris.
Left: ***Zemi*** (detail). 1903–04. Dominican Republic. Wood. 33.15". Private Collection, Paris. Reproduced in the 25th Annual Report of the Bureau of American Ethnology, Washington.

Cave painting depicting a funerary ritual. On the left, a figure of a shaman.
Cueva de las Maravillas, San Pedro de Macoris, Dominican Republic.

When Christopher Columbus discovered the New World, the "Tainos" (an inappropriate term since it in fact designates an ethnic group, indeed even a specific social class) occupied most of the Greater Antilles, that is, Puerto Rico, almost all of Hispaniola (present-day Santo Domingo), and eastern Cuba. Admiral Columbus's first observations were as follows: "So kindly, tractable and free from covetousness are these good Indians, that I swear to your highnesses that there is no better people nor better land. They love their neighbors as themselves, and their conversation is the sweetest that can be conceived, always pleasant and always smiling. It is true that both men and women go entirely naked, yet your highnesses may rest assured that they have very commendable customs." He, in fact, drew a clear distinction between those he

Three-pointed stone (front and back). La Romana, Dominican Republic.
H. 9.1". Fondación Garcia Arévalo, Santo Domingo.

considered "good Indians," that is, the Tainos, who gave him a warm welcome, and the cannibalistic Caribs, in whom he already saw a possible source of profit through their sale as slaves. The discoverer of the New World went into raptures over the exuberant beauty of the island he baptized "Hispaniola" (the Latin transcription of La Española), singing the praises of its heavenly beaches, rivers overflowing with fish, multicolored birds, etc., whilst considering that the kindness and cowardice of its inhabitants would make them excellent servants. Yet all the Spanish chroniclers (the sole and inevitably subjective and fragmented source of information enabling us to decipher the rare objects that have survived) all agree on the extreme refinement of Taino civilization, certainly the most complex and organized in the Antilles. Arawak society in the islands, dominated by lords or caciques, developed a mainly agrarian economy. The centralization of power in the hands of one man seems to have also been a Taino tradition since they named Columbus *guamiquina,* or "supreme lord of the Spanish," that is, sole chief, and presented him with the symbols of this authority: tobacco, duhos, and cotton belts decorated with pearls or shells reminiscent of North American wampum (seashell beadwork). The chiefs of tribes were assisted by dignitaries or *nitainos* (a term whose abbreviated form came to designate the cultures of the Greater Antilles as a whole), while the *naborias* occupied the lowest rungs of the social ladder. The insularity of the Caribbean peoples did not prevent them from making contact with the populations of other islands by using high-speed dugout canoes, which the Spanish admired as much as they did their hammocks. According to some chroniclers, including Bartolomeo de Las Casas, the Tainos lived in villages, whose population of one to two thousand people lived in twenty to fifty *bohios* or *caneys,* multifamily dwellings reminiscent of Oceanian communal houses. Peter Martyr d'Anghiera, Queen Isabella the Catholic's chaplain and a friend of Christopher Columbus, described with wonderment the large residence of one of the caciques of the Cap-Haïtien region, whose roof was made out of multicolored reeds interwoven with complex patterns. This house probably opened onto a rectangular courtyard used for social or religious ceremonies, such as the famous *batey* ceremonial ball game. Most likely related to its Amerindian equivalent, this game could be either a merely playful pastime (but which the Aztecs feverishly gambled on), or an extremely religious ceremony involving human sacrifice. Derived from the wooden or leather belts worn by batey players, the stone belts illustrate the degree of perfection the Tainos attained in stone poli-

Anthropomorphic pestle. Puerto Rico. Stone. H. 11". Museo de la Universidad de Puerto Rico, Río Piedras.
Following pages: **Anthropomorphic inhaler** (front and back). La Cucama, Dominican Republic. Manatee bone. H. 3.4". Fondación Garcia Arévalo, Santo Domingo.

shing. These may have been trophies offered to victors. According to the great Americanist ethnologist Christian Duverger, these ellipsoidal belts may have symbolized a fundamental dyad, such as the union between Earth and sky.

Once they had gotten over the initial culture shock, the Europeans of the First Encounter very soon came up against a world light-years away from their own thought and belief systems. Convivial by nature, the Tainos also showed a generosity that astounded the gold-hungry Spanish. They even offered their sisters or daughters as tokens of affection. Yet they had a profound aversion to incest and could punish thieves by subjecting them to particularly barbarous tortures.

Like all the Amerindian peoples, the Tainos seem to have been profoundly idealistic dreamers. They believed in the resurrection of the dead, whom they saw as living in an eternal springtime, a kind of Garden of Eden populated with animals of all species and full of rivers teeming with fish. They were respectful

Vomitive spatula in the form of a bat. Dominican Republic. Manatee bone. W. 9".
Fondación Garcia Arévalo, Santo Domingo.

of nature, tending their gardens with a care that filled Christopher Columbus with such admiration he exclaimed, "One could find none as beautiful in Castile in the month of May."

The Tainos also lavished great care on their bodies, which they decorated with paintings for festive and religious occasions with dyes made from crushed *jagua* and *bija* seeds, or with charcoal soot. Their jewelry and body ornaments, associated with tropical bird feathers, were just as intricate. Ironically, most of these treasures, so priceless for the Tainos—amulets, necklaces, pectorals, diadems heightened with strips of gold, belts in plaited cotton decorated with pearls and shells (such as the magnificent example in the Museum für Volkerkunde in Vienna)—would end up in the Spanish hands of Catholic kings who considered them merely as modest gifts.

This rather idealized vision of an Eden-like world in which people lived in their natural state and never went hungry or worried about tomorrow is in contradiction to the stone and wood sculptures their inspired yet anonymous artists left us. Taino art, steeped in animist beliefs, has a power often verging on

Anthropomorphic handle of an oval dish (detail). Dominican Republic. Wood, teeth, and shell. H. 19.9". Formerly in the collection of Archduke Leopoldo of Tuscany (1617–75). Museo Nationale di Antropologia e Etnologia, Florence.

expressionism. What do these painfully stiff figures, skeletal after days of fasting, represent if it is not fear of death, its last convulsive spasm?

"Zemi" is the generic term designating both the god itself and its representation in wood, stone, ceramic, shell, or cotton. "Each plant, tree, or animal species has its zemi, whereas the human species has its tribal, family, or individual zemi," explains the ethnologist Christian Duverger. He continues, "Some zemis were probably associated with precise hierarchical functions, such as those of the chief or witch doctor. Depending on their type, zemis were buried in fields, beneath houses, or shut up in temples. Domestic zemis were hung from the roofs of huts, some inside, others outside" (Duverger, 1999).

Anthropomorphic statuette. West Indies. Black basalt. H. 8.7". Formerly in musée de l'Homme. Musée du Quai Branly, Paris.

Pectoral. Dominican Republic. Shell. H. 3.4".
Private Collection, USA.

The forms of these stone, wood, or cotton statuettes could therefore vary greatly, from geometric to abstract to strikingly realist depictions. The stupefying anthropomorphic idol today at Turin University was once displayed in front of Saint Peter's Basilica in Rome as a symbol of the victory of Christianity over paganism . . . whilst turning a conveniently blind eye to relic worship in Europe.

Contrasting with this willfully Baroque art, given the range of the materials used, is the sublime perfection of the *trigonoliths.* These three-pointed zemi figurines, which the sculptor Constantin Brancusi would have been proud of, were laden with a symbolism closely linked to fertility. They were buried in the ground to make the yucca plant grow. The yucca, the Tainos's staple diet, was worshipped as Yucahu Bagua Maorocoti, the supreme, immortal, and invisible

Reliquary (zemi). Early 16th century. Dominican Republic. Cotton, shell, rhinoceros horn, mirror, beads/seeds, glass paste, bone, gold, and resin. H. 12.5". Museo Nazionale Preistorico Ethnografico Luigi Pigorini, Rome.

Skull amulet. Higuey, Dominican Republic. *Strombus gigas* (queen conch) shell. H. 3.7". Fondación Garcia Arévalo, Dominican Republic.

being living in the sky. According to chroniclers, these mysterious zemi stones, combining the images of the breast and vulva, also helped women in childbirth. Their triangular, bulging form evokes the beak of the inriri bird, a kind of green woodpecker believed to have opened the vulva of an asexual creature to transform it into a woman. These extremely sacred stones were also used to dig up the first clods of fertile Earth.

Another remarkable group of zemi figurines was closely linked to the taking of *cohoba.* This powder, obtained by crushing and pulverizing seeds containing toxic and hallucinogenic alkaloids, enabled direct contact with the dead and spirits. The highly codified cohoba ritual was a privilege reserved for the elite: The caciques, but above all the *behiques,* shamans who, because they acted as healers, wielded immense power. After a long and arduous initiation involving prior purification by ritual vomiting, the behiques entered a trance during which they conversed with the spirit world. The Tainos must have greatly admired these shamans who journeyed into the beyond on their behalf; they created poignant wood, stone, and clay idols modeled on their likeness, their eyes hollow and their bodies skeletal. Indeed, one is moved by their expressive power. The Tainos's Y-shaped inhalers and vomiting spatulas, sculpted in the graceful form of the bat or *opia* (spirit of the dead), are also poignant testaments to the extent to which man will go to transcend his body and become a spirit.

But if there is an obsessive theme in Taino art—and one shared by the other Amerindian civilizations—it is the head. The Tainos customarily decapitated their dead, burying the body but keeping the head for ritual purposes. Cephalomorphic depictions are sometimes double, evoking the legend of the twins Boinayel and Marohu, gods of the Sun and rain. Taino sculptors also showed their prowess in sculpting faces on surfaces as small as the canines of dogs or tropical seals. Few cultures have experimented as fully with ways of depicting the skull. "The invention of the Tainos, when it comes to depicting death, is as vast as Picasso's," Jacques Kerchache so rightly pointed out in the splendid catalog of the Petit Palais exhibition (Kercharche, 1994).

The tragic irony is that the Greater Antilles was the theater both of the First Encounter, and its following genocide. Massacres, diseases, and mass suicides would, in the next ten years, decimate the Indians whom Columbus and his companions had described as "people of excellent heart who know nothing of cupidity."

STONE, WOOD, AND COTTON ZEMIS

"Most of the people of the island of Hispaniola own many zemis of different types. Some contain the bones of their father, their mother, their family, and ancestors; they are made from stone or wood," noted the chronicler Ramon Pané. If we now consider these objects to be remarkable sculptures, we should not forget their original use as funerary urns, most probably reserved for high-ranking dignitaries, caciques, behiques, and nitainos.

These stone, wood, or cotton ossuaries were especially venerated by the Tainos and hidden in caves during the Spanish conquest. As fate would have it, some crossed oceans to be exhibited in distant lands as vibrant incarnations of a particularly fearsome paganism. Father Francisco Ruiz saw them as "the horrific form of the spirits of evil."

Funerary urn (zemi). Front and back. Sierra de Bahoruco, Dominican Republic. Wood. H. 37.4".Fondación Garcia Arévalo, Dominican Republic.

RUPESTRIAN PAINTINGS AND PETROGLYPHS: THE SOURCES OF AN ART

Since the dawn of time, man has constantly expressed his doubts, questions, and anxieties on cave walls and rock faces. The inhabitants of the island today called Santo Domingo were no exception, as countless petroglyphs (engraved stones) and cave paintings dating back to 2,500 BC attest. Anthropomorphic and zoomorphic figures and mysterious scenes that probably evoked funerary or shamanic rituals seem to have been the favorite motifs of these artists, whose inspired drawing is the equal of their distant counterparts at Lascaux. The Tainos and their ancestors used mineral pigments made from substances oxidized in salt, which took on beautiful black, reddish, and brown hues. They were usually combined with charcoal. If the memory of body paintings remains only in explorers' accounts or on a few clumsy engravings, stone, on the other hand, has preserved the genius of these island peoples, immortalizing their artistic repertoire, one that boldly exists on the frontiers of the unconscious.

Monoliths and petroglyphs decorated with zemis. Utuado, Puerto Rico.

SEATS FOR THE AFTERLIFE

It is perhaps the duhos, sadly usually deprived of their original incrustations, that best reflect the creative genius of the Taino sculptors, distant precursors of the modern furniture designer. Use of these ceremonial seats, probably derived from the metate grinding stones of Central America, was the exclusive privilege of caciques, behiques, and nitainos, during Cohoba rituals or ball game ceremonies. The Conquistadors' official chronicler, Gonzalo Fernández de Oviedo, notes that when the caciques died they were wrapped from head to foot in "bands of woven cotton, like saddle girths, very long, very tight," and that "they were placed on a duho," while another duho was handed down to the eldest son and successor.

Chroniclers recount that the Tainos, as a welcoming gesture, invited the Spanish to sit on these prestigious seats. On the island of Hispaniola, the cacique Anacuona even offered fourteen of them to Bartolomeo Columbus, the admiral's younger brother. Yet the conquistadors, obsessed as they were with gold, scorned these extraordinary thrones. They were carved from a single block of stone, in the form of strange animals with stubby legs and arms and their tails raised as armrests and on whose enormous heads the ears and eyes sparkled with gold. They were undoubtedly unaware of the highly symbolic value of these representations of the zemi Opiyelquoviran—a wild spirit who, in his wanderings, embodies the faculty of displacement. It was therefore logical that the shaman sat on a duho during his trances: It greatly facilitated his ecstatic journey in the spirit world. Whatever these seats signify, their formal perfection is the hallmark of a great designer, a kind of precursor to the works of Le Corbusier and Charles Eames.

Duho (ceremonial seat). 13th–14th century. Haiti or Dominican Republic. Wood. H. 16.4" L. 30.4" L. 11.9". M. and Mme David Weill Donation. Formerly in musée de l'Homme. Musée du Quai Branly, Paris.

MESOAMERICA

An Art of Blood and Fury

Chichimec, Mixtec, Olmec, Aztec . . . names with barbarous overtones that could deter the novice explorer from discovering the rich and hermetic universe of the Mesoamerican civilization. A host of preconceived ideas and clichés warp our perceptions of these peoples and their beliefs. These erroneous ideas also fire the imagination: Mayan pyramids lost in the jungle, newborn babies sacrificed on the altars of ferocious, bloodthirsty deities, and undeciphered calligraphies.

With every new archeological dig and its accompanying exhibitions and publications, the traditional "sensationalist" view of these peoples is being discarded in an effort to better understand the intrinsic originality of each cultural region, whose complex religions and sophisticated rituals never cease to intrigue, and whose prodigious art dazzled Albrecht Dürer and frightened Charles Baudelaire.

When one tries to sketch the distinguishing traits of what we call "Mesoamerica," one generally refers to the seminal definition drawn up in 1943 by the Americanist Paul Kirchhoff. He compiled a list of technological advances that he considered constitute a kind of idealized "Identikit" portrait. Kirchhoff cataloged the following

Mask. Circa 100–200 BC. Colima region of Mexico. Tremolite, actinolite, chlorite. H. 3.8". Museo Barbier-Mueller de Arte Precolombino, Barcelona.
Following pages: **Mictlantecutli, god of death.** Aztec. Circa 1480. The House of the Eagles. Ceramic. H. 69". Museo del Templo Mayor, Mexico City.
Offering in the form of a human skull decorated with inlay and sacrificial knives. Aztec. Circa 1250–1521. H. 9". Museo del Templo Mayor, Mexico City.

shared traits among the various civilizations from this vast geo-cultural region: Growing of squashes, corn, beans, and pimentos; the wearing of cotton and agave fiber garments; the making of pottery and stone and wood and bone tools; knowledge of the principle of the wheel (but not of how to use it); the building of pyramidal platforms and mounds; the practice of a mysterious ball game; the use of a dual calendar combining astronomical, astrological, and mathematical knowledge; the worship of gods organized into a crowded pantheon governed by the principle of metamorphosis; the foundation of city-states based on a theocratic and military ideology; the large-scale practice of human sacrifice; and a highly stratified society, as the rich contents of their tombs illustrate.

Chupicuaro (front and back). 18th–17th century BC. 7th–2nd century BC. Mexico. Terra-cotta. H. 12.1". Formerly on Guy Joussemet collection. Musée du Quai Branly, Paris.

This is an impressive kaleidoscope whose continuity as a cultural entity is just as remarkable—Mesoamerican civilizations existed for around four thousand years, dating from the appearance of the first Neolithic hamlets until sixteenth-century conquistadors. These civilizations, of course, did not develop without conflicts and breaks: Some died out while others rose to take their place. Regions dominant during one period were eclipsed by others and vice versa. And yet, benea th its fluctuating frontiers and empires, this civilization, whose roots indisputably lie in the Mexican ensemble, can above all be defined by its symbolic yet naturalistic, poetic but terrifying vision of the world. But then this is probably true of every great culture.

It was precisely the profoundly pessimistic nature of the Mesoamerican civilization, which its art in many ways reflects, that first struck Western observers and

still does today. This radical, irreversible, and cosmic pessimism was encapsulated in a mysterious 260-day calendar that enabled one to read the future or allot a person a name at birth. Composed of thirteen numbers associated with some twenty signs, it nourished this fatalistic belief in predestination. As the ethnologist Christian Duverger so magnificently sums up, "In Mesoamerica, one was what one was born." The "eagle" sign predisposed one to war, the "rabbit" to agriculture, and the "flower" governed artistic abilities. There was no escaping the pitiless machinery of Mesoamerican destinies. In the face of one's destiny, the universe, and the gods, man was a fragile, anguished, and crushed creature. His earthly life mattered little compared with the smooth workings of the cosmos.

If one word sums up this relationship with the holy, it is "sacrifice." There is not a shadow of a doubt: The whole of Mesoamerica was sacrificial in tradition from its very outset. Sacrifice by tearing out the heart (it was taken, still beating, from victims' ribcages), sacrifice by beheading (the heads were placed for all to see on platforms near the main sanctuaries), sacrifice by arrow (an apparently northern tradition), and so on—the imagination of the officiating priests seems to have been almost limitless. Over the millennia, these practices, initially reserved for exceptional circumstances (the founding of a city, the crowning of a sovereign, etc.), and which so horrified Spanish missionaries, degenerated. A host of macabre artworks graphically illustrate this: Skulls and crossbones, rosaries of heads and severed hands, faces contorted by pain, torture instruments, terrifying monsters. There is not a smile in sight . . . the art of Mesoamerica seems to revel in horror. And despite our modern detachment, one is at a loss to understand why these statues of grimacing gods, originally daubed with the blood of their victims, and the terracing of these towering pyramids, which one can imagine running with the precious liquid, instill such fear.

Preceding double page: **Mask.** Teotihuacán III period. Mexico. Ochre and cream terra-cotta. H. 3.9". Museo Nacional de Antropologia, Mexico City.

In Mesoamerica, the gods had an insatiable thirst for blood, which man constantly had to quench with his own blood and that of others. If he failed in this implacable duty, the cosmos and the whole of humanity were condemned. There was nothing gratuitous, let alone sadistic about these sacrifices, which the conquistadors considered satanic. For the ancient Mexicans, it was merely a means of "thwarting the phenomenon of the dissipation of energy" (Duverger, 1999). This is, indeed, a complex reality that can be understood only if one bears in mind that cosmic energy was perceived not as a limitless source but as a limited stock liable to run out. As ecologists of the cosmos, it was the Mesoamericans' duty to literally nourish their voracious and predatory divinity, the Sun. A luminous and life-giving star, but also an all-consuming fire, the Sun, if not perpetually fed, would go out—a metaphor that takes on its full meaning when one thinks of the human kebab roasted to slake the Sun's never-ending thirst.

It is only by keeping this in mind that one can interpret, or decode, most of the imagery in Mesoamerican art. There is no interest in anecdote, nothing amiable in this art entirely dedicated to an idea that seeks only to be meaningful. A jaguar drinking human blood is simply an allegorical depiction of the Sun drinking the "precious water" by night. For the Mesoamericans, even the apparently harmless image of a flower branch was an explicit allusion to human sacrifice poetically called "flowering death."

How many visual mistranslations have our moralizing, Eurocentric eyes fabricated by wanting to see only what they wanted to see? For instance, what we generally consider to be delightful depictions of vegetables (squashes, cacti, cocoa beans, etc.) are, in fact, holy representations, as are many images of crocodiles, jaguars, toads, armadillos, dogs, and even turkeys. Mesoamerica extolled the interdependence of the realms and existential fluidity. A man or a woman could also be a bat, puma, peccary, anteater, owl, bee, or tortoise just as a god or goddess could take on the appearance of a mountain, cloud, plumed head-

Yugo, a protective belt worn during the ball game. AD 500–950. Veracruz, Mexico. Stone. L. 16.2". Museo Amparo, Puebla.

dress, jade ornament, or tobacco plant.

"Mesoamerican civilization, like so many others, had no conception of pure aesthetic experience," the Mexican poet and essayist Octavio Paz observed in an enlightening text published in France in *Le Signe et le mémoire* in 1993. He writes: "Beauty, not a value in its own right, could sometimes be associated with religious values or utility. The work of art was not an end in itself but a bridge or talisman. A bridge: The work of art transports one from the here and now toward a there in another time. A talisman: The work exchanges visible reality for another. Thus, the effigy of the deity Coatlicue is the Earth, the Sun a jaguar, and the Moon the face of a beheaded goddess. The work of art is a conduit, a transmission vehicle for forces and sacred, alien powers. Art's purpose is to open the doors to the other side of reality."

"The other side of reality." What could be more "realist" than the art of Mesoamerica? Yet, it definitely belongs in the "wild arts" category, as André Breton and his Surrealists suggested. The ability to metamorphose, a propensity

Lady Xoc, kneeling before her husband, Itzam Balam, who holds a burning torch. Classic Maya. AD 726. Yaxchilan, Chiapas, Mexico. Limestone. H. 43" W. 314".

for symbolic associations, visual puzzles, and a tendency to sometimes build on abstractions—these are just some of the facets of a visual language that for too long has been defined solely by its austere and macabre dimensions. We forget the pure visual delight of the wildly free graphic games in Mayan codices, the hypnotic presence of funerary masks with eyes inset with rocks, crystals, or precious stones, and the amazing refinement of a palette of rich carmines and vivid blues, strident yellows, and deep greens.

Yet many of the masterpieces we admire in the protective sanctuaries of those modern temples—the museums—were not made for the eyes of the living but for the oblivion of the tomb. These statues and objects are symbolic offerings, provisions for the next world, not trinkets, and certainly not works of art.

It is not by chance that in every Mesoamerican civilization the artist remained anonymous. There is no urge to sign a work. To do so would be imposture, or, quite simply, philosophical and spiritual nonsense. Religion and politics were one and the same thing. The artist was an agent in the service of the clergy or sovereign. "Modern authors who are convinced that some Mayan glyph or calendar date is an artist's signature are definitely mistaken about the time and place. They are confusing Yaxchilan with the Bateau-Lavoir," Christian Duverger caustically remarks.

A second mistranslation, probably just as pernicious, consists in reproaching Mesoamerican art for its apparent monotony and sepulchral coldness. But what, then, did the ancient Mexicans think when they saw, invariably in the form of pictures or sculptures, a crucified man and his cohort of so very "human" saints? The criticism that pre-Hispanic art is monotonous is all the more unjustified given that it is capable of freeing itself of all realist constraint: Plump babies with jaguar's fangs, serpents covered with plumage, clouds full of human faces, warriors jumping out of an eagle's beak, and so on. One should not forget that these

The Lord of Las Limas (Olmec statuette found in a motel in Texas and returned to Mexico). Mid-preclassic Olmec. Las Limas, Veracruz, Mexico. H. 21.5". Museo de Antropologia de Xalapa, Veracruz.

Pyramid of Kukulkan. Circa 987.
Yucatán, Mexico.

gray stone sculptures we now consider so brutal were once adorned with sumptuous finery: Extravagant plumed headdresses, garments made of paper or fabric, and pupils inlaid with precious stones to brighten their gaze. But one must also imagine these severe effigies brandishing flamboyant decorations, jingling bells, and beautiful feather shields. Nothing, therefore, could be more reductive and false than this black-and-white image of pre-Colombian art.

One merely has to read the first awestruck conquerors' accounts of the wondrous refinement and luxuriousness of the cities, the prodigious skill of the craftsmen, and the extravagant lifestyle and finery of the nobles. "There are large

Drawing of the pyramid at Texcoco, with the temples Tlaloc and Huitzilopochtli. 17th century. From *Codex Ixtlilxochitl* (attributed to Fernando de Alva Ixtlilxochitl, 1578–1650), dating from the first years of the Spanish conquest. 8.20 x 12.1". Bibliothèque Nationale de France, Paris.

Collection E. Eug. GOUPIL à Paris
Nº 65-71.
Ancienne Collection J. M. A. AUBIN

towns and marvelous edifices and great markets and riches, among these towns there is one, the most marvelous and richest of all, called Tenustitlan, which has been marvelously and artfully built on a large lagoon; the great lord of the town and the province is a king called Mutezuma," Hernán Cortés wrote in a letter to the King of Spain in 1520. But this did not prevent the fiery conqueror with the soul of an aesthete from eradicating all trace of the Aztecan civilization without the slightest remorse. The barbarians are not always those we think.

Adolescent, known as the "Young Man of Tamuin," carrying a dead child on his back.
Huaxtec. Circa AD 1300. San Luis Potosi. Sandstone. H. 56.5".
Museo Nacional de Antropologia, Mexico City.
Preceding pages: **Hieroglyph.** Maya. AD 526. Museo Nacional de Antropologia, Mexico City.
Stone depicting a ball game player. Maya. AD 591. La Esperanza. Chinkultic, Mexico.
Limestone. Ø 0.22". Th. 0.05". Museo Nacional de Antropologia, Mexico City..

A JOURNEY AFTER DEATH

To say that Mesoamerica is an archaeologist's paradise would be an understatement. Thousands of sepulchers have been unearthed, all of them testaments to these pre-Hispanic peoples' obsession with ensuring the best possible conditions for their journey into the next world. The variety of funereal items is astounding: Single or multiple tombs, in pits or stone chambers, sarcophagi, and urns. The Mesoamericans buried their dead but also cremated them. If there is one constant with all these peoples it is their conception of death as a rite of passage or metamorphosis. The tomb is therefore merely the departure point of the deceased's odyssey through the land of the dead. The departed has the choice of three different solutions or routes:

– the celestial journey, reserved for heroes killed in battle and women who died in childbirth;

– the journey through hell, during which the deceased has to pass a daunting series of tests (crossing deserts and steep mountains, competing with a lizard at a ball game, crossing the nine rivers of this "Mesoamerican Hades" on the back of a dog, and so on);

– the earthly journey, during which Tláloc, god of water, ruled over the drowned, dropsical, pestilent, and victims of water-born "fevers." Is this the distant fantasy of a people of farmers, whose paradise resembles a land of perpetually green fields?

The length of these funerary journeys was symbolically fixed at four years. To accompany and provide sustenance for the deceased during his ordeals, food and drink and, depending on his social rank and wealth, finery and precious jewelry were placed beside him. This practice continues today: Some Indian peoples still slip a few pesos between the fingers of the dear departed.

From Teotihuacán jade funerary masks (probably intended to protect the deceased from the glacial wind that blew through the underworld) to delightful sugar or papier-mâché skeletons and skulls that are still displayed today during the Feast of the Dead, Mexican art has always flirted with the world of the dead.

Ornated mask with two intertwined snakes: Tlaloc (?) Aztec/Mixtec. 15th–16th century. Wood covered with turquoise and mother-of-pearl mosaic. H. 6.7". British Museum, London.

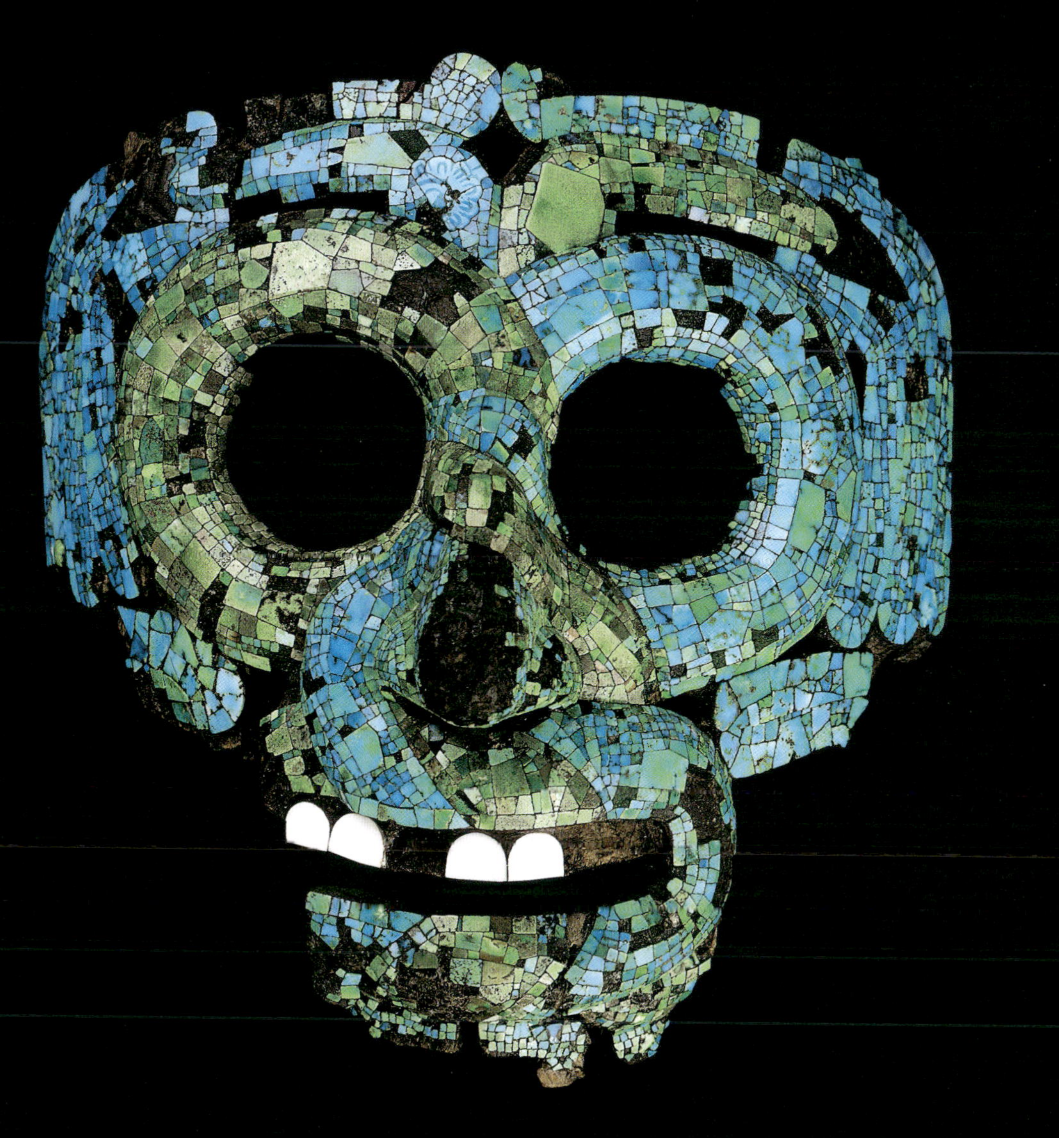

A CROWDED PANTHEON

Few civilizations have forged a pantheon as rich and crowded. It is as if in ancient Mexico there had to be a god for everything: Games, hunting, fertility, harvests, war, love, journeys, childbirth, corn, the Sun, the Moon, and so on. And this is not counting the string of tutelary divinities whose remit was to protect with their powers a whole array of professions: Sorcerers, soldiers, goldsmiths, musicians, shopkeepers, scribes, etc. Some gods were terrible, others soothing, some visible, others impalpable. There were anthropomorphic gods and hybrid gods made up of partially animal or vegetable anatomies.

It was, in fact, several indigenous traditions that built this complex and perplexing brethren over several millennia. Victors adopted the deities of the defeated and vice versa. One of the stars of this "Mesoamerican Olympus" was the figure of the Old God, who must certainly have originated in the first agricultural populations. The god of fire and volcanoes, he sat enthroned with his wife. She embodied the Earth and plant fertility and was, like him, also wrinkled and toothless. There is another god who tops Mesoamerican popularity polls: The mysterious Quetzalcóatl or "feathered snake." Originally an animal deity and fundamentally aquatic (the snake, as it slithers across cultivated fields, is in permanent contact with water), it gradually mutated into a celestial deity identified with the planet Venus. Another obsessive figure and one of the most spectacular in Mesoamerican religion is Xipe Totec or "Our Lord the Flayed One," who was initially perceived as a god of the renewal of nature, before engendering one of the religion's most disturbing acts: Humans were ritually flayed in his honor. Priests and sometimes even ordinary citizens then sported for forty days the skin of the unfortunate victims in their commendable desire for mortification. The so-called erotic deities, apparently more amiable, celebrated more the regeneration of the forms of the cosmos than the hedonistic, carnal pleasures of sex. One should not forget that the Mesoamericans were not great ones for pleasure.

The god Xipe Totec. Polychrome ceramic. H. 37.8".
Museo Regional de Antropologia Historia, Puebla, Mexico.

THE MEZCALA "IDOLS": MIRACLES OF SIMPLICITY

Of the many mysteries still shrouding the history of pre-Colombian civilizations, the Mezcala culture, which developed during the third and second millennium BC in the state of Guerrero, is still one of the most intriguing. How can one explain the extraordinary profusion of statuettes carved in serpentine, limestone, and jadeite, whose formal purity and geometric abstraction are so reminiscent of the Cycladic "idols"? Should we see them as personifications of honored ancestors, as substitutes for the deceased, or amulets for gaining the favor of good and evil spirits? In the absence of texts that could shed light on them, these little miracles of simplicity amidst the resolutely baroque art of the pre-Colombian civilizations continue to puzzle us.

Three statuettes from the Mezcala region. 300–100 BC. Mexico. Museo Barbier-Mueller de Arte Precolombino, Barcelona.
Preceding pages: **Huehueteotl, god of fire.** Circa AD 800–600. El Zapotal, Veracruz, Mexico. Terracotta. H. 22.6". Museo Barbier-Mueller de Arte Precolombino, Barcelona.
Chalchihuitlicue, goddess of water and fertility. Post-classic Aztec period (1300–1521). Mexico. Basalt. H. 16". Museo Barbier-Mueller de Arte Precolombino, Barcelona.

The Olmec Mystery, or the Disturbing Smile of the Child-Jaguar-Changeling

Olmeca,"the rubber people," was the Aztecs' poetic name for the mysterious peoples who lived along the inhospitable shores of the Gulf Coast, in the region of the present-day states of Veracruz and Tabasco. Archaeologists are still arguing about their precise origin. Some believe they came from Central America, while others trace them to the Mayas.
But regardless of this enigma, the originality of the Olmec visual language is undeniable. The chubby-cheeked "child-jaguar-changeling" with its disturbing smile dominates Olmec art and serves as a reminder of this distinct artistic originality.

One doesn't have to be a specialist to be able to recognize the Olmec style. One is immediately struck by its false naivety and serenity. It is as though all human representation was subjected to extreme rigor, taboo even: Smooth skulls have a strange sugar-loaf form (probably a depiction of a physical deformation practiced for a social or ritual purpose), and faces seem to be contorted in suffering, the corners of their mouths frozen in a tragic grimace. There is no sexual differentiation or erotic depiction, and, even if the Olmecs modeled statuettes of small children in clay, they took care to never suggest any "promise" of either male or female sex organs. The same severity

Anthropo-zoomorphic axe. La Venta archeological site, Tabasco, Mexico. Jade. Traces of cinnabar. Museo Nacional de Antropologia, Mexico City.
Following pages: **Anthropo-zoomorphic axe.** Unknown provenance. Jade. British Museum, London.
Detail of a stele with a stylized face of a man. Bas-relief. Museo de Antropologia, Jalapa, Mexico.

seems to govern that thematic icon of Olmec art, the jaguar. Stylized to the point of abstraction, anthropomorphized, and represented (more rarely) in an even more zoomorphic form, the great American wild cat reigns like a leitmotif over the whole Gulf Coast and even further afield.

Yet it would be wrong to reduce the whole Olmec religion to the figure of this cat alone. As early as this distant era (circa 1,200 to 500 BC), the theme of the jaguar seems to have acquired the status of a complex symbol that can be interpreted on different levels. One generally finds the cat associated with the Earth, or more precisely, the subterranean depths of its caves and caverns. A creature of darkness, it is the

ally par excellence of the night and the nocturnal world. As a predator, it joins forces with the eagle, who is represented by the Sun. (One should remember that in Mesoamerica, the Sun was above all the great consumer, an insatiable devourer of energy.) As an explicitly subterranean and telluric creature, the Olmec jaguar thus embodies the Sun during its nocturnal course, while the bird of prey symbolizes its diurnal trajectory. And it isn't by chance that the jaguar is also associated with fire—

Offering no. 4 at La Venta: ceremony comprising 16 figurines gathered around 6 steles.
Olmec. La Venta archeological site, Tabasco, Mexico. Jade.
Museo Nacional de Antropologia, Mexico City.

Anthropomorphic mask. Olmec. 850–450 BC. Guerrero, Mexico. Wood with jade inlay. H. 6.6". American Museum of Natural History, New York.

a cosmic power, a vector of movement, and both a creative and destructive energy. It follows from this disquieting dimension that the jaguar is also the great devourer of lives. Some anthropologists have postulated that there may have been an ancient tradition involving offering human prey to the divine predator to appease its wrath and hunger. If there is every reason to presume that babies were sacrificed, it can hardly be excluded that the Olmecs also ritually offered prisoners of war to these deified wild cats. In which case, they were neither the first nor last Mesoamericans to have indulged in such practices.

If there is an omnipresent, even obsessive figure in Olmec art, it is definitely the one archeologists have poetically baptized the "child-jaguar-changeling." But these ambiguous half-human and half-cat creatures, baring their fearsome teeth, are usually shown . . . weeping. Yet there is no trace of psychology or pathos in this puzzling

Figurine, probably a rain spirit. Olmec. 800–300 BC. Las Boscas archeological site, Puebla, Mexico. Ceramic. H. 13.2". Nelson A. Rockefeller Collection. Metropolitan Museum of Art, New York.

Olmec male statue. Olmec. 1200–800 BC. Pre-classical period. Mexico. Green serpentine. H. 3.9". Museo Barbier-Mueller de Arte Precolombino, Barcelona.

image. On the contrary, Christian Duverger sees these tears as the "very link in the jaguar/child symbolism." The other major figure in Olmec art is the "lit tle baby" with chubby cheeks and a plump, even bloated body, often shown sitting with its legs slightly apart and with no trace of genitals. For the French ethnologist, there can be no doubt that young children were indeed sacrificed, as they were the primary intermediary between man and the gods for bringing rain. "And while these children were being taken to the place where they would die, if they cried, if they shed a great many tears, those who saw them crying rejoiced because they saw this as a sign that rain would come in abundance," the Spanish chronicler Bernardino de Sahagún wrote about the children the Aztecs sacrificed to Tláloc, the god of rain.

But it would be wrong to consider the mysterious Olmecs merely as bloodthirsty bar-

Small Olmec mask (detail). Olmec. 800–400 BC. Las Choapas, Veracruz, Mexico. Serpentine. H. 4.7". Museo Barbier-Mueller de Arte Precolombino, Barcelona.

barians. These men, who seemingly sprang out of nowhere, built huge metropolises, sculpted colossal stone heads (thought by some to be effigies of ancestors or sovereigns, but were, most likely, the decapitated heads of enemies displayed as trophies), erected steles, which, in many respects, foreshadowed those of the Mayas of Copan and Quiriga, and above all, polished magnificent axe blades, which they buried as offerings. It is as if the Olmec culture already contained all the ingredients that would fashion the Mesoamerican identity over the next millennia.

A single material exemplifies the aesthetic in which art and the holy are one and the same thing: Jade, a beautiful rock with emerald green veins. Figurines, masks, ear ornaments, necklace beads, stilettos, "spoons," spear throwers, curious scale models of zoomorphic pirogues: there is hardly an Olmec object that was not fashioned from the divine stone. The choice to use this material was not gratuitous. Jade was believed by many Mesoamerican peoples to be a perennial substitute for blood, its solid and durable equivalent. And it was not by chance that it was the material for funerary offerings. Through symbolic associations and attributes, which only Mesoamerica seems to have created, the green stone was linked to water and its corollary, fertility. It was the stone of life and death and of sacrifice and rebirth.

Contrary to popular belief, the Olmecs did not suddenly disappear without a trace around 500 BC. Some rather fanciful archeologists have suggested there may have been a volcanic eruption that eradicated the group. Others have postulated that there were violent uprisings and sacked cities. Mutilated monuments and a series of seven deliberately buried sculptures were unearthed at San Lorenzo. But irre- spective of these enigmas (Mesoamerican archeology is still only its very early stages), there will always be the expressiveness of Olmec art, one of the most powerful that humanity has ever created.

Jaguar mask. Olmec. Jade. H. 7".
Peabody Museum of Archaeology and Ethnology, Harvard University.

INGENIOUS TOWN PLANNERS

Olmec tomb built with basalt columns. Discovered in Mound A-2 at La Venta. Now in the Villahermosa Archaeological Museum, Tabasco, Mexico.

The Olmecs were not only highly skilled sculptors but also remarkable town planners, as revealed by the excavations carried out in 1941 on the site at La Venta. Apart from the famous colossal heads mentioned above (carved from basalt blocks between 1,200 and 800 BC, with their surprisingly chubby features, disdainful mouth, and snub nose), the American archaeologists unearthed an important ceremonial center spread over huge artificial platforms. During this very early period, when the evidence of pyramids, slopes around ball game fields, and altars and sepulchers had already emerged, other excavations on the sites at San Lorenzo and Tres Zapotes revealed the extraordinary sophistication of Olmec sacred architecture. The Olmecs also seem to have paid great attention to the problems of storing water (networks of underground canals and tanks were unearthed), and, in doing so, followed in the footsteps of their farming forefathers.

Detail of a colossal head. Olmec. San Lorenzo, Veracruz, Mexico. Basalt. H. 111″. Museo de la Universidad de Veracruz.

A SKILLFULLY CODIFIED DEPICTION OF THE BODY

Although Olmec faces and bodies are almost mechanical in their coldness, their garments and finery reached rarely equaled heights of refinement. They also practiced piercing, stretching, distending, filing, cranial deformation, and used bands to compress the arms and ankles, labrets to dilate the lips, and perforated the ears and nose. As well as these mutilations, which denoted distinct social differences, there were probably also sacred body paintings and tattoos. A great many jade and basalt statuettes are covered with an iconography that is both cosmic and cosmetic. Certain Olmec figurines have strangely smooth skulls and, originally, probably sported removable headdresses, too perishable to have survived down the ages. There is every reason to think that the Olmecs did not go bareheaded. The hopelessly naked sculptures we know today must surely once have been decked in shimmering cloth, feather, and basketwork finery.

Female statue. Olmec. 800–400 BC. Gulf region, Mexico. Chlorite, with traces of cinnabar indicating a funerary use. H. 2.8". Museo Barbier-Mueller de Arte Precolombino, Barcelona.

Pyramid of the Sun. View of the fortress.Teotihuacán, Mexico. H. 213 ft. L. 719 ft.

In the Shadows of the Pyramids of Teotihuacán

Between 200 BC and AD 650, on the vast, volcano-studded plain in the north of present-day Mexico, there flourished the majestic and all-powerful holy city of Teotihuacán, a twenty square kilometer metropolis of avenues, ceremonial squares, residential quarters, and sacred edifices.
But in the early eighth century, by one of those strange twists of history, this glorious city and the civilization that created it suddenly and inexplicably went into economic and cultural decline, whose reasons archeologists have still not entirely elucidated.

By what whim of destiny did a handful of farming hamlets scattered over an arid valley, in only a few centuries become a harmonious city of temples, the magnificent sight of which left every visitor dumbstruck? On the eve of the third century AD, Teotihuacán, with its quadripartite plan dominated by the overbearing masses of its Pyramid of the Sun and Pyramid of the Moon, already had the air of a ceremonial center. There later sprung up houses of such extraordinary refinement and such a far cry from the rustic dwellings of the past that they could almost be considered palaces. At the same time, the city seems to have had a corporative topography. Pottery was produced and obsidian carved in certain quarters, while other districts were reserved for stonemasons or artisans who fashioned objects in stucco, shell, or slate. Some areas seem to have been given over to foreign populations—the Oaxaca Valley, for instance, if their funerary remains are evidence.

Scene on a tripod. A priest king and four men with spears.
Teotihuacán, Mexico. From *After Expedition*, vol. 2, 1960.

It was also around this time that the iconography of the main deities seems to have become fixed, such as the dreamlike and baroque image of the famous Quetzalcóatl. One only has to admire the exuberant decoration of the temple dedicated to him in the very heart of the citadel (the presumed residence of the supreme chief). Everything seems to bear the signature of the flamboyant feathered snake: Coils undulate between polychrome shell friezes, while on the façade, at regular intervals, the head of the divine reptile alternates with that of another hybrid figure: Tláloc, the god of rain. This decoration is a cosmic representation in stone, unifying sky, Earth, and water.

But if it appears to modern-day viewers to be dark and implacably austere, the temple of Quetzalcóatl must originally have been a blaze of color. At Teotihuacán, as in many other places in Mesoamerica, public edifices and sanctuaries gleamed with stuccoed and painted surfaces. This orgy of decoration had to be carefully maintained; otherwise, as soon as it lost its dazzle, it was covered over with another layer of stucco colored with vivid pigments and dyes. A dark red obtained from hematite superseded the white of the ancient temples. Pyrite black, malachite green, but also a deep blue and a bright yellow and orange later enriched the palette of these painters, who vied with one another in their virtuosity and experimentation

Brazier (detail). Nahua, Teotihuacán, Mexico. Polychrome ceramic.
Museo Nacional de Antropologia, Mexico City.

with materials. Ever eager to obtain even more shimmering, brilliant colors, they began introducing clay into their pigments, as a fixer but also to enable them to be polished. One even finds mica, a component of volcanic rock, in the famous and unmistakably lustrous Teotihuacán red.

But this hunger for materials had disastrous effects on the city's surroundings. To produce the lime needed for the mortar, thousands of tons of limestone were fed into ovens fuelled by thousands of trees—an ecological catastrophe that the bald hills surrounding Mexico City today illustrate. But these materials were not for utilitarian constructions but for acts of worship and little heed was paid to environmental preoccupations. One suspects that behind these dazzling effects and gaudy colors, there lay a concerted ambition to impose the city's own vision of the world. Teotihuacán was a truly ideal city. Its huge edifices were deployed over vast perspectives. One principle—horizontality—predominated, as if to ensure the stability of their pyramidal forms, which were themselves embodiments of the powers of the gods they were dedicated to. The homogenization of the city's buildings, their sense of order and symmetry, and a grid system of long avenues (including the nicely named north-south artery, the Avenue of the Dead) completed the solemnity and grandiloquence of this concerted urban planning. Another leitmotif was the architectural style archaeologists refer to as "talud-tablero," which designates a stepped pyramidal structure consisting of flat, horizontal planes or tableros, and angled sides sloping at forty-five and fifty degrees called taluds. By emphasizing their structures' horizontals, the architects of Teotihuacán spread out their volumes, which was another way of stressing their adherence to the Earth and accentuating their solidity. The pyramids of ancient Mexico therefore seem squashed compared with their Egyptian counterparts.

Mask. Teotihuacán, classic period. AD 200–900. Ceramic. H. 7.4". Museo Nacional de Antropologia, Mexico City. Preceding pages: **Wall of the Temple of Quetzalcóatl.** Teotihuacán, Mexico. **Plumed serpent** (detail). Temple of Quetzalcóatl, Teotihuacán, Mexico.

But Teotihuacán demonstrated its genius not only in its clear and planned architecture. A colossal statue, echoing the squat forms of the pyramids, was discovered close to the Pyramid of the Moon. Now in the National Museum of Anthropology in Mexico City, the three-meter-high Great Goddess, a barely hewn block of basalt, from whose stiff skirt emerge vaguely sculpted, stump-like legs, seems to look each visitor severely up and down.

Ceramics (tripod vases, vases with long thin necks, and statuettes with bizarrely articulated limbs) attempted to be more amiable, however. A warm orange color came into use, probably around AD 300. But here again, one should be prudent: Some archaeologists see this beautiful, thin-walled ware as a marker of the Teotihuacán civilization, others suggest, on the contrary, that these pieces were imported from the State of Puebla. Mexican fantasy explodes, however, with an extraordinary piece the Mexicanists call the *pato loco,* or the "mad duck," a strange winged creature with a jagged crest, bulging jadeite eyes, and gaudy orange, white, and red shell ornaments.

Alas, this ceramic oddity, which one could almost take for a fake, would soon be superseded by mass-produced ware that gradually became increasingly standardized. Even the famous hard stone funerary masks gradually lost their macabre opulence. A coating of stucco often concealed the clumsiness, even negligence of the lapidary.

Teotihuacán's exterior and interior mural paintings attained heights of exuberance. They depict a dreamlike and refined universe made up of ritual processions of priests or warriors that sport the attributes or appearance of their tutelary animal (jaguar, eagle, coyote, etc.), feathered snakes that fly over rows of trees of different species, and birds armed with shields or spears (it is tempting to evoke the Aztecan belief that soldiers killed in action were reincarnated as birds with flamboyant plumage). Divinities and sovereigns

Preceding pages: **Funerary mask.** AD 300–600. Teotihuacán, Mexico. Green stone. H. 9.4". Museo Nacional de Antropologia, Mexico City.
Funerary mask. Stone and obsidian. H. 7.8". Museo del Templo Mayor, Mexico City.

alike wore sumptuous attire, adorned with priceless jewelry on embroideries, feathers, and precious stones. The excavation of a residence among a group of houses to the west of Tepantitla unearthed an extraordinary mural of Tlalocan, paradise of the god Tláloc, which showed, on the banks of its rivers, a host of small figures dancing and singing amidst trees and butterflies.

When they discovered these charming and flowery pictures, many specialists went into raptures about the pacific nature of this theocracy. But this failed to recognize many of the symbols and allusions that covered the walls of Teotihuacán. If one looks closer, many of these birds are in fact eagles drinking human blood, and many of the coyotes are about to devour human hearts. As for the glyphs painted on the floor of a vast patio, "It is reasonable to see them as the names of conquered cities to be symbolically downtrodden by the warriors who gathered there for commemorative ceremonies" (Duverger, 1999).

By its apogee in the third century AD, the stylistic and spiritual influence of the huge capital of the high plateaus had spread far afield. One can discern its mark in the Gulf region and also in the vast northern spaces of Mexico, where merchants searched for turquoise, which, like jade, had virtues linked to fertility. In the fourth and fifth centuries, Teotihuacán seems to have asserted its ascendancy a thousand kilometers further south, over the city of Kaminaljuyú in the highlands of Guatemala, and as far as Tikal, the prestigious capital of the Mayas. From then on the Mesoamerican identity seems to have been widely established, with Teotihuacán as its driving force. It was not by chance that the Aztecs, many centuries later, constantly invoked its tutelary divinities and monuments. And yet at the dawn of the seventh century, the first signs of decline began to appear: Artistic creativity seemed to dry up, as though a kind of torpor had overcome the city and its population. Here again, some have suggested a hypothesis of a cataclysm, others of internecine uprisings. The answer may be much simpler and crueler: The great metropolis of Central Mexico may have gradually lost its raison d'être—its cosmological and spiritual belief system—and died a metaphysical death.

THE CHARMING "FUNERARY URNS" OF THE ZAPOTECS

In the heart of the present-day Oaxaca State, at the confluence of the Atoyac and Salado rivers, the archeological zone of Monte Albán, listed as a UNESCO World Heritage site in 1987, covers an area of some forty square kilometers, only six of which have been explored. Between around 150 BC and AD 650, it was covered with a grandiose ensemble of temples and sanctuaries generally attributed to the Zapotecs. But their origin is certainly more complex, as the site has revealed a mosaic of diverse cultural influences. At its apogee, Monte Albán had a population of some thirty thousand. The wealth and refinement of this culture can be seen in the extraordinary ceramics found in the tombs, which have incorrectly been thought to be funerary urns. They were, in fact, probably effigies of important figures or gods, easily recognizable by their ritual ornaments. Sitting cross-legged and decked in their sumptuous jewelry and feathered headdresses, they either gaze at the viewer intently or hide behind bat or jaguar masks. Roughly sculpted arms and legs, hardly more than stumps, emerge from their thickset bodies.

Did these watchers over eternity, placed in the tombs of the kingdom's dignitaries, protect the sleep of the deceased? Among the most depicted deities are Cocijo, the god of rain; Huehueteotl, the god of fire; Murciélago, the bat god, who reigned over the dead; and Xipe Totec, the god of spring and new vegetation.

Since their discovery in the mid-nineteenth century, fake "Zapotec urns" have been produced by the thousand. To cater to the increasing European demand (in 1842, a selection of objects unearthed at Oaxaca was exhibited in Seville), indigenous peoples rediscovered the skills of their ancestors and began producing urns as perfect as their prestigious models. The market was also soon flooded with authentic pieces discovered during the construction of the railroad between Mexico City and Oaxaca in 1880. Thermoluminescence dating is the only means of distinguishing a genuine Zapotec urn from a beautiful curio of dubious origin.

Funerary urns. Zapotec. AD 200–800. Oaxaca State, Mexico.
Museo Nacional de Antropologia, Mexico City.

The Mayan Golden Age

The Mayas are often referred to as "the Greeks of the New World," and indeed few peoples have exercised such fascination over the general public. There is hardly a mass-circulation magazine that does not periodically run a rapturous feature on the archeological discovery of one of their cities in the heart of the jungle, the deciphering of their writing, the "science" of their astronomy, or their mysterious disappearance. But recent remarkable studies of the Mayas have made quite a dent in this romantic vision and its deep-rooted clichés and myths. The inhabitants of present-day Guatemala, Belize, the western fringes of Honduras and Salvador, the Mexican states of Campeche, Yucatán, and Quintana Roo, and part of Chiapas and Tabasco certainly did create a profoundly original and extremely refined civilization. The Mayas were the only pre-Colombians to have systematically faced their religious edifices and palaces with stone. They built soaring pyramids in which they buried their sovereigns with great pomp, recorded their rituals and the results of their scientific observations in sumptuous codices, and modeled all the actors of their society in clay, decked in all their magnificent finery. And their frescoes are among the most beautiful pre-Colombian civilization produced.

Jaguar Bird receiving the jaguar helmet he will wear in combat from his wife, Lady Xoc (detail of a door frame). Maya. AD 726. Yaxchilan, Chiapas. Museo Nacional de Antropologia, Mexico City.

Yet behind this idyllic picture lies another truth. The Mayas were warriors and, like many other Mesoamerican civilizations, obeyed a military and sacrificial ide- ology focused on the quest for power and territorial expansion. Their art, utterly dominated by the obsessive figure of the sovereign and profoundly religious, was a vehicle for both power and the sacred. And as for the Mayas' supposed Golden Age, the least that can be said is that it was remarkably short-lived—yet another reason to reexamine their masks, jade statuettes, and stucco and stone altar effigies in a different light.

But those in search of exoticism and thrills have come to the right place. There are all the right ingredients: Shipwrecked Spanish sailors, the heroic resistance of several cities against their invaders, their conquerors' despair, and, finally, abandonment of lands deemed too unproductive. For many a century, neither the jungle of Yucatán nor the tropical forests of Petén seemed to attract the treasure-hungry and, even less, the missionaries. Only a handful of evangelists ventured into these lands peopled with infidels. After the initial mutual fascination came stake burnings and a brutal repression that would leave an indelible stigmata and force the Mayan peoples into radical and definitive isolation.

It was not until the mid-eighteenth century that these regions again aroused any curiosity—a curiosity that this time was tinged with romanticism and not colonial or purely mercantile considerations. It was a priest, Father Antonio de Solís, who first drew attention to the ruins next to his small village in Palenque. The King of Spain reacted immediately, dispatching an armada of officers and draftsmen to explore, describe, draw, and pillage the site. *Mexican Antiquities,* which was published in 1823 and featured a preface by François-René de Chateaubriand, also had an immediate effect. All manner of adventurers and explorers flocked to these tropical lands of the New World. The journalist John L. Stevens, accompanied by the talented draftsman Frederick Catherwood, enthusiastically roamed the length and breadth of Honduras and the highlands of Guatemala and went as far as

Yucatán. His description and Catherwood's virtuoso sketches and drawings cloaked the Mayas in an extraordinary aura. But the paths of the explorers would soon cross those of the archeologists. The sensitive photographs Désiré Charnay took of monuments between 1857 and 1859 are all the more moving because some of these edifices have since disappeared. Alfred P. Maudsley laid the foundations of a rigorous methodology during the excavations he carried out in 1889 on the site at Chichén Itzá. The distinction between archaeologist and adventurer is often blurred, and it was the independent explorer Giles Healey who made one of the most spectacular discoveries: The flamboyant frescoes at Bonampak.

Then, at the very beginning of the twentieth century, the great universities, mostly American—the Peabody Museum (the ethnological museum of the University of Harvard) and the Carnegie Institute in Washington—entered the fray. They concentrated on the excavation of the major sites (Mayapán, Copán, and Uaxactún) and established an initial chronological framework. Yet it was not until the 1950s that the full complexity of the Mayan world began to emerge. The excavations on the site at Tikal, carried out over some fifteen years, created a picture of a colorful and lively city of around seventy thousand inhabitants. Recently, European (German, French, and Spanish) teams have focused their attention, and spades, on increasingly coveted archaeological sites—local authorities have unfortunately become increasingly aware of the economic value of these grandiose sites as tourist destinations. In some regions, untimely regional development programs and oil exploration have ruined the work of archaeologists forever. All of which would be almost tolerable were it not for the pillaging. Countless pyramids have been emptied of their contents and steles and monuments sawn off or dynamited. Trafficking in artworks is big business in this part of the world. Fortunately, however, scientific publications and exhibitions (including the memorable one at the

Following pages: **Fuchsite mask** (front and inside). Maya. AD 400–500. Guatemala. H. 7.7".
Museo Barbier-Mueller de Arte Precolombino, Barcelona.

The Temple of the Sun, Palenque. Maya. Chiapas, Mexico.
Right: **Priest.** Maya. Wood. H. 49.2". Nelson A. Rockefeller Collection.
Metropolitan Museum of Art, New York.

Palazzo Grassi in Venice in 1998) are constantly revealing a Mayan world infinitely more complex and ambiguous than previously thought.

For someone visiting these regions for the first time, the overriding impression is one of diversity, confusion even. Each archaeological site—its sculpture, construction, and manner of occupation—seems to unearth a new experiment. It is as if each city wanted to prove its ingeniousness and extravagance and invent its own artistic language. In only a few centuries, the Mayas, whose civilization reached its peak in the seventh or eighth centuries, covered their land with pyramids, ball game fields, and palaces. Much has been written about this one-upmanship, the frenetic "keeping up appearances" that would become a lasting record of the rivalry between the many small Mayan city-states. As Christian Duverger explained, "the Mayan world did not awaken to civilization on its own but under the pressure of neighboring Mesoamerican peoples."

Anthropomorphic figure emerging from a flower.
Maya. Jaina Island, Campeche, Mexico. Terra-cotta.
H. 4.7". Museo Nacional de Antropologia, Mexico City.
Right: **Female figurine with a *huipil* (cape) and scarifications around the mouth.**
Maya. AD 600–800. Jaina Island, Campeche, Mexico.
Terracotta, Kurt Stavenhagen Collection, Mexico City.

Attacking Warriors. Maya. Late pre-classic period. Chiapas, Mexico.
Reconstruction of Chamber 2 of the Bonampak frescoes.

But it was not until Mayan civilization's third phase (from 600–650 to 800 AD, according to Duverger) that its creative genius fully bloomed. "The great sites experienced a second life; they interbred and spread at a frenetic rate. The dense tropical forest was colonized by innumerable groups led by power-hungry chiefs. These tribes deforested, built, and sculpted, imitating the great cities. Everyone strove to leave their mark, create a style, forge myths, and consolidate their legitimacy, using ever more imagination, effort and creativity . . . One can easily imagine and follow this fantastic blooming and the qualitative changes it brought about. It was not a sudden change in population that triggered this frenzied activity but their very idea of life which changed. The Mayas threw themselves into a race for riches and power. Everyone now invested all their capacities in a competition which does not seem to have been simply tribal rivalry. The stakes were higher. The Mayas were intent on conquering Mesoamerican supremacy."

Bas-relief on the flagstone in the crypt of the Temple of Inscriptions (detail).
Maya. Palenque, Mexico.

The vision of a Mayan civilization existing as a Garden of Eden, forged by tropical indolence and sensuality, is suddenly obsolete. There is no doubt in Duverger's mind that the period of Mayan expansion coincided exactly with the weakening of neighboring Mesoamerican peoples. "The aura of Teotihuacán had paled; the city of the gods was half abandoned, Monte Albán was on the decline, and Tula was not yet born. This was the trough of the wave. The Mayas saw their chance and seized it." Duverger's brilliant explanation throws new light on many of the frescoes that decorated their temples and palaces, and on many a hook-nosed profile of a prince or priest. It is often the language of force and domination that is glorified on steles and in bas-reliefs. And one obsessive all-powerful figure dominates all others: The sovereign. The king is literally every- where, alone or accompanied by servants, captives, or ancestors, depicted in majesty or in action and on lintels, crest tiles, stucco panels, façades, ceramics, and the stone marker discs used in ball games. The explanation of this frenetic image worship is simple: The Mayan king was an omnipotent sovereign protected by the Sun. As a cosmic power, it was he who had to ensure the survival of his community and people. And as chief of his warriors, he exposed himself to the perils of armed combat. On the lintels of Structure 1 at Bonampak, one can see him capturing an enemy by seizing him by the hair. There is no concern with anecdotal details: The main aim of war was to obtain ever more sacrificial victims. The image of the warrior-king is accompanied by that of the priest-king, who offers his blood and the blood of others' to the powers of other worlds. Self-sacrifice by mutilation (by piercing his ears, tongue, or penis), particularly well illustrated at Yaxchilán, was also one of the Mayan sovereign's duties.

But the king's responsibilities were just as overwhelming in peacetime. He had to ensure that the universe functioned smoothly and it was he who performed the rituals that brought rain to ensure good harvests. During festivals celebrating the ends of *katuns* (twenty-year cycles), he is depicted with small pearls falling from his open right hand, which some specialists believe to be corn seeds, incense, or even drops of his own blood. According to the eminent Americanist Claude-François Baudez, the Maya perceived the sovereign's body itself as a microcosm: His feathered headdress refers to the bird, an incarnation of the daily Sun, and his jade ear ornaments, necklaces, and pectorals symbolize fertilizing rain. His belt, adorned with celestial symbols, established the division between the upper and lower worlds of this corporal cosmography. And his jaguar pelt skirt and the wild cat's mask, which decorated his loincloth, clearly referenced the nocturnal Sun and the underworld.

In many respects, the grandiose, oversize architecture of the pyramids and palaces also appears to be a dazzling example of the theatrical staging of dynastic power. Even when the sovereign was absent, his image was manifest in vertiginous flights of steps, crest tiles, steles, and altars. It was the Mayas who built the tallest edifices in the New World. Some temples at Tikal and El Mirador are over seventy meters high—a height surpassed only by Teotihuacán's Pyramid of the Sun and Mexico's Templo Mayor. But inherent in their sheer size is their terrifying verticality. If the imposing massiveness of the monuments of Teotihuacán petrify, Mayan monuments dominate with their sheer height. Some archaeologists even think that the *cresteria* (crests) of the temples were an architectonic addition, merely to heighten the sensation of verticality. And so it comes as no surprise that this architectural headdress often represents the sovereign in a majestic or stylized face of a jaguar god.

Whatever the symbolism of the Mayan pyramids and palaces (megalomaniac demonstrations of power or "trampolines" to Heaven), one can only admire the technical achievement of these vertiginous edifices. Sometimes even the architec-

Following pages: **Lithograph of a stele** (AD 731. Copán, Honduras. H. 142") of a woman with headdress and two-headed snake scepter. By F. Catherwood published in *Views of Ancient Monuments in Central America* (1884). **Cylindrical vessel with anthropomorphic lid.** Maya. AD 600–800. Tikal, El Petén, Guatemala. Jade. H. 9.4".Museo Nacional de Arqueología y Etnología, Guatemala City.

Enthronement of Yax Pak (detail). Maya. AD 775. Copán, Honduras. Limestone. British Museum, London.

ture itself becomes sculpture when masks of monsters or celestial snakes spring dramatically from the façades. The Mayas' consummate mastery of trompe l'oeil achieved its most grandiloquent expression in the style adopted by the cities of Río Bec and in the Chenes region. Here, the palace itself becomes a gigantic demonic creature: The door is its wide open mouth and the threshold and lintel its jaws. If one looks carefully, in the middle of the façade, one can make out this terrestrial monster's muzzle and its bulging eyes, staring out over the square in front of the palace. Innumerable motifs (such as ear ornaments and the god's attributes), covering the walls like a beautiful and gigantic tattoo, complete this metamorphosis. But it is definitely in their steles that the Mayas showed all their originality and

Facade of the left wing of the Palace of the Nuns. Chichen Itzá, Mexico. Photograph by Désiré Charnay (1857–59) published in *Cités et ruines américaines,* no. 28, Gide, Morel & Cie, Paris, 1863.

expressed themselves to the full. In the city of Calakmul alone, 113 were found. From one to two meters high (except for certain types, which can be up to ten meters), these ornately decorated rectangular blocks were usually carved out of soft limestone. The front was devoted to royal effigies, while the sides were covered with columns of glyphs. These imposing and eminently sacred sculptures were placed at regular intervals in front of temple pyramids or in squares and were brought offerings and dedicatory gifts. They were erected at the end of each katun.

Mayan sculptors also showed their extraordinary virtuosity in small pieces carved in wood, jade, shell, bone, and stucco. The most beautiful, discovered in the tombs of high-ranking dignitaries, are exquisitely refined. Funerary masks made from sewn-together plaques, articulated earrings, necklaces, pectorals, pendants, bracelets, and ankle ornaments, all combining materials and colors as much for their beauty as for their symbolism, further enhanced the prestige of the deceased.

Mayan ceramics, with their varied repertoire of delightful scenes whose symbolism sometimes escapes us, are just as exquisite: The plaited pigtail motif, signifying royal power or a series of semicircles, invoking the Sun or the silhouette of the king-priest, writing down a scientific observation or recording a cabalist ceremony. On vases, one sometimes even sees mysterious masked figures, bleeding stags, or jaguars pierced with arrows. Much has been written about these enigmatic comic strips, whose accompanying glyphs probably served as subtitles. Are they the formal equivalent of the codex, describing the mythology of the hells, or do they reveal some scene from the next world?

A host of other just-as-original pieces, like a manual of fashion and customs, provide a mine of information about the Mayas' clothing, tattoos, and finery.

Preceding pages: **Murals discovered in 1946 in the Templo de las Pinturas.** Maya. AD 790–792. Maya. Bonampak, Chiapas, Mexico.
Seated figure. Simojovel, Chiapas. Clay. 11.3" X 6.4".
Museo Regional de Chiapas, Tuxtla-Gutiérrez, Mexico.

Individuals, irrespective of their sexual dimorphism, are generally depicted in profile, with a receding forehead, elongated sugar-loaf skull, slightly hooked nose, and almond-shaped eyes. Was this out of a concern for social or ethnic differentiation, or an aesthetic canon? Nobody knows. One thing is clear, though: Not anyone could be a Maya. Those not belonging to the community were portrayed with markedly straighter foreheads and more prominent chins.

The island of Jaïna (some thirty kilometers north of the town of Campeche), explored by Désiré Charnay in 1886, yielded innumerable small-modeled or molded figurines, still with their original vivid colors. Enchanted specialists and collectors discovered a world of lords dressed in heavy finery, women bent over their looms, warriors in ceremonial dress, musicians shaking maracas, ball game players in action, prisoners being tortured . . . Suddenly there was the whole of Mayan society before their dazzled eyes. But the provenance of some of these pieces, too beautiful and too realist to be true, is definitely suspicious. The excavations carried out in 1964 may have filled the display cases of the National Museum of Anthropology in Mexico City a little too generously.

But there is nothing at all suspicious about the magnificent "pieces of painting" that have miraculously survived. Just like architecture and sculpture, of which they were an integral part, frescoes participated in the proclamation of the order of the world and glorification of the sovereign. There is little anecdote, and their aesthetics are entirely subordinated to expressing triumph. Although most paintings decorated the interiors of buildings (as at Bonampak, where the frescoes could be seen only by a privileged few), they were nevertheless glorification and propaganda vehicles, depicting fantastic figures and battle scenes in astonishing detail.

Following pages: **Monumental mask at the base of the Great Pyramid at Izamal.** Yucatán, Mexico. Photograph by Désiré Charnay (1857–59) published in *Cités et ruines américaines,* no. 25, Gide, Morel & Cie, Paris, 1863. **Sculpture.** Maya. Late classic period (7th–10th century). Palenque, Chiapas, Mexico. Stucco. H. 9.5". Gift of Désiré Charnay. Formerly in musée de l'Homme. Musée du Quai Branly, Paris.

And their palette was just as strident. Judging by the best-preserved vestiges, Mayan edifices must have gleamed with dazzling colors that today we would find shocking. Like Greek temples and medieval cathedrals, the stucco monuments at Palenque were originally Technicolor spectacles. Each color had its precise symbolism: Red evoked death and rebirth, green represented the feathers of the quetzal or jade jewelry (symbols of fertility), and yellow and black the jaguar skin (an attribute of the sovereign).

But these are just tiny fragments of our incomplete and distorted picture of Mayan civilization. How many wooden sculptures have crumbled to dust, how many feather headdresses have been destroyed, and how many glyphs and codices have been effaced? Perhaps only the spectacle of a Mayan market, heady with scents and colors, could still give us a glimpse of the grandeur of a civilization whose sudden decline around the eighth century continues to puzzle us. Here again, specialists have come up with the wildest explanations and hypotheses. Gradual decline? Foreign invasions? Internecine struggles? Cultural aporia? Whatever the truth is, today, the Mayas are still living all over the vast territory their ancestors conquered over three thousand years ago and continue to speak their many languages and dialects. And their heroic political and cultural resistance is epitomized by one, tiny woman and her decorative clothes: Rigoberta Menchú, winner of the Nobel Peace Prize in 1992.

Fragment of an incense burner. Maya. AD 550–950. Rio Usumacinta Valley, Mexico, Terra-cotta, H. 9.9". Museo Barbier-Mueller de Arte Precolombino, Barcelona.

WRITING: AN ACT CLOSE TO DIVINATION

For the Yucatán Mayas, the center of the world was called Xocen—"Read me"—and the book was the origin of the world. "It is a natural book and was not made by anyone. The book turns its own pages. Each day a new page is turned, and if someone tries to turn it themselves, it bleeds because it is alive" (myth of the origin of the glyphic book quoted by the ethnologist Henri-Michel Boccara).

Names of gods, cities, dignitaries, sovereigns, dates of enthronements, ceremonies, births, deaths . . . the Mayas, like other Mesoamerican peoples, recorded everything, from the most minor to the most major of life's events, with glyphs or abstract symbols. But their love of signs was part of a genuine aesthetic in which writing was considered an art form in its own right, an autonomous medium in which scribes competed with painters and sculptors, on stone, wood, ceramics, jade, and shell.

Codex Troano and Codex Cortesianus *(Madrid Codex).* The Storm Goddess makes water with her breasts and from her vulva comes the the rain that soaks the earth. Classic period. Paint on paper and chalk engraving. Museo de América, Madrid.

But it was undoubtedly in their flamboyant codices that the Mayas showed their talent for calligraphy to the full. These books, made from deerskin or bark fiber, took the form of long strips and were folded like accordion bellows. Their very long texts meticulously recorded calculations or astrological observations and contained representations of deities. They were highly complex, and it was the priest's or soothsayer's task to write these glyphs and interpret them. There is nothing gratuitous about Mayan writing; it was essentially sacred and its use was divinatory.

Sadly, many codices must have been destroyed by the conquistadors and, later, by the ravages of time. Three examples of this liturgical literature have survived, however: One is in Dresden, another in Paris, and the third in Madrid. They are extremely difficult to read, as are most Mayan inscriptions, which seem to be deliberately ambiguous and hermetic.

It took relentless effort and perseverance to decipher Mayan writing. The Englishman J. Eric S. Thompson, who dominated research in the field from 1940 to 1960, made one of the most remarkable contributions. According to him, Mayan writing was based on a kind of puzzle, that is, the signs could be used for their phonetic sounds and not just their meaning. In the late 1950s, Tatiana Proskouriakoff and Heinrich Berlin definitively established that the content of Mayan inscriptions was principally historic. At the same time, the Russian Yuri Knorosov demonstrated that the Mayan system of writing was partly phonetic. In his view, the alphabet book recorded in Yucatán in the sixteenth century by the Franciscan bishop Diego de Landa and abusively considered the Rosetta stone of Mayan writing, was in fact merely a list of syllables.

But these two different approaches—structural and phonetic—both proved to be effective and productive. Many questions remain unanswered, though: What was the language of the inscriptions of the classical period? Yucatec, Chol,

Chorti, or Mopan? Could there have been a common, official language? This seems unlikely given the particularities of each city-state. The inscriptions and codices and the instruments of power and the sacred, give us an inevitably incomplete and fragmented vision of the Mayan world. Whatever the precise meaning of a Mayan text, it is an artistic message, a quest for immortality, a surpassing of oneself.

Mayan hieroglyphs. 8 of the 18 month signs and 8 of the 20 day signs. After Miguel Covarrubias in H.D. Disselhoff and S. Linné's *The Art of Ancient America*, Crown Publishing, New York, 1960.

Atlantes and Warriors: Toltec Military Art

Around AD 800 to 900, the whole of Mesoamerica seems to have experienced a period of profound upheaval. As the great sacred metropolises of Teotihuacán and Monte Albán were tottering under the assaults of invaders, a new era in Central Mexican history was dawning, starting with the rise of the Toltecs and their imposing capital, Tula, to the north of the Mexico City basin. Although Aztecan legends spread the myth of a fabulous city with palaces of gold, silver, and priceless feathers, archeologists have unearthed only modest vestiges, mainly figures of proud atlantes.

The art of the Toltecs attained its finest expression in the city of Chichén Itzá, capital of the Yucatán Peninsula until around 1220, in a perfect symbiosis of military aesthetics and the luxuriant Mayan tradition.

Chichén Itzá. Yucatán, Mexico.
Statue on top of the Temple of the Warriors, probably the rain god Tlaloc.

The god Chac-mool, guardian of the Temple of Chichén Itzá. Toltec. AD 900–1250. Yucatan, Mexico. Museo Nacional de Antropologia e Historia, Mexico City.

In the sixteenth century, the Spanish missionary Bernardino de Sahagún wrote *Historia general de las cosas de Nueva España* and stated: "At Tula, there abounded birds with rich plumage, the blue cotinga, the green-feathered quetzal, the zaquan with its yellow tail, the roseate spoonbill, and many other birds with sweet and melodious calls. Quetzalcóatl [sovereign of Tula] possessed all the riches of the world, gold, silver, green stones, and a thousand other priceless things. And cacao trees of different colors grew in abundance. All Quetzalcóatl's vassals were rich, never lacking in anything and knowing not hunger. There was such a profusion of corn they burned the small cobs to heat the steam houses."

It is hard to understand how, in only three centuries, a horde of uncouth, warlike nomads could take control of the whole of Mesoamerica and lay the foundations of a civilization with which the proud Aztecs would still identify many centuries later. The Toltecs, a people who spoke Nahua, were in fact former barbarians from the north, who gradually assimilated the cultures of the peoples they encountered during their

The god Chac-mool. Toltec. Temple of the Warriors, Chichén Itzá, Yucatán, Mexico.

Pyramid of Quetzalcóatl. Toltec. AD 800. Tula, Hidalgo, Mexico.

long migration south. The term "Toltecatl" (inhabitant of Tula) was not at all derogatory but, on the contrary, synonymous with "learned," "skilled craftsman," even "artist." And yet when one contemplates the ruins, which, in 1885, the Frenchman Désiré Charnay identified as ancient Tula, one can only be amazed. True, the Toltecs' capital was probably destroyed around 1200 and its temples and sanctuaries demolished before it was later occupied by the Aztecs. Built on a rocky outcrop, this majestic site still fills one with uneasiness. Tula was a city of mostly covered spaces. Vast hypostyle rooms sheltered the crowds converging on the temples. Its architecture, although entirely dedicated to the sacred, could hardly be said to be amiable. Its language was pragmatic, almost totalitarian. One can only be struck by the martial character of the four famous colossal statues archaeologists have called Temple B. Standing at attention, their empty eyes gazing out of impassive faces at some distant horizon, these atlantes represent the god in his Tlahuizcalpantecuhtli form, that is, as

Atlantes at the top of the Temple of Quetzalcóatl (Edifice B). Toltec. AD 800.
Tula, Hidalgo, Mexico. Stone. H. 14.5 feet.

Venus or the morning star. Their hieratic forms fit perfectly into an elongated rectangle, and on their chest they sport a curious, stylized butterfly emblem, symbolizing the resurrection of sacrificed warriors. But the most original creation of Toltec art are the Chacmool sculptures (whose formal purity and power would so fascinate the English sculptor Henry Moore). The symbolism and use of these sculptures, depicting half-reclined warriors resting on their elbows with their knees bent and head turned to one side, are still points of conjecture among Americanists. Are they messengers charged with taking offerings to the gods? Certain specialists consider them to be effigies of sacrificial victims themselves, their chests pointing toward Heaven. Others have suggested these sculptures were in fact the sacrificial stones on which victims were laid before their heart was torn out. One thing is certain: The figure of a Chacmool seems to be closely linked to ritual sacrifice. It is not by chance that its unmistakable silhouette is always seen on the top of pyramids, at the entrances to

An atlas, Temple of Quetzalcóatl, with his feathered headdress (detail). Toltec. AD 800. Tula, Hidalgo, Mexico.

temples, or in those particularly sacred places where the ball game was played. The Chacmool's very advent in Mesoamerican sculpture corresponds to a new climate of thought or, more precisely, to a form of ideological radicalization: Under the Toltecs, the bloody aspect of pre-Colombian sacrificial ritual intensified considerably.

Even if the Mayas, as we have seen, practiced self-mutilation, blood offering, and the immolation of war prisoners, the bloody aspect of their worship never attained such macabre and grandiosely orchestrated excesses. There were benches decorated with bas-reliefs showing decapitations, platforms decorated with human skulls, processions of jaguars devouring hearts, and farandoles of tibias. All the sculpted decoration at Tula, and then later at Chichén Itzá, bore the same stigmata of death—a death devoid of all pathos and psychology, a pragmatic, quasi-disincarnate, inhuman death. Only the worship of the green-feathered snake Quetzalcóatl, symbol of vegetation

Atlantes once supporting the porticos of the Temple of Quetzalcóatl, holding spears and a spear thrower. Toltec. Tula, Hidalgo, Mexico.

Stone relief at ball court (detail). Chichén Itzá, Yucatán, Mexico.

and renewal, seems to have slightly tempered the military austerity of Toltec culture. The greatest god of the kingdom was none other than Tezcatlipoca, god of war. It was military clans, the orders of the Eagles and Jaguars, who controlled all aspects of society. Power seems to have surreptitiously changed hands from the priest clans to the soldiers. But Toltec military totalitarianism did not triumph bloodlessly. Many late pictorial codices record clashes between partisans of Quetzalcóatl and Tezcatlipoca at Tula. According to some Amerindian traditions, Quetzalcóatl, god of the morning star—whose very name was synonymous with a sovereign of Tula—was expelled from the city. He left to convert other peoples before announcing his imminent return. And it was this belief in a second coming that triggered the downfall of Emperor Montezuma II when the conquistadors landed in 1519.

Whatever truth there is in this myth, the influence of the Toltecs made itself felt to varying degrees as far as the coast of Veracruz (especially at El Tajín) before culminating in the perfect symbiosis achieved at Chichén Itzá, some two thousand kilometers from its origin. But instead of slavishly plagiarizing the architecture of the austere Tula, this city in Yucatán transcended the vocabulary of its model by infusing it with strong Mayan influences. In this respect, the quality of the sculpture and painting of Chichén Itzá attained rarely equaled peaks of virtuosity. The bas-reliefs along the path around the large ball game field describe in graphic detail two rival teams watching the decapitation of the chief of the beaten clan. Snakes symbolize the spurts of blood springing from his neck. The mural paintings in the upper Temple of the Jaguars show ranks of dignitaries attending a ritual of the Feathered Snake cult. Even more spectacular is the façade of the Temple of the Warriors (so-named after the depictions of soldiers in Toltec dress on the pillars of the portico leading to it), which has depictions of Quetzalcóatl-Kulkulkán as the morning star (Venus), associated with masks of the rain god Chac. In front of this sumptuous gateway stands another imposing Chacmool, on which the officiating priests made sacrifices.

Much has been written about the striking similarities between these two Toltec cities. This should probably be attributed to the existence of trade routes between Central Mexico, the Gulf Coast, and the Yucatán Peninsula. Despite the many different hypotheses, the magnificent city of Chichén Itzá perpetuated and increased the far-reaching influence of Tula after the capital of the high plateaus was destroyed by a new nomad invasion from the north in 1168. But soon the Aztecs would revitalize the fabulous artistic and cultural heritage of the people they proudly considered their brilliant ancestors.

Follwing pages: **Heads of plumed serpents.** Toltec. 11th century.
Portico of the Temple of the Warriors, Chichén Itzá, Yucatán, Mexico.

The Aztecs, or the Twilight of the Gods

One can imagine the amazement of the conquistadors when they reached the shores of the New World at the dawn of the sixteenth century and discovered the power and sophistication of the Aztec Empire. This bloodthirsty, warlike people saw itself as the heir to a long tradition and complex cosmogony that had established human sacrifice as indispensable to its survival. Aztecan art, which profoundly subordinated to this belief, is striking both for its propensity for the macabre and its disturbing interface between life and death.

So much has been written about the cruel, bloodthirsty barbarian Aztecs, a people whose myriad composite gods defy modern understanding. They were a race of warriors, not artists, who left behind only monotonous, stiff, and even slavishly imitative creations. But they were also a "Titan with clay feet," which it took only a handful of Spanish soldiers to pitch into oblivion. The spectacular excavations undertaken in the Templo Mayor, in the heart of present-day Mexico City, are still yielding vestiges of breathtaking beauty that are forcing us to reevaluate and often radically change our vision of the Aztec world.

Vase depicting the rain god Tlaloc (offering no. 21). Aztec. Late post-classic period. Polychrome ceramic. H. 13.6". Museo del Templo Major, Mexico City. Following pages: **Coatlicue, goddess of the earth and death.** Aztec. Calixtlahuaca. Basalt. H. 30". Museo Nacional de Antrolopologia, Mexico City. Tlazoltéotl. **"Mother of God," giving birth to the god Centéotl.** Aztec. 1300–1521. Mexico Valley. Jadelite. H. 8.2". Dubarton Oaks Museum, Washington.

As is often the case in archaeology, chance played a preponderant role. In February 1978, during construction work not far from the cathedral, in the heart of Mexico City's historic quarter, a major obstacle brought work to a halt. A few days later, archaeologists extracted a circular monolith over three meters in diameter: A formless and decapitated effigy of the goddess Coyolxauhqui, half sister (and victim) of the great Aztec warrior god of northern origin, Huitzilopochtli. The rest is history: One of the most gigantic but also fruitful archaeological digs of all time was undertaken with the support of the president of the Mexican Republic, José Lopez Portillo. Twenty-four archaeologists, historians, researchers, anthropologists, biologists, palynologists, and other scientists analyzed every piece of information the site yielded in a specially created laboratory directed by Professor Edouardo Matos Moctezuma. The inauguration of the site museum in 1987 didn't stop work continuing, far from it. Two of the most spectacular statues

Xipe Totec, "Our Lord the Flayed One" (front and back). Aztec. Basalt. H. 22".
Salomon Hale Collection, Mexico City.

were discovered two years ago in the House of the Eagles, located north of the Templo Mayor: Mictlantecuhtli, god of death, whose livers protrude from his emaciated ribcage (the Aztecs believed the liver to be the seat of the soul), and the menacing "warrior-eagle," whose face seems to spring from the beak of the all-powerful Sun god. Americanists are now trying to rewrite the "bad press" of the Aztecan people. To correct this rather simplistic and negative view of the culture, they are pursuing entirely new paths of inquiry, focusing on the human figure, the Aztecs' relationship with the natural world, religion, the emblems of power, etc. From these new reference points, there emerges an impression of breathtaking creativity and a variety of aesthetic languages one might never have suspected in a civilization traditionally disregarded by art historians. And yet one only has to read Cortés's lyrical descriptions when he discovered Mexico in 1519 ("the most beautiful city in the world, a new Venice") to realize the heights of refinement attained by its artists and craftsmen. Metalsmiths, weavers, and other artisans enjoyed special status, had their own quarters

Two-headed serpent (pectoral). Aztec or mixtec. Late post-classic period. 15th–16th century. Wood with turquoise inlay. W. 2".British Museum, London.

and their own festivals, temples, and even gods. The name, the Tolteca, reveals their prestigious ancestry: It was probably the Toltecs, a civilized people par excellence, who initiated them under the guidance of Quetzalcóatl, the feathered snake that was worshipped at Tula.

No matter how grandiose these painted stucco effigies (the corn goddess Xilonen brandishing her cobs) and no matter how spectacular these basalt statues of deities (the sublime Ehecatl-Quetzalcóatl and his extraordinary "beak wig"), anthropomorphic polychromed braziers, shields with fanning feathers (insignias of power), and obsidian masks with menacing grins may be, one should never forget the plain truth: What twenty-first-century Westerners perceive as works of art of extraordinary perfection were simply objects of worship, intended to manifest the political-religious power of the Aztecan people. "To capture a moment of a holy story in stone is to enclose the ephemeral in the definitive," Ignacio Bernal and Mireille Simoni-Abbat wrote about the Aztecs' profoundly "official" art. It is as if the Aztecs, in their deep-rooted desire to create legit- imacy for themselves, wanted to reconcile all powers, friendly or hostile, including, unfortunately for them, the god of the Christians.

But what strikes one straightaway in their powerful, dramatic art is precisely the sentiment of sacred horror. An unbearable anxiety seems to run through the procession of monsters and deities spawned by the Aztecan imagination. One can almost understand the terrified amazement of the Catholic clergy when they first set eyes on these cohorts of mysterious, chthonian images, these baroque tangles of skulls and reptilian knots. A single example is enough to convey this obsessive propensity for the terrifying: Coatlicue, the old goddess of the Earth, whose ancestral name can be translated as "she who has a snake's skin." To portray Coatlicue, an entity they considered the mother of their tribal god Huitzilopochtli, the Aztecs dreamt up this dreadful gorgon of the pre-Colombian world. The face is replaced by two snake heads, themselves made of spurts of blood, like that which must have showered decapitated victims during fertility rituals. Her massive and powerful body is covered with dreadful symbols: Offerings of severed human hands, human hearts, skulls in relief, eagles' claws, streams of blood, and tangles of snakes. "La muerte es madre de las formas" ("Death is the mother of forms"), wrote the great poet Octavio Paz. We will probably never entirely elucidate the mystery of the terrifying Coatlicue, or the symbolism of her son, the solar Huitzilopochtli, who, when he was born, killed his brothers and sisters, the shadows. One thing is certain, though: For initiates, they probably embodied the symbiosis of good and evil, life and death, and the earthly and celestial. For the vast majority of the faithful, they represented pure horror, absolute terror.

But Aztecan art could sometimes have great fluidity, a suppleness that is surprising within such a military, sacrificial aesthetic. The concept of metamor-

Following pages: **Coatlicue portrayed as an old woman.** Aztec. Cozcatalan, Puebla. Basalt. H. 66". Museo Nacional de Antrolopologia, Mexico City. **Xochipilli, prince of flowers, god of joy, music, and dance.** Aztec. Tlamanalco. Andesite (mask and tooth collar). H. 30.8". Museo Nacional de Antrolopologia, Mexico City.

phoses and the permeability of the world and kingdoms are embodied in depictions of jaguars and snakes (there is a very fine, turquoise-inlaid example of Aztecan art in the British Museum). Still more confusing is one of the most famous masterpieces of Mexican art: The head of the eagle-knight in the National Museum of Anthropology in Mexico City, which theatrically shows a very anxious-looking human face springing from the beak of a holy bird of prey.

And how should one interpret the mysterious stone effigies adorning a no less mysterious mouth mask? Is it the god itself or its effigy? Or could this be a depiction of a priest, wearing his ornaments for some ritual, or a sacrificial victim? These distinctions were probably meaningless for pre-Colombians, since all men and all effigies wearing the attributes of the god "became" that god himself. Chroniclers' accounts reveal that most Aztecan statues, originally nude, were decked with finery and feather and paper ornaments and banners.

Reconstructions in museums and sometimes even vestiges give us an inevitably truncated, distorted picture. All the conquest's chroniclers tell us how gold and blood adorned their lugubrious worship of death. Their hardly polychromed black basalt statues were instruments of anguish and horror. Their sumptuous flint knives with turquoise-encrusted handles were meant solely to be plunged into the heaving breasts of sacrificial victims. And the vertiginous flights of steps leading up the sides of their temples ran with blood. Like its Chichimec, Toltec, and Totonac predecessors, the purpose of all Aztecan architecture was to glorify these macabre rituals. The nauseating smell of blood hung everywhere. There were blood-splattered sacrificial stones, clotted blood dried on walls, bloody corpses thrown into open graves, and dismembered, flayed, and

Statues at the base of the pyramid of the Templo Mayor. They were unearthed during the excavations carried out by the Mexican archaeologist Eduardo Matos Moctezuma in the 1980s. Aztec. 15th century. Tenochtitlán, Mexico. Basalt.
Photograph by Jean Paul Barbier-Mueller in *Civilisations disparues,* Assouline, 2000.

The *tzompantli* or altar of skulls. Templo Mayor, Mexico.
Photograph by Jean Paul Barbier-Mueller in *Civilisations disparues*, Assouline, 2000.

decapitated bodies. Forty years before the conquest, Nezahualcóyotl, the philosopher-king of Texcoco, had expressed his unbearable anguish at the sight of this waning world and had a nine-story tower built to symbolize his "pure idea." It is as if, to borrow Henri Sterlin's fine metaphor, the children of the Sun had slowly and irremediably descended into night. But soon, to the sound of the cannon and the litanies of the priests, the Aztecs would begin their long and painful apprenticeship of Christianity and cultural exchange. Were the old pre-Colombian gods destined to die? Idols were indeed knocked down and thousands of codices were burnt and unfailingly replaced by crosses (which were immediately ripped out of the ground). But everywhere, also, holy Aztecan effigies were hidden in the bowels of the Earth, only to suddenly resurface centuries later in their original nudity. It was then that science and

Sacrifice to the Sun. From a Florentine codex. Circa 1540.
Museo Nacional de Antrolopologia, Mexico City.

52

Head of an Eagle Knight. Aztec. AD 1440-69. Mexico Valley. H. 14.8". Museo Nacional de Antrolopologia, Mexico City.

belief entered into fierce conflict. If today these "pagan relics" are on view to all in the museums, a little of the Aztec blood has pervaded Christianity. One example of this mischievous osmosis is the Festival of the Dead every November first, with its armies of skeletons and hollow-eyed, grimacing skulls. A final message from the gods, perhaps?

Eagle Knight from the House of the Eagles. Aztec. AD 1440–69. Terra-cotta, stucco, and pigment. H. 66". Museo del Templo Mayor, Mexico City.

TENOCHTITLÁN: THE VENICE OF THE NEW WORLD

When the conquistadors arrived, Tenochtitlán, the Aztecan capital, was a magnificent island city crisscrossed by the canals that linked it to the surrounding lake. Its population then was probably around seventy-five thousand. When the Spaniards first set eyes on the city and set foot in its artificial gardens, witnessing their flood barriers with regularly spaced openings and wooden bridges, they must have been spellbound. They, of course, immediately compared it to Venice.

The city was carefully maintained by its inhabitants. Each house had one or two levels, a roof terrace, and an orchard. Religious and official buildings competed in magnificence. The capital's mythical center had been built on the very spot where, according to tradition, an eagle had landed on a cactus to devour a snake—almost a premonition if one considers Tenochtitlán's catastrophic fate. At the height of its

development, the city was destroyed by the Spanish the day after the Aztecs surrendered on August 13, 1521.

While recent excavations of the Templo Mayor continue to uncover the various phases of the great sanctuary's construction, the palace and its huge hypostyle room (described by the Spanish chronicler Bernal Díaz del Castillo) have not yet revealed their secrets. One must content oneself with imagining the imperial pomp of the last Aztecan sovereign, an absolute theocrat who carried all his ceremonial finery on a palanquin amidst a host of servants. In many respects, this theatrical and solar staging anticipated the pomp of France's King Louis XIV, otherwise known as the Sun King.

Codex Fejervary-Mayer. 1500. Detail of a depiction of the four stages of a woman's life, presented by the goddess of magic. Here, she appears dressed as a man, her power emanating from her vulva. Liverpool Museum.

FRANÇOIS REICHENBACH'S "MEXICAN MADNESS"

"The contact between Mexico and me was immediate and definitive," François Reichenbach liked to say when asked about his passion for Mexican art. His all-devouring obsession led the French filmmaker to make repeated trips to Mexico, a place that became his second homeland. Not a week went by that he did not receive cartons of grimacing masks, or "trees of life" dripping with a thousand offerings, or ceramics, or paintings in multicolored wool. Every piece was listed, classified, labeled, and hung on the wall like a dazzling trophy. His collection, the fruit of four decades of frenetic, impassioned research, is extraordinary both in its eclecticism and quality. Composed of over three thousand so-called popular objects, it reflects the complexity of this multi-ethnic land, which oscillated between paganism and Christianity, madness and naivety.

In 1991, two years before he died, François Reichenbach announced that he wanted to donate his unique collection to a foundation or major French museum. The response was immediate. Marseille's Musée des Arts Africains, Océaniens et Amérindiens (the MAAOA), then close to opening, and its head curator, Alain Nicolas, became the proud trustees of the finest European collection of Mexican folk art. The time had finally come for these antipodean creators, disregarded by artistic officialdom for so long, to be recognized. The Musée National d'Art Moderne/Centre Georges-Pompidou, and also the Fondation Cartier in Paris, had already demonstrated the intense creativity of these modest artists who flirted with the supernatural and death, and the poetry of their ex-votos, whose magic is equaled only by their formal power.

Tiger mask. Decorated using the rayado technique, during which several different-colored coats of lacquered are applied then scratched away. Guerrero State, Mexico. Wood, yellow lacquer, teeth, and boar whiskers. H. 25.7". F. Reichenbach Collection, 1994. M.A.A.O.A., Marseille.

Coyote mask. Cora, Nayarit State, Mexico. Painted papier-mâché and fabric. F. Reichenbach Collection, 1994. M.A.A.O.A., Marseille.
Fisherman mask. Guerrero State, Mexico. Painted wood. F. Reichenbach Collection, 1994. M.A.A.O.A., Marseille.

Playing marvelously on the spectacular, the grotesque, and the terrifying, these troops of grimacing faces, chimerical *alebrijes* (papier-mâché creatures), and "psychedelic" paintings enchant collectors and museum curators, who are delighted with encountering these new forms. Jaguar and bat masks resurface from their pre-Hispanic past, along with colonially-influenced masks with blond hair and blue eyes, masks of the white-bearded "old man," and *diablitos* as red as Satan's fire. This fascinating mixture of the burlesque and macabre is typical of all Amerindian civilizations.

"In every Mexican, the child and the god merge," François Reichenbach remarked

Bat mask. Guerrero State, Mexico. Painted wood. F. Reichenbach Collection, 1994. M.A.A.O.A., Marseille.

in *Une passion mexicaine,* the admirable film he made about them in 1992. "In every Mexican, dream and reality mingle," one could add. To convince oneself of this one only has to immerse oneself in the *nierikas* (woolen rugs) of the Huichol Indians. These rugs, with their fluorescent colors and designs, represent the cosmogonic visions of the *maraacam* (shaman) or help decipher the "trees of life," peopled with dark deities and figures that look like Batman. But the first prize for artistic inventiveness has to go to the famous Linares family of Mexico State. Their very popular work is a dazzling denial of the tenacious cliché of the anonymity of the so-called folk artist.

Skull. Obsidian. H. 4.3". Wood. Bliss Collection, Washington.
Right: **Death mask.** Mexico, Painted wood.
F. Reichenbach Collection, 1994. M.A.A.O.A., Marseille.

SOUTH AND CENTRAL AMERICA

The Mirage of El Dorado

"Ahead of you lies fatigue, hunger, thirst, and perhaps death, but also gold; behind you, the easy life. Here, Peru and its riches; there, Panama and its misery. Make your choice like a good Castilian. As for me, I am leaving for the south." These heroic and peremptory words were spoken, according to chroniclers' accounts, by Francisco Pizarro himself, the very man who would annihilate one of the most powerful empires of the pre-Hispanic world, the dynasty of the Incas.

The rest is history: A handful of ill-disciplined Spanish soldiers hungry for wealth and glory tragically confronted the Indian people, who were amazed by these bearded, white-skinned men perched on strange animals with hooves, their weapons gleaming in the Sun. Like a giant with clay feet, "the Empire of the Four Earths" came tumbling down, the sovereign undermined by internecine struggles and his temples and sanctuaries pillaged. The ancient civilization of Peru came to an end on November 16, 1532, and with it millennia of ancestral traditions and myths. Galleons sped back to Spain, laden with statuettes and golden jewelry. More and more adventurers of all kinds dreamt of pursuing the same mirage, the hopeless and obsessive quest for El Dorado (the "Gilded One"), whose fabulous kingdom would never be found.

Coca bag. Mochica. 4th–8th century. Rio Moche Valley.
Gold (22 carats). H. 24.4" W. 10.5". Private collection.

But Peru, the fantastical, Utopian land of milk and honey, would bring Europe many a treasure as precious as the hypnotic yellow metal: The potato, quinine, coca, an infinite number of fruits, and much more. Archeologists' spades would unearth hundreds of monuments (the ruins of Tiahuanaco in Bolivia and at Chavin, and the grandiose Machu Picchu in Peru) and thousands of objects (textiles, ceramics, jewelry, and statuettes), gradually revealing the extraordinary complexity and cultural wealth of civilizations that preceded the magnificence of the Incas by several centuries.

And yet so many mysteries still cloud the cultural perceptions of the people that inhabited the five-thousand-kilometer-long Andes Mountain range. It is as if there were not one but several South Americas, determined by their natural environments (endless, monotonous plains to the east and soaring peaks of the Cordillera de Los Andes to the west) and the uneven development of their populations. Phases of cultural disintegration were followed by periods of maturation, unification, even standardization. No wonder that in different places and at different times one finds the strained smile of a god with cat's teeth that could almost be the signature of this vast empire. Just as, sculpted in lava at San Augustin, woven in *mantos* (funerary cloaks) at Paracas, and drawn on ceramics at Nazca, one sees the same terrifying figure of the sacrificer holding weapons and trophies of human heads up to the gods.

Our knowledge is far from exhaustive (many sites are still waiting to be excavated, or at least interpreted), but everywhere there is the magnetic presence of works in clay, gold, or feathers "invested with a power before being adorned with beauty," to quote Claude Roy: The "Venuses" of Valdivia (central coast of Ecuador), timidly fashioned in clay around 3,500 BC, whose ample breasts and stomach, suggest the beginnings of a fertility cult; the flamboyant compositions woven in Peru from the late second millennium BC, whose checkerboard patterns and stylized figures could have come straight out of a Paul

Funerary mask. Vicus or Mochica. BC 200–circa AD 600. Northern Peru. Copper and shells. H. 9.3". Museo Barbier-Mueller de Arte Precolombino, Barcelona.
Preceding pages: **Machu Picchu**. Inca. Cúzco, Peru.
Statue found in the tomb of the Lord of Sipán. Inca. Sipán, Peru. Gold. Museo Brüning, Chiclayo.

Lamas galloping down to a river. Peru.
From *L'Empire du Soleil,* Paris, Hachette, 1957.

Klee painting; gorgon masks and other fantastic creatures cast in the priceless yellow metal by goldsmiths with shamanic powers (Quimbaya and Calima jewelry from Colombia; the La Tolita culture in Ecuador), and many other strikingly realist, even furiously erotic figures (even if it is now known that the orgiastic scenes depicted were rituals); and the Mochica ceramics so prized by museums and collectors (Peru, circa first century BC).

But if modern sensibilities have gradually tamed this eclectic and inspired imagery (sometimes purified, sometimes stylistically affected), many a question remains as to their precise use. There is no inscription or date in the clay or stone and no mention of a name (except during very late periods) to cast any light. As Danielle Lavallé, who understands these cultures well, so succinctly summed up, "The pre-Incaic Andes is a land with no history" (Lavallée and Lumbreras,1985). It is with no history because there was no written

Repoussé gold statuettes. Chimu. North coast of Peru.
H. 2". W. 2.3". Formerly in musée de l'Homme. Musée du Quai Branly, Paris.

word. Perplexed archaeologists and anthropologists have pored over countless mysterious scenes painted on vases, scrutinized many a terrifying two-headed or masked monster, wondering whether they are fantastic creatures, deities, or people dressed up in fancy dress. It matters little, in one respect: In Mesoamerica, the real and mythical worlds seem to reflect one another in a fascinating game of mirrors. One thing is certain, though: Many Andean creations bear the mark of the supernatural, the stamp of terror. Wide-eyed stares, bared teeth, menacing fangs, chimerical creatures, and feline masks are seen alongside the tortured grimaces and dismembered bodies of prisoners just as one encounters the same snake devil—an aquatic, chthonian creature that embodies power

Following pages: **Textile**. Huari. AD 600–1000. Tiahuanaco, Bolivia. Cotton and wool.
Vase. Huari. Rio Grande Valley. Polychrome clay. H. 5.5" W. 3.5". Figure wearing a shirt decorated with geometric motifs. Banco Credito del Perú En La Cultura Collection.

but also symbolizes fertility—running like a leitmotif through every period and land.

We will never ever completely understand the spiritual and mental universe of the potters, sculptors, and goldsmiths who fashioned these visual ravings. Yet Andean archaeologists constantly emphasize the extraordinary connections that exist between the artists of Peru, Mexico, and Ecuador, like some koine of visual languages and myths still yet to be explored.

Central America, so often disregarded by art historians and anthropologists, continuously reveals its role as the obligatory conduit between north and south. In many respects, it seems to have been a veritable nerve center, subject as much to Mexican and Mayan influences as southern trends from Colombia, Ecuador, and Peru. Due no doubt to its rugged topography, Central America seems not to have known a great civilization comparable to that of the Chimus or Incas. On its fragmented terrain there is not the slightest trace of a town or state worthy of the name, merely of minute fiefdoms locked in internecine struggles. Yet one should not underestimate the cultural dimension of a zone today encompassing Honduras, Salvador, Nicaragua, Costa Rica, and Panama. If other peoples, including their powerful neighbors, erected proud mud, brick, or stone pyramids and monumental steles, the peoples of Central America were content to create on a more modest and human scale. But if one contemplates their admirable metates (grain grinding bowls), sculpted in the form of an armadillo, crocodile, or wild cat, their work is just as striking. And what should one make of the tripod altars whose legs support birds with razor-sharp teeth and triangular wings? Only an African sculptor could rival their formal purity. Their ceramics also attain summits of inventiveness: A veritable cosmic laboratory teeming with amphibians and reptiles against a backdrop of violet-hued designs. Art, here, is hypnosis, shamanic flight, as light as a feather, as the flapping of wings.

Here again, so many questions remain unanswered. Why, for instance, did some civilizations prefer jade and others gold? Why did some disappear so suddenly, only to be replaced by others? And how can one explain the iconographic development of that ubiquitous Mesoamerican motif, decapitation? From the trophy head brandished by Aztecan priests to Panamanian sacrificers, this obsession with offering dismembered bodies as food to the gods is written in blood. The Amerindian scalp is the ultimate metamorphosis of this, its most perfect expression.

Putting aside moral judgments and preconceived ideas, one should remember this simple historical fact: Decimated by smallpox, robbed of its beliefs and gods, and hastily converted to the "true religion," pre-Hispanic America, its life-substance bled out of it, died a sudden death. Righteous-minded Europeans even refused the Indians the simple right to be human beings.

In the bloodthirsty and violent sixteenth century, a single voice cried out in the torment: "I fear that we have greatly hastened its decline and ruin by our contagion, and that we have sold it our opinions and arts at far too great a price. It was an infant world" (Montaigne, *Essays,* book 3, chapter 6).

Metates (left, from Nicaragua; right, from Costa Rica). AD 500–1500. Andesite. W. 23.4". Museo Barbier-Mueller de Arte Precolombino, Barcelona.
Following pages: **Loincloth.** Nazca. South coast of Peru. Cotton and feathers. Black dots on yellow. H. 35" W. 27". Banco Credito del Perú En La Cultura Collection.
Head of a fardo (mummy bundle). Nazca/Huari. South coast of Peru. Cotton and feathers. H. 8.6" W. 21.5". Banco Credito del Perú En La Cultura Collection.

THE "VENUSES" OF VALDIVIA

Sometimes sculpted in soft stone but usually made in ceramic, the small "Venuses" created around 3,500 AD on the equatorial Pacific Coast are hauntingly erotic and gentle visions of femininity. It is as if, over five thousand years ago, their anonymous sculptors tried to explore every facet of the female body and its infinite formal variations.

Never more than ten centimeters high, these figurines, with legs reduced to mere stems, arms pressed to their sides or crossed above a small, bulging stomach, small buttocks but swollen breasts, are probably expressions of an ancestral cult linked to the concept of fertility. Some researchers have suggested that their voluminous helmet-like hairstyle with a center parting, when seen from behind, represents a penis. Whatever their meaning (fertility idols or propitiatory amulets), these charming statuettes are a happy accident in an otherwise resolutely warlike, even phallocratic world of pre-Colombian art.

The "Venus". Valdivia. 3500–1500 BC. Ceramic. H. 2.2" W. 1.2". Museo Nacional del Banco Central del Ecuador, Quito.

MOCHICA CERAMICS: A SCALE-MODEL WORLD

Who has never contemplated, in an art or museum exhibition, the lively, multicolored microcosms so delightfully illustrated by Mochica vases? They are like wonderful illustrated dictionaries of the civilization that emerged in the Chicama region at the beginning of the first century BC. Hunting, fishing, war, even passionate lovemaking scenes (complete with starkly erotic depictions of fellatio and masturbation) are represented with a realism quite rare in pre-Colombian art.

But after this initial impression, one feels slightly uneasy in front of these "face-portraits." Their serene, laughing, anxious features are a catalog of stereotypical expressions rather than a likeness of some real-life model. Each expression seems to have its corresponding category of tattoos and finery. And the many sacrifice and mutilation scenes confirm, if need there was, the highly bellicose nature of the Mochica people.

Portrait. 1939–46. Acomayo, Cúzco, Peru. Fundación Pierre Verger, Salvador.
Right: **Stirrup-spouted portrait vase**, depicting a high-ranking warrior wearing a curious birdlike hat. Mochica. Ceramic. Museo Nacional de Antropologia y Arquelogica, Lima.

Bottle in the form of a feline's head. Late Chavin. 700–500 AD. Jequetapeque Valley, North Peru. Ceramic. H. 12.2". Nelson A. Rockefeller Collection, Metropolitan Museum of Art, New York.
Vase. Huari. AD 600–1000. Pachamac expansion. Sculpted ceramic with zoomorphic head. Polychrome decoration; H. 6.9" W. 4.7".Banco Credito del Perú En La Cultura Collection.

LUGGAGE FOR THE NEXT WORLD

The Paracas culture on the southern coast of Peru, discovered in 1925 by Julio C. Tello, revealed one of the most extraordinary textile treasures of the pre-Colombian world. In a vast funerary complex Tello quite logically called a "Necropolis," 429 corpses were found wrapped in a shroud that formed a conical bundle called a *fardo.* Apart from their ritual and protective use, these multiple layers of thick fabric are also extraordinarily refined and beautiful. According to Daniell Lavallée, "Never, in the history of Peruvian weaving, did

Fragment of a textile. Paracas, BC 800- AD 200. Peru. Formerly in musée de l'Homme. Musée du Quai Branly, Paris.

artists have such freedom in developing their aesthetic gifts, even if their models are inspired by preestablished religious or magic models."

Under the Incas, textile production also underwent a spectacular development. Not limited to the funerary and religious domain, fabrics denoted prestige and political and economic order, in the rigorous, geometric aesthetic language of the Incas.

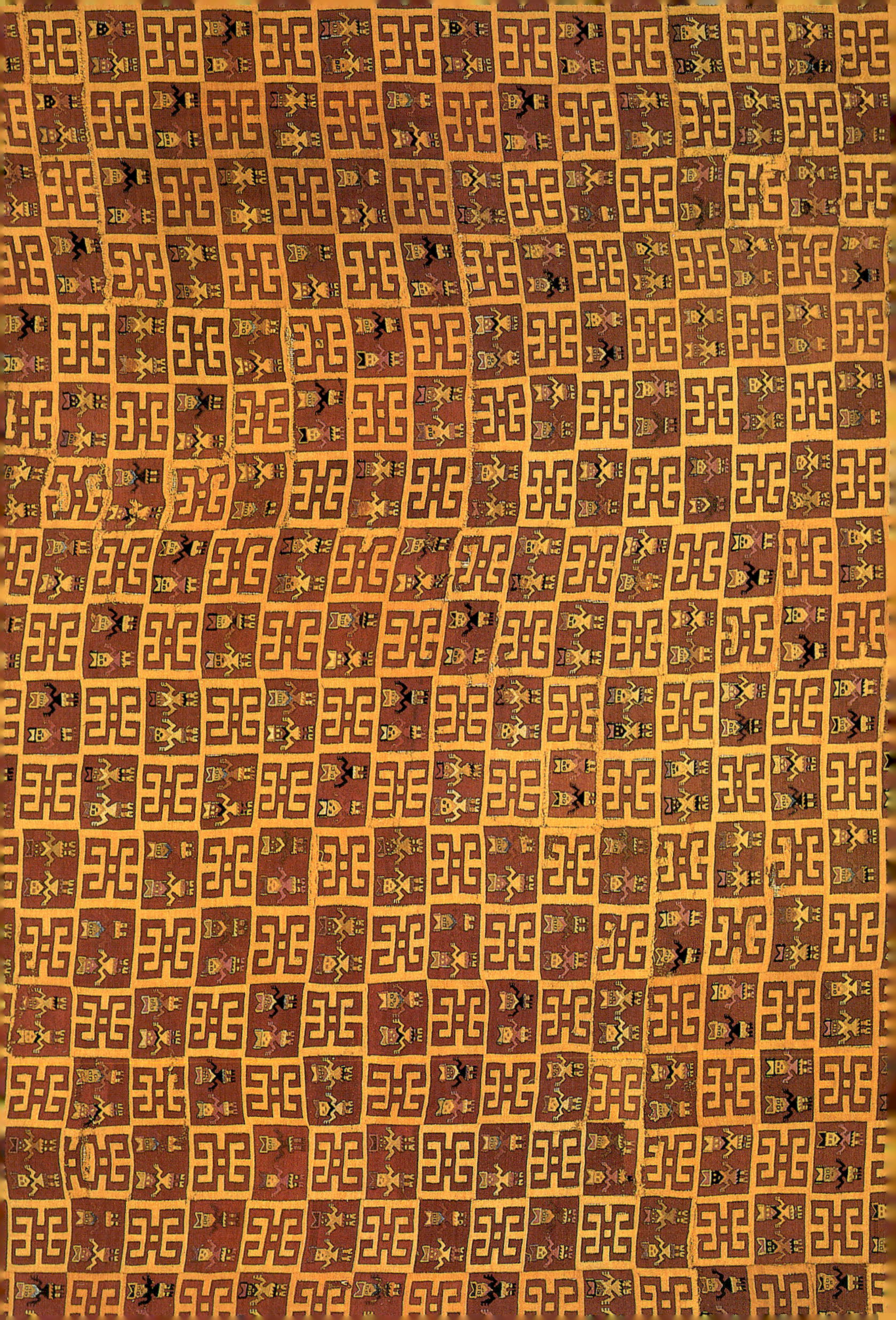

Alpaca quadricorn hat. Wari. AD 600–800.
Museo Chileno de Arte Precolombino, Santiago.
Left: **Cotton and alpaca textile.** Chancey. AD 1200–1450.
Fundación Museo Amano, Lima.

THE INCA EMPIRE: "NAVEL OF THE WORLD"

In less than a century, the Incas built one of the most important empires in the history of humanity. Despite their late arrival on the stage of Andean history (around 1538, Pachacutec, the "reformer of the world," unified what was still just a cluster of fiefdoms), they left such splendor and magnificence behind them that they almost eclipsed the previous four thousand years of cultural tradition.

So much has been written about the "Children of the Sun." They have been hailed as paragons of the "good savage" and of every virtue, only to then be scorned and belittled. Philosophers and other Utopian thinkers have compared the Incan state to the Egypt of the pharaohs, ancient Greece, the Roman Empire, and even the Europe of the cathedral builders—an example of the Eurocentric tendency to superimpose mental schemas on a culture that, in many respects, appears so diametrically different.

But behind these intellectual quarrels, there lies the genius of the Incan people, so perfectly summed up by Incan architecture and religious town planning. The Incas showed little interest in sculpture (only a very few gold or silver statuettes, discovered in unplundered tombs, have been found), but one can't help but admire their intricate network of roads, bridges, temples, fortresses, and garrisons. The Spanish were dumbstruck by Cuzco, the capital—a lasting, tangible expression of their centralized state—and its cut-stone edifices, paved streets, water system, and largely underground road network. "The city of the sovereigns of this country is so large and so beautiful that it is worthy of Spain. It is full of palaces and poor people are unknown there," wrote Pedro Sancho de la Hoz, Francisco Pizarro's secretary in 1534. Cuzco, whose name in the Quechua language probably meant "navel of the world," appears, in many respects, to have been an ideal city. Its regulated construction, purity of line, and rigorous planning were close to perfect. Harmoniously espousing the slopes of the Andes, its cut-stone buildings, relatively modest in size and height, were built with remarkable precision, without even the use of mortar—a technical feat all the more remarkable in regions often ravaged by violent earthquakes.

Incan edifices were massive but their niches, doors, and windows attenuated their austere appearance. The most sumptuous (the Coricancha or "Garden of Gold," where Inti (the Sun), Quilla (the Moon), and Quoyllu (the Stars) were worshipped, was cloaked in a gleaming shroud of thick gold leaf. But the building that undoubtedly exercises the most fascination and has been interpreted the most widely is definitely Machu Picchu. One is immediately struck by the majesty and grandeur of the site Hiram Bingham discovered in 1911, especially if one considers the Incas' artistic ambition to build on such a grand human scale. Although many interpretations now seem obsolete, it is certain that Machu Picchu was both a ceremonial and residential site. Was it a gigantic royal mausoleum, or a proud fortress barring access to Cuzco to the wild peoples of the forest? It has even been suggested that it may have been a convent for the "virgins of the Sun," vestal virgins of the Andean world. And there will be many more such fantasies.

Machu Picchu. Inca. 1450-1532.
Cuzco, Peru.

Tears of the Sun

"The Sun was an ugly little man.
'Do you want to be the father of the world?' he was asked.
When he said yes, he was dressed in pure gold, gold clothes, gold bag, gold cap,
everything gold . . . And when he got up, night ended."
—Kogi Indian myth

Few civilizations, except for the Ancient Egyptians, seem to have been as fascinated by gold as the cultures which bloomed in the Northeastern Andes between 1,000 BC and AD 1,500. The myth of El Dorado ("the Gilded One"), which appeared in the writings of the conquistadors, reflected the gold-hungry Spaniards' total incomprehension of the indigenous peoples and their "satanic" rituals.

Searching beneath this naive belief, ethnologists are now endeavoring to interpret the extraordinary symbolism attached to gold—the "sweat and tears of the Sun" and instrument of power and the divine.

Pure, dazzling gold: The stuff of so many dreams and fantasies since the dawn of time, the metal has been used everywhere as a sign of power or to symbolize eternity or wealth, in the saint's halo or the king's crown, as the ground of a Byzantine mosaic, or to coat a Buddha. And the Amerindian world is no excep-

Funerary mask. Nazca. BC 200– AD 600. Cordillera Central, Peru. Repoussé Gold. H. 0.09". Formerly in musée de l'Homme. Musée du Quai Branly, Paris.
Following pages: **Rectangular gold nariguera.** Inca. "Lord of Sipán" tomb site, Peru. Museo Brüning, Chiclayo. **Necklace of sixteen convex gold discs.** Inca. "Lord of Sipán" tomb site, Peru. Ø 1.8". Museo Brüning, Chiclayo.

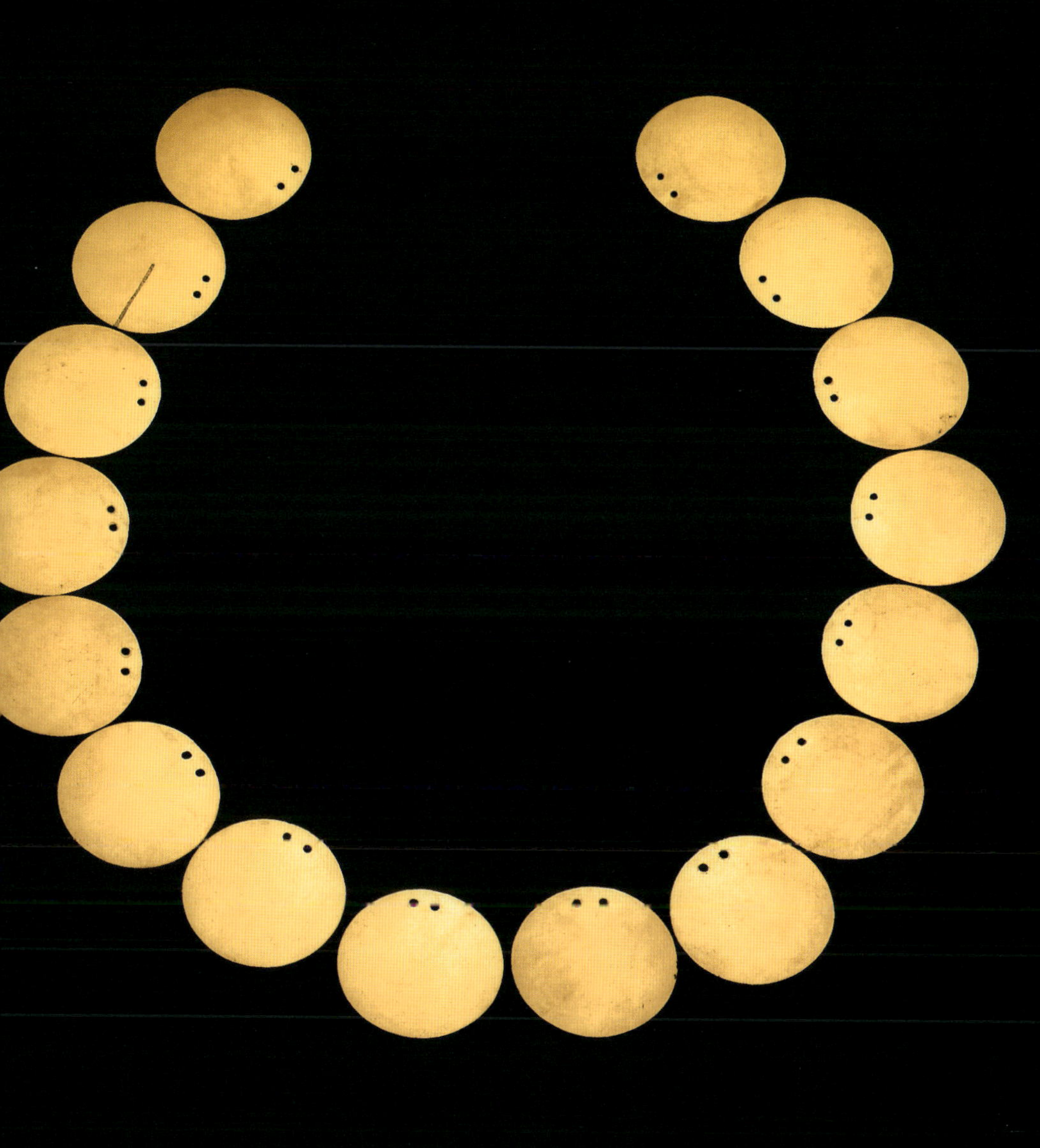

tion. Gauging by the countless ornaments archaeologists constantly retrieve from the bowels of the Earth, its civilizations had profound veneration for gold.

Yet there is nothing ostentatious, no flaunting of wealth, in what one can rightly describe as their frenetic worship of the "god gold." As receptor of the life-giving energy of the Sun (the masculine entity of the universe at the heart of all things and which re-creates the world each time it reappears), gold became a divine substance, an offering. It embodied the beneficial power that makes the corn grow, and gives strength and good health to all those who wear it. In the Amerindian world, particularly in the rosaries of the ancestral cultures that emerged in Colombia, Peru, and Ecuador, gold was far more than a precious metal to be bartered or sold. It was a magical talisman with sensual and quasi-hypnotic power, to be admired in the dazzling rays of the Sun. Spanish chroniclers recorded their amazement when they saw the doors of caciques' residences covered with gold discs burning like Suns. And the spectacle of these Indian dignitaries with their capes covered with gilded plaques must have been just as grandiose.

But what most went to the heads of the gold-thirsty conquistadors was not, as one can imagine, the mystical and quasi-carnal union of gold and Sun. One term came to epitomize the fantasies these cultures and their beliefs engendered: El Dorado (the "Gilded One"), a figure whose extraordinary origin has been long forgotten. During the coronation ceremonies of sovereigns on Lake Guatavita (some ninety kilometers from Bogotá), the caciques appeared decked in all their sparkling jewelry, with their naked bodies entirely coated with gold powder. This was all it took to fire the imagination of Spaniards transplanted into a universe of beliefs they often only perceived superficially. "On the lake, they made a large raft with reeds, adorned and decorated as sumptuously as possible . . . They stripped the heir naked, daubed him with sticky clay, then covered him with gold powder and sequins, so that he was completely coated with this metal. The gilded Indian made his offering by throwing all the gold and emeralds he was wearing into the middle of the lake; the four caciques who were with him did the same, and, once the raft had returned to land, celebrations began, the bagpipes, horns, long chants, and dances in their manner welcoming the newly elected, who was recognized as a prince and lord. From this ceremony comes the very famous name of El Dorado" (Freyle, *El Carnero,* 1636). Although one can imagine this Spanish chronicler's amazement at such a spectacle, ethnological research has since helped us interpret this complex ritual. For present-day Kogi Indians, who have inherited the customs of their ancestors, the lake is still "the uterus of Mother Earth," which the Sun fertilizes by sowing his seed.

And when pre-Colombian men embarked on their ultimate journey, they did so accompanied by an impressive "mortuary trousseau" of gold and light: Earrings, nose ornaments, pectorals, and other finery, pieces which are now admired merely as relics in modern-day temples, the museums. Although the myth of El Dorado is by no means dead, one should bear in mind this observation by the ethnologist Gerardo Reichel-Dolmatoff: "In fact, the time that has passed since the Conquest is so short, so insignificant that the treasures in the Museo de Oro (Gold Museum) in Bogotá still have the same power over the native population today. This is why it is unlike other museums: It is a pre-Colombian aboriginal sanctuary (*Precious Metalwork and Shamanism,* 1986).

And it is precisely in the light of this remark that one should regard the sublime finery and ornaments of the Indian peoples both as instruments of worship and messengers of the divine. Whether in the form of a frog or a bat, the menacing jaws of a jaguar or the emblematic image of a shaman metamorphosed into a birdman, gold had no mercantile value for the Indians. It was at once the "sweat

Following pages: **Tumbaga gold pectoral depicting a flying shaman birdman.**
Muisca. 600 BC–AD 1600. Guatavita, Cundinamarca, Colombia. H. 8.2" W. 8.8".
Museo del Oro, Bogota.
Zoomorphic gold pectoral plaque depicting a flying shaman birdman.
Tolima. Museo del Oro, Bogota.

Part of a necklace. Conch decorated with mosaic. H. 2.3" W. 1.2".
Banco Credito del Perú En La Cultura Collection.

of the Sun," light, heat, semen, and power. Only individuals belonging to the ruling classes had the right to possess or exhibit gold finery, jewelry, and objects. The recent discovery on the north coast of Peru of the tomb of the Lord of Sipan is a striking example of this.

But beyond these ornaments' seminal fertilizing, vital, and poetic meaning, there is also an aesthetic dimension. Their savage, hypnotic beauty never ceases to amaze us: The masks of the Chimu culture in Peru, with their slightly almond-shaped eyes, look as though they were hammered directly on to the face of a dead prince, like a piece of skin torn off and offered to eternity; *tumis* (sacrificial knives), whose formal perfection, bordering on abstraction, seems to seal the

Gold and silver ceremonial knife. Chimu. AD 1100–1200. Peru. L. 10.7". Private collection.
Following pages: **Male statuette.** Inca. Andes, South Peru. Silver and colored paste inlay. H. 7.6". Formerly in musée de l'Homme. Musée du Quai Branly, Paris. **Gold leaf antrhropomorphic figure with a platinum eye.** BC 300- AD 300. El Angel, Carchi province, Ecuador. H. 5.1". Formerly in musée de l'Homme. Musée du Quai Branly, Paris.

Votive statuettes with gold and bone jewelry. Quimbaya. 200 BC–AD 500. Antioquia, Colombia. Museo del Oro, Bogota.

fundamental and cosmic union of the Moon and the Sun; Nascan gorgons, shooting their serpentine rays like sunbeams, their globular eyes like some chimerical batrachian's; and, in Ecuador and Colombia, a miniature, hybrid people of lizard-men, jaguar-men, and caiman-men whose radiant, golden splendor immortalizes the original unity of the cosmos.

The Indians believed that in the beginning there was no difference between men and animals. Only when the Sun and Death appeared did a division take place and the human species found itself excluded from the primordial world and its power and knowledge. Only through ritual—by dancing, chanting, and wearing masks—could man regain contact with these original forces. And this is certainly what these fantastical creatures cast in gold, neither animal nor human but both at the same time, remind the viewer.

Funerary mask. Chimú. Hammered and repoussé gold.
Trujillo site, Peru.

This perpetual capacity to metamorphose oneself, to explore other realms and interact with the spirit world, is concentrated in one man: The shaman. In Amazonia, the Andes or Siberia, among the Inuit or the peoples of Korea, this "voyager of the invisible" (as Maurice Godelier so aptly described him) is usually redoubtably intelligent. It is he who penetrates the different strata of the cosmos, who acts as mediator, healer, caster of spells, and initiator, and who is often also a consummate artist or artisan. Depending on the Amerindian culture, the role of shaman could be inherited or revealed in a vision or dream. It was also possible for a person to become a shaman simply by pursuing his vocation. According to Gerardo Reichel-Dolmatoff, "The apprenticeship, under the guidance of an older practitioner, can last several years and ends with the initiation. As an almost universal rule, the neophyte has to die symbolically in order to be reborn with

certain supernatural faculties. To attain this goal, the apprentice spends a long period in complete isolation, fasting until he reaches a critical degree of initiation and enters hallucinatory states during which he imagines himself changed into a bird, flying through the air and visiting unknown dimensions of the cosmos."

Colombia, as we know, is particularly rich in psychotropic plants. For the shaman, a hallucinogenic substance is a gift of the gods. In the trance it induces, he can enter the supernatural world, where he can conquer the allies, that is, the spirits of animals and plants, which will later become his auxiliaries. Such beliefs and practices still endure in many Colombian tribes, for whom the shaman remains the great transformer. "Thus when he dons the mask of a wild cat, he is seeing the world through the jaguar's eyes. So he behaves like a true predator, for whom the others play the role of prey," explains the ethnologist Roberto Pineda Camacho in the catalog of the very fine exhibition "Spirits, Gold, and the Shaman," at the Grand Palais in 2000. But if there is

Tunjos (ex-voto). Muisca. AD 650–1550. Gold. Museo del Oro, Bogota.

one animal with whom he is irrevocably associated, it is the bird. Whether as a bird of prey, a night bird, or a seabird, with a long or hooked beak, and sometimes as a human bird, too, the shaman becomes the Birdman who rises into the air wearing a bird's mask and feather diadem, sometimes even imitating a bird's mysterious song. One only has to consider the predilection with which pre-Colombian goldsmiths depicted the shaman's feathered counterparts in all their diversity, on nose rings, earrings, pectorals, and headdresses, all of which have the same spread wing motif, the symbol of shamanic flight.

The Birdman journeys over a territory stretching far beyond the confines of Colombia, from North America to Easter Island and including the Andes and the tropical forests. His image lives on in archaeological testaments, but also in the mythology of many present-day Indian tribes, whose shamans still take flight. What better way of crossing the threshold of dreams to converse with the spirit world than through the air?

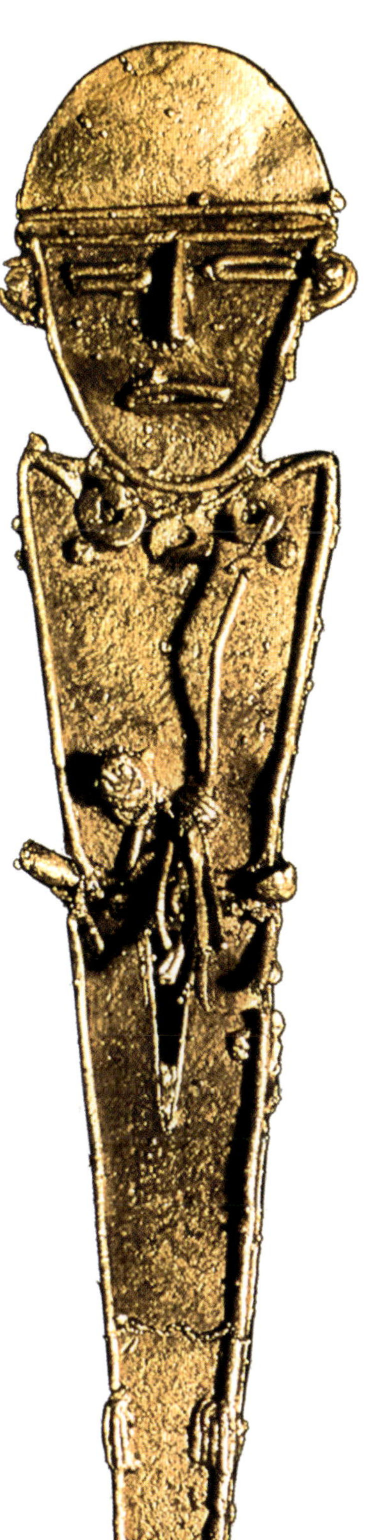

Pendant. Yocoto, Calima.100 BC–AD 1000. Restrepo, Cauca Valley, Colombia. Lost wax-cast iron, gold. H. 2.8″. Museo del Oro, Bogota.
Juana Ventura, shaman. 1999. Chichicastenango, Tikal, Guatemala.

THE TOMB OF THE LORD OF SIPAN: A PRICELESS TREASURE

Most ancient gold artifacts currently in the public domain come from the intensive clandestine digging carried out over recent years. When unearthed with no scientific concern whatsoever, objects immediately lose much of their archeological value and become merely treasures. The irremediable loss of precise context this entails, which only rigorous archaeological excavation can reconstruct, has seriously hindered study and identification.

In 1987, however, the discovery of the tomb of the Lord of Sipan, on the northwest coast of Peru, by the archaeologist Walter Alva enabled enormous advances in our knowledge of the Mochica culture (200 BC–AD 600) and its precious metalwork. For the first time, it was possible to scientifically excavate a wealthy sepulcher and extract all the information necessary for the reconstruction of its context. The two women lying at the head and feet of the "Lord of Sipan" were probably his wives or concubines. On either side of him lay two men around forty years old. A number of ornaments had been piled inside the coffin, objects that had never been found together before: A gold, pearl, and turquoise standard or pectoral; a pectoral with pink shell sequins; several ear ornaments, depicting ducks and deer, others portraying warriors; a great many necklaces; a gold and silver scepter; several ceremonial knives; a rattle with little spherical bells; and a coxal protector—in short, priceless archaeological treasures that had miraculously escaped the attention of the *huaqueros* (tomb pillagers).

Tomb of the "Lord of Sipán." Mochica. BC 200- AD 600. Gold jewelry, ritual objects, and human remains. Photograph taken for the archives of the Proyecto Arqueológico, Sipán.
Museo Brüning, Chiclayo.

Following pages: **Two feline heads.** Mochica. BC 200- AD 600. Sipán, Peru. Gold leaf.
Museo Brüning, Chiclayo.

Bird. Chimú. Peru. Repoussé and hammered gold.
Gold shark. Museum für Völkerkunde, Munich.

MAN AND ANIMAL IN SYMBIOSIS

One of the main points that all pre-Colombian societies have in common is the close relationship that the Indians maintained, and still maintain, with nature, which they consider a universal and generous mother. The Indian can therefore not conceive, as Western man does today, of a separation between the human world and the animal kingdom. To a large extent, his very survival depends on nature, and the control he has over it depends on the knowledge he acquires from it. The interaction between the human and the animal is so close it can be considered truly symbiotic. Man feels the animal, respects, lives the animal; and the animal in turn can exteriorize human facets and behavior. Among the actors, the most represented in pre-Colombian cosmogony and precious metalwork are:

– The bat. Associated with darkness and sometimes also blood, this nocturnal predator plays a major role in the mythology of the Kogi Indians. It embodies both the ancestral world and its taboos (including homosexuality and incest), and life and fertility. When a girl has her first period, the Kogi still say, "The bat has bitten her."

– The crocodile. This amphibious animal often evokes the subterranean world of the dead.

– The frog and the toad. Everything opposes them to birds. Birds fly, have warm

Gold frog pendant. AD 1000–1530. Chiriqui, Panama. H.2.3". Nelson Rockefeller Collection, Metropolitan Museum of Art, New York.
Crocodile pendant. Quimbaya. 900-1600. Restrepo, Cauca Valley. Museo del Oro, Bogota.

blood, sing melodically, and have multicolored plumage, while batrachians are cold-blooded amphibians, have monotonous voices, and prefer shady places. The bird and the frog and toad are used to express the opposition between air and water, light and dark, dry and wet. Toads also have a powerful hallucinogenic substance in their parotid glands and characteristically have very violent sexual behavior.

– The jaguar. This animal is the feared and dreaded carnivore omnipresent in Andean mythology. When a shaman puts on a mask or collar with jaguar's teeth, he becomes a jaguar and acquires his strength. In certain cultures, the jaguar represents the Sun and his voice can be heard in thunder.

– The bird. Andean precious metalwork is teeming with stylized herons, ducks, humming-birds, eagles, and vultures. Their plumage, song, different beak shapes, and piercing eyesight make them the preeminent shamanic creatures. The image of the bird flying with spread wings symbolizes the shaman's ability to ascend into other worlds or levels of the cosmos.

– The snake. The snake is cold-blooded, both terrestrial and aquatic, and associated with the underworld. The fact that the snake periodically sloughs its skin makes it a symbol of eternal rebirth.

The Kingdom of the Birdmen

For centuries, the Amazonian Indian tribes, still largely isolated from the outside world, have been making finery from feathers that would turn most couturiers green with envy. Their amazingly and chromatically daring "sacred trinkets" state the sex and rank of their wearers and their belonging to the cosmos and to a tribe. The fragile, immaterial feather is also the shamanic instrument par excellence, the ideal doorway through which to enter the world of spirits and dreams.

"To be naked is to be without speech," say the Dogons of Mali. "To be a 'real man' one has to dress oneself with birds' feathers," is the reply of the Amazonian Indians. In these Conradian forests infested with insects and snakes, along the immense river that the Spanish so aptly baptized with the rebel name Amazone, there are still ethnic groups who, in their style of dress, preserve their untainted and constant desire to capture beauty and deploy it. Is it the sticky heat of this green hell which pushes men and women to wear only feathers as light as the breeze? Kayapos, Bororos, Karajas, Urubu Ka'apors, Jivaros . . . each tribe and group has its own distinctive palette and range of nuances and textures. Nothing is gratuitous: Whether brilliant, mottled, satiny, velvety, even metallic, the feather is transformed into a universal language. It marks the stages in life, recounts births and deaths and indicates sex and rank and also tribal membership. Flamboyant or diaphanous, majestic or modest, it

Indian from the Matto Grosso. 1880. Ministère des Affaires étrangères, Paris.

Shaman Cofan. Amazon, Brazil.
Feather diadem. Ikpeng culture. Xingu, Brazil. H. 8.6" W. 35.5". Vilma Chiara and Niede Guidon Expedition. Formerly in musée de l'Homme. Musée du Quai Branly, Paris.

Bororo Indian. Amazon, Brazil. Photograph by Claude Lévi-Strauss (1935).
Preceding pages: **Position of the hand holding the arrow.** Bororo. Mato Grosso State. Brazil. Claude Lévi-Strauss Collection and photograph. Formerly in musée de l'Homme.Musée du Quai Branly, Paris.

is gracefully slipped into armbands, necklaces, diadems, and earrings. Its vocabulary is immense, its grammar limitless: The entire bird kingdom—parrots, macaws, toucans, japus, curassows, partridges, eagles and falcons—all play their part. But not content with satisfying the prodigality of such a generous and exuberant nature, the Amazonian Indians invent other expressive ranges and harmonies: A solar yellow, a strident red, cascades of turquoise and orange, or an emerald green clashing with a deep blue, and so on. In *Tristes Tropiques,* Claude Lévi-Strauss wrote admiringly about the creativity of these dressmakers of the New World: "Even if they are not in ceremonial dress, the taste for ornament is so strong that men are constantly improvising new finery. Many wear crowns: Fur headbands decorated with feathers, basketwork rings, also feathered, collars of jaguar's claws mounted on a wooden hoop. But they are content with much less: A ribbon of dried straw, picked up from

Basketwork and feather headdress worn for the *macheteros* dance. 20th century.
Mojos de Llanos Indians, northeast Bolivia. H. 31" W. 60". Formerly in musée de l'Homme.
Musée du Quai Branly, Paris.

the ground and rapidly rounded and painted, makes a fragile headdress which the wearer will parade until he prefers some other novelty inspired by another find." And the ethnologist, with his peerless wit and intelligence goes on to describe that "one has to enter the men's house to understand the energy these strapping fellows spend on making themselves beautiful. In every corner, they are cutting out, fashioning, chiseling, gluing. Shells from the river are cut up into fragments and vigorously polished on stones to make necklaces, and fantastic constructions of bamboo and feathers are assembled. With the application of a dressmaker, men built like blacksmiths transform each other into chicks by gluing down to their skin." But make no mistake, nothing could be less profane than these antipodean fashion shows and parades. And nothing less natural, too. By the very choice of feathers and the manner in which they are assembled, the Indian states his identity and his belonging to a tribe, clan, and society. "A piece of finery can signify power or courage," emphasizes Roberta Rivin, curator of the sumptuous exhibition at the Fondation Mona Bismarck in Paris. "Each tribe has its own distinct ornaments and styles, each with its own specific symbolism and meaning. Jewelry is used for different purposes, such as puberty rituals or the ceremony of the giving of names, whose magic and spiritual dimension express man's bond with the cosmos" (*L'Art de la plume en Amazonie,* Somogy, 2001). Wreaths of aigrettes, diadems, halos, armbands, necklaces, and visors identify the man, and are made from different types of feather (down, tail, wing, or small feathers that cover the back or abdomen), each of which has a precise function on the bird: Regulating temperature, flying, attracting a mate, etc. And just as in the bird realm the males are often more colorful than the females, it is usually the Amazonian Indian male who wears the jewelry and finery. Women spend their time tilling the fields, weaving cotton, and educating their children. The activity of indulging in ceremonial and sacred haute couture is exclusively reserved for men. It is the job of these dandies to aim blowpipes with rhomboidal points, make traps, and throw nets to capture birds with the ideal plumage for their finery. And these feathered Amazonian virtuosos constantly invent new languages and ever more subtle harmonies, much like a painter increases the range of his palette, selecting and composing colors and forms, textures and materials.

The Kayapo and the Bororo favor long feathers, which they fix to grandiose, rigid frames. The Jivaro prefer to stick small down feathers into fragile fiber or cotton supports. One technique alone sums up the ingeniousness of these grand couturiers: tapirage. A sophisticated technique still practiced today, it consists of modifying the color of a bird's plumage while it is alive. "The chest feathers are plucked and the

Single man's feather crown. 20th century. Río das Arraias, Para State, Brazil. Kayapos Indians. Ø 8.8". Jean Vellard Expedition. Formerly in musée de l'Homme. Musée du Quai Branly, Paris.
Following pages: **Namikwara boy with a feather in his nose.**
Photograph by Claude Lévi-Strauss (1938).
Feather. Urubu-Ka'apor, Maranhao region, Brazil. Private collection.

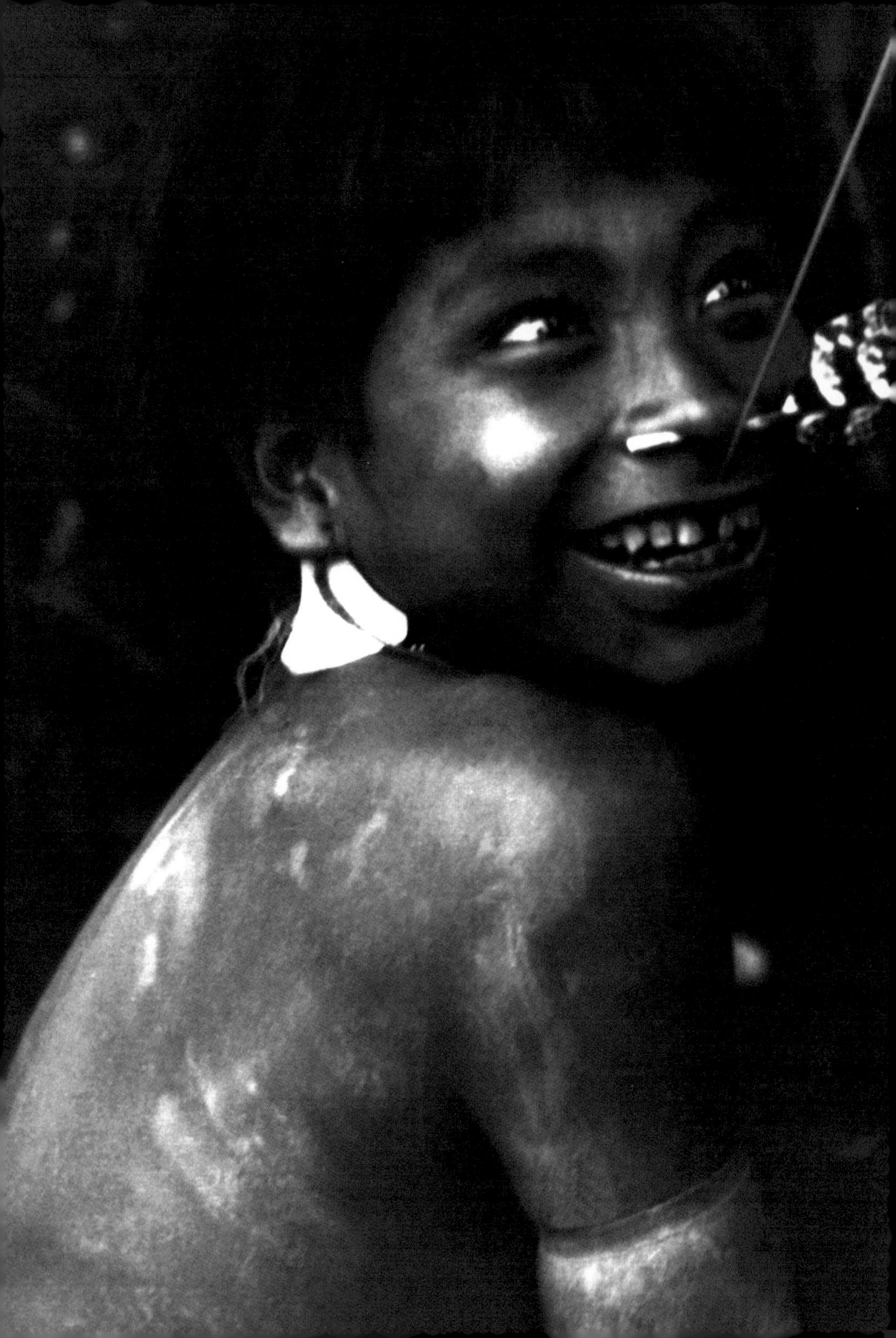

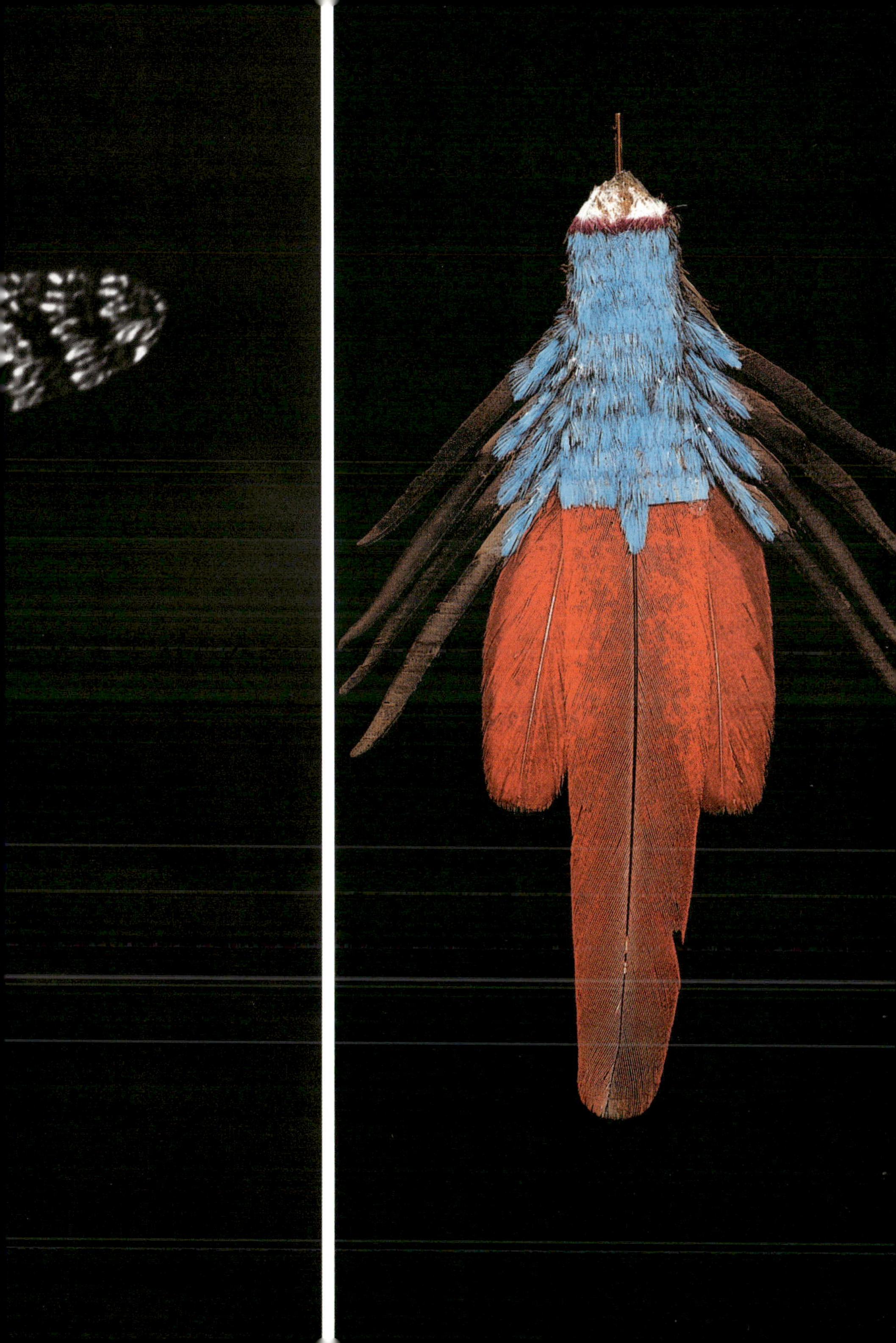

bird's skin is rubbed with the blood of a frog or the fat of a certain fish. When the feathers grow again, they are orangy yellow instead of green," explains Roberta Rivin. This eminent specialist of the Amazonian Indians adds, "There are other methods of coloring feathers, used to enlarge the chromatic range or simply to remedy a lack of feathers for a particular design. One of these methods consists in boiling large white feathers in a decoction of brazilwood, then dyeing them red. Another simpler technique involves exposing feathers to the heat of a flame or steam" (op. cit.).

In fact, for the Indians there is nothing less disturbing than ambiguous tints. They are the allies of doubt and chaos. There are no subtle monochromes and half tints. Blue-orange, red-green, yellow-violet—everything is a harsh, strident clash of color. "In order that the world should be thinkable and the mind find comfort in its spectacle, there has to be difference," sums up Claude Lévi-Strauss. Selected, classified, composed, colored, and reused, the feather, as a medium, uses the colors of the bird world to differentiate itself from them. It is this artificial plumage that states the man's racial identity or species, it is this illusion of nature that expresses the apprehension of differences and all the possibilities of creation. The Amazonian feather, an "expression of intelligence and the intelligible order of the world," according the Swiss ethnologist Daniel Schoepf, is also an immaterial material, a shamanic instrument, a vehicle of spirits and dreams. To become a birdman is an ideal means of leaving the world of the living and attaining the kingdom of the gods. It is also the most spectacular way of showing off in front of everyone. Such fiery plumage would make Thierry Mugler or John Galliano go green with envy.

Karaja occipital fan. Mato Grosso, Brazil. Tucum palm sticks, cotton thread, resin, tuiu, ara, parrot feathers. Ø 62.5". Collected by Luis Donisete Benzi Grupioni. Cid Collection, San Paolo, Brazil.
Following pages: **Yanomami Indian.** Wiramabiu-Theri, Roraima State, Brazil. Photograph by Sebastiao Salgado Amazona. **Feather decoration on a straw crown.** Waura Indians, Brazil. H. 18.3". Vilma Chiara and Niede Guidon Expedition. Formerly in musée de l'Homme. Musée du Quai Branly, Paris.

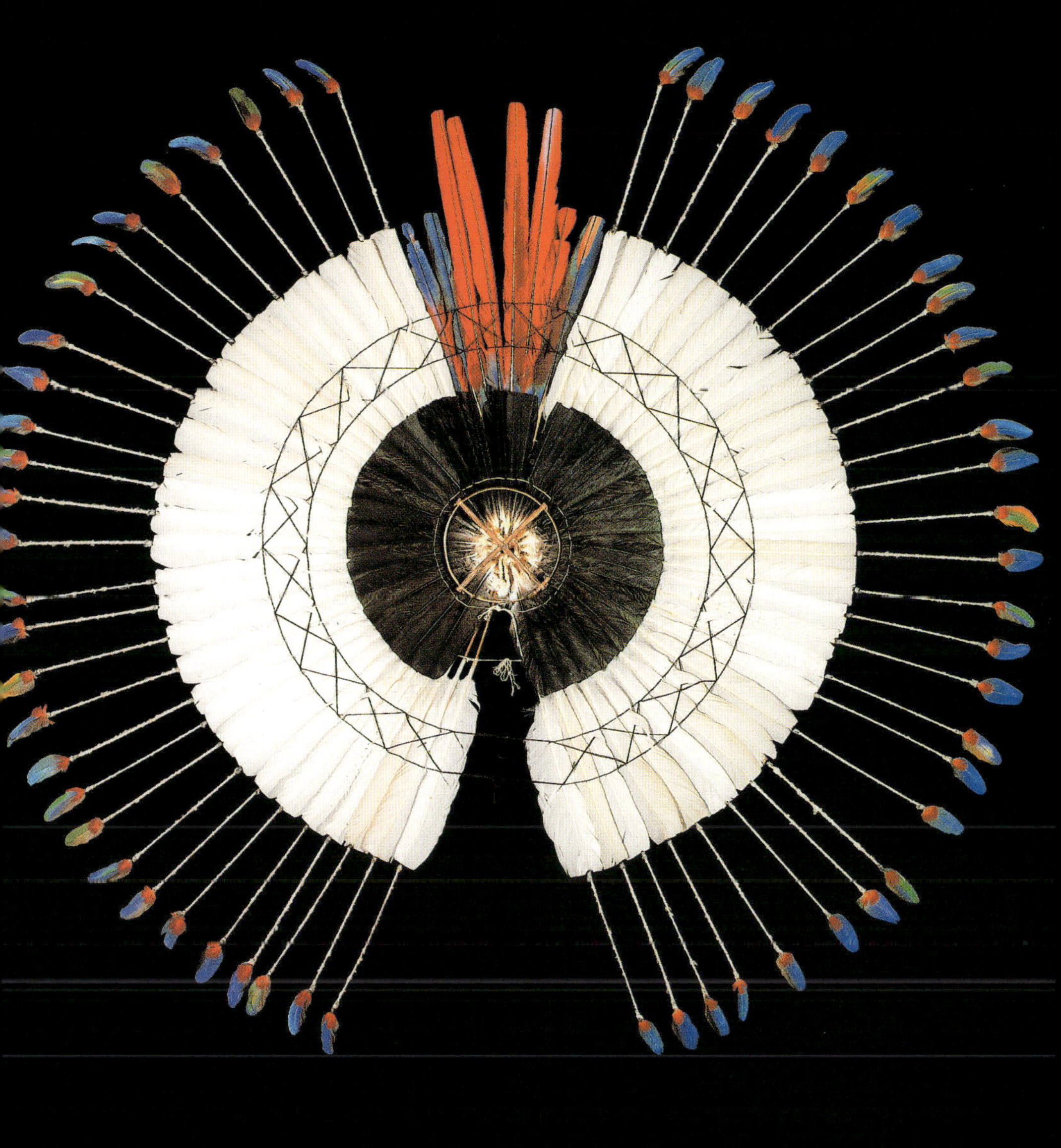

SENSITIVE SKIN

As Claude Lévi-Strauss noted in Tristes Tropiques, for the Caduevo Indians, "A body which is not painted is a stupid body, one has to be marked to be a man." Although nearly all the peoples of South America have adorned their bodies with colors and an infinite variety of motifs, the masters of this pictorial practice are undoubtedly the peoples of the Amazonian forests and savannas. "To give an idea of the luxury of these naked Indian body decorations, I note that an adult in the prime of life obtains in exchange for fifteen days of work just enough chica to paint himself red. Like poor people from temperate countries who complain about not having enough to buy clothes, here one hears the Orinoco Indians declare themselves so miserable that they cannot even paint half their body," wrote the German naturalist Alexander von Humboldt in his journal, Journey to the Equinoctial Regions of the New Continent on April 9, 1800. But despite several centuries of persecution, epidemics, and genocides, the Indians of Brazil have not forgotten the refined art of their ancestors, with its stunning, decorative grammar and sophisticated palette.

With amazingly daring acts, these innate artists borrow the language of nature and reinvent it: A few dots on the face are all that's required to slip into the skin of a snake, black and brown marks imitate the jaguar, and abstract wings painted on the cheeks suddenly metamorphose a human into a bird of prey, the lord of the air. There is nothing fortuitous in this dizzyingly beautiful pictorial alchemy: Conciliating the cunning spirits of forest and thicket; interceding for the fertility of the fields; performing the cyclic rituals accompanying the harvests; hunting and fishing; treating the sick; warding of scourges and illness; and miming the mythical events that created the world are just some of the uses of this teeming cutaneous iconography. In these societies, hastily labeled "primitive," the ornamentation and transformation of the body is an ideal means or form of language for communicating with the supernatural

Caduveo Indian woman. Brazil. Photograph by the Italian explorer Guido Boggiani (August 8, 1897). Fric Collection, Prague.

Preceding pages: **Yanomami Indian women.** Lgarape River, Roraima State, Brazil. Photograph by Sebastiao Salgado Amazona.

Anthropomorphic burial urn. Circa 1000. Lower Amazon, Brazil. Terra-cotta. H. 15.2″.
Museo Barbier-Mueller de Arte Precolombino, Barcelona.
Young Caduveo woman with paintings on her face, shoulders, and chest.
Photograph by Claude Lévi-Strauss (1935).

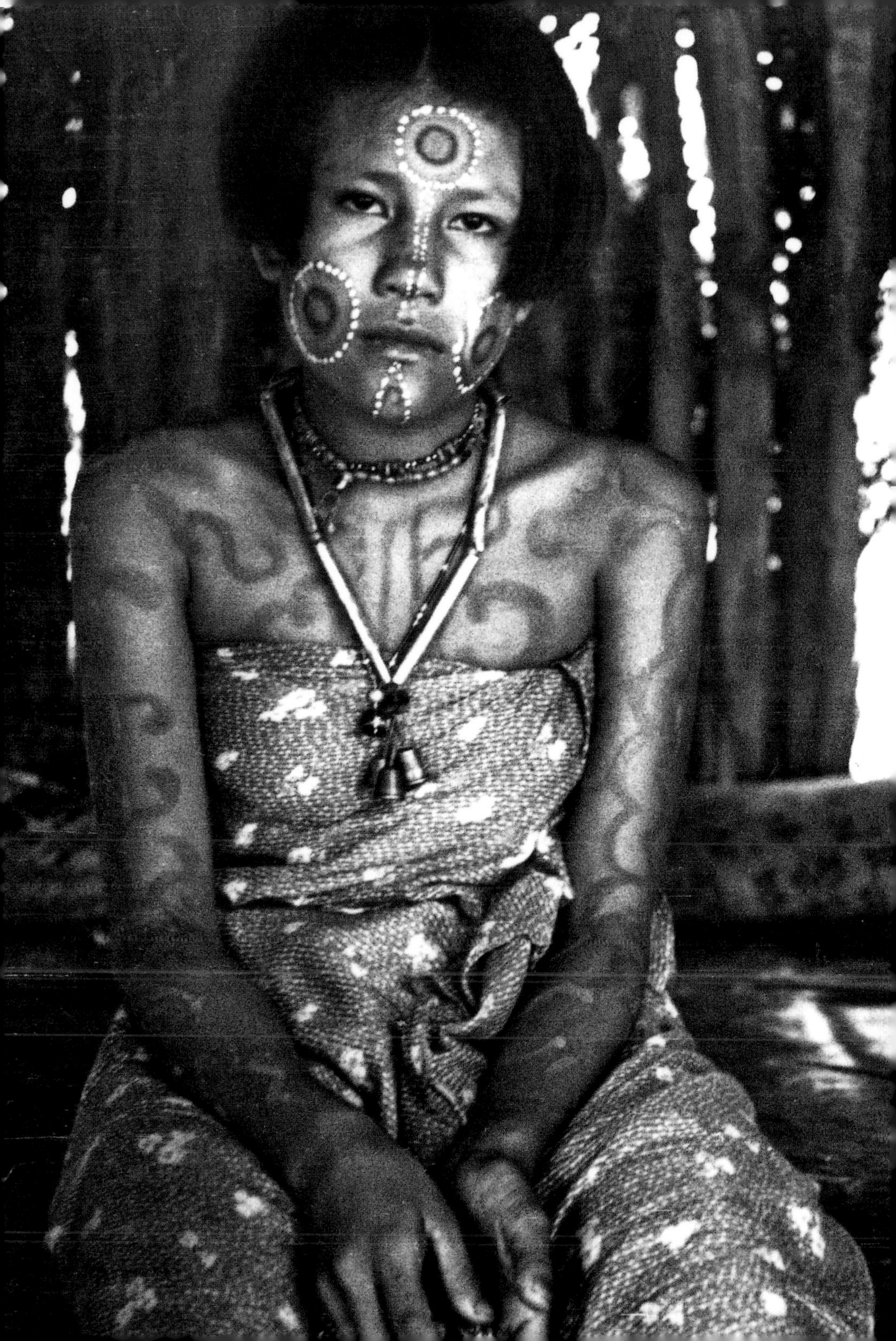

world. Body painting, the act of superimposing on one's naked biological skin a second, social skin, expresses the socialization of the human body while assigning it its place in the cosmos. Only Kayopo–Xikrin and Caduveo women paint themselves, while feathered dress is reserved exclusively for men. Innumerable designs and motifs spring forth from the expert hands of these inspired artists: Straight or broken lines, triangles, quadrilaterals, and ocelli that suggest jaguar's spots or furtive steps of an animal. Most of these highly stylized motifs are incomprehensible without the artist's explanation. A women painter wears the insignia of her role as artist on her body: A black hand dyed with genipapo represents the palette, while the other hand, painted white, holds the brush. True, these marks act as an insignia. To push back the limits of appearances, to favor the cosmic encounter between the earthly and spirit worlds, to produce a work of art capable of giving aesthetic pleasure while increasing the status of the group: These are the conscious aims of these body decorations, which no exhibition could ever really re-create. An exhibition will never be able to fully capture the shamanic dimension of metamorphosis rituals, the vividness of the perfumes and chants, and the dance of these motifs on bodies, spinning and jumping like magnificent birdmen.

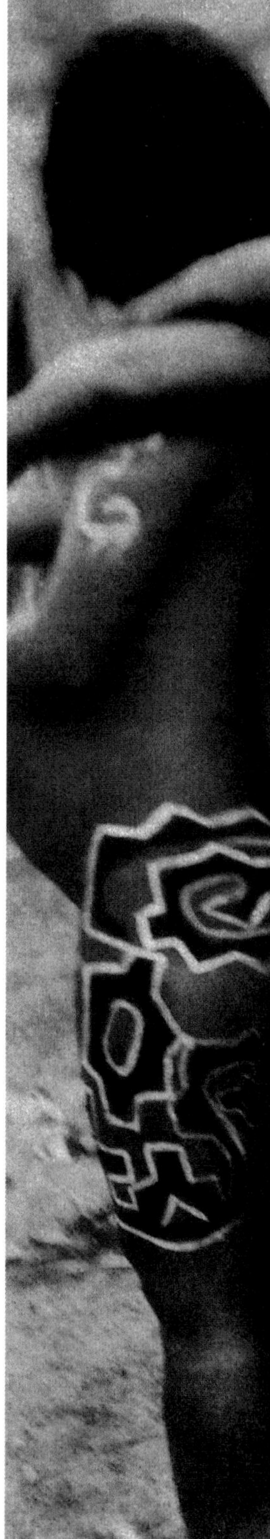

Ocaina girls with body painting. Photograph by Major Thomas Whiffen (1896). BNF/Sociéte de géographie, Paris.
Following pages: **Cubeo mask.** Amazon. H. 55".Museo Barbier-Mueller de Arte Precolombino, Barcelona.
Person wearing a jaguar mask, blowing into a ceramic pot. Photograph by Theodor Koch-Grünberg (1910).

Panamanian Psychedelic Ceramics: Art in a State of Ecstasy

A crab motif with a diamond-shaped vulva symbol inside it and with the symbol of the toothed vagina as a mouth; a poisonous stingray's backbone; a shamanic iguana with a visible embryo; a figure with a birdlike head and winged arms, and so on . . . phantasmagorical creatures straight out of a Surrealist poem? No, merely a list of motifs on ancient Panamanian ceramics.

These unusual pieces are like no other and are of an extreme asceticism, clarity, and fluidity that is alien to pre-Colombian art, and which many have taken little interest in or ignored. Tripods and dishes conjure a dreamlike world, located somewhere at the margins of reality; their formal repertoire is still an enigma for ethnologists and their style is revered by only a few enthusiasts, above all the Swiss collector Jean Paul Barbier-Mueller, who, over the last ten years, has amassed a quintessential selection of these terra-cotta pieces that defy rigid classification and simplistic interpretation.

Vase. AD 950–110. Gran Cocle region, Panama. Ceramic. H. 7.8" Ø 11.7". Museo Barbier-Mueller de Art Precolombino, Barcelona. Left: **Polychrome dish.** AD 700–850. Gran Cocle region, Panama. Ceramic. Ø 10.4". Museo Barbier-Mueller de Art Precolombino, Barcelona.

There is not the slightest ferocity, violence, or formal religiosity in this art from the frontiers of Mesoamerican civilization, a culture usually so obsessed with blood and sacrifice. The liberty of these drawings seems so complete and indicative of such frenzied modernism that they could have been painted by a contemporary artist. And yet archaeologists working in these exuberantly tropical regions are certain that most of these ceramics are over a thousand years old. The soberly expressive stone statuary and sumptuous metalwork of ancient Panama first attracted the attention of collectors and scholars in the nineteenth century. The French explorer Louis Catat, on a reconnaissance expedition in the Darien province in 1889, was clearly struck by the Panamanian archaeological remains he saw there, and which he considered clear signs of an ancient civilization. It was not until the very early twentieth century, however, that the first genuinely archaeological excavations were carried out there. The first expedition, led by the famous anthropologist Sigvald L. Linné, was Swedish-backed. But the ceramics of these fertile Pacific regions soon aroused the curiosity of major North American institutions. On the site at El Caño, the writer Alpheus Hyatt Verrill, a likeable crackpot who prided himself on his knowledge of archaeology, discovered a ceremonial area with ten sculpted basalt anthropomorphic and zoomorphic columns, and in true Romantic spirit, promptly concocted woolly theories as to why the presumed temple was abandoned. But the far more levelheaded Peabody Museum of Archaeology and Ethnology at Harvard University sent Samuel Kirkland and his team to carry out extensive excavations, which were so successful that the University of Pennsylvania soon followed suit. Dozens of sepulchers were unearthed, all packed with offerings: Ostentatious finery, gold, emerald, ivory, and agate jewelry, and hundreds of polychrome ceramics revealed the great refinement of these highly hierarchical societies and much more. The archaeologists marveled at the extraordinary cosmology they discovered on these multicolored terra-cotta, in which the real mingles with the supernatural and the animal with the

Detail of a polychrome dish. AD 250–1500. Veragas or Tonosi, Panama. Terra-cotta. Ø 16.4". Museo Barbier-Mueller de Art Precolombino, Barcelona.

human. This was the art of a waterlogged region of marshlands and snaking rivers whose inhabitants—crocodiles, tortoises, sawfish, shellfish, and scorpions—were gods, spirits, and heroes. This steamy, tropical world was one in which visions, reality, myth, and the supernatural so easily dissolved into one another, and one in which drugs were sovereign. There is indeed something of the psychedelic in the hallucinatory drawings, overexcited spirals and trembling stripes of ancient Panamanian ceramics. Was the inspired artist who drew these meandering lines revolting against the boredom of geometry? And who is this haggard, wide-eyed antipodean gorgon scornfully brandishing arm stumps with razor-sharp claws? Like her distant Greek counterpart, her face is simian, her body squat, and her limbs puny. She is a monster, both horrifying and grotesque, animal and human, repellent and disturbing, and an embodiment of the irrational. And why are these four tortoises, seen from the sky, dancing some macabre farandole around a petrified lizard? And who are these grimacing spiders, basking crocodiles, snakes and scorpions, crabs and crustaceans staring at with bulging eyes? Could this terrifying yet painstakingly lifelike menagerie be some mysterious clan symbolism? It matters little to the eye, which is swept away, hypnotized by its spirals, volutes, meanders, zigzags, and stripes. Art here is all illusion, trompe l'oeil, and imposture, just as on archaic Chinese bronzes, the mask of the ambiguous t'ao-t'ieh monster, with its stiff profile, squatting legs, and coiled tail, could be shying away from the viewer or deceiving him. Or, just as two figures in the same motif can reappear independently of one another, or a false-negative drawing can disappear into a white background. One obsessive anthropomorphic face with a carnivorous smile dominates this extraordinary artwork. Does it belong to a priest, cacique, or shaman? The third possibility seems the most likely, given the immense power of these men—half sorcerers half spirits—in these regions. The shaman is the very embodiment of metamorphosis, the mediator between humans, animal powers, and superior forces. By taking psychotropic substances, the shaman can become a jaguar, bird, or spirit. His trances and fevers take him on a journey of initiation, one which enables him to see into the future, cast spells, and also cure

Polychrome bowl. AD 700–850. Gran Cocle region, Panama. Ceramic. Ø 16.4". Museo Barbier-Mueller de Art Precolombino, Barcelona.

and heal. The shaman, master of the beyond, was both respected and feared. So was this why clandestine diggers smashed these vases and bowls when they emerged from the shadows in all their convulsive beauty. The reason is unfortunately much more mundane. As Jean Paul Barbier-Mueller has pointed out, tomb pillagers, disgusted at not finding any gold jewelry, smashed these ceramics, which they regarded as worthless. The task of saving these magnificent pieces fell to archaeologists, and, in particular, to a handful of collectors intrigued by their bizarre repertoire and the formal simplicity of their designs. Who did them? A question all the more intriguing given that ancient Panamanian ceramics seems to have been an accident of Central American art. There is not the slightest reminiscence or trace of Mayan or Aztecan culture. Whether geometric or floral, brightly colored or strikingly sober, their motifs do have something rebellious about them. "Like a Pollock canvas explodes out of the frame, escapes from its stretcher, the ceramics of Gran Cocle Culture area—where they are particularly beautiful—extend out into space," Jean Paul Barbier-Mueller enthusiasticaly points out. They make exuberant use of that most delicate of colors, violet, which breaks with the original three-color scheme. It is tempting to see the hand of "possessed" artists in them. "Were the male or female potters who painted these other-worldly drawings and hues on clay depicting themselves in their moments of ecstasy?" wonders Jean Paul Barbier-Mueller, who describes his favorite motif as "a sawfish revised and updated by some nutty professor."

CUNA MOLAS:
"EMBROIDERIES OF THE WORLD"

"Mola is the Cuna Indian word for any piece of fabric, all clothes and, in a literal or metaphoric sense, anything that covers: The foliage of a tree, the clouds in the sky, a bird's plumage, skin. It is also the name of the pictures embroidered on the front and back of women's garments," explains the ethnologist Michel Perrin, who regularly lives with these people scattered over the tiny coral islands off the Panamanian coast. He speaks their language and has been observing and studying them for almost twenty years. He also admires their extraordinary textiles, ignored, even regarded with contempt by many, but which, largely thanks to him, are now considered as works of art in their own right. Their graceful volutes and labyrinthine meanders and arabesques take one back into a primordial age when man, beast, mountains, plains, rivers, and seas were one.

Although their origin is still shrouded in mystery (Michel Perrin emphasizes the strange link between some of these embroideries and the pre-Colombian ceramics discovered in the Gran Cocle Culture area in central Panama), their formal power is stunning. Molas, which are almost exclusively the work of women, have the lightness and gaiety of a Paul Klee, the geometricality of a Victor Vasarely, and sometimes even the fear of the void of a Robert Combas.

Kuna Indian women threading beads. 1984. Panama.
Following pages: **Mola.** 1925. Kuna Indians. Panama. Private collection.

NORTH AMERICA

More Indian Than Indian

"The Indians of the different tribes living in the Upper Missouri region are undoubtedly the most handsome looking, and have the best equipment and finest clothing of all their kind on the North American continent. They live in a region abounding in bison and wild horses, which procures them health and longevity. Of all the Indians I have met, they are the most independent and happiest; they live entirely in their natural state, and consequently are almost indescribably beautiful and pleasant to behold. Nothing in the world can surpass the beauty and grace of some of their games, pastimes, festivities and parades, which I will later discuss and paint" —George Catlin, *North American Indians* (reedition Albin Michel, 2004)

In the first half of the nineteenth century, the paintings of George Catlin, the young American artist who wrote this idyllic description of the peoples of the Great Plains, had already began propagating the myth of the proud, noble Indian. But he was, of course, ignoring the ravages of the American conquest. There was another, far less rosy side to the picture. Smallpox and other diseases brought from Europe were decimating entire tribes, and the freedom of the Indian people was melting away. And yet every account by the first European travelers, lost in wildernesses traversed by buffalo herds, contributed to this myth. The Sioux, Crow, Blackfoot, and Comanche seemed to epitomize Europe's vision of this primitive, noble race of the New World.

Navajo Indians in Canyon de Chelly, northeast Arizona.
Photograph by Edward S. Curtis (1904).

While Fennimore Cooper was glorifying *The Last of the Mohicans* (published in 1826), two young artist-explorers were recording the haughty faces of Indian chiefs and their subjects on canvas and paper. In 1832 and 1833, the Swiss painter Karl Bodmer, accompanying his Russian patron (Prince Maximilian of Wied-Neuwied), covered some eight thousand kilometers in thirteen months, while from 1830 to 1836, George Catlin spent six springs and summers studying the nomadic tribes of the Great Plains: The Mandan, Sioux, Cree, Assiniboine, Gros Ventre (Big Belly), and Crow. No tribe eluded their feverish, methodical study. If Bodmer seems to have worked in the grand manner of the Renaissance masters (doing numerous sketches and drawings of his subjects before coloring them), Catlin worked more rapidly, driven by a greater sense of urgency. Catlin could paint six paintings a day, without a single sketch, thinning his oil paint so that it would dry quicker. Apart from their undeniable documentary value (for ethnologists, their works are still manna from Heaven), these works reflect an undeniable aesthetic emotion. But while Bodmer seemed to remain detached from his subjects, like a scientific observer, Catlin—the young American—showed genuine empathy for his subjects: His colorful pictures magnify the beauty and dignity of these natural men; his heart bleeds "because of the fate awaiting the survivors of this unfortunate race." His portrait gallery was shown all over Europe and acclaimed by artists and writers, including Charles Baudelaire, Eugène Delacroix, Charles Dickens, Victor Hugo, and George Sand. King Louis Philippe of France ordered fifteen copies for Versailles, and even allotted them an exhibition room in the Louvre. Despite this, Catlin died a few years later, riddled with debt and his wonderful Indian dream in ruins.

The American Edward S. Curtis, heir to a generation of photographers anxious to record the last moments of a dying race, also spent all his money and energy on cataloging the customs of over eighty North American tribes. But the veritable visual encyclopedia he published between 1907 and 1930 was a commercial flop despite its great aesthetic merits. Curtis was accused of being more interested in emotion than scientific rigor. After all, had he not given his subjects typical Indian clothes when they no longer had their traditional costumes or were already dressing in the European style? Steeped in the ideals of the nineteenth-century Romantics, Curtis even retouched his prints to make a sky more dramatic or efface all trace of modernity. But in their choice of expressions, poses, settings, and accessories, these late-nineteenth-century photographs depict larger-than-life Indians. His pictures awakened many a fantasy and dream well before the rise of filmmakers and advertisers, but the reality behind the myth was infinitely more complex and tragic. In December 1890, the last Sioux died in the snows of Dakota, the great chief Sitting Bull was murdered, and a few days later the massacre of Big Foot and his men at Wounded Knee seemed to seal the fate of American Indian peoples. Confined to reserves and deprived of freedom of speech and their collective memory and rituals, the peoples of the forests and plains perished slowly amid indifference and contempt. For many Americans, they were merely the ghosts of a bygone past. And the story may well have ended there had it not been for the courage and energy of these peoples who, although they have no written language, libraries, or temples, have left the rest of humanity their vision of the world and heritage of dances, chants, and ceremonies, all of which cry out their pride in being Indian. Their culture is the result of twelve thousand years of adaptation to their natural and social environment.

Despite their diversity, a single ideal seems to bind all these communities together: Their respect for nature, the Mother Earth that is both the origin and the culmination of everything, the sacred place where the bones of their ancestors rest. These men and women were ecologists before their time, also great artists, whose works, only recently admired in museums, are still laden with

Buffalo Bill posing with Indian chiefs
wearing traditional beaded leather clothes and headdresses.

dreams. One only has to look at the magnificent bead decoration on Iroquois bags, the graceful "butterfly" hair sticks of Arizona, or Navajo blankets of dazzling modernity, or even—infinitely more baroque—flamboyant Cheyenne feather headdresses that would turn the monarchs of the world green with envy. They seem now like a warning to all the gravediggers of history, to all the shadow snatchers. After all, according to one Indian song, still sung today, "We have all death to sleep."

The shaman Little Big Mouth outside his tent near Fort Sil, Oklahoma, in 1869. Photograph by William S. Soule.
Left: ***Mandeh-Pachu, a young Mandan Indian.*** Color lithograph by Huerlimann after a watercolor by K. Bodmer (1809–93). Nordamerika Native Museum, Zurich.

***Mu-ho-she-kaw* (White Cloud).** George Catlin, 1845–46. Oil on canvas. 31.4" x 25.3".
Commissioned by King Louis-Philippe of France.
Formerly in musée de l'Homme. Musée du Quai Branly, Paris.
Left: **A Pigean dandy.** 1900.

Masks and Totems: The Heraldic Art of the Northwest Coast

"It is in New York, a magical place where childhood dreams gather to meet, where secular tree trunks sing and speak, where indefinable objects watch the visitor with the anxious fixity of faces, where animals of superhuman kindness join their little paws like hands, praying for the privilege of building a beaver's palace for the elected one, to be his guide in the kingdom of the seals or teach him with a mystical kiss the language of the frog or kingfisher. This place, on which outdated but singularly effective curatorial methods have conferred the added prestige of cave-like chiaroscuro and heaps of lost treasures, can be visited daily from 10:00 A.M. to 5:00 P.M., at the American Museum of Natural History. It is the vast room on the ground floor devoted to the Indian tribes of the north Pacific coast, which stretches from Alaska to British Columbia" —Claude Lévi-Strauss, extract from *The Way of Masks*, 1979.

In 1778, the explorer James Cook was probably the first European to encounter these strange men dressed in flowing robes woven from cedar bark, their bodies tattooed, their noses ringed, their lips decorated with bone labrets, and their artificially deformed skulls adorned with huge hats. But these autochthonic peoples of the northwest weren't uncivilized "barbarians." They lived in magnificent painted wood dwellings decorated with totems, produced art of great sophistication and complexity, and performed ceremonies and rituals whose magnificence was rivaled only by their theatricality. The highly hierarchical Indians of the forests and lakes, lovers of the beautiful, had elaborated an aesthetic language on the frontiers of the real, which teemed with strange forms and was reigned by the disturbing figures of the wolf, bear, and crow.

Potlatch dancers. 1904. Klinkwan, Alaska.

Mask of a woman. Tlingit. 19th Century. British Columbia, Canada. Painted wood, beads, and bone ear ornaments. H. 7.8". Formerly in musée de l'Homme. Musée du Quai Branly, Paris. Left: **Tlu'wulahu costume.** Photograph by Edward S. Curtis (1914).

When white men first landed on this narrow strip of land stretching from Alaska down to Oregon in the second half of the eighteenth century, they were astounded by the highly stratified societies they discovered there. These tribes of fisher-hunter-gatherers, composed of slaves, commoners, and high-ranking people, and ruled by chiefs whose authority and prestige far outreached village or clan boundaries, benefited from an exceptionally rich environment—rivers full of fish, and deep fjords and dense forests—which ensured them their comfortable lifestyle.

Until the early twentieth century, these communities lived in extended families in spacious communal houses, sharing a cultural heritage of rituals and beliefs and also a system of artistic representation unlike any other in the Amerindian world. Teeming with monsters, supernatural creatures, and innumerable semiabstract signs, their artworks had both a religious and social meaning, affirming the power of a family or clan, or the ancestry of a greatly venerated lineage. In all their art, from the totem poles in front of their houses to the decoration of their robes, spoons, and chests, ones sees the same horror of the void, the same swarms of hybrid forms in which the practiced eye gradually learns to make out a beak or the exaggeratedly large eyes of a bird. But there is no improvisation in these carpets of imagery. They played the role of family coat of arms. Everywhere, one sees the obsessive and ancestral motif of the crow—a creature more dreamlike than real—with a broad face, dilated nostrils, mouth, ears, spread wings, and plumed tail. A subtle game of sinuous combinations and contrasting color complements the labyrinthine aesthetic of these canvas shields. As the French ethnologist Marie Mauzé, a specialist in the art of these regions, has explained, the primary line was accompanied by a secondary line, painted in

Preceding pages: **Masks of the fish devil and octopus hunter.**
Qagyuhl. Photograph by Edward S. Curtis (1914).
Statue of a shaman. 20th Century. British Columbia, Canada. Red cedar and fish teeth.
Formerly in the Claude Lévi-Strauss Collection, and musée de l'Homme. Musée du Quai Branly, Paris.

red, which enhanced the main motif; the "tertiary" spaces, so-called because they were delimited by the primary and secondary lines, were either sculpted in bas-relief or painted in blue. Symmetry was obtained using the "double-image" method, which consisted in giving a single figure a double profile, and thus both a frontal and exaggeratedly dilated appearance. Faced with these representations composed of distortions and reinterpretations of the real, one is immediately reminded of archaic Chinese bronzes, haunted by the tutelary, "gluttonous" figure of t'ao t'ieh. A discreet reminder of the Amerindians' Asian origins perhaps?

One finds the same jubilant creativity and formal profusion in the haughty silhouettes of their totem poles, reaching up into the cloud vault of the sky. The Haida totem poles, teeming with heads and bodies of bears, crows, killer whales, salmon, and sometimes even humans, are particularly exuberant, and proclaim loud and clear the prestige and wealth of the families who erected them.

But it is perhaps in their masks and their play of metamorphoses that the Indians of the Northwest Coast, these puppeteers of the imaginary and conjurers of the subconscious, excelled the most. Masks of crows snapping their beaks; a mask representing the Sun; bird masks suddenly opening to reveal a human face of stupefying hypnotic power: These are celestial mechanics for conversing with the spirit world. Claude Lévi-Strauss praised the genius of these visionary artists capable of shaking up the placidness of everyday life, disregarding beaten tracks and forever seeking new improvisations.

One figure dominated this society with all his aura and prestige: The shaman. Mediator between the real and supernatural worlds, healer, intercessor, and medium all in one, the shaman played a vital role in the tribes along the Northwest Coast, especially the Tlingits, famous for their sacred ceremonies. The climax of a shamanic ritual was the masked dance, in which the shaman donned his various masks (eight in all), in turn, embodying a celestial or marine creature,

a bird, or a dead warrior—a symbolic and ostentatious means of showing his ability to reign over the worlds of the living and the dead.

Just as spectacular, although nonreligious, were the potlatch ceremonies, which celebrated a chief's power and reinforced interfamily relations.Unbelievably magnificent, these celebrations included festivities (mimed dances and satirical sketches) and demonstrations of wealth (guests were showered with gifts). Missionaries and the authorities were swift to condemn them, seeing them as

Transformation mask. Kwakiutl. 19th century. British Columbia, Canada. Wood. H. 13.3" W. 20.7" (closed) 50.7" (open). Formerly in the Claude Lévi-Strauss Collection, and musée de l'Homme. Musée du Quai Branly, Paris.

useless and expensive wastes of abundance. What they did not see was the intrinsic purpose of these social gatherings: To bind the community.

The inhabitants of the Northwest Coast have always been an artist people. Far from remaining static, certain styles have traveled, evolved, and even found admirers outside their clan—the vast majority of this new clientele are Euro-Americans. And over the last thirty years there has been a genuine revival. The totem peoples have not yet said their last word.

Following pages: **Tlingit dancers' masks.** Qagyuhl. Mountain goat horn, cedar bark. Photograph by Edward S. Curtis (1914). Pages 272–73: **Detail of a blanket worn by certain dancers during *potlatches* (ceremonies).** The central motif depicts a bear with four bird's heads (crows and eagles). Circa 1860. British Columbia, Canada. Formerly in musée de l'Homme. Musée du Quai Branly, Paris.

The Painted Buffalo Hides of the Plains Indians

"During our stay in Paris we met people at the ethnological department of the Musée de l'Homme, and the curator was kind enough to show us their famous collection of painted hides. I had already heard about them, but this was the first time I had seen them first hand. I was so moved that I began blurting out a continuous flow of words about hide painting, describing the way in which the hide was cut and worn, the way the motifs were organized and the tools used to paint them . . . to my knowledge, they are the most ancient robes in the world" (Vitart, 1993).

This moving account was written by George Horse Capture, great grandson of a famous chief of the Gros Ventre (Big Belly) tribe on the Fort Belknap Reserve in Montana, and one of the most eminent American curators of Amerindian art. But knowledgeable as he was, he was suddenly confronted with a whole chunk of history, dislocated, like so many of his brothers, from its roots and traditions.

Resuscitated by ethnologists and deciphered by Indian lore, these garments of prestige, power, and dreams poetically reflect the lost grandeur of the cultures of the Plains Indians and the wealth of their spiritual universe dominated by the tutelary figure of the buffalo god.

"Lies Sideway." Crow Indian, Montana.
Photograph by Edward S. Curtis (1908).

Detail of a painted buffalo (?) hide. 18th century. USA.
Formerly in musée de l'Homme. Musée du Quai Branly, Paris.

Their colors are vivid and strident: A red extracted from wild berries; a green from lichen, moss, and other plants; a yellow from a particular type of Earth; and, of course, the famous ultramarine blue, obtained, according to the Indians, from a mineral mixture, or a decoction of duck excrement cooked in an oven. No matter what the secrets of their making, the sure drawing, flamboyant colors, and masterful compositions of the Plains Indians' painted robes are enthralling. What inner urges prompted these virtuoso painters to wield their brushes so freely on these hide canvases? Was it the desire to record—for future generations—their clan's memory, the grandeur of its myths, its war sagas, and betrayed alliances? It has often been said that the Indians have no past because they have no written language. One only has to look at these mantles, covered with hoof prints, stars, and other hieroglyphs—instantly understandable by the entire community—to realize that the opposite is true. Of course the Indians' violent colonization and

Sioux shaman painting the winter tale of the Missouri. Chronicle of his tribe on a deer hide.
Photograph taken around 1923.

***Ee-ah-sa-pa* (Black Rock)**, George Catlin, 1845–46. Oil on canvas. 32 x 25.4". Commissioned by King Louis-Philppe of France. Formerly in musée de l'Homme. Musée du Quai Branly, Paris.
Left: **Three villages mantel.** Painted buffalo hide from Illinois. 74 x 57".
Formerly in musée de l'Homme. Musée du Quai Branly, Paris.

Buffalo hunting in winter, George Catlin (1845–46). Oil on canvas. 32 x 25.4". Commissioned by King Louis-Philippe of France. Formerly in musée de l'Homme. Musée du Quai Branly, Paris.

the equally destructive effects of assimilation destroyed so many symbols and signs. One's puzzled gaze now roams over the forests of circles and diamonds whose hypnotic brilliance illuminates the center of many a robe.

The mystery of these stylized memory-paintings may one day be solved. Indians and whites, ethnologists and museum curators are studying these objects and their visions in an attempt to decipher the Indians' vivid chronicles of a world still at the height of its powers. They were painted at a time when, on the plains and elsewhere, the rhythm of existence depended on the wanderings of a giant hairy relic of prehistory, the terrifying but providential bison. Few animals have fashioned the life and beliefs of a people so completely as this enormous creature, weighing over a ton and measuring up to four meters long. The Indians depended on this prince of the prairies for their principal resources and most of their rituals and

Geronimo cutting up a buffalo. 1885.

beliefs. Its flesh sustained them: They made their tools and weapons from its bones, and their blankets and clothes from its skin. Its hooves, attached together, rang like cowbells; its skull was used as a potent medicine; its nerve fibers as bowstrings and thongs; its tendons as sewing thread; its horns as recipients for liquids; its tail as a paintbrush or flail for steam baths; and its gall stones were crushed to make paint. And, of course, its enormous, mythological outline inspired statuettes and effigies and the propitiatory amulets used in secret ceremonies. One of the Sioux's most important religious objects was a sacred pipe carved from the tibia of a young bison. Women revered the bison's model maternal behavior. And during that fundamental ceremony of the Indian peoples, the Sun Dance, all the participants ritually ate its tongue, believing it was a protective animal and patron of generosity and hospitality.

The tribes of the Plains modeled their entire existence on the buffalo god. They moved their tepees and families with each migration, dividing into smaller groups in the autumn to pass the winter in some deep valley sheltered from the cold, then reemerging in the spring to reassemble for the summer. These nomads had no use for superfluous objects. Instead of a fixed abode, they had a lightweight, easily dismountable, and erectable dwelling, the tepee. Their only possessions were their everyday light, unbreakable, and easily transportable utensils and implements. And for art, they had their clothes, finery and accessories: Shirts, belts, moccasins, headdresses, leggings, rings, and cushions, in which they concentrated all their aspiration for beauty.

One of this migrant people's most ambitious creations were the paintings they did on the hide of the mythical buffalo, and also sometimes on the hide of the elk, bighorn, deer, and, more rarely, horse. But it was in their ceremonial and protective dress that the sacred pact between the Plains Indian and the buffalo achieved its fullest expression. Women were responsible for preparing the hides. It was a codified, seven-stage process: Skinning, scraping, tanning, drying, then humidification with warm water, rinsing on a frame, and, finally, sanding. The hide, now immaculately smooth, was ready to be painted. Artistic expression was both a male and female activity, but each had their own motifs and languages. Women favored abstract forms. They decorated objects and garments with geometric symbols (parallel lines, diamonds, and triangles) and cabalistic signs. Did they inherit the exclusive right to use them from their mother? They may well have done, as certain motifs are specific to certain tribes. Men, on the other hand, used a figurative language based on pictograms (horses, men, buffalo, etc.) intended to glorify the tribe's feats of war or to depict shamanic dreams and visions. Many symbols, initially expressing intimate and intense relationships with the spirits of nature, gradually took on martial and almost heraldic meanings. As the French ethnologist Anne Viart has emphasized, they were probably meant to be examples for generations to come: "The Plains societies were essentially warlike. War was a glorious game with set rules in which braving risk and danger was more important than killing one's adversary. To approach an armed, unwounded enemy and merely "touch" him with a whip or a stick was braver than killing him. An individual's ascension of the social hierarchy depended on his moral value and warlike acts" (Vitart, 1993).

As in body paintings and tattoos, the scenes depicted on the robes of the Plains Indians were a kind of nonalphabetic writing, an illustrated chronicle of the tribe's collective memory. Yet there is nothing gratuitous in these combinations of solar motifs, silhouettes of tepees, and humans with puny limbs. They are the actors of a secret opera whose score has been lost. One can never overestimate the devastating effects of colonization on the collective memory of these tribes. Very often one can only guess at the meaning of these images. It has been thought that the geometric outline of these robes is the decomposed shape of a buffalo, as in a Surrealist drawing. Anne Viart suggests that "the painted robe thus becomes, using a thinking close to European logic, the mnemonic recall of a communication between men and the holy, in the same way that the statues of saints in Catholic churches recall the pacts between men and God" (op. cit.).

One particularly recurrent motif that has fascinated ethnologists is the thunderbird. For many tribes, this easily identifiable slender figure with outspread wings whipping up the storm is the ideal mediator between man and Creator—with whom the warrior would like to enter into secret alliance when on dangerous buffalo hunts.

But when contemplating these miraculously well-preserved pieces of pure painting, what delights divinely destabilized Western eyes is their curious mixture of innocent freshness and false simplicity. The willfully economical art of the Amerindians revels in ellipsis, in the subtle game of understatement. The appearance of U-shaped hoof prints indicates a herd of horses, a single finger indicates that the warrior probably lost his hand in combat, a feather headdress symbolizes tribal identity, and a scalp represents victory. And what could possibly be more allusive and effective than a mere line to express the linearity of a story.

Figurative, abstract, realist, and visionary, these memory strips plunge one into the primordial world of wanderings and dreams, in which men converse with the powers of darkness and the Sun, warriors wear feather headdresses as high as the sky, and birds have the power to carry prayers to the Supreme Being. Soon, however, these Iliads and odysseys of the Indian world would begin to include a vaguely comic figure: A tiny white man wearing a hat and armed with a rifle. The rest is history.

Buffalo hide robe (detail). Thunderbird motif. Illinois Indians. 18th century (?).
H. 47.2" W. 42". Formerly in musée de l'Homme. Musée du Quai Branly, Paris.

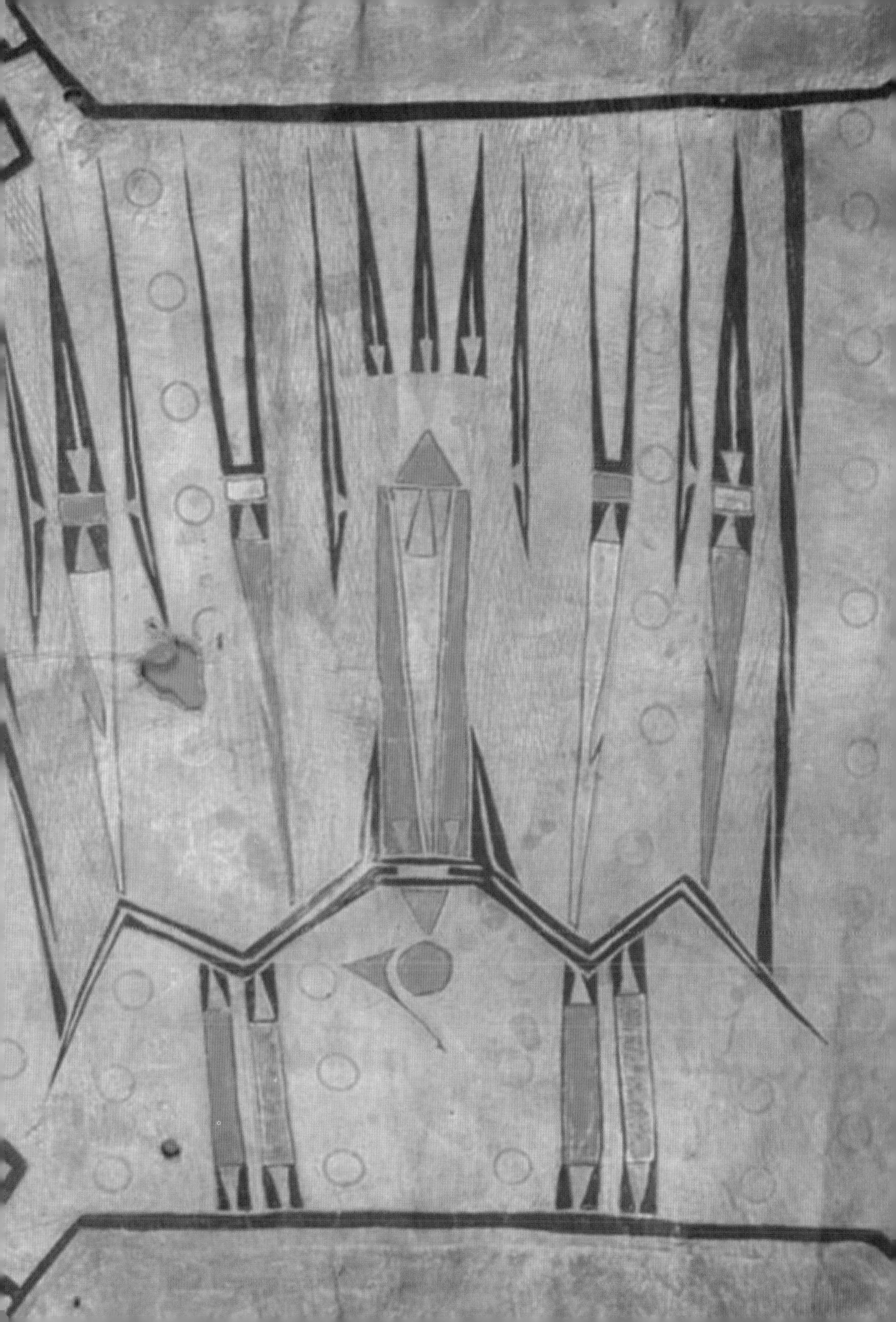

"THE SKY DOGS"

When the Blackfoot of the Northern Plains first saw a herd of horses thundering toward them, they could not believe their eyes. They decided it was the Supreme Being himself who had sent them these strange creatures that, in their minds, were larger and much faster dogs.

There is the legend, but there is also the very real impact the advent of the horse had on Amerindian cultures in the early seventeenth century. The mustang, the result of anarchic crosses between the mounts of the Spanish colonists and their adaptation to the environment, literally revolutionized the lives of these tribes. The horse was a rapid means of transport and also a bartering currency. It stimulated the emergence of a nomadic culture specific to the Great Plains, based essentially on buffalo hunting and war. One can't help but admire the saddles women embroidered with porcupine spines, the decoration of their harnesses, and the extraordinary masks that covered the horse's head, all of which illustrated the Indians' love and veneration for their mounts. For the Indians, the horse was an essentially holy creature with supernatural powers. For many tribes, it also became a symbol of prestige and wealth, and the Comanche and Cheyenne tribes became legendary in this respect.

Unfortunately, the same fate awaited the proud mustang as the buffalo herds. Both fell victim of American government policy, intent on eradicating all forms of Indian culture, and were almost completely exterminated.

Sioux Indians. Great Plains, Dakota.
Photograph by Edward S. Curtis (1905).

The Dance of the Kachina Dolls

André Breton's studio, rue Fontaine, Paris, 1955.

"This Hopi doll evokes the corn goddess: In the crenellated frame of the head, you can see clouds over the mountain; in the small checkerboard in the middle of the forehead, the corncob; around the mouth, the rainbow; in the vertical grooves of the dress, rain falling in the valley. Tell me, is this or is this not poetry as we continue to understand it?" —André Breton interviewed by the journalist Jean Duché in *Le Littéraire*

From the dawn of the twentieth century, the kachina dolls of the Hopi and Zuni Indians fascinated Emil Nolde, Marcel Duchamp, André Breton, Paul Éluard, and others. In no time, these ritual and pedagogical objects became fashionable gifts prized by ethnologists, Surrealist artists, and tourists alike. Yet irrespective of this enduring infatuation, these figurines continue to provide a multicolored and touching chronicle of the visible and invisible world of the Hopi Indians and their myriad spirits.

Kuwan Heheva kachina. 1900–10. Arizona. Poplar, feathers, and natural pigments. H. 12.5". Formerly in the collections of Claude Lévi-Strauss and Jacques Lacan. Galerie Flak, Paris.

Stiff as tin soldiers, daubed with paint, and dressed up in their party finery, they have flat or potbellied tummies and their eyes either bulge or slit. Their "familiar strangeness" is riveting. Who are these singular, deceptively, crudely drawn dolls, these ravishing little monsters made of wood, fur, and feathers? "Kachina": three sonorous, poetic syllables that evoke supernatural beings, half men/half gods, and the masked dancers embodying those spirits. They are also the sculpted cottonwood effigies given to children to familiarize them with their culture's complex and many-faceted pantheon. These figurines, sculpted in the shadows of a ceremonial room, embody the very essence of the Hopi and Zuni Indians, the inhabitants of an arid universe of sand and rocks, scorpions and snakes, whose pitilessly blue sky is only rarely visited by clouds bearing life-giving rain. For at least a thousand years, these peoples of the high plateaus and mesas of New Mexico and Arizona have been influencing the cosmos with their ceremonies, ensuring the perpetuity of their race. Yearly, from December to July, the dances of the kachina, veritable visual prayers to the heavens, reenact the primordial gestures that enable the Sun to continue on its course. Because, what are these dolls whose clumsy and poetic charms are such a pleasure to behold, if they are not a cosmic, joyous, and insolent inventory of a protean and mischievous universe?

These dolls—exact replicas of the masked dancers down to the very last detail—are neither idols nor toys. Their purpose is above all to familiarize young Indians with their people's many spirits. Eototo, for instance, is one such spirit. With his lunar, stupefied-looking face, he is immaculately dressed all in white (a sign of his importance) and holds the sacred gourd with which he "fills the water tanks." Or there is the more disturbing Mastop, the Death Fly Kachina, his chest tat-

Hopi Indian dressed for a sacred dance. From *Die Sitten der Dölker* by Dr. Georg Buschan (Union Deutsche Verlagsgesellschaft). Preceding pages: **Zuni woman wearing a tableta.** Photograph by Edward S. Curtis. **Angakchina mask with a tableta**. Zuni, Arizona. Poplar, red, black, and brown polychrome, leather, and beads. H. 26". Formerly in the Volz Collection. Private collection.

Mongwu Wuhti (woman owl with horns) kachina, by the Hopi sculptor W. Tawaquaptewa. 1930s. Arizona, United States. Poplar and natural pigments. H. 9.2". Galerie Flak, Paris.
Right: **Hopi Indians, New Mexico.** Photograph by Edward S. Curtis (1906).

tooed with the imprints of white hands, the signature of the Bear Clan and its talented painters. There are countless others: Long-Beaked Kachina, Whipper Kachina with his menacing beard, Sorcerer Kachina with his curious mask traversed by multicolored dominos, and so on. There are also the Lady Kachinas, with their elegant, coiled hair-styles and the Butterfly Girl Kachinas with their extraordinary stepped headdresses (staircases to the sky) symbolizing the clouds, whose cheeks are striated with red chevrons to evoke the slanting morning rains. One sometimes wonders whether one should laugh or grimace at the Ogre Kachinas, brandishing their long saws, broad knives, and hatchets dripping with blood. Less threatening are the Clown Kachinas, known as "jester men with mud heads," the bulging-eyed Mocking Kachina, the Rattle Kachina, with his strangely ovoid skull, the Rabbit Stick Kachina, with his yellow antennae pointing skyward like two question marks. The inventory of these prodigiously inventive hybrids of vegetable and

Mastop (Death Fly) kachina (front and back). Circa 1920–30. Arizona. Poplar, feathers, twigs, and natural pigments. H. 7.2". Galerie Flak, Paris.

mineral, human and animal, masculine and feminine, laughter and fear, is far from complete. Duck, owl, eagle, the entire winged race, with its long tapered beaks, feathered scalps, and collars has turned out in force to persuade the spirits to bring their life-nurturing rain clouds. Bear, badger, antelope, cow, an entire Noah's ark. But plants and vegetables, so primordial for these inhabitants of the high plateaus, also have their part to play in the visual orgy of forms and colors, in a vegetable masquerade in which the cactus's guests are the red pepper, corncob, bean, squash, and multicolored flowers.

"Today, 22 August 1945, at Mishongnovi, from the bottom of the ladder that descends mysteriously into the kiva, the sacred Hopi subterranean chamber, I salute you as the snakes are indicating with a final knot that they are ready to accomplish their union with the human mouth . . . From the most distant ripple of the echo which awakens the foot that imperiously stamps on the ground to seal the alliance with the powers which cause the seeds to germinate." The author of these archaic and passionate lines addressed to the Indian people is none

The saguaro. The white flower of this giant cactus is the emblem of Arizona.
Photograph by Barry Goldwater (1940).
Ygya kachina. Hopi. Painted wood. H. 15.2". Horst Antes Collection.

Zuni dance. Photograph by George Wharton James.

other than André Breton, pope of Surrealism and defender of the redskin cause. Almost twenty years before, he wrote *Ode à Charles Fourier* and proclaimed that "the eye exists in a wild state." He and Paul Éluard, then an art dealer, were already collecting these strange dolls "decorated with blue zigzags." And it was Breton who, in 1936, organized a large Surrealist exhibition to display kachina dolls, Oceanian pieces, and works by the mentally ill and insane at Galerie Charles Ratton, the leading primitive art dealer of the day. In parallel, the painter and sculptor Max Ernst, in exile in New York like Breton and so many other European artists at that time, also fell in love with Indian culture. He went to Hopi country in the summer of 1941 and returned there to live with his wife Dorothea Tanning at Sedona in the Arizona desert from 1946 to 1956. We know the huge influence these grandiose and timeless landscapes had on Max Ernst's painting: His petrified forests are testaments to the blistered Earth of the Indian desert. We know less, however, about the painter's mystical and amorous communion

Kachina dance during the Powamu festival. Walpi. Photograph by James Mooney (1893).

with Hopi culture and its ceremonial rituals and forms, traces of which are to be seen in his famous sculptures *Capricorn* (1948) and *King Playing with the Queen* (1944).

And it was not by chance that several other Surrealists were, in turn, inspired by the Hopis' dreamlike and poetic universe, a shady world oscillating between extreme rigor (each color on the dolls indicates a cardinal point, a function, a clan, etc.), and fantasy (their humor often degenerates into subversive, even scatological eroticism). The dolls, which were initially sculpted in the womblike shadows of a ceremonial chamber before being hung from the beams of an Indian household (or, more prosaically, in the display cases of collectors), found themselves, by one of those somersaults that art history so often performs, in Joan Miró's huge ethereal canvases, and the inspired gouaches which Marc Chagall produced in 1945 for Stravinsky's *Firebird* (according to a study by Francis Ndiaye, one of the models for the costumes was directly inspired by the

speckled figure of Kokosori, the "Young God of Fire"), or, more recently, in the violent and primitive canvases of the Argentinean painter Jorge Camacho.

Today, kachina dolls have become the fashionable prizes of novice collectors, whose eyes are not always as astute as André Breton's or André Malraux's. Some are magnificently sober, others stridently vulgar. Yet the stylistic evolution of these ritual effigies is by no means recent. In the nineteenth century, the earliest figurines (completely flat and summarily carved in cottonwood roots) were gradually superseded by highly realistic sculptures in the round. Legs began to protrude from beneath the rounded skirt, arms sprouted from the trunk, and accessories appeared. Although a ritual object at the outset, the kachina doll soon became a tourist souvenir. Some sculptors even began introducing deliberate errors into their works (inversions, additions or omissions of symbols, colors, etc.) to protect their secret culture. As early as 1910, the feet grew larger to increase the figurine's stability when stood on a shelf instead of hung on a wall—a market-driven innovation that would gradually transform the kachina doll into a curio. And, of course, erotic subjects, a characteristic trait of Hopi humor, disappeared to comply with the morals of the Euro-American market. Pigments also began to be replaced by the industrial paints that would sound the knell of traditional colors. As yet another concession to collectors, kachina doll sculptors began to sign their works. The ultimate heresy came when women began sculpting dolls. Mary Shelton became famous for sculpting an Aya Kachina one and a half centimeters high. To please an increasingly broad clientele, artists began catering to the most ephemeral fashions—the latest fad is for a fanatical hyperrealism combined with the most caricatured pornography. This acculturation went a step further with the intrusion of strangers into the Hopi pantheon such as White Bison, the Snake Dancer, and a bizarre little rodent strangely reminiscent of Mickey Mouse.

Alo Mana kachina. Hopi. Circa 1920. Painted wood and string. H. 8.6". Museum of Indian Arts and Culture, Sante Fe, New Mexico.

What is the state of the art of the Hopi Indians today, at the dawn of the twenty-first century? A vulgar caricature of a people sucked into the American maelstrom? The blooming of kachina doll exhibitions and festivals would seem to contradict this. Some Hopi sculptors—Alvin James Makya, Von Monongya, and Dennis Tewa—are now considered as full-fledged artists in their own right. But despite these metaphors, the true kachina dolls are still those which continue to spiritually and viscerally unite the Indian to the Earth of his ancestors.

Anthropomorphic figure. Pueblo, New Mexico. Poplar root and natural pigments. H. 14". Private collection. Galerie Flak, Paris.
Left: **Patung kachina.** Hopi. 1950. Painted wood. H. 10.9". Horst Antes Collection.

A STRICT VOCABULARY OF FORMS AND COLORS

Just like the costumes and masks of the dancers, the making of kachina dolls obeys rules as strict as those governing Tibetan mandalas. There is no anecdotal detail, nor the slightest embellishment in the choice of their attributes or the elaboration of their decoration. The Hopi Indians' basic material is the root of the cottonwood tree, well-known for its ability to descend deep in search of water—a quality bound to please a people perpetually praying for rain.
Once it has been sculpted, the root is coated with a clay-based paste on which the colors are then applied. These were once all vegetable or mineral pigments but have since been replaced by acrylic paints, and if many symbols and accessories are no longer understood by the Hopis themselves, many rules are still obeyed. The colors always refer to the six cardinal points: Yellow for north, blue-green for west, red for south, white for east, black for the zenith, and gray or multicolored for the nadir. Hues can also symbolize the kachina doll's provenance, function, or belonging to a specific category. The doll's accessories are often its finishing touches. But here again, modernity has taken its toll. Formerly made out of leaves, and therefore perishable, their collars are now represented by a circle painted in green, and often include plastic. Mouse or squirrel fur has replaced other furs and leather. To preserve certain bird species, the use of feathers is now severely regulated by the hunting and fishing authorities. Hopi artists, instead of clothing their dolls in the sumptuous plumage of the eagle, now have to content themselves with pigeon or sparrow feathers. Some sculptors, afraid of being fined, have even stripped ancient dolls of the very feathers that gave them their original power and symbolism, thereby committing a dual artistic and spiritual sacrilege.

Kwasai Taka kachina. Hopi. Circa 1930. Arizona. Poplar, turquoise, feathers, and natural pigments. H. 8.6". Formerly in the Claude Lévi-Strauss Collection. Galerie Flak, Paris.

MASKS AND MASQUERADES: A WHIRLWIND OF PRAYERS

The Hopi world is a strictly codified universe in which nothing seems to be left to chance. Whether animal or vegetable, living or dead, human or supernatural, all creatures and things are linked to one another. This belief in reciprocity is so strong that it seems to govern every interaction. And the supernatural world—the realm of deities, demigods, kachinas, monsters, and ancestors—appears in many respects to be a replica of the Hopi world. Therefore, one has to treat with the greatest respect all these powers venerated by ceremonies and prayers in designated places of worship. In return, the spirits invoked bestow upon humans good health, rain, abundant corn, and livestock.

The kachinas, personified by masked dancers, can only make their appearance in Hopi villages during the first part of the year. The spirits descend on the plateaus at the end of December and live there until the end of July. During the semester that they are absent, they live as earthly beings, cultivating their fields and rejoicing with their families. When the spirits appear in Hopi villages, they are always warmly welcomed and showered with flour and gifts of food, tobacco, pine branches, paho prayer sticks, etc. Some villagers even sprinkle a few drops of precious water on them so that these Messengers of the Gods will summon the clouds to fertilize the fields. Kept well away from prying eyes, the masks of the *wyuya* (ancestors) are fed daily in the houses of the clans.

Nothing is too beautiful to gain the favor of the kachinas. From March to July, there are spectacular ritual dances in the village squares. In her superb book, *Kachina des Indiens Hopi,* Elisabeth Laniel-Le François wrote, "If once in your life you have contemplated the kaleidoscopic tableau of masked figures with their castle-like headdresses pouring their treasures (kachina dolls, fruits, and toys) out onto long green corncobs, you will never forget this firework display."

Zuni dancers. New Mexico. Photograph by John K. Hiller (1879).

Yet there is absolutely nothing gratuitous in these ballets-prayers, vital to the proper functioning of the cosmos. To take on the role of the masked dancer is a serious and totally binding act. The dancer has to submit to a whole range of obligations: No salt, meat, fat, or water during the dance, and, above all, total sexual abstinence during the four days preceding the festivities, during the festivities themselves, and during the four ensuing days. To not respect these rules could unleash the most terrible catastrophes.

But beyond these codes and rules, there is the intrinsic beauty of these dances, whose extraordinarily synchronous and grandiose choreographies, meted out by each stamping dancer, symbolize the rain pounding down on the rocks of the Mesa.

Following pages: **Talavai mask**. Circa 1900. Arizona. Galerie Kevin Conru, Paris.
Pages 312–13: **The goddess Haschebaad.** Photograph by Edward S. Curtis (1904).
Navajo Yel mask. Circa 1900. Arizona. Galerie Kevin Conru, Paris.

THE ARTIC WORLD

The Call of the Far North

Seamen, whalers, explorers, ethnologists, poets, and scholars have all succumbed to the beauty of these virgin, windblown wastes, and been moved by the pride of these peoples whose lifestyles and beliefs have remained untouched. The purity of their sublime and ferocious world has been a cathartic revelation for all.

"Eskimo" . . . three syllables which instantly conjure a vision of a primordial, uniformly white universe, a virginal land of dreams and fantasies. The ancient Greeks believed the souls of the dead were swept away to these distant climes by Boreas, god of the North Wind. Despite the geographic descriptions brought back by the first explorers, the Far North paradoxically came to epitomize an ideal place, peopled by pacific and brotherly inhabitants. Every year, Apollo, the most beautiful, youngest, and also most mysterious of the Greek gods, went on a strange pilgrimage to these distant lands populated with seals and sea monsters. The son of Zeus and Leto was a master of prophesy, and his priestess, Pythia, perched on her tripod, delivered oracles and predictions while chewing bitter plants (which no doubt induced her trances). So it is hardly surprising that on Greek vases one sees the terrifying, sepulchral figure of a shamanic crow, like

Young Eskimo made up to "play the mask." Kangerlussuatsiaq, Alaska.
Photograph by Paul-Emile Victor (1936).

Eskimo women building an igloo. June 1926. Alaska.

some discreet but disturbing reminder of the celestial and boreal acquaintances of the most seductive of Greek gods.

The Icelandic sagas also describe the exploits of the Viking Eric the Red, the first European to land on the island he christened Greenland to distinguish it from Iceland, the "Gray Land." According to Nordic literature and also Eskimo oral tradition, relations between the two communities were anything but pacific and there were even violent conflicts. Oddly, and for still obscure reasons—famine due to climatic cooling, the degeneration of the population due to intermarriage, massacres, enemy raids?—Europeans gradually deserted these regions in the late fifteenth century. For over two centuries, Greenland was again Eskimo land, whose shores were only occasionally visited by the whalers who ventured into Baffin Bay, or by a ship hopelessly trying to reach India by the Northwest Passage. Soon, though, missionaries and merchants were fighting for supremacy

Natives of Kotzebue Sound, Kamchatka, Siberia.
Illustration from Otto von *Kotzebue's Picturesque Travels Around the World,* 1822.

over these icebound shores, the former keen to harvest souls, the latter its untold riches. Meanwhile, at the other end of the Eskimo world, Russians greedy for more territory had reached Siberia by river and sea. The Bering Strait was discovered in 1648 by the Cossack Zemen Dezhnev. A few decades later, Czar Peter the Great sent a maritime expedition from the Kamtchatka Peninsula on Russia's far eastern coast. The rest is history: Russian and Siberian fur trappers and traders flocked to this new icebound El Dorado, bringing with them the Russian Orthodox religion, vodka, epidemics, depletion of its species, and the displacement of its populations.

In the nineteenth century, whaling increased the influx of Westerners eager to make their fortune in these Arctic waters. Scotsmen ventured into Melville Bay and Baffin Land, then, in the second half of the nineteenth century, American whaling ships from New England began mooring in Hudson Bay. This had a

disastrous effect on local populations and brought with it alcoholism and moral and spiritual despair.

The first anthropologists would, however, do much to alter this desperate situation. The Eskimos, scorned and considered barely human savages, would gradually acquire the more enviable status of primitives worthy of study. The exploration of the coastlands (especially by the Danish explorer Gustav Holm, who arrived at Ammassalik in 1884 and collected numerous everyday objects for the National Museum in Copenhagen) and the discovery of the hinterland (Fridtjof Nansen in 1895 and Ludvig Mylius-Erichsen in 1906–09), did much to deepen this growing fascination. In 1910, the Danish explorer Knud Rasmussen founded his legendary Thule station, which became a fabulous Eskimo conservation and research center. Throughout his life, Rasmussen was fascinated by Arctic myths and legends and was anxious to preserve shamanic rituals—food taboos, wife swapping, sharing of sexual activities—from the dictates of the Church. This young administrator, ethnologist, expedition chief, and poet passionately defended the inhabitants of this small village nestled in the bay of the North Star. He was a visionary pioneer in understanding the importance of the cinema and immortalized on film the extraordinary scenes he witnessed on the east coast of Greenland at the beginning of the twentieth century.

The French ethnologist Jean Malaurie, Rasmussen's spiritual son in many respects, acknowledged his huge debt to his illustrious predecessor. "Rasmussen's shadow envelops you on the tracks around Thule, wherever you go. For me, he was an example and a model, and I gradually discovered him through the remarks of the Inuit [the Eskimo people of North America and Greenland], that is, after my first expedition to Thule . . . Peter Freuchen, his closest friend, described him as 'the man whose laugh preceded him.' I would put it differently: 'the man whose charm preceded him,' using the shamanic meaning of the word 'charm,' that is, 'encharmed'" (Malaurie, 1990).

But other lovers of the icecap would also succumb to the vertigo of the Far North. Another familiar visitor to Ammassalik was the mythical Paul-Emile Victor. On July 11, 1934, the *Pourquoi Pas?,* captained by Jean-Baptiste Charcot, left Saint-Servan for the east coast of Greenland with the young French ethnologist at the head of an expedition that included Robert Gessain (doctor and anthropologist), Michel Perez (geologist), and Fred Matter (film-maker). Their aim was to collect typical Inuit objects before their culture was wiped out by Westernization. Despite the village's few inhabitants (some nine hundred), the expedition returned with an exceptional harvest. Over four thousand pieces entered the Musée d'Ethnographie du Trocadéro, the precursor the Musée de l'Homme.

On August 8, 1936, the *Pourquoi Pas?* deposited Paul-Emile Victor at the small village of Kangerllugssuatsiak, where during the winter he continued his research alone, living with an Eskimo family. In fine weather, his friends even taught him the rudiments of seal and bear hunting, skills fundamental to any understanding of the daily life and spiritual universe of these Arctic peoples. Captain Charcot was less lucky. He and all but one of his crew perished on September 16, 1936, in a storm off the coast of Iceland. As fate would have it, all the movie footage Paul-Emile Victor had shot during his expedition to Greenland and many documents destined for the Musée de l'Homme, sank with them.

Preceding pages: **Eskimo woman wearing sealskin clothes with a baby in the hood of her jacket, outside her snow-covered communal hut.** Winter 1936. Kangerlussuatsiaq, Alaska. Photograph by Paul-Emile Victor.

Following pages: **The explorer Jean Malaurie at Thule.** June 20, 1951.

Kangerlussuatsiaq Fjord. Photograph by Paul-Emile Victor (1936).

The Hallucinatory Art of the Arctic People

"We do not believe, we fear . . . We fear the Weather Spirit of the Earth, whom we must fight against to wrest our food from land and sea. We fear Sila (the Weather Spirit). We fear dying from hunger hunting in the cold snow. We fear Takanakapsaluk, the Great Woman down at the bottom of the sea who rules over all the beasts of the sea. We fear the sickness we meet daily around us; not death, but suffering. We fear the evil spirits of life; those of the air, of the sea, and of the earth that can help wicked shamans harm their fellow men. We fear the souls of dead human beings and of the animals we have killed. This is why our fathers inherited from their fathers all the rules of life based on the experience and wisdom of generations."

—Shaman from the Canadian Arctic

These Arctic "Ten Commandments," passed on to the great Danish explorer Knud Rasmussen by a shaman from the Canadian Arctic in the early twentieth century, wonderfully sum up these northern peoples' intimate, carnal, obsessive bond with nature, the nature that embraces them, nourishes them, and snaps them up. The art of the Inuit scattered over Alaska and Siberia, of the Samis or Lapps of northern Scandinavia and some twenty-six northern Siberian peoples expresses the cosmic power of the universe and the metaphysical grandeur of these infinite snowbound spaces, scattered with forests and swept by moaning winds whose disturbing voices weave themselves into one's thoughts and haunt one's nightmares and dreams.

Amulet in the form of a woman's face. Inuit. 1900. Ivory and glass beads. Alaska Gallery of Eskimo Art, Chicago.

Who are these last nomads of the icecap, torn between a heritage stretching back into prehistory and their legitimate aspiration to modernity, these men and women who still carve their doubts, anxieties, impulses, and fantasies in ivory, wood, and stone?

There is nothing gratuitous about the aesthetics of these immemorial languages laden with ancestral tradition. Art is an apprenticeship, a metaphor, and a magical or propitiatory spell. As mediator between the worlds of the living and the dead, art opens the door to dreams and trance. Reconciling the visible and invisible, and the animal and human realms, it becomes their communal breath, pulse, and hypnosis. It is, therefore, hardly surprising that the Surrealists, led by André Breton, were the first to take an interest in the rituals of these peoples "hungry for the holy," to cite that great defender of the Inuit cause, Jean Malaurie. André Masson, Marc Tanguy, Max Ernst, and, of course, Claude Lévi-Strauss all wanted to pass through the looking glass, and collected Eskimo masks whose disturbing, epileptic grimaces are like questions thrown to the gods.

"Most of them were based on shamans' visions," wrote the ethnologist Dorothy Jean Ray. "They were mainly worn during ceremonies, when the community gathered to honor certain animals and flatter their spirits before the hunting season, but there were also purely social gatherings, during which dances told ancient tales and enabled one to simply appreciate the beauty of the masks and the dancers' movements." She continues, with a hint of bitterness, "Traditional Yupiit masks were used until the 1910s, but only in certain villages, due to the pressure exerted by missionaries eager to put an end to these 'pagan' practices. Later, certain masks were made for films or as art objects to be hung on the wall . . . They were not sold as souvenirs until the 1950s." One could never denounce strongly enough the damage done to these peoples of the Far North: Stalin's deportation of Siberian shamans to the gulags, the banning of the American Indians' potlatches, burned masks, eradicated religions, devastated landscapes, polluted forests and rivers, collective memories annihilated, talents smothered, and artistic languages contaminated and trivialized. The list of poisoned gifts that colonization brought these primitive peoples of the icecap and tundra is long. But although the balance sheet is overwhelmingly negative, there have been glimmers of hope over recent decades. In 1969, the first international Pan-Inuit Congress of these peoples, who have lived scattered from Asia to Greenland for ten thousand years, was organized in Paris by the Centre d'Etudes Arctiques (EHESS/CNRS). This exceptional event enabled these communities to meet their respective administrations on an equal footing for the first time in their history. Alongside these peoples' legitimate struggle to assert their identity, archaeologists and ethnologists all over the world continue to compare and publish their research. Attention has been increasingly focused on Asia, the communal cradle, it now seems, of most of these civilizations. Jean Malaurie noted in the preface of the same admirable book he edited: "Studying the engraved ivories of the high Eskimo culture of the Bering Straits in the fifth century BC, one is struck by its stylistic relationship with Neolithic Chinese jade and the complex art of the Indians of the Northwest Coast. There is the same split representation from one continent to another. The similarities are clear, and yet the distances, geography, and history suggest one should be extremely prudent." The answer to this enigma is perhaps to be found in the spectacular archaeological discoveries made in the heart of eastern Siberia, the crossroads of all these cultures and their migrations. But one also merely has to look at these objects and sculptures, at these little miracles of humor, subtlety, inventiveness, and poetry with a fresh eye. The French artist Annette Messager, who confessed to spending hours gazing at reproductions of Eskimo masks, remarked that "with two or three feathers, two

Following pages: **Handle in the form of a seal.** Inuit. 1900. Ivory and pearl. British Museum, London.
Figurine. Inuit. Ivory and glass beads. Alaska Gallery of Eskimo Art, Chicago.

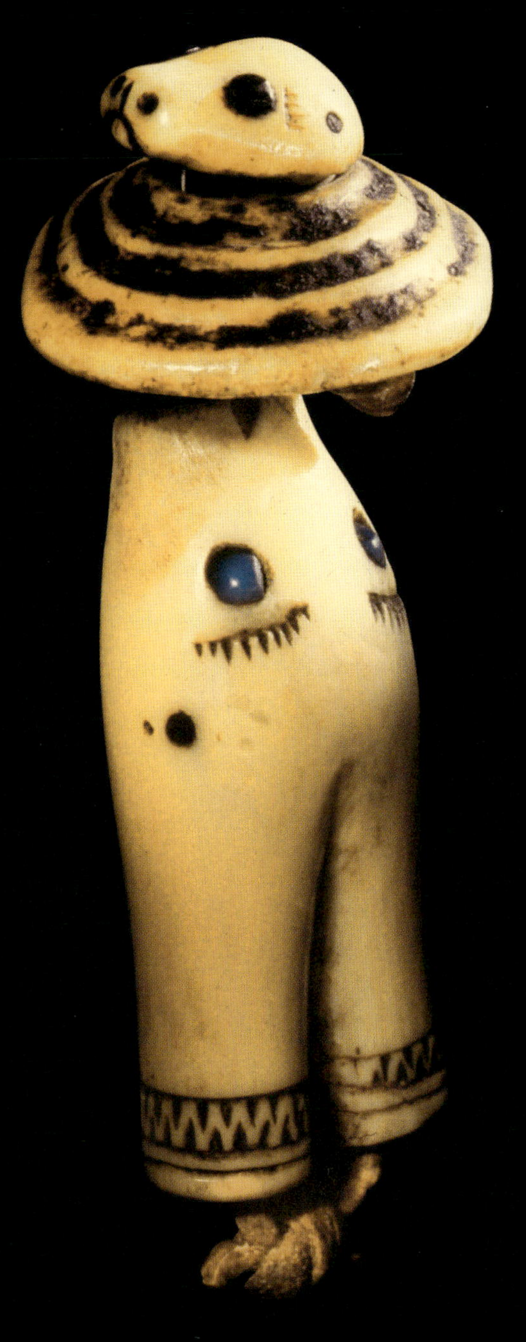

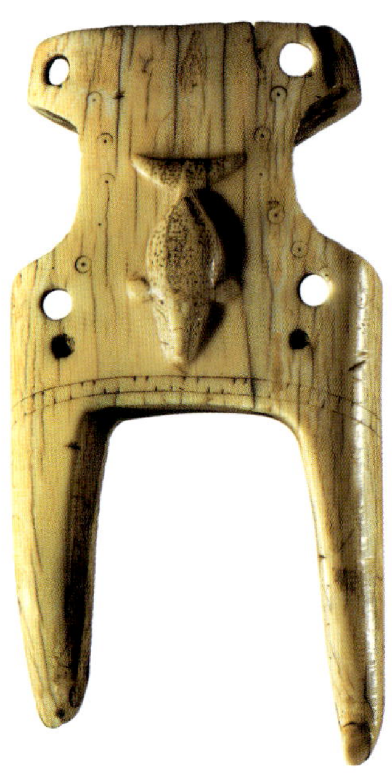

Harpoon fork. Inuit. Circa 1900. Northwest Alaska.
Walrus tusk. British Museum, London.

or three bits of wood, they talk to us about the Moon and the Sun." It is an art dressed up in children's rags, giving a miniaturized, mirror image of an adult world. But it is also an art of anguish and horror, an art of grimaces frozen in ivory and wood, and an art of the supernatural, completely summed up by those nightmarish, malevolent gris-gris of the arctic world, the Tupilak figurines. Although the word "artist" does not exist in the Eskimo language, one does not have to be a specialist to appreciate the beauty of their smallest tools, of the most modest piece of their basketwork or jewelry. In Aleut culture, the cap is decorated with geometric motifs and also pearls, feathers, and seal silk, denoting the prowess and rank of the hunter. Similarly, the refinement of the decoration and sophistication of the materials (animal tails, fur, and glass beads) of Yupiit and Inupiat parkas, made by women for their husband or sons, denote the wearer's rank. Until the late nineteenth century, the ultimate luxury was to wear a spotted

Comb. Inuit. Circa 1900. Ivory. Alaska Gallery of Eskimo Art, Chicago.

reindeer fur imported from Siberia. But if male garments primarily denote social status, women's are genuine works of art. Yupiit women's parkas are usually decorated with a mosaic of motifs in contrasting colors, demanding months of work, sometimes even a year to complete. Inuit women's parkas are just as elaborate. Intended to protect both mother and child, they have wide shoulders and a deep cape covering the traditionally ornate embroidered skirt and trousers. Coins, cartridge case, pieces of spoon or other metallic fragments, chosen for the sounds they make, complete these highly alluring outfits. But it is probably their tattoos that most profoundly surprised missionaries who strayed into these icy regions. Done as soon as a girl has her first period, these "seduction wounds"

Following pages: **Labradorian Eskimo girls with dolls** (gifts offered by the Donald B. MacMillans Expedition to Greenland, November 1926).
Statuette. Inuit. 18th–19th century. West Alaska. Ivory. H. 2.8". Musée Barbier-Mueller, Geneva.

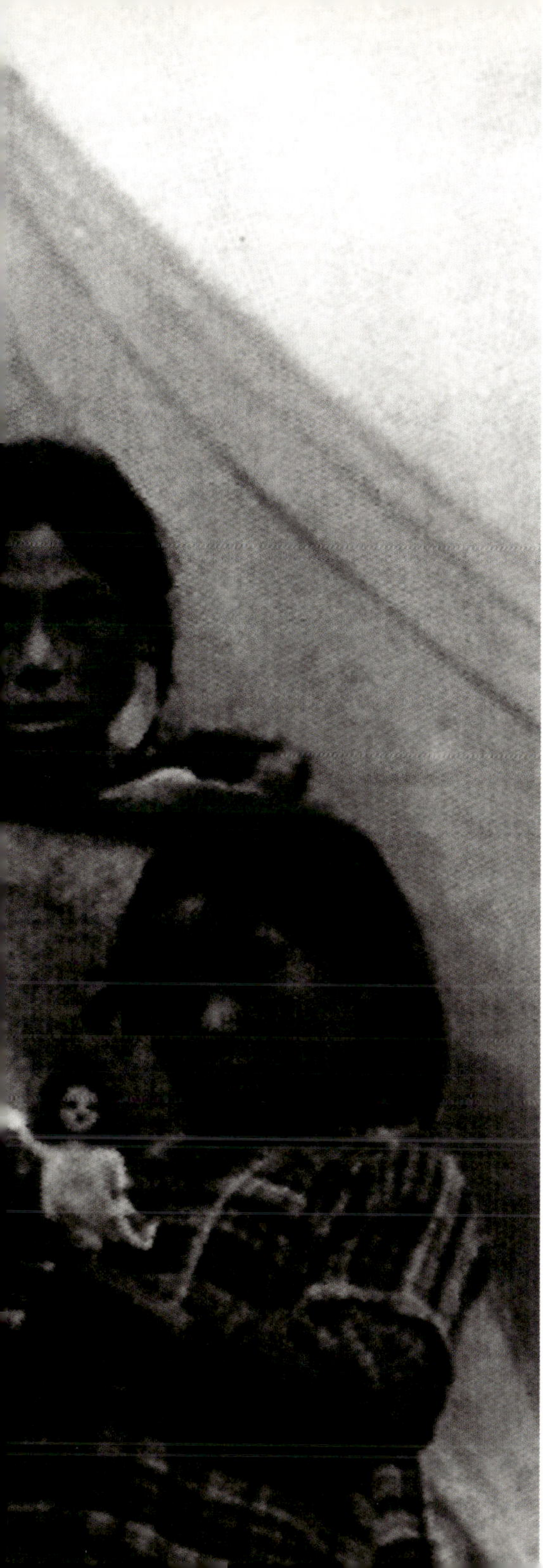

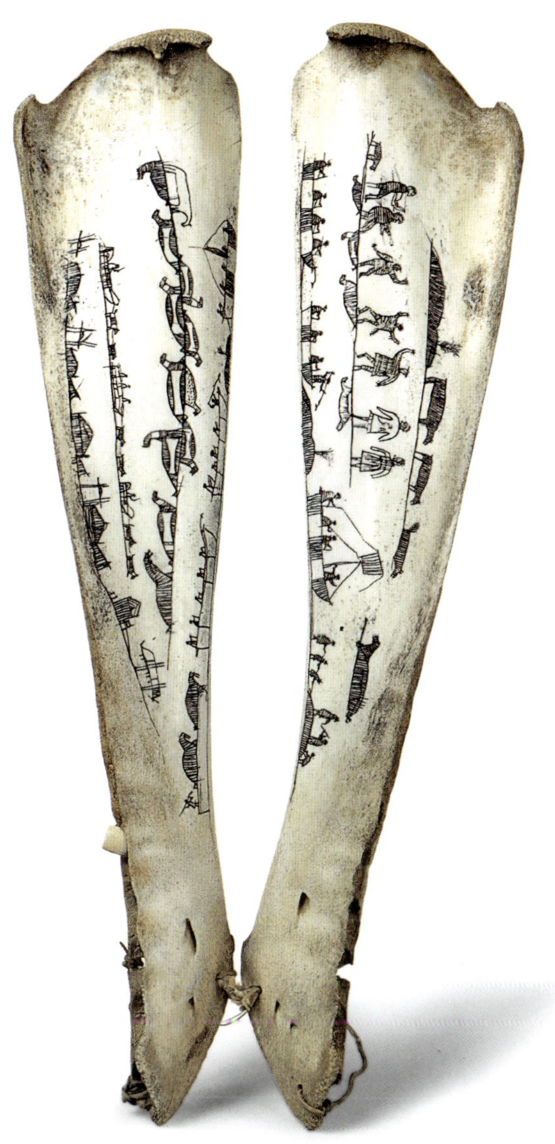

Commemoration of a hunt on a beluga jaw. Cape Prince of Wales, Alaska. L. 18.3". Formerly in musée de l'Homme. Musée du Quai Branly, Paris.
Left: **Eskimo in 1928.** Nunivak, Alaska.
Photograph published in *The North American Indian* by Edward S. Curtis (vol. 20), 1930.

are usually concentrated on the forehead, cheeks, and chin, and sometimes at the corners of the eyes. Depending on regional custom, the legs and arms are also tattooed.

The formal power of Eskimo animal sculpture, a distant descendent of Paleolithic traditions (?) and a nomadic artistic language, traces of which have been found in Scytho-Siberian archaeological remains, no longer needs any proving to Westerners, even if the work of inspired sculptors is often confused with the mediocre imitations made for tourists. On the other hand, the hypnotic and incantatory splendor of their tales and dances is still largely unknown. Hearing these guttural chants in the cocooned, womblike matrix of the igloo is an extraordinarily intense sensorial and aesthetic experience. The Inuit do not yet practice the art of declamation amongst themselves, or even that equally jubilatory art, the insult. Dancing and chanting are elegant and convenient ways of settling disagreements but, as we have seen, they are also a means of entry into the ecstasy and elevation of the trance, incontestably the most poetic means for these Arctic peoples to exorcise their fears and anxieties, to transcend the condition of simple mortality, and fly high, far, far away into the aurora borealis.

Pastolik spirit mask. Circa 1890. Painted wood and moveable elements from the lower Yukon. H. 13.8". Phoebe Apperson Hearst Museum of Anthropology, Berkeley.

Preceding pages: **Eskimo woman's parka.** The very wide collar enables her to carry her baby on her back and breastfeed it without exposing it to the cold. West Greenland. National Greenland Museum and Archives, Nuuk.

Noatak child. Alaska. Photograph by Edward S. Curtis (1929).

IN THE BEGINNING, THERE WERE THE PALEO-ESKIMOS

Today, it is generally accepted that the Eskimo people are Mongoloids whose ancestors came from Siberia across the Bering Strait and populated the American Arctic and Greenland from west to east. The common language of these nomadic hunters was Eskaleut. But the development and diversity of their art suggests that these cultural groups did not take quite the same routes.

In the Canadian Arctic and Greenland, the so-called Dorset culture appeared around 1,000 BC, and died out two thousand years later. Despite their extremely harsh environment, these populations had an acute artistic sensibility. They sculpted minute animals in ivory, wood, and stone and life-size masks. The quality of their execution is such that it has been suggested that they were produced by specialized artists or even shamans. Certain motifs specific to the Dorset culture corroborate this: Networks of lines depicting skeletons, with X marks emphasizing the joints. The anthropologist Yvon Csonka interprets this as the need to show both the visible and invisible aspect of beings. More disturbing are the bunches of human heads, sculpted in antler or wood. They appear to evoke a universe populated by obscure spirits and dreams, and continue, even behind glass in museum display cases, to exert their shamanic power.

Around AD 1,000, a new migration swept through the Dorset culture, bringing with it different aesthetics and practices. The Thule Eskimos, thought to be the ancestors of the present-day Canadian Inuit, were whale hunters and preferred decorating functional objects (combs, snow goggles, and bow drill handles) to traditional sculpture. The choice of material had a symbolic meaning: Antler was associated with men, the Earth, and summer and ivory with the female world, the sea, and winter.

The Inuit conception of art as an integral part of everyday life, practiced by all, lived on untainted until it became affected by a new constraint: The dictates of the contemporary art market.

Animal tooth figurine. Bering Straits.
Edmund Carpenter Collection.

THE NIGHTMARISH GRIMACES OF THE TUPILAK

Their stares are wide-eyed and they stick out their chest or, on the contrary, curl up into the fetal position. One is showing his skeleton and walking on bear's paws, another is crawling on two articulated arm stumps, another is part seal and part human. Where does this anxiety spring from? From the metamorphosis taking place before the viewer's very eyes? From this blurring of realms and categories? From these terrifying bare-teethed grimaces, from these hallucinating ivory eyes? The answer is from all this. It is as if these Arctic Brancusis, as in many respects these Eskimo sculptors were, deliberately distorted their forms and subtle harmonies.

A Tupilak is a hybrid creature carved in bone or wood, used primarily as a malevolent spell. Any Eskimo with enough knowledge and an adherence to strict rules could fashion one of these disturbing fetishes, capable of harming and even killing an enemy. The effectiveness of these arctic voodoo dolls depended on their ingredients: Parts of animals hunted by the victim, skeleton fragments, earth, birds' feet, pieces of skin and placenta, body parts of stillborn babies, and also the victim's hair and pieces of his or her clothing.

For these recipes to work, they had to be activated by magical chants and incantations, and these malevolent creatures were thought to grow daily in power and size by sucking the genitalia of the person who made them. Once its enemy had been designated, the Tupilak threw itself into the water and swam away to terrify its unfortunate victim to death. But this magic could also be extremely dangerous for the person who made the Tupilak. If it failed in its mission, it could turn against him. Fortunately, the life of these charming monsters was usually very short, as the Tupilak died once it had accomplished its mission.

Tupilak. Inuit. East Greenland. Wood, walrus tooth, and bone. William Channing Collection.

Tupilak. Inuit. Ammasalik, Greenland. Wood. L. 6.2".
Formerly in musée de l'Homme. Musée du Quai Branly, Paris.

The advent of Christianity in these desolate lands would drastically upset these animist beliefs, which missionaries considered particularly barbarous. But if countless masks and amulets were burnt and many religious traditions perished in the flames with them, their dreamlike dimension remained profoundly etched in the collective imagination of these arctic peoples. At Ammassalik, on the east coast of Greenland, many contemporary sculptors are still celebrating the marriage of sky and sea and of man and magic, even if they are doing so to cater to new invaders—tourists eager to take home a thrillingly scary Eskimo souvenir. Now, in even the remotest parts of Alaska, one can find pale imitations abusively called Tupilaks.

Tupilak, half-man half-quadriped. Inuit. Ammasalik, Greenland. H. 2" L. 5.5". Formerly in musée de l'Homme. Musée du Quai Branly, Paris.

Tupilak, half-man half-animal. Inuit. Ammasalik, Greenland. H. 1.4" L. 2.3". Formerly in musée de l'Homme. Musée du Quai Branly, Paris.

MAN AND ANIMAL: THE INDISSOCIABLE COUPLE

The Inuit ("true men" or "real people), as they call themselves—as opposed to the term "Eskimo" ("raw-meat eater")—have had to use every last ounce of their energy and ingenuity to survive in the pitiless Arctic environment. The permafrost (permanently frozen ground), the lack of vegetation, and the year's two harshly contrasting seasons (a long, dark, glacial winter and a short, radiant summer) have forged these peoples' capacity to adapt and their profound knowledge of nature, which is reflected in their every activity. Nomads or seminomads, they depended chiefly on hunting and fishing, and developed a highly sophisticated communal sharing of resources, ensuring the social cohesion and survival of small isolated groups. It is, therefore, hardly surprising if this ancestral dialogue between man and animal lies at the very heart of their art and oral tradition of dances, chants, rituals, and legends.

From northeast Siberia to east Greenland, the polar bear plays a major role in Eskimo mythology. A host of magico-religious practices (mixtures of taboos and offerings) surround polar bear hunting. Its flesh and fur were highly prized, and conferred great prestige and the status of hero on the man who brought it home. Myriads of statuettes and amulets of this fearsome creature have been carved in bone, ivory, and wood since prehistory. The polar bear embodied the ideal mediator between the forces of nature, the supernatural and the world of men.

Seal hunting was also a vital activity for the Eskimo peoples, who depended on its meat, blubber, and blood for their survival. For the hunter, the daily rendezvous between sea and sky on the frozen wastes of the icecap was a solemn and feared one. After hours of waiting, the seal would finally emerge from the hole drilled in the ice to offer him its warm blood. In exchange, he sprinkled a handful of snow over it so that its soul could return to the depths from which it came. This symbolic gesture says so much about the Inuit's respect for his prey—so necessary for their interdependency and mutual survival.

Polar bears hugging. Inuit. 19th century. Northwest coast of Alaska. Walrus tooth. H. 3.12". Alaska Gallery of Eskimo Art, Chicago.

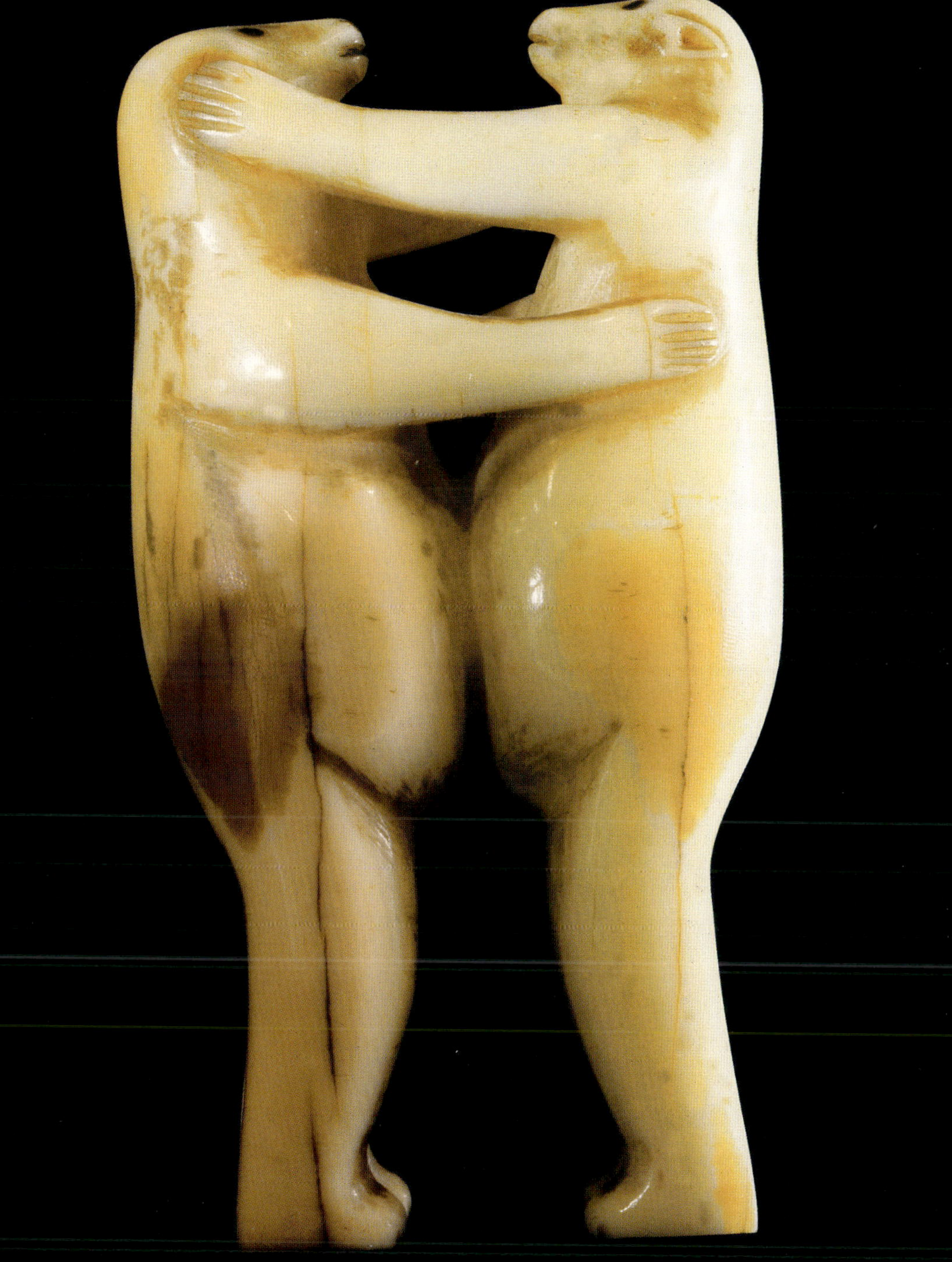

Shamanic Icons: The Extraordinary Destiny of the Alphonse Pinart Collection

"From Shakespeare's theater there remains his plays and words; from the Eskimo theater, there remains its masks and forms, a résumé of a daring existential and universal language."
—Danièle Amez, *Masques eskimos d'Alaska*

Celebrating rituals, seasons, and rites of passage, Eskimo spirit masks, collected in the late nineteenth century by the French explorer Alphonse Pinart, subjugate one with their vivid polychromy and expressionist grimaces midway between hypnosis and ecstasy. The tale of their discovery and their miraculous resurrection is an incredible one.

An ovoid wooden mask haloed by a string of small arrow- and feather-shaped batons stares with two round pupils. The perfectly balanced face is divided horizontally into three parts emphasized by the bright three-color palette: A chalky white, a brownish red, and a subtle green midway between emerald and turquoise. Were it not for the outrageously dilated nostrils (a seal's?), its features would be unequivocally human. And yet a hint of mystery wreaths this strange face enigmatically tattooed with a network of dots: Following the semispherical eyebrows, a horizontal fringe brutally divides the zones of the mouth and nose, and tears flow down each cheek.

From what exotic climes could this flamboyantly polychrome and daringly sculpted miracle of an icon have come from? Whose chisel carved its convulsive, neither

Mask representing the sun. Kodiak Islands, Alaska. Painted wood, fur, string, and tendon. H. 16.8" W. 10.1". Collected by Alphonse Pinart in 1871. Château-Musée de Boulogne-sur-Mer, France.

Nunivak ritual mask. Photograph by Edward S. Curtis (1928).

male nor female, half-human and half-animal features? The answer is to be found in the French port of Boulogne-sur-Mer, in the archives of its castle-museum. One fine day in 1986, the museum's curator, Françoise Camille Halley-des-Fontaines-Poiret, woke some seventy of these miraculous faces from their slumber. They had been left in the sepulchral darkness of a store cupboard, carefully wrapped in paper. Each had an inventory number, stating its provenance and identity. There was not a shadow of a doubt! This was the extraordinary collection of Eskimo masks Alphonse Pinart brought back from the Kodiak Archipelago in Alaska at the very end of the nineteenth century. The intrepid explorer had bequeathed this priceless harvest to his hometown.

Mask. Inuit. West Alaska. The face in the middle symbolizes the "spirit of the moon," the rim is the "spirit of the air," the outer circles the cosmos, and the feathers the stars. Smithsonian Institution, Washington.

Maskettes. 1928. Nunivak. Alaska. Photograph published in *The North American Indian* by Edward S. Curtis (vol. 20), 1930.
Left: **Small mask for dancers.** Inuit. Alaska. Wood, beads, and feathers. British Museum, London.

Noatak seal hunter in a kayak.
Photograph by Edward S. Curtius (1929).

And the vagaries of taste had consigned them to oblivion. It had taken a century for the masks Pinart had collected to cease to be mere "curios" and become "artworks," to quote the museum's curator. Duly identified, classified, and restored, these magnificent pieces could now receive the supreme consecration: The magnificent exhibition organized in 2002 by the Musée du Quai Branly. But now that they have been rehabilitated, how should one interpret these faces? Their accompanying chants, rituals, and dances have been extinct for decades now, and Alphonse Pinart's unmethodical, muddled notes in a mixture of French, English, and Russian, often shed little light on this. When this apprentice ethnologist wintered on Kodiak from 1871 to 1872, its inhabitants were going through

Blower mask. Kodiak Archipelago, Alaska. Wood. H. 11.9".
Collected by Alphonse Pinart in 1871. Château-Musée de Boulogne-sur-Mer, France.
Following pages: **Eskimo woman showing her tattoos.**
Sleepy mask. Kodiak Archipelago, Alaska. Wood. H. 14.8". Collected by Alphonse Pinart in 1871. Château-Musée de Boulogne-sur-Mer, France.

a crucial phase of their history. This grandiose island has remained largely untouched by man but its religions have gradually disappeared. As a result of the Russian colonization and the inevitable epidemics brought with it, the great winter hunting festivals and their accompanying rituals slowly lost their meaning. Ineluctably, the spirit masks lost their raison d'être and became mere inanimate objects. Was Pinart's collection a desperate attempt to save this imperiled heritage? Sven Haakanson Jr., curator of the Alutiiq Museum and Archaeological Repository on Kodiak, has formulated the disturbing hypothesis that some of these masterly faces may have been carved at the young Frenchman's request, like last Mohicans of a religion already close to extinction.

But such doubts in no way affect the extraordinary formal vigor of these mute testaments to a specifically Kodiak artistic canon, with its stylish and improbable synthesis of realism and abstraction. Alphonse Pinart tentatively described this magnificent Arctic gorgon, whose radiating effect is masterfully created by its crown of luminous feathers, as a "Moon Spirit." He wrote "Sun Spirit" on another mask emerging from a board with its mouth slightly open, as though thrown forward. Its severe face with prominent brows and a perfectly straight nose are covered with the same tattoos.

These hypnotic Alaskan faces, unearthed or saved from the flames of some obscure shamanic ceremony by a rookie explorer, were stowed away in a ship's hold and made the long voyage back to France, only to be entombed in a museum. Who could ever sufficiently praise the "diabolical" science and formal inventiveness of these visionary sculptors? The closer one looks at this strange family of "polar Pinocchios," the more one is filled with a mixture of wonder and stupefaction. There is not the slightest repetition nor asphyxiating constraint in this procession of convulsive faces, with domed and receding foreheads, thin lipped or contracted mouths, shut and wide-open eyes, and severe or laughing expressions. They are like a catalog of all the possibilities of creation or, more precisely, the full range of variations at the sculptor's disposition. Mask-shields with skinny profiles whose mimicry wavers between the tragic and the burlesque; baby masks with every grimace and buffoon-like expression imaginable; Cubist masks whose sharp angles seem to push back frontiers; board masks as radical as they are spellbinding; and deeply etched faces whose painful grimaces express the most poignant of human comedies.

Many of the identifications proposed seem risky, as most of these orphan faces have lost the memory of their chants and rituals. But reading through Alphonse Pinart's confusing, wandering notes, the fog sometimes lifts. "The nocturnal traveler," "he who has lost his mind," "the clown," "the old man," "he who pays a visit," "he who seeks," "he who protects the body," "the hunter of the aurora borealis," "the idiot," "he who knows not," "the woman who pays (or surfaces?)," and also "the one with a turned-up nose," "the one with the big nose," "the one with big lips": these are just some of the mysterious epithets Alphonse Pinart gathered from his informers. But there is nothing coquettish or lighthearted in these seemingly comical appellations. Each is a precise identification of a role to play, a position to take, a role to assume. These mask-sculptures of amazing power, which Western aesthetes delight in admiring as works of art, were the actors (instruments?) of ceremonies whose shamanic purpose vied with their theatrical dimension. One only has to read the accounts of the Russian explorers of these icy regions. Everything is scrupulously recorded: The large lantern in the middle of the room, the men frenetically beating the drum, girls in outfits made from seal intestine, glass beads hanging from their lower lip and their ears, their noses pierced with a bone. Then there are those figures who suddenly appear: Disturbing little devils with their faces painted red and their back

Following pages: **Serene mask.** Kodiak Archipelago. Hardwood, tendon, and feathers. H. 10.1". Collected by Alphonse Pinart in 1871. Château-Musée de Boulogne-sur-Mer, France.

Mask. Kodiak Archipelago. Polychromed hardwood. H. 4.7. Collected by Alphonse Pinart in 1871. Château-Musée de Boulogne-sur-Mer, France.

and head sprinkled with eagle down. A kayak, stuffed animal hides, and hunting weapons hang from the ceiling of the ceremonial house. "Land ahoy!" the chief shouts. "Prey will come to he who has not yet killed anything. There they are, there are the animals!" wrote the Russian navy officer Gavrila I. Davydof about a performance (or "game") he watched on Kodiak Island on December 8, 1802. "Then everyone cried out in different voices, imitating animals; they blew whistles prepared beforehand. In short, they made quite a din. The performance was coming to an end; a few minutes later the hunters began swaying, shaking rattles in time" (from an account published in two volumes in Saint Petersburg in 1810 and 1812).

In a journal published by Saint Petersburg's Archives of the Academy of Sciences, the folklorist I. G. Voznessiensky also wrote accounts of these theatrical rituals, both performances and propitiatory ceremonies involving demonic spirits. "A single dancer appears, crawling out of a pile of hides in a corner, to the left of the entrance to the *barabora.* His back was covered with a bird skin parka and the front of his body with a *kamleyka.* He was wearing a high hat and he was masked. Music. A sweet song, with nothing abrupt about it." How could one then consider these opaque, mute faces merely as charming curios? Their faces would be obscenely naked without their wooden hoops or feather corollas, pathetic fossils of a forgotten, outlawed religion, pitiful icons emptied of their substance.

Pointed masks in the form of a bird's beak, thin masks shaped like spearheads (the whale hunter's weapon), and miniature masks probably worked like marionettes, today so desperately inert. And what should one make of the masks Davydof described as "sorts of pointed helmets made out of curved twigs, one of them entering the mouth of the men like a horse's bit," and those made of woven grass covered with black fabric, and the masks striped with reddish intestines, forming semicircles on the face? Ghosts, organic imitations gone forever, disappeared into nowhere.

One thing is sure: The hypnotic power of these wooden portraits remains long after their death. Listen to Jean Malaurie auscultate the face of one such convulsive beauty with a terribly living presence: "It is the very being itself in its inner energy. The mask, whose personality with a frontal gaze, is a genealogy of thought.' To stare at it for a long time has its consequences: The eyes stare right through you. Creased, hollow eyes calling out to you. They menace you if the eyes are closed, the mouth twisted between bared castrator's teeth. These holes continue to question your innermost self . . . These savage masks, most of which were destroyed after ceremonies, have that primal power that leaves no one who beholds them unmoved, otherwise it would be a purely aesthetic exchange. This is the peril any hasty visitor to a museum brings upon himself. Hell is reserved for the timid." And this coryphaeus of the peoples of the icecap concludes, "One has to look and look at primitive masks to see them, as one listens and listens to music to try and understand between the notes" (Malaurie, 2001).

Allow yourself to be bewitched . . .

Following pages: **Mask.** Inuit. Point Hope, Alaska. Wood with natural patina, traces of polychromy. Chin partially restored. W. 8.2". Formerly in the André Breton Collection. Private Collection.
Mask, half-man half-whale. Inuit. 1900. Wood. Mask used during the ceremony marking the beginning of the whale hunt. Field Museum of Natural History, Chicago.

THE DRUM DANCE

One would be mistaken to consider the masked dances of the Arctic peoples as merely severe and hieratic religious ceremonies. The laughing and chanting that rang through the communal dwelling broke the monotony of the long winter nights. Reenactments of traditional themes, brimming over with that provocative humor so typical of the Inuit, were improvised to the rhythm of the drum. The first European observers were quick to condemn their often lewd gestures and verbal license.

The erotic dimension of these masked dances played an important social role: It was at the end of this type of performance that the Eskimos ritually exchanged partners, a ceremony poetically called "the putting-out-the-lights game."

Many a European has fantasized about these sexual practices, but for the Inuit, they were part of the renewal of the universe's fertilizing powers.

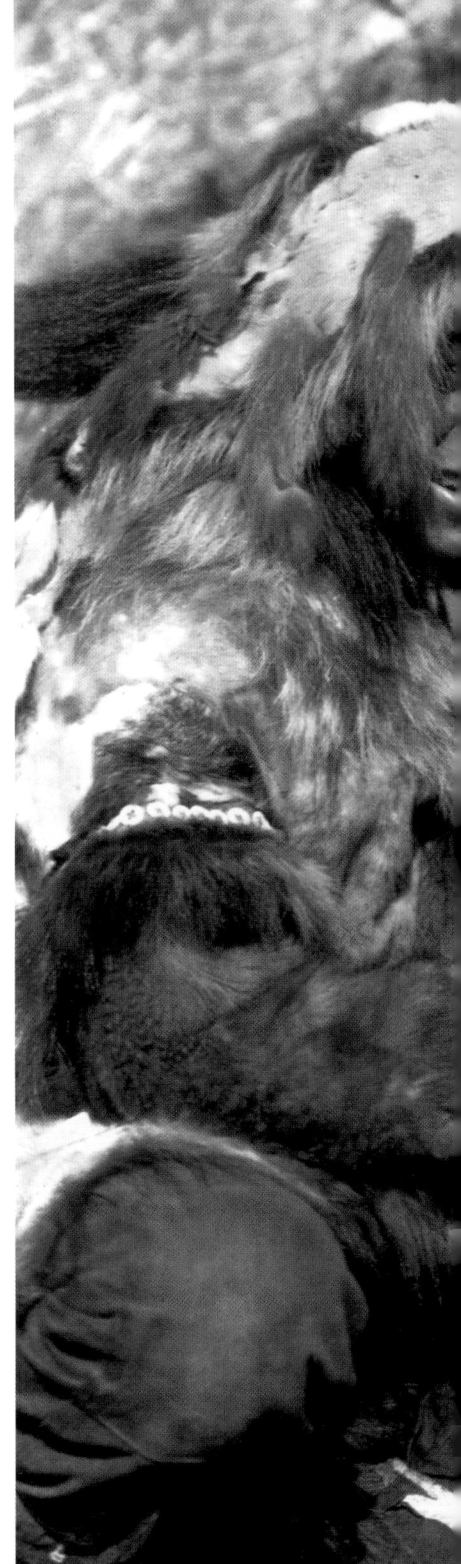

Indian with a drum. 1928. Nunivak people. Alaska. Photograph published in *The North American Indian* by Edward S. Curtis (vol. 20), 1930.
Following pages: **Eskimo girl resting by KangerLussuatsiaq Fjord, Alaska.** Photograph by Paul-Emile Victor (August 1936).

EPILOGUE

THE CONSECRATION OF ABORIGINAL ART

Torn between prehistory and modernity, Aboriginal art is captivating, both in the inventiveness of its forms and the richness of its repertoire. Yet these painters, now celebrated by the world's greatest museums, have remained faithful to their tradition, rituals, and cosmogony vibrant with poetry and invention.
Their ultimate consecration came when the Musée du Quai Branly invited eight Aboriginal artists to create their own space in the heart of the new museum in Paris—a symbolic, artistic, and political gesture that deserves recognition.

John Mawurndjul creating his own space in the heart of the Musée du Quai Branly. September 2005.
Left: **Aborigine artist painting on bark.** 1977. Maningrida. Arnhem Land, Northern Territory.

Potato Dream, Kangaroo Dream, Boomerang Dream, Dream of the World, and *Red Ochre Dream.* The canvases are even more mysterious than their cabalistic titles: Flamboyant, striated, hatched, dotted with white marks, tattooed with curves and meanders, traversed by lightning and balls of fire, haunted by skeletons and footprints. Colors seem to have emerged from some Edenic time, or a dream: Pinks evaporate into mauves, subtle shades of ocher and gray, delicate greens, canary yellow. From what celestial cartography did these Milky Ways, peopled with luminous signals and stars, spring? Out of what primal Earth did this grammar of circles and dots, a language of the infinitely possible, emerge?

Flashback to the 1970s, to the middle of the Australian Desert, an insolently beautiful, red ocher desert, to a town of corrugated iron huts surrounded by barbed wire. It was in Papunya, the Aboriginal Florence, a location straight out of a Wim Wenders movie, that one of the most revolutionary artistic phenomena of all time took place. For the first time in their history, Aborigine-initiated artists revealed their "painted dreams" to protest against the assimilation policies of the federal government in Canberra, and in so doing unwittingly founded a school of painting of unprecedented fertility and modernity. But it was a white man who unleashed this outburst. Geoffrey Bardon, a young art teacher newly posted to this government-run camp, where around a thousand nomadic Aborigines (Arrernte, Anmatyerre, Luritja, and southern Warlpiri) had unceremoniously discovered the quintessence of civilization: A police station, gas station, grocer's store, church, and school. And it was on the walls of that school that one day in July 1971, a handful of initiated artists, encouraged by Bardon, dared to defy white culture by painting a fresco, showing ritual motifs dating back over twenty thousand years. In three large circles linked by lines, they painted the *Honey Ant Dreaming.* It was both an act of self-defense and a political statement, a reappropriation of their land as much as it was an artistic gesture. And like a trail of fluorescent powder, more paintings sprang from the desert, revealing new repertoires of signs and colors in all their magnificence. Schools and styles emerged and—as with every artistic movement—its masters were soon identified by Western collectors and museum curators. Art dealers flocked, canvases were exported, prices soared, and the artist Rover Thomas triumphed at the 1990 Venice Biennale. And yet there could be nothing less unnatural, nothing less acculturated than this aboriginal art torn between prehistory and modernity. Is this due to the timeless grammar of its signs, the hypnotic power of its colors, the vitality of its fascinating repertoire, like so many paths to be explored—all techniques and materials—so as to better hijack them? Nothing could be less antiquated than these paintings from Australia's Central Desert, whose artists have swapped natural pigments for acrylic paint and transposed onto a flat canvas or cardboard surface mythical episodes once painted on sand or skin.

Yet the same primordial desires subtend all these works: To preserve the beauty of the world and to ensure that its original spirit lives on. Each painting is a kind of identity card of a sacred place, a sort of property deed. The Aborigines say, "To not paint one's land is to allow oneself to die, to give in to darkness." Because what Western eyes initially perceive as seductive pictograms are, in fact, painstaking transcriptions of mythical episodes handed down from generation to generation, according to strict rules of sacred filiation. Nothing is left to chance in these alternations of rhythms and colors, there is nothing whimsical about these volutes and meanders. Each story—and therefore each painting—corresponds to a territory and to one or several families. Woe betide anyone who steals (paints without permission) a segment of a mythical episode or piece of a dream. "In this painting, I am evoking the myth I inherited from my father, from my father's father, and my paternal aunts. My painting is the *Dreamtime*," Judy Granites told the French ethnologist Françoise Dussart in 1985. Tim Leura Tjapaltjarri said five years earlier:

Following pages: **Aborigines.** Copper plate engravings, published in *Bilderbuch für Kinder* by Carl Bertuch (vol. 8), Weimar, 1813.

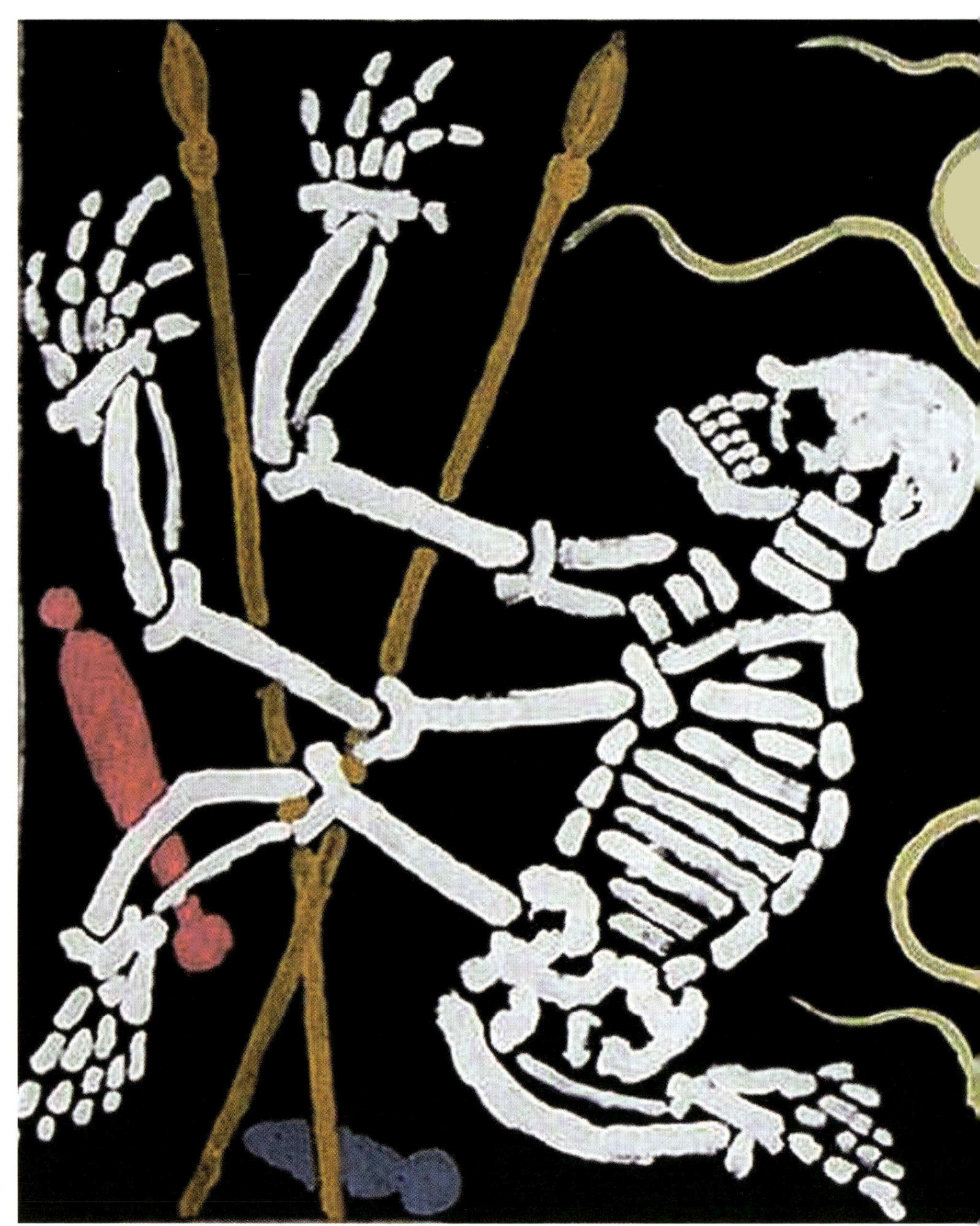

Preceding pages: **Yumu aborigine, on the last day of the baptism of blood ceremony.** Roger-Viollet Collection. ***Women's Dream,*** Ronnie Tjampitjinpa. Kintore culture. Circa 1940. Central Desert. Northern Territory. Acrylic. 35.5 x 23.8". Musée du Quai Branly, Paris.

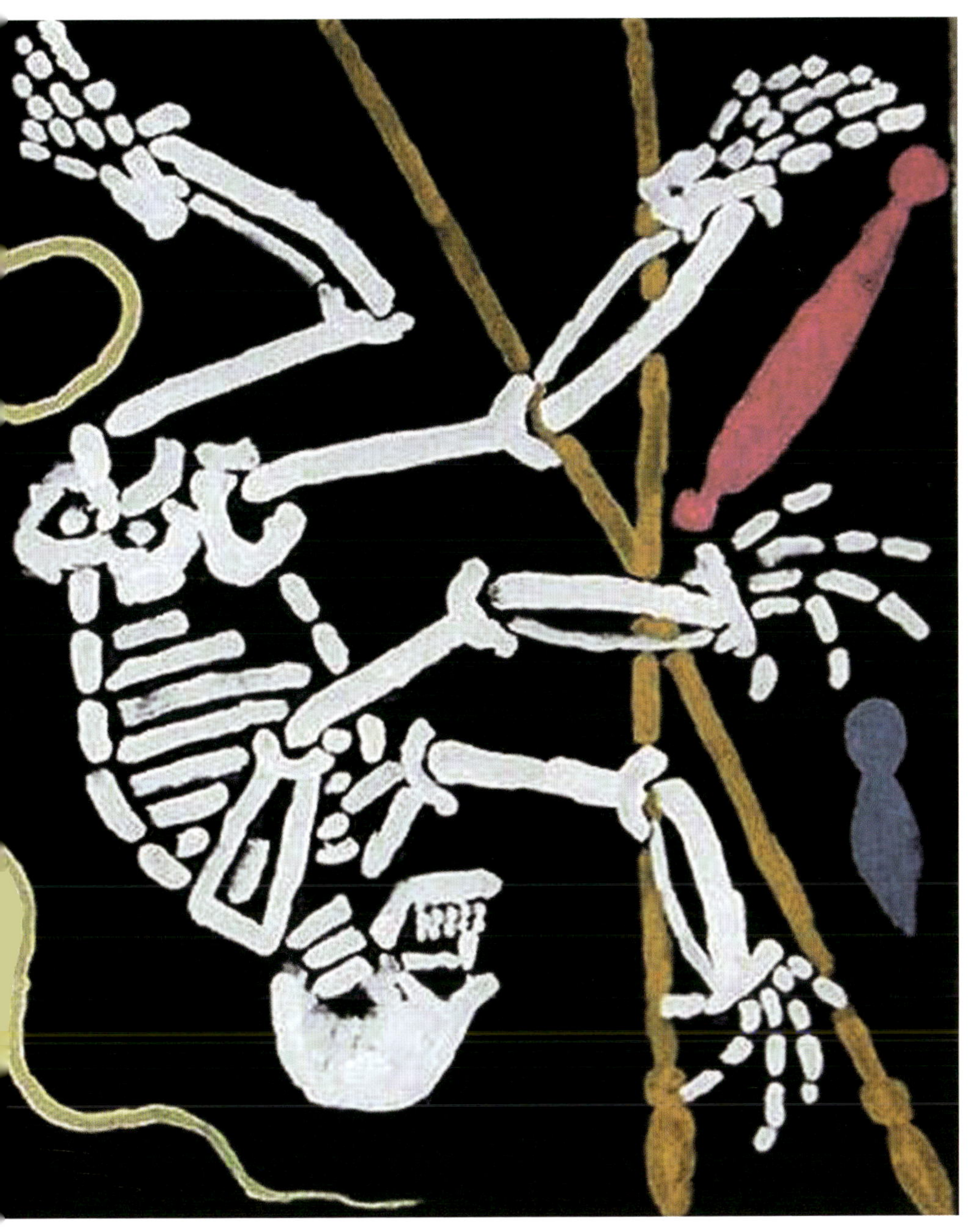

First Dreaming, Clifford Possum Tjapaltjarri. School of Papunya. Alice Springs. Acrylic on linen. 35 x 57".

"When I pick up my brush, I think of my 'dreams,' about the 'dream of the sun, moon, and morning star,' about the 'water dream' and the 'dream of food in the outback,' about the 'old man's dream,' the 'children's dream.'" *The Dreamtime,* is far too poetic an expression to have not attracted Western ethnologists and art historians like bees to honey. In fact, as Françoise Dussart explains, it expresses a fundamental notion of Aborigine religion. It designates "the immutable and ancestral period during which male and female mythical beings such as the Dingo, the Eucalyptus, the Emu, and the Crocodile emerged from the Earth, then still flat . . . They journeyed over the Earth, leaving physical imprints of their extraordinary acts. They sculpted the landscape and the sky. They then appeared in the dreams of the first human beings to tell them in detail the routes they had taken and their acts and the socio-religious organization humans had to adopt." And so it was that for millennia, generation after generation of men and women of the same clan perpetuated and reactivated these dreams which, strictly speaking, are their property. Like archaic control panels teeming with signs, chants, and prayers, they recount the long voyage of their ancestors across the Australian continent. Because what do these arcs, lines, and dots describe if it is not that sacred route endlessly begun again, endlessly relived?

The Australian anthropologist A. P. Elkin described the Aborigines as "an artist people." "Australia? An infinite mosaic of paintings, chants, and ceremonies, but also a mosaic of languages and cultures," wrote Sylvie Crossman and Jean-Pierre Barou, curators of the memorable exhibition of Aboriginal painting in the Grand Halle de la Villette in Paris in 1997. How can one embrace such a host of symbols and images, an aesthetic of a desert that is itself protean? "A map of Australia is an amalgam of superimposed paintings," explains Jean-Pierre Barou. "Each region has its codes and style. In the West, the rhythms are solemn, severe, like Gregorian chants. In the South, on the contrary, one witnesses a multiplicity of color." The young French collector Arnaud Serval, curator of the magnificent exhibition in the

Passage de Retz in Paris in 2002, has boundless admiration for the blend of rigor and creative inventiveness of these "born teachers." Having worked as "their assistant, preparing their colors, canvases, stretchers, and brushes," he admits to "having brought myself with them, thanks to them." "They are true teachers, they guide you; their paintings are teaching aids, explicit revelations. Like Tibetan mandalas, they take you to other levels of consciousness."

It is therefore hardly surprising that painters are also, and above all, the great masters of ceremony, the guardians of Aboriginal knowledge. "If Picasso had been born in the land of the Aborigines, he would probably have been a great initiate," Jean-Pierre Barou notes seriously. And this ardent defender of Aboriginal culture cites the painters of the desert worthy of the greatest museums: Rover Thomas, of course, who in a few decades has become the star of the Pacific museums, the darling of the art critics and dealers and the great Clifford Possum Tjapaltjarri, decorated by Queen Elizabeth of England and so admired his work is forged. But there are also the less well-known women painters of the Utopian community, such as Emily Kwementway Kngwarreye, a kind of magical reincarnation of Matisse. When will a European museum permanently and without the slightest discrimination, show Aboriginal and Western artists side by side? The Musée Tinguely in Basel has just shown a magnificent exhibition of the internationally famous painter John Mawurndjul, and the Musée du Quai Branly has integrated the work of Aboriginal artists into the very heart of its architecture and museum plan. There could be no greater tribute to Australia.

Following pages: **John Mawurndjul**, in the Musée du Quai Branly. September 2005.

AUSTRALIA : TERRA INCOGNITA

Australia was the last continent to be discovered by Europeans, but for its aboriginal peoples it is the original Earth, the land they have been living on for at least sixty thousand years. One can therefore easily understand the mixture of reciprocal revulsion and fascination of representatives of these diametrically opposed cultures when they first met in the late seventeenth century. "All they [the Aborigines] seem to want is that we leave," Captain James Cook wrote laconically in his logbook on April 29, 1770. First contact: first misunderstanding. The Aborigines initially thought that these men with white skin who had suddenly appeared in their world were their ancestors returning to visit them. The same Aboriginal term designates European invaders and the spirits of the dead, whose bodies lose their pigmentation and become white.

But curiosity soon gave way to hostility and confrontation. From their ethnocentric viewpoint, the Europeans considered these nomadic and seminomadic hunter-gatherers as primitive peoples, examples of mankind in its savage state. It was not until the 1930s and the enlightened work of the German anthropologist Franz Boaz, and later the research by the French ethnologist Maurice Leenhardt, that the aesthetics of the Aborigines were fully appreciated. In the 1960s, Claude Lévi-Strauss studied their kinship systems, which are as complex and sophisticated as mathematical languages. For these "intellectual aristocracies," kinship is both biological and classificatory. Exchanges of gifts, mutual support, participation in ritual ceremonies, and the attribution of marital partners are all regulated by social rules determined by the place of each person within the group. Thus only men and women of great learning have access to the esoteric dimension inherent in all things.

A young Czech living in France, Karel Kupka, was largely responsible for the revelation of Aboriginal art in Europe. During his many stays in Australia, especially in Arnhemland, and thanks to his friendships with initiated artists in certain regions, this painter and ethnologist collected, first for the Basel Museum then for the Musée National des Arts Africains et Océaniens in Paris, magnificent paintings on bark and posts, and funerary sculptures of stunning poetic power.

Hatched, striated, as though X-rayed, these pieces of dreams, peopled with spirits so fragile that a breath of wind could break their bones, have now entered the collections of the Musée du Quai Branly like a benevolent echo of the paintings of John Mawurndjul.

Seven *Mimi* (rock spirits) by Nangunyari-Namiridali (detail). 20th century. Paint on eucalyptus bark. 25.7 x 19.5". Musée du Quai Branly, Paris. Following pages: **Karel Kupka in 1956**, at the exhibition of aboriginal art at the East Sidney Technical College. Photograph in the Sydney *Morning Herald*. ***Pregnant Maam Ghost Spirit*** by Namatbara. 20th century. Millingimbi, Arnhem Land, Northern Territory. Paint on eucalyptus bark. 28.5 x 21.8". Musée du Quai Branly, Paris.

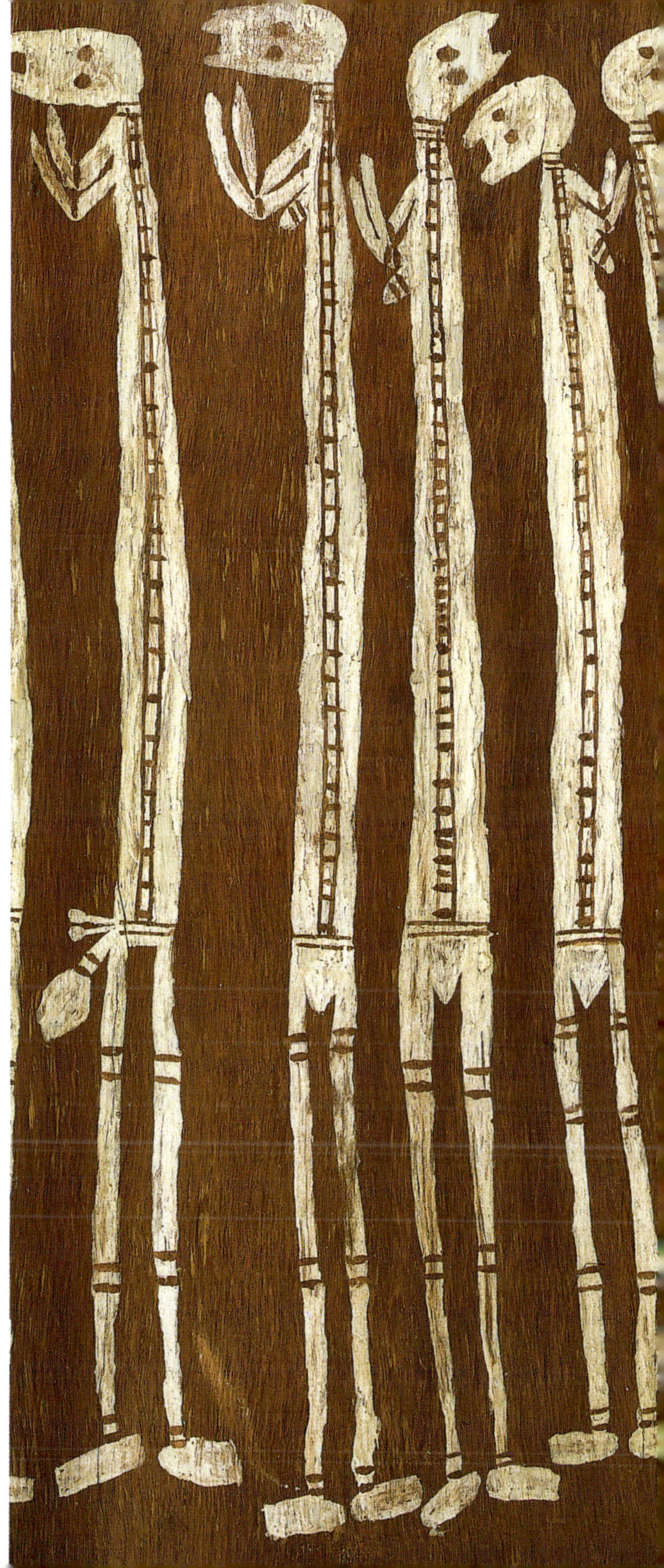

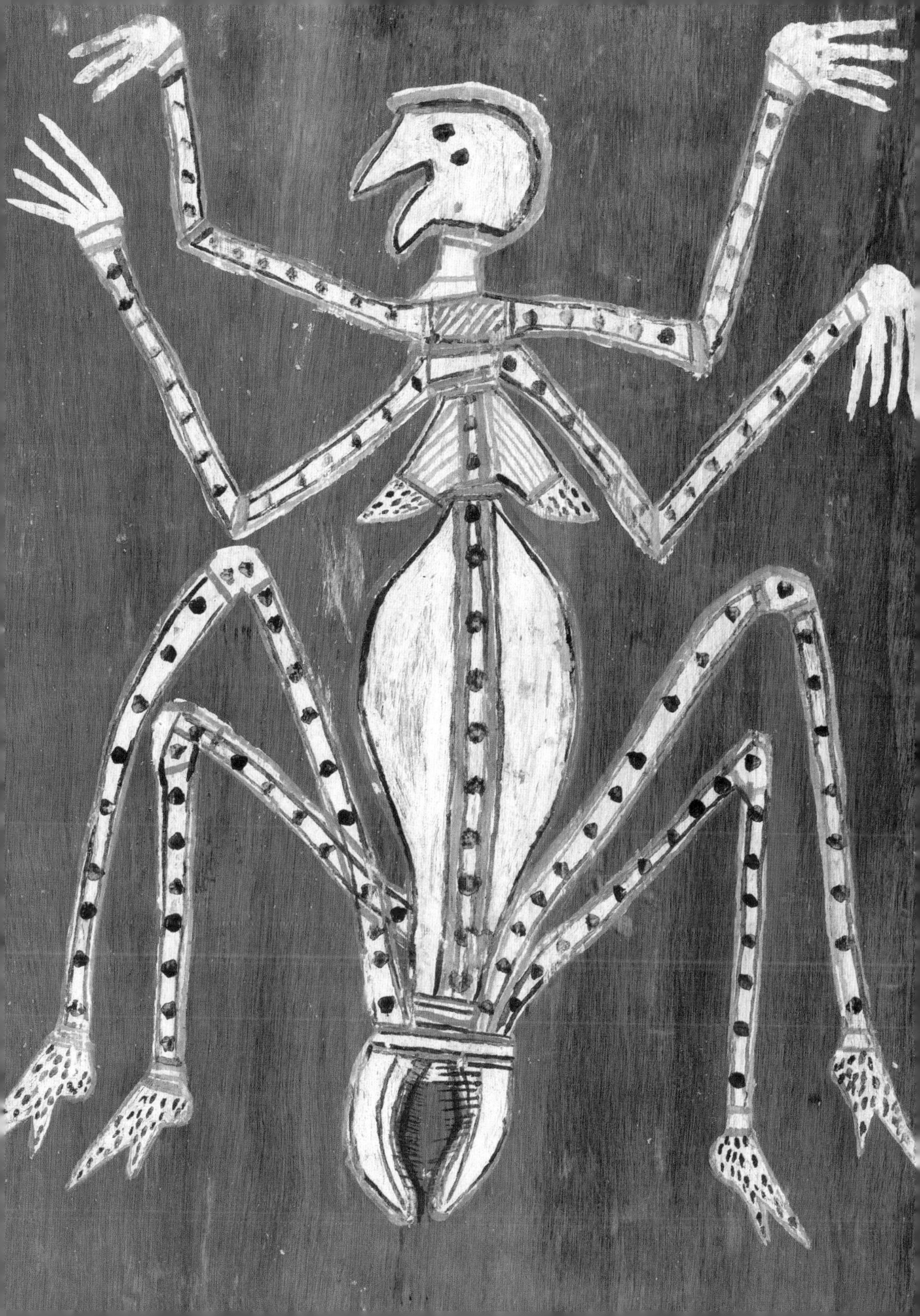

□ site
• town

MESOAMERICA

GULF OF MEXICO

SOUTH AND CENTRAL AMERICA

NORTH AMERICA

Nawarran **(The Rock Python)** by Jimmy Midjaw Midjaw, 1959. Arnhem Land, Northern Territory. Earth pigments on eucalyptus bark. H. 78 cm. L. 41,5 cm. Private collection

AUSTRALIA

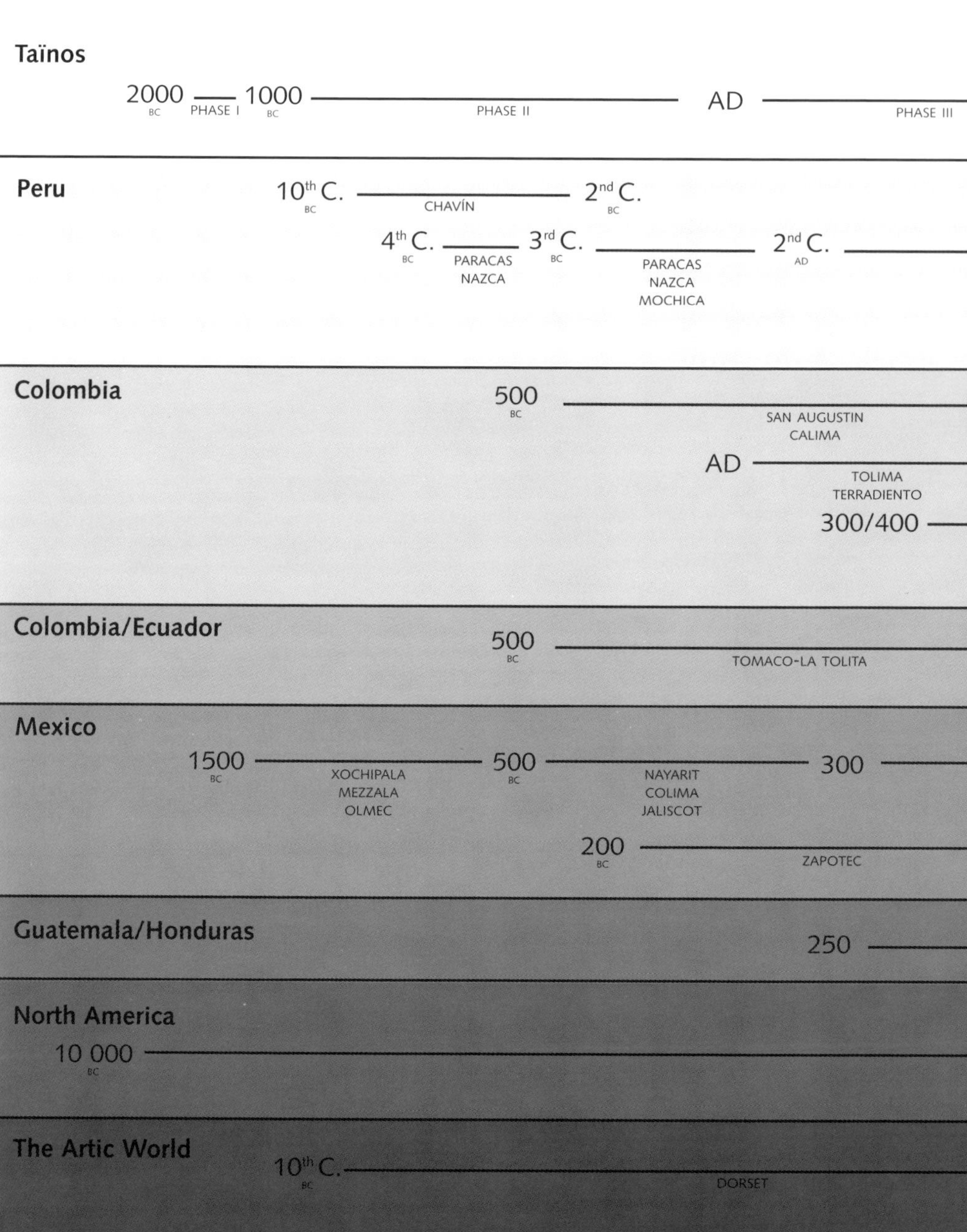

Taïnos
2000 BC
PHASE I
1000 BC
PHASE II
AD
PHASE III
Peru
10th C. BC
CHAVÍN
2nd C. BC
4th C. BC
PARACAS
NAZCA
3rd C. BC
PARACAS
NAZCA
MOCHICA
2nd C. AD
Colombia
500 BC
SAN AUGUSTIN
CALIMA
AD
TOLIMA
TERRADIENTO
300/400
Colombia/Ecuador
500 BC
TOMACO-LA TOLITA
Mexico
1500 BC
XOCHIPALA
MEZZALA
OLMEC
500 BC
NAYARIT
COLIMA
JALISCOT
300
200 BC
ZAPOTEC
Guatemala/Honduras
250
North America
10 000 BC
The Artic World
10th C. BC
DORSET
The Aborigine World
Prehistory

COMPARATIVE CHRONOLOGY

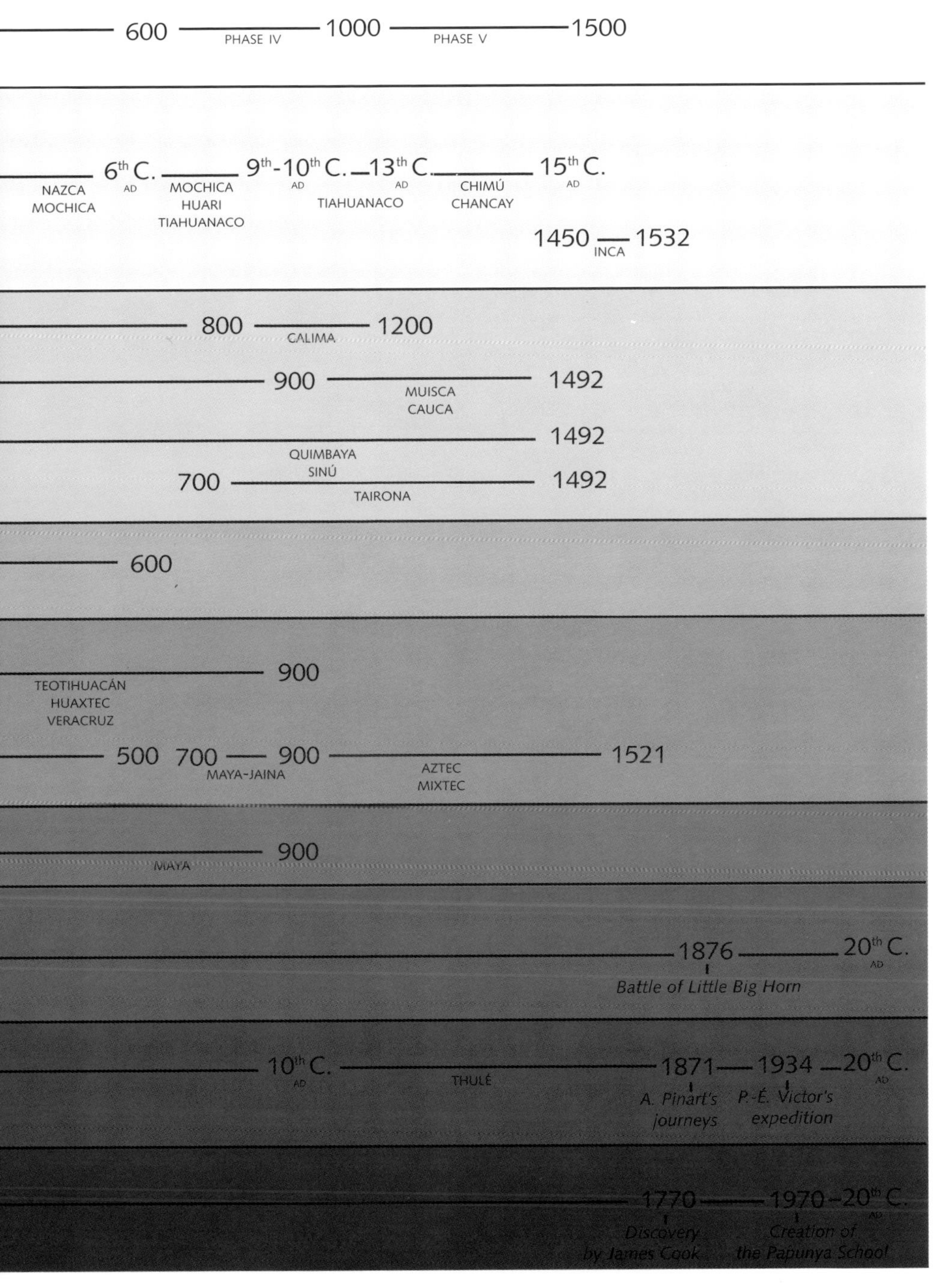

BIBLIOGRAPHY

THE PRIMAL ARTS

Breton, A. *Entretiens (1913–1952)*. Paris: Librairie-Gallimard, 1952.
Dagen, P. *Le Peintre, le Poète et le Sauvage: Les voies du primitivisme dans l'art français*. Paris: Flammarion, 1998.
Degli, M. and Mauzé, M. *Arts premiers: Le temps de la reconnaissance*. Paris: Gallimard/RMN, 2000.
Malraux, A. *La tête d'obsidienne*. Paris: Gallimard, 1974.
Roy, C. *Arts sauvages*. Paris: Nathan/Delpire, 1998.
Rubin, W. (ed). *Primitivism in 20th-Century Art*. London: Thames & Hudson, on behalf of the Museum of Modern Art, New York, first published, 1988.

FIRST-HAND ACCOUNTS

Carelli, M. *À la découverte de l'Amazonie: Les carnetsdu naturaliste Hercule Florence*. Paris: Gallimard, 1992.
Catlin, G. *North American Indians*. London: Penguin Books, 2004.
Curtis, E. *The North American Indian: The Complete Portfolio*. Koln and New York: Taschen, 1997.
La Condamine, C.M., de. *Voyage sur l'Amazone*. Paris: La Découverte, 1994.

GENERAL

Abel, B., Bihl, C. Pierre, J., Rousselot, J.L. *Masques Eskimos d'Alaska*. Paris: Éditions Amez, 1991.
Alcina Franch, J. *L'Art précolombien*. Paris: Citadelles & Mazenod, 1978.
Barbier-Mueller, J.P. *Guide de l'art précolombien*. Milan: Skira, 1997.
———, *Civilisations disparues*. Paris: Assouline, 2000.
Baudez, C. F., Becquelin, P. *Les Mayas*. Paris: Gallimard, 1984.
Bernal, I., Simoni-Abbat, M. *Le Mexique, des origines aux Aztèques*. Paris: Gallimard, 1986.
Boas, F. *Primitive Art*. New York: Dover, 1955.
Camacho, J., Laniel-Le François, M. E., Pierre, J. *Kachina des Indiens Hopi*. Paris: Amez, 1992.
Caruana, W. *Aboriginal Art*. London and New York: Thames & Hudson, 1994.
Désveaux, E. *Quadratura Americana: Essai d'anthropologie lévi-straussienne*. Geneva: Georg, 2001.
Dupaigne, B. Robbe, B. *Chez les Eskimo avec Paul-Emile Victor et Robert Gessain*. Paris: Éditions du Museum National d'Histoire Naturelle, 1989.
Dussart, F. *La Peinture des Aborigènes d'Australie*. Marseille: Éditions Parenthèses, 1993.
Duverger, C. *La Méso-Amérique: L'art préhispanique du Mexique et de l'Amérique centrale*. Paris: Flammarion, 1999.
Eliade, M. *Le Chamanisme et les techniques archaïques de l'extase*. Paris: 1951.
Faugère-Kalfon, B., Taladoire, E. *Archéologie et art précolombiens: La Mésoamérique*. Paris: École du Louvre/RMN/La Documentation Française, 1995.
Fauvet-Berthelot, M.F., Lopez Lujan, L. *Aztèques: La collection de sculptures du musée du quai Branly*. Paris: Musée du quai Branly, 2005.
Feest, C. F. *Native Arts of North America*. London: Thames & Hudson, 1992.
Fohlen, C. *Les Indiens d'Amérique du Nord*. Paris: PUF, 1992.
Glowczewski, B. *Rêves en colère: Alliances aborigènes dans le Nord-Ouest australien*. Paris: Plon, 2004.
———, *Pistes de rêves: Voyage en terres aborigènes*. Paris: Éditions du Chêne, 2005.
Jacquin, P. *Sur la terre des Peaux-Rouges*. Paris: Gallimard, 1987.
Kerchache, J. (ed.). *Sculptures: Afrique, Asie, Océanie, Amériques*. Paris: RMN, 2000.

Lavallée, D., Lumbreras, L. G. *Les Andes: De la préhistoire aux Incas*. Paris: Gallimard, 1985.
Lefébure, A. (ed.). *Indiens et explorateurs, 1825–1930*. Paris: Éditions La Découverte, 2005.
Lévi-Strauss, C. *The Savage Mind*. New York: Weidenfeld & Nicolson, 1966.
———, *The Way of Masks*. Seattle: University of Washington Press, 1982.
———, *Tristes Tropiques*. New York: Atheneum Publishers, 1974.
———, *Saudades do Brasil*. Paris: Plon, 1994.
Lévi-Strauss, C., Lévine, D. *Amérique: Continent imprévu*. Paris: Bordas, 1992.
Malaurie, J. *Les Derniers Rois de Thulé*. Paris: Plon, 1955.
______, *Ultima Thulé*. Paris: Bordas, 1990.
———, *L'Appel du Nord*. Paris: Éditions de La Martinière, 2001.
Malaurie, J., (ed.). *L'Art du Grand Nord*. Paris: Citadelles & Mazenod, 2001.
Métraux, A. *Les Indiens d'Amérique du Sud*. Paris: A.M. Métailié, 1982.
Muecke, S., Shoemaker, A. *Legendary Tales of the Australian Aborigines*. Melbourne: University of Melbourne Press, 2001.
Newton, D., (ed.). *Sculpture: Chefs-d'œuvre du musée Barbier-Mueller*. Paris: Imprimerie Nationale, 1995.
Paz, O. *Le Signe et la Mémoire*. Paris, Gallimard, 1993.
Perrin, M. *Le Chamanisme*. Paris: PUF, 1995.
———, *Tableaux Kuna: Les Molas, un art d'Amérique*. Paris: Arthaud, 1998.
Taladoire, E. *Les Mayas*. Paris: Editions du Chêne, 2003.
Talayesva, D. *Sun Chief: The Autobiography of an American Indian*. New Haven: Yale University Press, 1942.
Victor, P.-E. *La Vie des Eskimo*. Paris: Nathan, 1976.
Victor, P.-E., Robert-Lamblin J. *La Civilisation du Phoque*. Paris: Armand Colin, 1989.
Zimmerman, L. J., *Les Amérindiens*. Paris: Albin Michel, 1997.
———, *Native North America*. Oklahoma: University of Oklahoma Press, 2003.

EXHIBITION CATALOGUES (in chronological order)

Équateur: La Terre et l'or, Maison de l'Amerique latine. Paris: Librairie Séguier, 1989.
Art millénaire des Amériques, texts by Octavio Paz, Michel Butor, Jean-Paul Barbier, Henri Stierlin, Danièle Lavallée, Conceiçao G. Corrêa, Iris Barry. Geneva: Musée Barbier-Mueller, 1992.
Parures d'histoire: Peaux de bison peintes des Indiens d'Amérique du Nord, Anne Vitart, (ed.). Paris: RMN, 1993.
La Peinture des Aborigènes d'Australie de Françoise Dussart, Musée des Arts d'Afrique et d'Océanie. Marseille: Éditions Parenthèses, 1993.
L'Art des sculpteurs Taïnos: Chefs-d'œuvre des Grandes Antilles Précolombiennes. Jacques Kerchache (ed.). Musée du Petit Palais. Paris: Éditions Paris-Musées, 1994.
Kachina, Poupées rituelles des Indiens Hopi et Zuni. Musées d'Arts Africains, Océaniens, Amérindiens, Marseille. Musées de Marseille: RMN, 1994.
L'Or des dieux, l'Or des Andes, Pérou, Colombie, Équateur, Daniel Lévine (ed.). Metz: Éditions Serpenoise, 1994.
Comme un oiseau, Hervé Chandès (ed.). Fondation Cartier pour l'art contemporain. Paris: Gallimard/Électa, 1996.
Peintures aborigènes d'Australie, le Rêve de fourmi à miel. Jean-Pierre Barou, Sylvie Crossman (ed.). Grande Halle de la Villette. Paris: Indigène Éditions, 1997.
La Danse des Kachina, Poupées Hopi et Zuni dans les collections surréalistes et alentour. Pavillon des Arts. Paris: Éditions Paris-Musées, 1998.
I Maya, Palazzo Grassi. Venice: Bompiani, 1998.
Mexique, Terre des Dieux, trésors de l'art précolombien. Cäsar Menz (ed.). Geneva: Musée Rath, 1998.
Indian Summer: Les premières nations d'Amérique du Nord. Musées royaux d'Art et d'Histoire. Brussels, 1999.

Art des Indiens d'Amérique du Nord dans la collection d'Eugene et Clare Thaw. Fenimore Art Museum, New York, Mona Bismarck Foundation, Paris. Mona Bismarck Foundation/Somogy Éditions d'Art, 2000.
Australie: Le temps du Rêve. Amiens: Musée de Picardie, 2000.
Indiens des Plaines: Les peuples du bison. Michel Le Bris (ed.). Centre Culturel Abbaye de Daoulas. Éditions Hoëbeke/Abbaye de Daoulas, 2000.
L'Art de la plume en Amazonie. Paris: Mona Bismarck Foundation/Somogy Éditions d'Art, 2001.
Arts précolombiens de l'Amérique centrale dans les collections du musée Barbier-Mueller de Barcelone. Somogy Éditions d'Art, 2001.
Amazonie précolombienne dans les collections du musée Barbier-Mueller d'art précolombien de Barcelone. Éditions 5 continents, 2002.
Aztecs, Edouardo Matos Moctezuma, Felipe Solis Olguin (ed.). London: Royal Academy of Arts, 2002.
Les Esprits, l'Or et le Chamane. Musée de l'Or de Colombie, Clara Isabel Botero Cuervo, Jean-François Bouchard. Paris: RMN, 2002.
Kodiak, Alaska: Les masques de la collection Alphonse Pinart. Émmanuel Désveaux (ed.). Paris: Adam Biro/Musée du Quai Branly, 2002.
Symboles sacrés: Quatre mille ans d'art des Amériques. Evan M. Maurer, Molly Hennen (ed.). Paris: RMN, 2002.
Esprit kachina: Poupées, mythes et cérémonies chez les Indiens Hopi et Zuni. Paris: Galerie Flak, 2003.
Plumes d'éternité: Parures funéraires de l'Ancien Pérou. Collection Georges Halphen. Paris: Maison de l'Amérique latine/Somogy Éditions d'Art, 2003.
Trésors de la céramique précolombienne. Collections Barbier-Mueller. Fondation de l'Hermitage. Lausanne/Somogy Éditions d'Art, 2003.
Yanomami: L'esprit de la forêt, Bruce Albert. David Kopenawa (ed.). Paris: Fondation Cartier pour l'art contemporain/Actes Sud, 2003.
Brésil indien: Les arts des Amérindiens du Brésil. Luis Donisete Benzi Grupioni, Regina Polo Müller, Cristiana Barreto (ed.). Paris Galeries nationales du Grand Palais. Paris: RMN, 2005.
Rêves d'Amazonie. Michel Le Bris, Pascal Dibie (ed.). Centre culturel Abbaye de Daoulas. Editions Hoëbeke/Centre culturel Abbaye de Daoulas, 2005.

House pillar. Kwakiutl Indians. 2nd half of the 19th century. British Columbia, Canada. Cedar wood. H. 10'6". Formerly in musée de l'Homme. Musée du Quai Branly, Paris.

ACKNOWLEDGEMENTS

This book would never have been possible without those priceless "encounters" that guided my gradual and still ongoing discovery of the "primal arts." I would like to thank, first of all, my late father, Henri Geoffroy, whose intellectual virtuosity was equaled only by his profound erudition. I was brought up on his bedtime tales of "savages" (the appellation was used affectionately, in the sense in which André Breton and Claude Roy understood it). Many years later, men and women would in turn leave their mark on me with their open-mindedness and intelligence: Jean-Paul Barbier-Mueller, my debt to whom I have already emphasized in Volume 1 of this edition; Christiane Falgayrette-Leveau, director of the Musée Dapper and formerly my publisher; Jacques Kerchache, whose inspired vision I shall never forget; Stéphane Martin, president of the Établissement public du Quai Branly, who has always shown rare benevolence; Jean Malaurie, the prestigious founder of the "Terre Humaine" series; Claude Lévi-Strauss, whose writings deeply moved me as a young student; and Aube Breton, who so kindly showed me around her father's studio in rue Fontanie. I have of course not forgotten the many museum curators and ethnologists I have met during my research, but the list of their names would be far too long to include here. I hope they will forgive me.

I would like to express my sincere and affectionate gratitude to Martine Assouline, my faithful publisher, who has supported this project from the very beginning, to Valérie Tougard, who edited the text, to Mathilde Dupuy d'Angeac, who designed the layout, and to Stéphanie Guarneri, who researched the illustrations. My heartfelt thanks to you all.

Finally, I would like to thank the members of my family and close friends who helped and supported me through the writing of this book: Laurent and Cassandre Schneiter, my "sentinels of daily life," of course, my mother, Denise Geoffroy, who knows my anxieties inside out, Josette and Jean-Louis Schneiter, who so generously lent me documents, and also Guenaëlle Hastings, Isabelle Hernio, Aliona Chotova-Mottet, and Marie-Anne Mattard-Bonucci, whose affectionate presence are worth all the libraries in the world . . .

The Publisher would particularly like to thank Anne-Joelle Nardin from the Barbier Mueller Museum; Antoine Lefébure, Christine Maine and Clair Morizet from Musée du quai Branly; Daphné Victor for Paul-Emile Victor Fund; Nadia Behmen, Calmels Cohen, Raymonde Arrmati from Musée de la Charité in Marseille as well as the AKG Agency; Claudia Andujar; Apolline Cohen and John Mawurndjul; Professor Horst Antes; Dirk Bakker, Carlos Blanco and Marco Antonio Pacheco (Instituto Nacional de Antropologia e Historia, Mexico); Aube Breton; the British Museum in Londres; Benjamin Charignon (Éditions Plon); Kevin Conru; Contact Press Images Agency; Corbis Agency; Mr. B. Devos, Javier Ferrand, the Galerie Flak (Paris); Véronique Garrigues, ADAGP; Pierrick Jan (Réunion des Musées Nationaux); Mrs. Kelmester (Fondation Cartier pour l'Art Contemporain); Jennifer Kramer (Christopher Cardozo Fine Art, Inc); Claude Lévi-Strauss; Matthieu Lévi-Strauss; David McNeece (Museum of Indian Arts and Culture, Santa Fe); the Metropolitan Museum of Art in New York; Mr. Meunier (Les Films du Prisme); the French Foreign Policy Office (Archives Department); Céline Raniaud (Chateau-musée de Boulogne-sur-Mer); Rapho/Top Agency; Roger Viollet Agency; Yves Simart for Gisèle Freund Succession; Paul Swendsen and Michel Zabé.

PHOTO CREDITS

Abm-archives Barbier-Mueller-Studio Ferrazzini, Geneva: p. 40, 64-66, 76-77, 83, 102, 122, 169, 175, 234, 238, 240-245, 333.
Aboriginal Artists Agency Limited, Clifford Possum: p. 378-379.
Akg-images: p. 24-26, 32, 51, 56, 70-71, 84, 112, 114-116, 120, 124, 130, 132-134, 138, 156-157, 196-197, 202, 204-206, 246-250, 256-257, 274, 281, 287, 309, 332, 336-337, 347, 351-352, 354, 370, 374-375, 393; photo Veintimilla, p. 50; photo Werner Forman, p. 57, 98, 324, 328-331, 338-342, 365; photo François Guénet, p. 106-107, 190; photo Andrea Baguzzi, p. 113.
All Rights reserved: 172, 199, 212 (top left), 386; photo Miguel Covarrubias, p. 86; photo Underwood & Underwood, p. 292; photo George Wharton James, p. 300; photo Jean Malaurie, éditions Plon, p. 322; photo Raold Ammunbjen, p. 356; photo Theodor Koch-Grönberg, p. 239.
Archives du Projecto Archeologico Sipan (Museo Bruning), Bill Bellenberg, Martha Cooper et Nathan Benn (National Geographic) et Javier Ferrand: p. 209.
Assouline: p. 166, 189, 388-392.
Azusa, Denver: p. 277.
Barry Goldwater, 1940: p. 298.
Bibliothèque Nationale de France, Paris: p. 55.
Calmels Cohen: p. 291, 364; André Breton archives, p. 9, 11.
Château-Musée de Boulogne-sur-Mer Collection, photo B. Devos: p. 348, 355, 357-361.
Christopher Cardozo Fine Art, photo Edward Curtis, p. 258, 262, 264, 270-271, 290, 312, 350.
Claude Lévi-Strauss: p. 14, 220, 224, 235.
Contact Press Images, photo Sebastião Salgado Amazonas: p. 228, 230.
Corbis: p. 6, 54, 108, 136, 152, 207, 254, 260, 334, 366; photo Stéphanie Maze, p. 36; photo Danny Lehman, p. 80; photo Charles & Josette Lenars, p. 81; photo Bettmann, p. 316; photo Edward Curtis, p. 353.
Dagli Orti: 52, 63, 87, 93, 155; art archive/museo del Templo Mayor, p. 46; art archive/Navy Historical Service Vincennes France, p. 317.
Dirk Bakker, 1993: p. 20-23, 28-30, 35.
Enrico Gras & Marios Craveri: p. 170.
Fondation Cartier pour l'Art Contemporain, photo Claudia Andujar: p. 16.
Fundação Pierre Verger, photo Pierre Verger: p. 180.
Galerie Flak, photo Thierry Malty: p. 288, 294, 297, 305, 306.
Galerie Kevin Conru: p. 310-311, 313.
Gisèle Feund Estate: p. 4, 79, 88-89, 92, 104, 109, 117, 128, 135, 142, 144-145, 148-149, 154, 162.
Hélène Hoppenot: p. 131.
Hugo Maertens, Bruges: p. 159, 160-161, 163.
Ilona Ripke, Berlin/ADAPG, Paris 2006: p. 299, 304.
INAH, 1999: photo Carlo Blanco-Raíces, p. 42-43; photo Marco Antonio Pacheco-Raíces, p. 68.
Irmgard Kimball: p. 97.
Jaume Blassi & Jordi Blassi: p. 182-183.
Javier Ferrand: p. 164, 167, 173, 176-177, 181, 187, 192-193, 198, 203, 210-211.
Jean Paul Barbier: p. 151.
Judy Anderson de Bustamente: p. 178-179.
Laurent Schneiter: p. 371, 382-383.
Metropolitan Museum of Art: p. 75, 105, 186, 213 (left).
Michel Zabé: p. 72, 140.
Miguel Covaruubias: p. 127.
Musée de l'Homme: p. 265; photo coll. M. Delaplanche, p. 19, 39, 171, 200-201, 259, 278-280; photo coll. D. Ponsard, p. 29, 217, 221, 223, 276; photo coll. B. Hatala, p. 184-185, 263, 272-273, 335, 344-345.
Musée du Quai Branly: 218-219, 285; photo Hugues Dubois, cover, endpaper, p. 8, 44-45, 121, 268-269, 399.
Musée Pigorini, Rome: p. 31.
Museo National de Antropologia e Historia, Mexico: p. 91, 153.
Museum Fur Volkerkunde, Munich: p. 212 (top right)
Museum of Natural History, Smithonian Institution, Washington D.C.: p. 74.
Otto Stupakoff: p. 59.
Paul-Émile Victor Fonds: p. 15, 314, 318-319, 323, 368.
Paul Swendsen, all restoration © 2005: p. 216, 236-237; Ministère des Affaires Etrangères, Direction des Archives, p. 214; photo Guido Boggiani, p. 233.
Rapho/Top: p. 12-13; photo Sabine Weiss, p. 289.
RMN: photo Rudolph Schrimpf, p. 213 (right); photo Jean-Gilles Berizzi, p. 377, 385; photo Hervé Lewandowski, p. 387.
Robert Woods Bliss Collection, Washington D.C.: p. 143.
Roger Viollet Collection: p. 376.
Shango Productions, photo Igor Delmas: p. 18.
Smithonian Institution, Washington, D.C., photo James Mooney: p. 301.
Studiensammlung Horst Antes, Berlin: p. 225
Trustees of the British Museum: p. 61, 146.
xxx. miaclab. org, photo Blair Clark: p. 302.
Zé de Boni: p. 227.